Pro Spring Boot

Felipe Gutierrez

Apress®

Pro Spring Boot

Felipe Gutierrez
Albuquerque
New Mexico, USA

ISBN-13 (pbk): 978-1-4842-1432-9   ISBN-13 (electronic): 978-1-4842-1431-2
DOI 10.1007/978-1-4842-1431-2

Library of Congress Control Number: 2016941344

Managing Director: Welmoed Spahr
Lead Editor: Steve Anglin
Technical Reviewer: Manuel Jordan Elera
Editorial Board: Steve Anglin, Pramila Balan, Louise Corrigan, Jonathan Gennick, Robert Hutchinson, Celestin Suresh John, Michelle Lowman, James Markham, Susan McDermott, Matthew Moodie, Douglas Pundick, Ben Renow-Clarke, Gwenan Spearing
Coordinating Editor: Mark Powers
Copy Editor: Kezia Endsley
Compositor: SPi Global
Indexer: SPi Global
Artist: SPi Global

Distributed to the book trade worldwide by Springer Science+Business Media New York, 233 Spring Street, 6th Floor, New York, NY 10013. Phone 1-800-SPRINGER, fax (201) 348-4505, e-mail orders-ny@springer-sbm.com, or visit www.springeronline.com. Apress Media, LLC is a California LLC and the sole member (owner) is Springer Science + Business Media Finance Inc (SSBM Finance Inc). SSBM Finance Inc is a Delaware corporation.

For information on translations, please e-mail rights@apress.com, or visit www.apress.com.

Apress and friends of ED books may be purchased in bulk for academic, corporate, or promotional use. eBook versions and licenses are also available for most titles. For more information, reference our Special Bulk Sales–eBook Licensing web page at www.apress.com/bulk-sales.

Any source code or other supplementary materials referenced by the author in this text is available to readers at www.apress.com/9781484214329. For detailed information about how to locate your book's source code, go to www.apress.com/source-code/. Readers can also access source code at SpringerLink in the Supplementary Material section for each chapter.

Printed on acid-free paper

To my wife, Norma Castaneda.

Contents at a Glance

Contents

About the Author

Felipe Gutierrez is a solutions software architect, with bachelor's and master's degrees in computer science from Instituto Tecnologico y de Estudios Superiores de Monterrey Campus Ciudad de Mexico. Gutierrez has over 20 years of IT experience, during which time he developed programs for companies in multiple vertical industries, including government, retail, healthcare, education, and banking. He currently works as a principal technical instructor for Pivotal, specializing in Cloud Foundry, Spring Framework, Spring Cloud Native Applications, Groovy, and RabbitMQ, among other technologies. He has worked as a solutions architect for big companies like Nokia, Apple, Redbox, and Qualcomm, among others. He is also the author of the Apress title *Introducing Spring Framework*.

About the Technical Reviewer

Manuel Jordan Elera is an autodidactic developer and researcher who enjoys learning new technologies for his own experiments and creating new integrations.

Manuel won the 2010 Springy Award—Community Champion and Spring Champion 2013. In his little free time, he reads the Bible and composes music on his guitar. Manuel is known as dr_pompeii.

He has tech reviewed numerous books for Apress, including *Pro Spring, 4th Edition* (2014), *Practical Spring LDAP* (2013), *Pro JPA 2, Second Edition* (2013), and *Pro Spring Security* (2013).

Read his 13 detailed tutorials about many Spring technologies and contact him through his blog at http://www.manueljordanelera.blogspot.com or follow him on his Twitter account at @dr_pompeii.

Acknowledgments

I would like to express all my gratitude to the Apress team—to Steve Anglin for accepting my proposal; to Mark Powers for keeping me on track and for his patience with me; to Matthew Moodie and the rest of the Apress team involved in this project. Thanks to everybody for making this possible.

Thanks to my technical reviewer, Manuel Jordan, for all the details and effort in his reviews, and the entire Spring Boot team for creating this amazing technology.

Thanks to my parents, Rocio Cruz and Felipe Gutierrez, for all their love and support. Thanks to my brother Edgar Gerardo Gutierrez. Special thanks to my girls who keep me on track: Norma, Nayely my "Flaca," and Ximena my "Gallito". I love you girls!

—Felipe Gutierrez

CHAPTER 1

■ ■ ■

Introduction to Spring Boot

It has been almost 13 years since the first beta release of the Spring Framework, which proved that you could create Java Enterprise applications without the complicated architecture that Sun Microsystems exposed to the world with the release of J2EE.

The Spring Framework was released as an open source project and was accepted well. It became the best open source framework for creating enterprise applications in a fast, reliable, and elegant way by promoting the use of design patterns and becoming one of the first frameworks to use the Dependency of Injection pattern. The Spring Framework has won a lot of awards in the open source community and keeps up to date by creating new features and embracing new technologies. This helps developers focus only on the application business-logic and leave the heavy lifting to the Spring Framework.

This chapter introduces the Spring Boot technology and gives you a very small taste of what it is and what you can do with it. You will learn about all its features and the associated "how-tos" during the course of the book. Let's get started.

Spring Boot

I can easily say that Spring Boot is the next chapter of the Spring Framework. Don't get me wrong, though; Spring Boot won't replace the Spring Framework. That's because Spring Boot *is* the Spring Framework! You can view Spring Boot as a new way to create Spring applications with ease.

Spring Boot simplifies the way you develop, because it makes it easy to create production-ready Spring-based applications that you can *just run*. You will find out that, with Spring Boot, you can create standalone applications that use an embedded server, making them 100% runnable applications. I will talk about this in several chapters of the book. One of its best features is that Spring Boot is an "opinionated" technology in that it will help you follow the best practices for creating robust, extensible, and scalable Spring applications.

You can find the Spring Boot project at `http://projects.spring.io/spring-boot/` and very extensive documentation at `http://docs.spring.io/spring-boot/docs/current/reference/htmlsingle/`. You can see the Spring Boot home page in Figure 1-1.

Electronic supplementary material The online version of this chapter (doi:10.1007/978-1-4842-1431-2_1) contains supplementary material, which is available to authorized users.

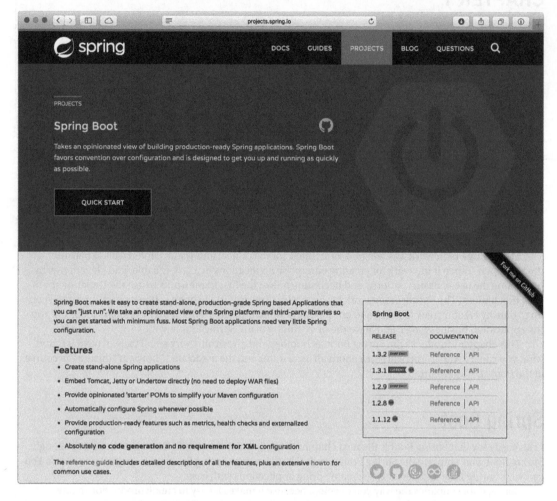

Figure 1-1. Spring Boot home page (http://projects.spring.io/spring-boot/)

Spring Applications

If you are a Spring developer like me, you already know that in order to create a simple Spring web application, you must follow certain rules of the J2EE stack and some of the Spring Framework. Those rules include the following:

Create a folder structure that contains your WAR (Web ARchive):

- It must contain a `WEB-INF` folder with `lib` and `classes` subfolders that contain the third-party libraries and your web application classes, respectively.

- Some JSP (if needed), HTML, CSS, images, and JavaScript (if needed) files.

- A file named `web.xml` that will contain the Spring `org.springframework.web.servlet.DispatcherServlet` class.

- Your Spring beans in the form `<servlet-name>-servlet.xml` (of course, you can override this and add the complete location and name of your Spring beans).

Use a utility to package your WAR file. You can use the jar tool, but most people are more used to running Apache Maven, Gradle, or, if you are "old-school," Apache Ant to compile, test, and create the WAR file.

Use an application server or container to run your WAR file, such as Tomcat, Jetty, Jboss, or WebSphere. Sometimes you need a dedicated server for deploying J2EE applications.

Even though it's only a few steps, the reality is a more painful when you have a lot of resources and classes and a bunch of Spring beans that you need to include, wire up, and use. I'm not criticizing the way Spring web applications are developed, but I think it is more about what tool you use to help you avoid this particular hassle. Tools range from an IDE such as the STS tool (https://spring.io/tools) that helps you include the correct Spring XML schemas for declaring your beans, to external tools like YEOMAN (http://yeoman.io/), which helps you create the structure and avoid the boilerplate to set everything up.

I'm talking about a simple Spring web application, but what happens when you need to include some persistence, or messaging, or perhaps you need to include security? Then you need an easy way to manage your dependencies. Of course, the easiest way is to download each dependency, but this can become a nightmare, at which point you'll start looking for tools like Apache Maven or Gradle (a Groovy DSL for compile, build, and deploy use) to help you with these dependency management tasks.

Believe me, at some point it gets more difficult, and there should be a better way to develop Spring applications, right?

Spring Boot to the Rescue

Thanks to the amazing hard work of the Spring team, the first beta released two years ago gave amazing results. I was lucky to test it, and now with more added to it, it has become the "de facto" way to create Spring applications.

Instead of reading more about Spring Boot and how easy it is to use, take a look at the simplest Spring web application possible. See Listing 1-1.

Listing 1-1. app.groovy

```
@RestController
class WebApp{
     @RequestMapping("/")
     String greetings(){
       "<h1>Spring Boot Rocks</h1>"
     }
}
```

Listing 1-1 shows you a Groovy application and the simplest possible Spring web application. But why Groovy? Well, Groovy removes all the boilerplate of Java and, with a few lines of code, you have a web app. How do you run it? You simply execute the following command:

```
$ spring run app.groovy
```

You should have something like the following output:

```
  .   ____          _            __ _ _
 /\\ / ___'_ __ _ _(_)_ __  __ _ \ \ \ \
( ( )\___ | '_ | '_| | '_ \/ _` | \ \ \ \
 \\/  ___)| |_)| | | | | || (_| |  ) ) ) )
  '  |____| .__|_| |_|_| |_\__, | / / / /
 =========|_|==============|___/=/_/_/_/
 :: Spring Boot ::        (v1.3.1.RELEASE)
```

```
INFO 62862 --- [runner-0] o.s.boot.SpringApplication        : Starting application on
INFO 62862 --- [runner-0] o.s.boot.SpringApplication        : No active profile set,
falling back to default profiles: default
...
INFO 62862 --- [runner-0] s.b.c.e.t.TomcatEmbeddedServletContainer : Tomcat initialized with
port(s): 8080 (http)
INFO 62862 --- [runner-0] o.apache.catalina.core.StandardService   : Starting service Tomcat
INFO 62862 --- [runner-0] org.apache.catalina.core.StandardEngine  : Starting Servlet
Engine: Apache Tomcat/8.0.30
INFO 62862 --- [ost-startStop-1] o.a.c.c.C.[Tomcat].[localhost].[/] : Initializing Spring
embedded WebApplicationContext
INFO 62862 --- [ost-startStop-1] o.s.web.context.ContextLoader    : Root
WebApplicationContext: initialization completed in 1820 ms
INFO 62862 --- [ost-startStop-1] o.s.b.c.e.ServletRegistrationBean : Mapping servlet:
'dispatcherServlet' to [/]
...
INFO 62862 --- [runner-0] s.b.c.e.t.TomcatEmbeddedServletContainer : Tomcat started on
port(s): 8080 (http) ...
```

You may be wondering: Wait a minute, what is this `spring run` command? How can I install it? What else do I need? Don't worry too much; in the next chapter, you will install the Spring Boot CLI (Command Line Interface) and you will learn everything you need to know about this particular tool.

You can open a browser and point to `http://localhost:8080` to see the message: *Spring Boot Rocks*.

How does the Spring Boot know about a web application and how to run it? Spring Boot inspects your code and, based on the annotations `@RestController` and `@RequestMapping`, tries to execute your code as a web application. It does this by using an embedded Tomcat server and running the web app from within. That's it! It's very simple to create a Spring web application.

Now let's see the Java version, which is a minimal web app. I'll show you only the code for now; in the next chapter, you'll learn how to set it up. See Listings 1-2 and 1-3.

Listing 1-2. SimpleWebApp.java

```java
package com.apress.spring;
import org.springframework.boot.SpringApplication;
import org.springframework.boot.autoconfigure.SpringBootApplication;


@SpringBootApplication
public class SimpleWebApp {

    public static void main(String[] args) {
        SpringApplication.run(SimpleWebApp.class, args);
    }
}
```

Listing 1-2 shows you the entry point for a Spring Boot application in Java. It's using a `@SpringBootApplication` annotation and the `SpringApplication` singleton class in the `main` method that will execute the application. The `run` method call accepts two parameters—the class that actually contains the annotated `@SpringBootApplication` annotation and the application's arguments.

Listing 1-3. SimpleWebController.java

```java
package com.apress.spring;

import org.springframework.web.bind.annotation.RequestMapping;
import org.springframework.web.bind.annotation.RestController;

@RestController
public class SimpleWebController {

        @RequestMapping("/")
        public String greetings(){
                return "<h1> Spring Boot Rocks in Java too!</h1>";
        }
}
```

Listing 1-3 shows you the typical Spring MVC controller class, where you use the @RestController and the @RequestMapping annotations to tell Spring to use the SimpleWebController class as a web controller and to use the method greetings as an entry point for a HTTP request.

You can run this example by using the Spring Boot CLI, the same as you did with the Groovy version. In this case, though, you are using the .java extension:

```
$ spring run *.java
```

Or, if you add the structure for Maven, you can run this example by using the following command:

```
$ mvn spring-boot:run
```

Or, if you have the Maven wrapper (discussed in the next chapter), you can run it with the following command:

```
$ mvn spring-boot:run
```

Or, if you set up the structure for Gradle, you can run it with this command:

```
$ gradle bootRun
```

Regardless of the method you use, open a browser and point to the URL http://localhost:8080/. You should see the message: "Spring Boot Rocks in Java too!".

You may be wondering how to set this Java version up or how to use the Spring Boot CLI, right? Don't worry, in the next chapter, you will see how to install and use the Spring Boot CLI to prototype Spring apps in the awesome programming language called Groovy (like Listing 1-1) and you will learn how to use Spring Boot to run Java-based Spring applications (like Listings 1-2 and 1-3) and how Spring Boot works internally.

For now, I simply wanted to show you that, with a few lines of code, you can create a simple Spring web application using Groovy or Java instead of all that hassle from the J2EE stack.

■ **Note** If you want to use Spring Boot right away, feel free to use the book's companion source code. The Java example contains the structure and everything you need to run the Maven wrapper: $ mvnw spring-boot:run.

5

Why Spring Boot?

Spring Boot has many features that make it suitable for:

- Cloud Native Applications that follow the 12 factor patterns (developed by the Netflix engineering team at http://12factor.net/)

- Productivity increases by reducing time of development and deployment

- Enterprise-production-ready Spring applications

- Non-functional requirements, such as the Spring Boot Actuator (a module that brings metrics, health checks, and management easily) and embedded containers for running web applications (such as Tomcat, Undertow, Jetty, etc.)

The term "microservices" is getting attention for creating scalable, highly available, and robust applications, and Spring Boot fits there perfectly by allowing developers to focus only on the business logic and to leave the heavy lifting to the Spring Framework.

Spring Boot Features

Spring Boot has a lot of features that you'll learn about in the following chapters, and here is just a taste:

- The `SpringApplication` class. I showed you that in a Java Spring Boot application, the main method executes this singleton class. This particular class provides a convenient way to initiate a Spring application.

- Spring Boot allows you to create applications without requiring any XML configuration. Spring Boot doesn't generate code.

- Spring Boot provides a fluent builder API through the `SpringApplicationBuilder` singleton class that allows you to create hierarchies with multiple application contexts. This particular feature is related to the Spring Framework and how it works internally. If you are a Spring developer already, you'll learn more about this feature in the following chapters. If you are new to Spring and Spring Boot, you just need to know that you can extend Spring Boot to get more control over your applications.

- Spring Boot offers you more ways to configure the Spring application events and listeners. This will be explained in more detail in the following chapters.

- I mentioned that Spring Boot is an "opinionated" technology, which means that Spring Boot will attempt to create the right type of application, either a web application (by embedding a Tomcat or Jetty container) or a single application.

- The `ApplicationArguments` interface. Spring Boot allows you to access any application arguments. This is useful when you want to run your application with some parameters. For example, you can use `--debug mylog.txt` or `--audit=true` and have access to those values.

- Spring Boot allows you to execute code after the application has started. The only thing you need to do is implement the `CommandLineRunner` interface and provide the implementation of the `run(String ...args)` method. A particular example is to initialize some records in a database as it starts or check on some services and see if they are running before your application starts.

- Spring Boot allows you to externalize configurations by using an `application.properties` or `application.yml` file. More about this in the following chapters.

- You can add administration-related features, normally through JMX. You do this simply by enabling the `spring.application.admin.enabled` property in the `application.properties` or `application.yml` files.

- Spring Boot allows you to have profiles that will help your application run in different environments.

- Spring Boot allows you to configure and use logging very simply.

- Spring Boot provides a simple way to configure and manage your dependencies by using starter poms. In other words, if you are going to create a web application, you only need to include the `spring-boot-start-web` dependency in your Maven pom or Gradle build file.

- Spring Boot provides out-of-the-box non-functional requirements by using the Spring Boot Actuator, so you can see the health, memory, and so on, of your application.

- Spring Boot provides `@Enable<feature>` annotations that help you to include, configure, and use technologies like databases (SQL and NoSQL), caching, scheduling, messaging, Spring integration, batching, and more.

As you can see, Spring Boot has all these features and more, and you'll learn more about these features in the following chapters. Now it's time to start learning more about Spring Boot by seeing how it works internally.

Summary

This chapter provided a quick overview of the Spring Framework and covered one of its new technologies: Spring Boot.

The following chapters start showing you all the cool features of Spring Boot, first by creating simple applications and understanding the internals of Spring Boot and then by creating more complicated applications.

CHAPTER 2

■ ■ ■

Your First Spring Boot Application

In this chapter you are going to install the Spring Boot CLI, learn more a little about it, and create your first Spring Boot application. You will learn how Spring Boot works internally so you have a better picture of this amazing technology.

You can create Spring Boot applications by using the Spring Boot Command Line Interface (CLI) or by using Maven, Gradle, and even Apache Ant. This chapter has step-by-step explanations on what needs to be done to set up your environment from the command line through using Spring Boot on an Integrated Development Environment (IDE). Let's get started!

Installing Spring Boot CLI

Before you install the Spring Boot CLI, it's necessary to check your Java installation, because you must have JDK 1.6 or higher in your computer. Sometimes it's necessary to have the JAVA_HOME environment variable pointing to your Java installation and the java program in your PATH.

UNIX OSs: Linux, OS X, and Solaris

There are a lot of tools that can help you install the Spring Boot CLI. If you are using any UNIX environment, including Linux, OS X, or Solaris, you can use a very good tool named SDKMAN. You can find it at http://sdkman.io/. Open a terminal window and execute the following:

```
$ curl -s get.sdkman.io | bash
```

After it finishes, you can execute the following line to run the sdk command:

```
$ source "$HOME/.sdkman/bin/sdkman-init.sh"
```

Then make sure that the sdk command is working by executing this line:

```
$ sdk version
SDKMAN 3.2.4
```

Next, it's time to install the Spring Boot CLI, which you do by executing this command:

```
$ sdk install springboot
```

© Felipe Gutierrez 2016
F. Gutierrez, *Pro Spring Boot*, DOI 10.1007/978-1-4842-1431-2_2

Once the CLI is installed, you can check if everything went okay by executing this request:

```
$ spring --version
Spring CLI v1.3.2.RELEASE
```

You should get the latest version of Spring Boot; in my case it's release 1.3.2. Now you are ready to start using the Spring Boot CLI on a UNIX system.

■ **Note** You can use the same sdk command to install Groovy and Gradle. You can install those two by executing: $ sdk install groovy and $ sdk install gradle.

There is another UNIX-like OS option called *homebrew*. This tool was initially developed for OS X users so they could install missing tools from the UNIX/Linux world. One of the benefits of brew is that it has a sandbox that doesn't interfere with your system.

On OS X you can go to the http://brew.sh/ web site and read more about this particular tool. In order to install brew, you must execute this command:

```
$ ruby -e "$(curl -fsSL https://raw.githubusercontent.com/Homebrew/install/master/install)"
```

Once it finishes installing, follow the instructions to get it working from the command line. You might need to open a new terminal and/or do a source over the .bash_profile file to get it working, although if you have the latest version, you won't need to do this. Just follow the instructions on the screen after you install brew. You can then execute the following command to install Spring Boot:

```
$ brew tap pivotal/tap
$ brew install springboot
```

If you are a Linux user, you can install brew (you can get more info at http://brew.sh/linuxbrew/) by executing this command:

```
$ ruby -e "$(curl -fsSL https://raw.githubusercontent.com/Homebrew/linuxbrew/go/install)"
```

Then execute the same commands from above:

```
$ brew tap pivotal/tap
$ brew install springboot
```

That's it; it's very simple. One of the benefits of using the Linux version is that you don't need sudo, because all the software is installed in your home directory.

■ **Note** You can also use the brew command to install the software that we are going to use in the next chapters, including RabbitMQ, Redis, and MySQL.

Windows OS

If you are a Windows user or you don't want to use the previous methods, you can download the ZIP binary distribution and uncompress it. These are the links of release 1.3.2:

- `http://repo.spring.io/release/org/springframework/boot/spring-boot-cli/1.3.2.RELEASE/spring-boot-cli-1.3.2.RELEASE-bin.zip`

- `http://repo.spring.io/snapshot/org/springframework/boot/spring-boot-cli/`

These links are the binary versions, but if you wonder where those links are coming from, you can find them here: `https://docs.spring.io/spring-boot/docs/current/reference/html/getting-started-installing-spring-boot.html#getting-started-manual-cli-installation`. You must have the `JAVA_HOME` variable set (pointing to your Java SDK) and the `SPRING_HOME` variable pointing to where you uncompress the binary distribution. Also make sure to set up your `PATH` variable, which includes the `%SPRING_HOME%\bin` path (or, if you are using UNIX, it's `$SPRING_HOME/bin`). By setting these variables to the environment, you will have access to the `spring.bat` or `spring` scripts.

■ **Note** The binary distribution contains a Groovy version, so you are set if you want to run Groovy scripts. You can verify that your installation was successful by typing `$ spring --version Spring CLI v1.3.2.RELEASE`.

You have the Spring Boot CLI, so what's next? In the previous chapter, you saw a simple web application written in Groovy and Java, and the way that you run it is by executing this command:

`$ spring run *.groovy`

or

`$ spring run *.java`

But there is more to it. Not only is the Spring Boot CLI useful for running the application but it also initializes and creates the structure you need. For example, you can create a base or minimal project by executing the following:

`$ spring init --build gradle myapp`

This command will call the web service at `https://start.spring.io` (this is discussed in the following sections of this chapter) and will create a folder named `myapp`. The project is Gradle-based, although if you don't include the `--build gradle` option, it will by default create a Maven-based project. Figure 2-1 shows the structure of the project.

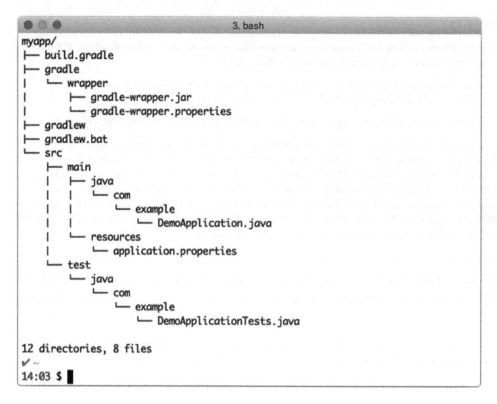

Figure 2-1. *Spring Boot project structure*

Figure 2-1 shows you the Spring Boot project structure created when you execute the spring init command. If you want to add more features—such as web, JPA, and Maven projects—you can execute the following command:

```
$ spring init -dweb,data-jpa,h2,thymeleaf --build maven myapp --force
```

This command will create a Spring Boot Maven project and will include all the necessary dependencies in the pom.xml file to run a Spring Boot web application. It will include libraries to handle web files (this will include the embedded Tomcat server), persistence (data-jpa), the H2 database engine (h2), and a viewer engine (thymeleaf). You need to use --force to override the previous myapp directory or you can change the name.

Don't worry too much about what are those dependencies or how they create this project; you'll learn more about this in the following sections.

Now you are set to start using the Spring Boot CLI with Groovy or Java and can create prototype applications. You can use the Spring Boot CLI to create "production-ready" apps, which will depend on how you set up your environment to use this tool. You'll learn more about using the Spring Boot CLI in this chapter and later chapters.

Spring Boot with Maven and Gradle

If you already use Maven (https://maven.apache.org/) or Gradle (http://gradle.org/) as tools for compiling, testing, and building, you can use also Spring Boot. And as you might guess, you need to include some dependencies in order to use Spring Boot. The following sections explain what you need for every project in Spring Boot. You must see these as requirements if you want to use Maven or Gradle to develop Spring Boot apps.

Using Maven

Listing 2-1 shows the pom.xml file that you use every time you need to create a Spring Boot app.

Listing 2-1. pom.xml

```
<?xml version="1.0" encoding="UTF-8"?>
<project xmlns="http://maven.apache.org/POM/4.0.0"
xmlns:xsi="http://www.w3.org/2001/XMLSchema-instance"
    xsi:schemaLocation="http://maven.apache.org/POM/4.0.0
    http://maven.apache.org/xsd/maven-4.0.0.xsd">
    <modelVersion>4.0.0</modelVersion>

    <groupId>com.example</groupId>
    <artifactId>myapp</artifactId>
    <version>0.0.1-SNAPSHOT</version>

    <!-- Spring Boot Parent Dependencies-->
    <parent>
        <groupId>org.springframework.boot</groupId>
        <artifactId>spring-boot-starter-parent</artifactId>
        <version>1.3.1.RELEASE</version>
    </parent>

    <!-- Add dependencies: starter poms -->
    <dependency>
        <groupId>org.springframework.boot</groupId>
        <artifactId>spring-boot-starter</artifactId>
    </dependency>

    <!-- Spring Boot Plugin for creating JAR/WAR files -->
    <build>
        <plugins>
            <plugin>
                <groupId>org.springframework.boot</groupId>
                <artifactId>spring-boot-maven-plugin</artifactId>
            </plugin>
        </plugins>
    </build>
</project>
```

Listing 2-1 shows you the minimum pom.xml that you can have for any Spring Boot application. If you take a closer look, there is a tag section where you need to include the spring-boot-starter-parent artifact. This particular dependency contains all you need to run your app. It contains all the descriptions of dependencies that a Spring Boot application needs, like all the dependencies of the Spring Framework (spring-core), Spring Test (spring-test), and more. You only need to use this parent pom.

Another section is the starter poms, where you declare the dependencies of the actual Spring Boot feature you want to use. Listing 2-1 shows the default starter, spring-boot-starter artifactId. The starter poms will bring all the dependencies that you need for your application, which is why you need to include just one starter pom. For example, if you are creating a web application, the only dependency you need is the spring-boot-starter-web artifact:

```
...
<!-- Add dependencies: starter poms -->
    <dependencies>
        <dependency>
            <groupId>org.springframework.boot</groupId>
            <artifactId>spring-boot-starter-web</artifactId>
        </dependency>
        ...
    </dependencies>
...
```

This dependency will include all the spring-core, spring-web, spring-webmvc, embedded Tomcat server, and other libraries related to the web application. A later section of this chapter explains more about the Spring Boot starter poms. At this point, you simply need to understand that you can include these dependencies in your main pom.xml file.

The last section is the Spring Boot Maven plugin, and it is included by declaring the spring-boot-maven-plugin artifact. This particular plugin will help you package your application as a JAR or WAR with the command: mvn package. It also has several goals/tasks that you can use, like the one in the previous chapter for running the Spring Boot app: mvn spring-boot:run. You can get more information about this plugin at its web site: http://docs.spring.io/spring-boot/docs/1.3.1.RELEASE/maven-plugin/.

You are set now with Maven. You are going to create your first Spring Boot app later, though. Right now I want you to know all the possible ways to use Spring Boot.

Using Gradle

You can use Gradle (http://gradle.org/) to compile, test, and build Spring Boot apps. Just as with Maven, you need to have a minimum description for creating Spring Boot applications. See Listing 2-2.

Listing 2-2. build.gradle

```
buildscript {
    repositories {
        jcenter()
        maven { url "http://repo.spring.io/snapshot" }
        maven { url "http://repo.spring.io/milestone" }
    }
    dependencies {
        classpath("org.springframework.boot:spring-boot-gradle-plugin:1.3.1.RELEASE")
    }
}
```

```
apply plugin: 'java'
apply plugin: 'spring-boot'

jar {
    baseName = 'myproject'
    version =  '0.0.1-SNAPSHOT'
}

repositories {
    jcenter()
    maven { url "http://repo.spring.io/snapshot" }
    maven { url "http://repo.spring.io/milestone" }
}

dependencies {
    // starter poms dependencies
    compile('org.springframework.boot:spring-boot-starter')
}
```

Listing 2-2 shows you the minimum build.gradle file that you need to use to run Spring Boot applications. The first section you need to look at is the buildscript, where you add the dependency of the Spring Boot Gradle plugin. This plugin contains the parent pom (which contains all the base dependencies) and the tasks that will help you compile, run, and package your Spring Boot apps. It declares a repositories section where the Gradle tool will look for *Maven-like* servers that provide all the libraries needed by the dependencies section that is declared.

Next is the section where you apply the plugins, in this case the apply plugin: spring-boot. This will add the tasks mentioned above. Then, either you are creating a jar or a war declaration that contains the baseName and the version. Next is the repositories section, where all the dependencies can be found to be downloaded into your environment. Finally there is the dependencies section, where you put all the starter poms in the form of org.springframework.boot:spring-boot-starter-<feature/technology>. Listing 2-2 shows the default spring-boot-starter artifact.

So, for example if you want to create a web application with testing, you need to add the following in the dependencies section:

```
compile("org.springframework.boot:spring-boot-starter-web")
testCompile("org.springframework.boot:spring-boot-starter-test")
```

If you want to use a starter pom, you have to add the following syntax.
For Maven:

```
<dependency>
    <groupId>org.springframework.boot</groupId>
    <artifactId>spring-boot-starter-[TECHNOLOGY]</artifactId>
</dependency>
```

For Gradle:

```
compile("org.springframework.boot:spring-boot-starter-[TECHNOLOGY]")
```

As you can see, the Spring Boot team created a very easy-to-follow naming convention for all the starter poms. Note also that you don't need to add any dependency version, because the starter poms will take care of that.

Now you are set to use Gradle for your Spring Boot apps.

■ **Note**   When using Gradle you can use the Gradle wrapper, which allows you to have a binary Gradle when you want to distribute your application and the computer doesn't have Gradle. See `http://www.gradle.org/docs/current/userguide/gradle_wrapper.html`.

Spring Boot Using External Tools

You have learned how to install Spring Boot CLI to use Groovy or Java for your apps, and you have seen the minimal declaration dependencies for using Maven or Gradle. You do need to create a directory structure as well. If you want to add more features, you also need the names of the starter poms. (I showed you only the minimum requirements for Maven and Gradle, right?)

Well, there is a tool that you can use without using an IDE. The Spring team created a reference architecture tool/service called Spring Initializr, and you can use it to create a complete project with all the dependencies that you need.

Spring Boot Using the Spring Initializr

You can find this reference architecture service at `http://start.spring.io`. It's hosted by Pivotal Web Services. Right now it's on its second iteration. It provides a simple version (Figure 2-2) and a full version (Figure 2-3) and both look great!

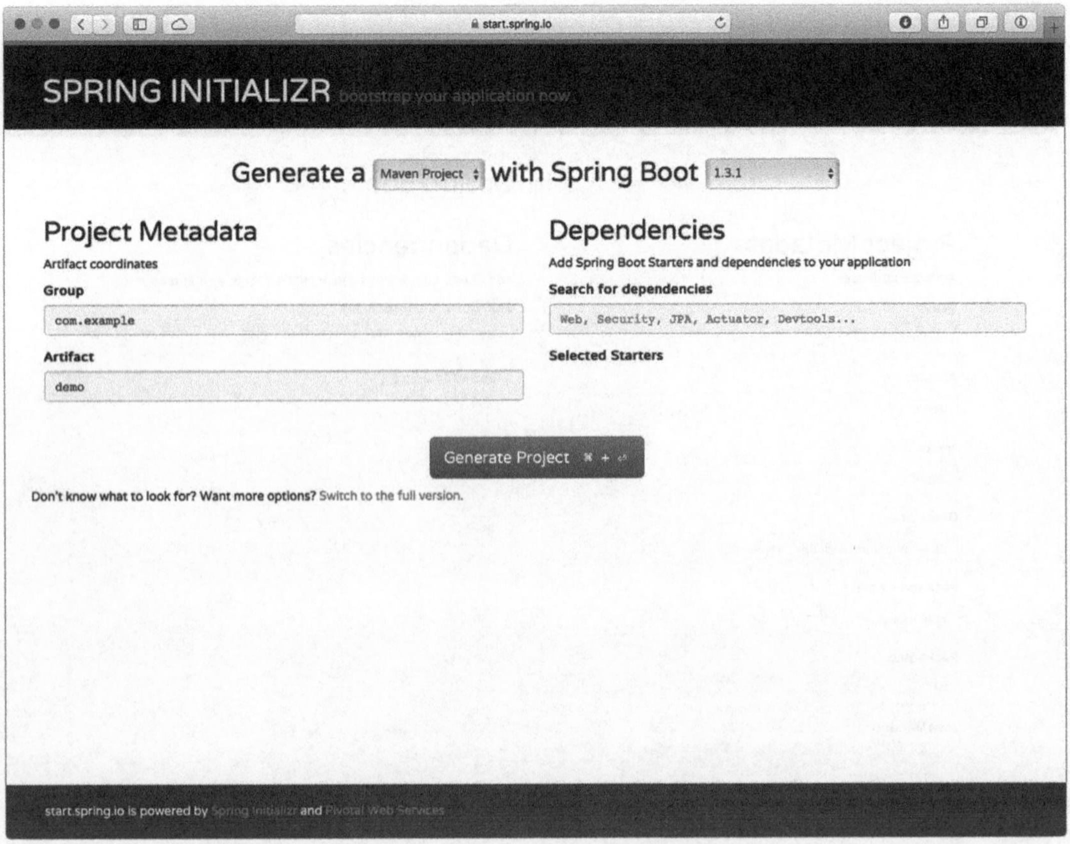

Figure 2-2. Simple view of the Spring Initializr (`http://start.spring.io`)

Figure 2-2 shows an interface where you can create your Spring Boot application. You can include all the dependencies by just typing *web*, *security*, or *jpa*. If you click the Generate Project button, you will get a ZIP file that contains the structure and the pom.xml or build.gradle file, depending on what project type you choose. You can also select the Spring Boot version and the programming language to use (Groovy or Java).

Figure 2-3 shows you the full version of the Spring Initializr, and if you keep scrolling down, you will find all the dependencies that you can add by clicking on the checkboxes. After you select the features you want to use, click the Generate Project button to get the ZIP file that contains your project.

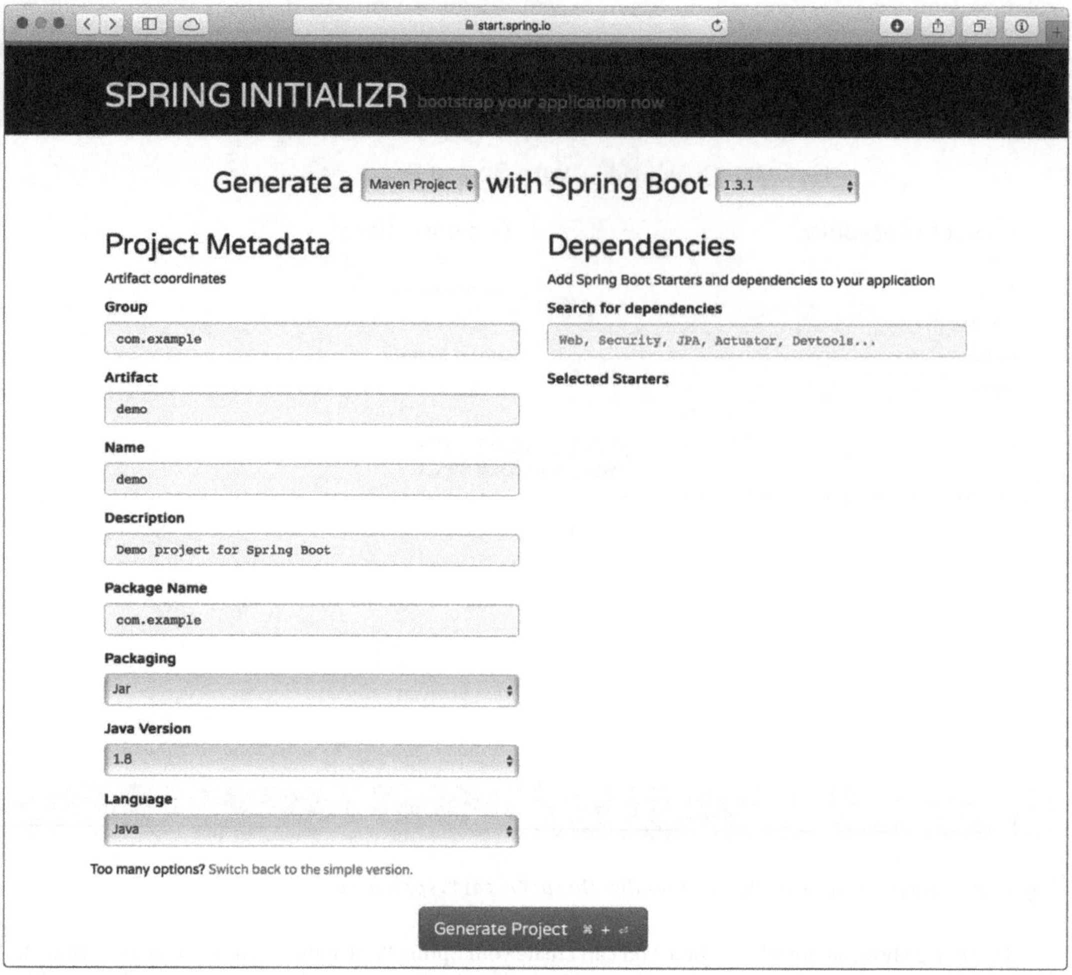

Figure 2-3. *Full version of the Spring Initializr*

Using the Spring Initializr with UNIX cURL

The Spring Initializr can be accessed using the UNIX cURL command because at the end it is a web service and it exposes a RESTful API. So, for example, if you wanted to create a simple project that contains just the minimum files, you could execute the following command:

```
$ curl -s https://start.spring.io/starter.zip -o myapp.zip
```

This command will create a myapp.zip file that contains all the structure for the Spring Boot app. And by default it contains a Maven project with its pom.xml file and a Maven wrapper. This means that you aren't required to have Maven installed, because it comes with it. You can easily use all the goals/tasks to compile, build, and run your Spring Boot apps.

If you want the minimum structure for a Gradle-based project, just execute the following command:

```
$ curl -s https://start.spring.io/starter.zip -o myapp.zip -d type=gradle-project
```

With this command you will have a build.gradle and a Gradle wrapper. They will help you to compile, build, and run your Spring Boot apps without having to install Gradle.

If you want to create a Spring Boot application with a web feature, you can execute the following command:

```
$ curl -s https://start.spring.io/starter.zip -o myapp.zip -d type=maven-project -d
dependencies=web
```

Using this command, you will have in your pom.xml file the spring-boot-starter-web artifact as a dependency. Sometimes you will want to see how the pom.xml or build.gradle file looks when you're adding some dependencies. You can generate these files by executing the following command if you want only the Maven pom.xml:

```
$ curl -s https://start.spring.io/pom.xml -d packaging=war -o pom.xml -d
dependencies=web,data-jpa
```

This command will generate only the pom.xml with a WAR package type and the spring-boot-starter-web and the spring-boot-starter-data-jpa artifacts. If you want the build.gradle file as well, you execute the following command:

```
$ curl -s https://start.spring.io/build.gradle -o build.gradle -d dependencies=web,data-jpa
```

This command will generate only the build.gradle as a JAR (this is the default option, unless you use the -d packaging flag) and it will contain the same starters from the previous command. So, as you can see, you have several options for creating a Spring Boot application.

■ **Note** You can get more details about what other options you can set when executing the cURL command. Just execute this command: $ curl start.spring.io.

Notice that the -s option is used in these examples. It allows you to force the cURL command to be silent, and you can remove it and see the progress of the ZIP file being downloaded. You can get more information about all the flags shown in the cURL examples by Googling them or executing the $man curl command.

Spring Boot Using Spring Tool Suite (STS)

If you are already using the Eclipse IDE, you can install the STS as a plugin or download it at https://spring.io/tools/sts/all. The STS is available for all the different operating systems. See Figure 2-4.

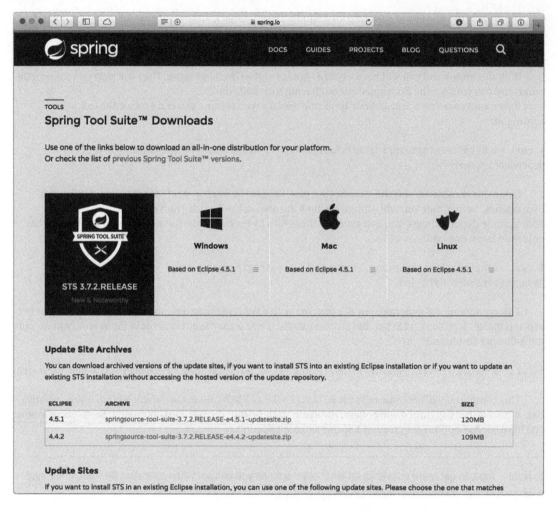

Figure 2-4. *Spring Tool Suite (STS) web page (https://spring.io/tools/sts/all)*

One of the benefits of using the STS is that it comes with Spring Boot support. Choose File ➤ New to see the Spring Starter Project option (it's the first option shown in Figure 2-5).

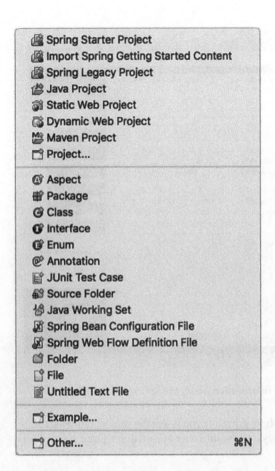

Figure 2-5. Choose File ➤ New ➤ Spring Starter Project

If you click on the Spring Starter Project option, the Spring Starter Project wizard will appear. This is where you put all the general information about your Spring Boot project. See Figure 2-6.

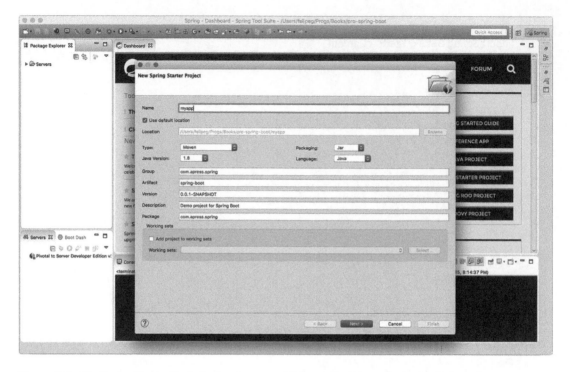

Figure 2-6. *The Spring Starter Project wizard—general information about the Spring Boot project*

Figure 2-6 shows you the first page of the wizard where normally you select the project type (Maven or Gradle), the Java version, the language (Java or Groovy), and some other Maven descriptors. If you click Next, the dependencies page appears. See Figure 2-7.

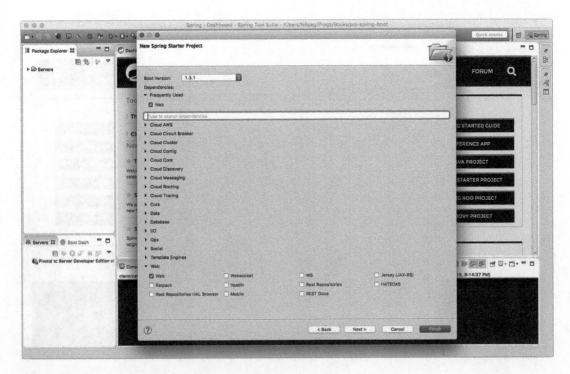

Figure 2-7. *Spring Starter Project wizard—dependencies selection*

Figure 2-7 shows you the next page of the wizard, where you select the dependencies for your application and the version of Spring Boot to use. You can choose the latest snapshot. And if you click Next, you can see the summary of your Spring Boot project. See Figure 2-8.

23

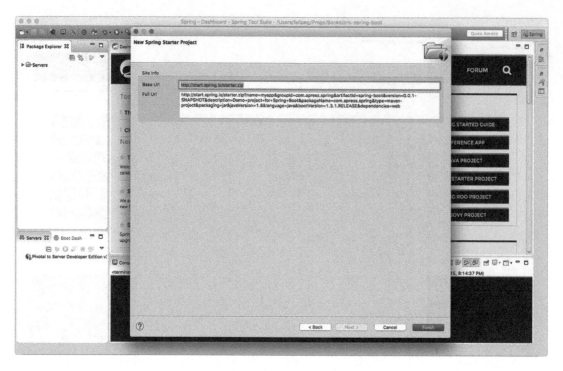

Figure 2-8. *Spring Starter Project wizard—summary page*

Figure 2-8 shows you the final step and summary of what the wizard will generate, because it gives access to the URL and all the parameters that you can use with the cURL command. You could even paste the whole URL in a browser and get the ZIP file.

The Spring Starter Project wizard will download and uncompress in the background and set the workspace with the Spring Boot project you created. As you can see, you have another option to create Spring Boot applications. One of the major benefits of using the STS is that it has support for Spring Boot. This means wizard support and code-completion support for the `application.properties` and the `application.yml` files, as well as cloud support and some other features.

Your First Spring Boot Application

It's time to create your first Spring Boot application. The idea of this application is simple—it's a journal application. You will start with something simple in this chapter, just enough to get to know the Spring Boot internals. During the rest of the book, you will modify it so at the end you have a complete and production-ready Spring Boot application.

Spring Boot Journal

This application is called "Spring Boot Journal" and it's a simple application in which you will have a collection of entries that shows the main ideas over a timeline.

You have installed Spring Boot CLI and you already know more about the different options for using Spring Boot with Maven or Gradle. You also know that you can use an IDE like the STS and use the Spring Boot project wizard. Regardless of the method you choose, it will be the same for this application. It's most important to describe the main concepts behind the Spring Boot technology.

These steps show you how to create the Spring Boot journal application using the STS:

1. Open the STS and select File ➤ New ➤ Spring Starter Project. You can add any package name or any group or artifactId if you want, just make sure to select Java as the language. I will use both pom.xml and build.gradle files, so you have all the dependencies this app needs. See Figure 2-9. After entering all the necessary information, click Next to move to the dependencies page.

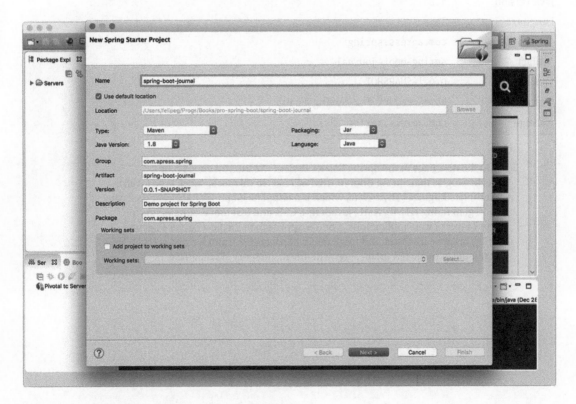

Figure 2-9. Spring Starter project—Spring Boot journal

Figure 2-9 shows you the first page of the Spring Starter Project wizard. As I said before, you can put whatever information you like. The important part are the classes you are going to use, but if you want to follow along, this is the information I used in the example:

Field	Value
Name	spring-boot-journal
Type	Maven
Packaging	Jar
Java Version	1.8
Language	Java
Group	com.apress.spring
Artifact	spring-boot-journal
Version	0.0.1-SNAPSHOT
Description	Demo project for Spring Boot
Package	com.apress.spring

2. On the next page of the Spring Starter Project wizard, you choose the technologies that Spring Boot Journal will use. In this case, check Web (Web), Template Engines (Thymeleaf, which is a template engine capable of processing and generating HTML, XML, JavaScript, CSS, and text that is suitable for the view layer of web applications, a better approach to the Java Server Pages or JSPs, because it's faster and more reliable), Data (JPA), and Database (H2). This example uses the JPA technology with the in-memory H2 database.

See Figure 2-10. After choosing your dependencies, you can click Finish.

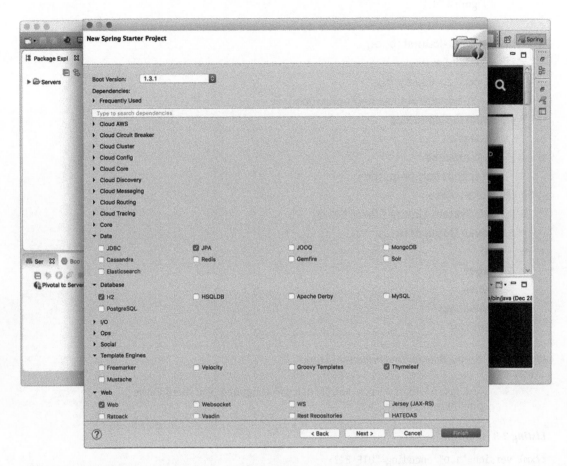

Figure 2-10. Spring Starter Project wizard —dependencies —Spring Boot journal

3. Take a look at the project's file structure. You should have something similar to Figure 2-11.

Figure 2-11. *Spring Boot journal project structure*

4. Next, take a look at the pom.xml file that was generated. You should have something like Listing 2-3.

Listing 2-3. pom.xml

```xml
<?xml version="1.0" encoding="UTF-8"?>
<project xmlns="http://maven.apache.org/POM/4.0.0"
xmlns:xsi="http://www.w3.org/2001/XMLSchema-instance"
    xsi:schemaLocation="http://maven.apache.org/POM/4.0.0
    http://maven.apache.org/xsd/maven-4.0.0.xsd">
    <modelVersion>4.0.0</modelVersion>

    <groupId>com.apress.spring</groupId>
    <artifactId>spring-boot-journal</artifactId>
    <version>0.0.1-SNAPSHOT</version>
    <packaging>jar</packaging>

    <name>spring-boot-journal</name>
    <description>Demo project for Spring Boot</description>
```

```
<parent>
    <groupId>org.springframework.boot</groupId>
    <artifactId>spring-boot-starter-parent</artifactId>
    <version>1.3.1.RELEASE</version>
    <relativePath/> <!-- lookup parent from repository -->
</parent>

<properties>
    <project.build.sourceEncoding>UTF-8</project.build.sourceEncoding>
    <java.version>1.8</java.version>
</properties>

<dependencies>
    <dependency>
        <groupId>org.springframework.boot</groupId>
        <artifactId>spring-boot-starter-data-jpa</artifactId>
    </dependency>

    <dependency>
        <groupId>org.springframework.boot</groupId>
        <artifactId>spring-boot-starter-thymeleaf</artifactId>
    </dependency>

    <dependency>
        <groupId>org.springframework.boot</groupId>
        <artifactId>spring-boot-starter-web</artifactId>
    </dependency>

    <dependency>
        <groupId>com.h2database</groupId>
        <artifactId>h2</artifactId>
        <scope>runtime</scope>
    </dependency>

    <dependency>
        <groupId>org.springframework.boot</groupId>
        <artifactId>spring-boot-starter-test</artifactId>
        <scope>test</scope>
    </dependency>
</dependencies>

<build>
    <plugins>
        <plugin>
            <groupId>org.springframework.boot</groupId>
            <artifactId>spring-boot-maven-plugin</artifactId>
        </plugin>
    </plugins>
</build>

</project>
```

Listing 2-3 shows you the pom.xml of the Spring Boot journal. The important part in this pom is the dependencies section, which contains all the starter poms that you selected in the wizard. Remember, you are going to use a web technology (your Spring Boot journal is a web application—spring-boot-starter-web), a template engine (Thymeleaf—spring-boot-starter-thymeleaf) that will render the HTML pages of the journal app, a Data (JPA – spring-boot-starter-data-jpa) technology that will take care of the data persistence, a Database engine (H2), an in-memory database, and a test unit framework (spring-boot-starter-test) that will help with all the unit and integration testing. For now, and for your first application, the H2 database engine will be enough. Later in the book you will switch to different database engines, such as MySQL, MongoDB, or Redis.

If you selected a Gradle project, Listing 2-4 shows you the build.gradle file.

Listing 2-4. build.gradle

```
buildscript {
    ext {
        springBootVersion = '1.3.1.RELEASE'
    }
    repositories {
        mavenCentral()
    }
    dependencies {
        classpath("org.springframework.boot:spring-boot-gradle-plugin:${springBootVersion}")
    }
}

apply plugin: 'java'
apply plugin: 'eclipse'
apply plugin: 'idea'
apply plugin: 'spring-boot'

jar {
    baseName = 'spring-boot-journal'
    version = '0.0.1-SNAPSHOT'
}
sourceCompatibility = 1.8
targetCompatibility = 1.8

repositories {
    mavenCentral()
}

dependencies {
    compile('org.springframework.boot:spring-boot-starter-data-jpa')
    compile('org.springframework.boot:spring-boot-starter-thymeleaf')
    compile('org.springframework.boot:spring-boot-starter-web')
    runtime('com.h2database:h2')
    testCompile('org.springframework.boot:spring-boot-starter-test')
}
```

```
eclipse {
    classpath {
        containers.remove('org.eclipse.jdt.launching.JRE_CONTAINER')
        containers 'org.eclipse.jdt.launching.JRE_CONTAINER/org.eclipse.jdt.internal.debug.
        ui.launcher.StandardVMType/JavaSE-1.8'
    }
}

task wrapper(type: Wrapper) {
    gradleVersion = '2.9'
}
```

Listing 2-4 shows the build.gradle file. The important part is to take a look at the dependencies sections where all the starter poms are declared. It's very similar to Maven. I only want to comment about the last section, where there is a Eclipse declaration. This will help you to get the correct runtime environment when you import this project to STS or any other Eclipse IDE version.

     5.   For this journal, you need to create a domain class. See Listing 2-5, which shows the Journal class.

Listing 2-5. com.apress.spring.domain.Journal.java

```
package com.apress.spring.domain;

import java.text.ParseException;
import java.text.SimpleDateFormat;
import java.util.Date;

import javax.persistence.Entity;
import javax.persistence.GeneratedValue;
import javax.persistence.GenerationType;
import javax.persistence.Id;
import javax.persistence.Transient;

@Entity
public class Journal {

        @Id
        @GeneratedValue(strategy=GenerationType.AUTO)
        private Long id;
        private String title;
        private Date created;
        private String summary;

        @Transient
        private SimpleDateFormat format = new SimpleDateFormat("MM/dd/yyyy");

        public Journal(String title, String summary, String date) throws ParseException{
                this.title = title;
                this.summary = summary;
                this.created = format.parse(date);
        }
```

```java
        Journal(){}

        public Long getId() {
                return id;
        }

        public void setId(Long id) {
                this.id = id;
        }

        public String getTitle() {
                return title;
        }

        public void setTitle(String title) {
                this.title = title;
        }

        public Date getCreated() {
                return created;
        }

        public void setCreated(Date created) {
                this.created = created;
        }

        public String getSummary() {
                return summary;
        }

        public void setSummary(String summary) {
                this.summary = summary;
        }

        public String getCreatedAsShort(){
                return format.format(created);
        }

        public String toString(){
                StringBuilder value = new StringBuilder("JournalEntry(");
                value.append("Id: ");
                value.append(id);
                value.append(",Title: ");
                value.append(title);
                value.append(",Summary: ");
                value.append(summary);
                value.append(",Created: ");
                value.append(getCreatedAsShort());
                value.append(")");
                return value.toString();
        }
}
```

Listing 2-5 shows you the `Journal` domain class. Because you are using the JPA technology, you need to use the `@Entity`, `@Id`, and `@GeneratedValue` annotations so this class gets marked as JPA entity and can be persisted to the database. You are going to see more of these classes in later chapters of the book. As you can see, there is also a `@Transient` annotation, which will indicate to the JPA engine not to persist that property, because it's only being used to format the date. This class has two constructors, one with no arguments and is needed for the JPA engine and the other with some arguments that you are going to use to populate the database.

There is an override of the `toString` method, which will be useful for printing the records.

6. Next, you need to create a persistence mechanism for the journal data. You are going to use the Spring Data JPA technology by creating an interface and extending it from the `JpaRepository` interface. See Listing 2-6.

Listing 2-6. com.apress.spring.repository.JournalRepository.java

```java
package com.apress.spring.repository;

import org.springframework.data.jpa.repository.JpaRepository;
import com.apress.spring.domain.Journal;

public interface JournalRepository extends JpaRepository<Journal, Long> { }
```

Listing 2-6 shows you the Spring Data Repository JPA technology, and it's easy to extend the `JpaRepository` interface. The `JpaRepository` is a marker interface that allows the Spring Data Repository engine to recognize it and apply the necessary proxy classes to implement not only the base CRUD (Create, Read, Update, Delete) actions, but also some custom methods. You can do this by having some naming conventions, such as `findByTitleLike` or `findBySummary` or even `findByTitleAndSummaryIgnoringCase`. All the actions will then be set as transactional by default. The `JpaRepository` also has some convenient behavior because you can add sortable and paging actions to your data.

Don't worry too much about this right now, because you'll learn more about the Spring Data (JDBC and JPA) in its own chapter. For now, the only thing you need to do is create the interface and extend from the `JpaRepository` marker interface.

7. Because this is a web application, you need to create a web controller. See Listing 2-7.

Listing 2-7. com.apress.spring.web.JournalController.java

```java
package com.apress.spring.web;

import org.springframework.beans.factory.annotation.Autowired;
import org.springframework.stereotype.Controller;
import org.springframework.ui.Model;
import org.springframework.web.bind.annotation.RequestMapping;

import com.apress.spring.repository.JournalRepository;

@Controller
public class JournalController {

        @Autowired
        JournalRepository repo;
```

```
    @RequestMapping("/")
    public String index(Model model){
            model.addAttribute("journal", repo.findAll());
            return "index";
    }
}
```

Listing 2-7 shows the web controller, which will send back all the journal entries. In this case the class is marked with the @Controller, which is a marker for the Spring MVC engine so this class is treated as web controller. The @Autowired annotation will instantiate the JournalRepository variable repo, so it can be used in the index method.

The index method is marked with the @RequestMapping annotation, which will make this method the handler for every request in the default route /. If you take a look, there is a Model class parameter that will be created, and it will add an attribute named journal with a value that is the result of calling the JournalRepository interface, repo.findAll() method. Remember that by extending a JpaRepository, you have by default different methods, and one of them is the findAll method. This method will return all the entries from the database. The return will be the name of the page index, then the Spring MVC engine will look for the index.html in the templates folder.

8. Then in the src/main/resources/templates folder, you need to create the index.html file. See Listing 2-8.

Listing 2-8. src/main/resources/templates/index.html

```
<!doctype html>
<html lang="en-US" xmlns:th="http://www.thymeleaf.org">
<head>
  <meta charset="utf-8"></meta>
  <meta http-equiv="Content-Type" content="text/html"></meta>
  <title>Spring Boot Journal</title>
  <link rel="stylesheet" type="text/css" media="all" href="css/bootstrap.min.css"></link>
  <link rel="stylesheet" type="text/css" media="all" href="css/bootstrap-glyphicons.css">
  </link>
  <link rel="stylesheet" type="text/css" media="all" href="css/styles.css"></link>
</head>

<body>
<div class="container">
  <h1>Spring Boot Journal</h1>

  <ul class="timeline">
   <div th:each="entry,status : ${journal}">
    <li th:attr="class=${status.odd}?'timeline-inverted':''">
      <div class="tl-circ"></div>
      <div class="timeline-panel">
        <div class="tl-heading">
          <h4><span th:text="${entry.title}">TITLE</span></h4>
          <p><small class="text-muted"><i class="glyphicon glyphicon-time"></i>
          <span th:text="${entry.createdAsShort}">CREATED</span></small></p>
        </div>
```

```
  <div class="tl-body">
    <p><span th:text="${entry.summary}">SUMMARY</span></p>
  </div>
    </div>
  </li>
  </div>
  </ul>
</div>
</body>
</html>
```

Listing 2-8 shows you the index.html file that will be rendered using the Thymeleaf engine, which is why you have an XML namespace in the html tag. What is important here is the th:each instruction. It will get the journal entries as a collection (by using the entry variable and the status variable in the index of each iteration) and it will iterate to create different tags based on the number of entries. To access the property for each entry, you use the th:text instruction.

9.   As you can see in Listing 2-8, there are some CSS defined. The important one is style.css. (I borrowed this style from Jake Rocheleau at http://blog. templatemonster.com/2014/04/23/tutorial-build-vertical-timeline-archives-page-using-bootstrap/.) I modified and added this style.css file to the book's source companion code. You can download it from the Apress web site. It's important to know that Spring Boot will look for the static/ path to collect all the public files that you want to expose to the web, this will be the case with JavaScript, image files, and CSS files.

10.   Now the important part, the main application. See Listing 2-9

Listing 2-9. com.apress.spring.SpringBootJournalApplication.java

```
package com.apress.spring;

import org.springframework.boot.SpringApplication;
import org.springframework.boot.autoconfigure.SpringBootApplication;

@SpringBootApplication
public class SpringBootJournalApplication {

    public static void main(String[] args) {
        SpringApplication.run(SpringBootJournalApplication.class, args);
    }
}
```

Listing 2-9 shows you the main application. You don't need to do anything, and this is the class that was generated when you use the Spring Starter Project wizard. You are ready to run it, but wait! Where is the data? You need to inject some data so you can see the result. Modify the SpringBootJournalApplication class to look like Listing 2-10.

Listing 2-10. com.apress.spring.SpringBootJournalApplication.java

```java
package com.apress.spring;

import org.springframework.beans.factory.InitializingBean;
import org.springframework.boot.SpringApplication;
import org.springframework.boot.autoconfigure.SpringBootApplication;
import org.springframework.context.annotation.Bean;

import com.apress.spring.domain.Journal;
import com.apress.spring.repository.JournalRepository;

@SpringBootApplication
public class SpringBootJournalApplication {

    @Bean
    InitializingBean saveData(JournalRepository repo){
        return () -> {
            repo.save(new Journal("Get to know Spring Boot","Today I will learn Spring
            Boot","01/01/2016"));
            repo.save(new Journal("Simple Spring Boot Project","I will do my first Spring
            Boot Project","01/02/2016"));
            repo.save(new Journal("Spring Boot Reading","Read more about Spring
            Boot","02/01/2016"));
            repo.save(new Journal("Spring Boot in the Cloud","Spring Boot using Cloud
            Foundry","03/01/2016"));
        };
    }

    public static void main(String[] args) {
        SpringApplication.run(SpringBootJournalApplication.class, args);
    }
}
```

Listing 2-10 shows the final version of the journal app. One thing to mention is the saveData method that is returning an InitializingBean. This particular class is always called when the Spring engine is creating the instance to initialize it. In this case, the method will be executed before the application finishes running.

In order to run it, select the SpringBootJournalApplication.java class from the Package Explorer view and right-click on it. Then choose Run As ➤ Spring Boot App. Once it's running you can open a browser and point to http://localhost:8080. You should see something like Figure 2-12.

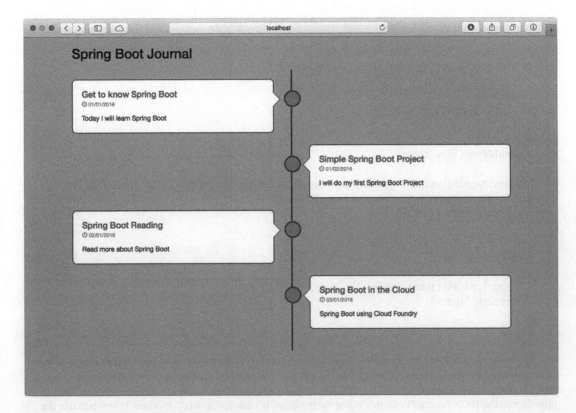

Figure 2-12. *The Spring Boot journal web application*

Figure 2-12 shows you the result of running the Spring Boot journal application. If you analyze it in more detail, probably what is most time consuming will be the graphic design rather than the code. With only a few lines of code, you have a very cool Spring Boot app. You will modify this app in the remaining chapters.

You can stop your application by pressing Ctrl+C in the terminal where the application is running.

What happens if you want to expose this journal as a service? It would be nice to have a request to the http://localhost:8080/journal and the response be JSON data. You need to modify the JournalController class. You are going to add a new method that will handle the /journal route and respond as JSON data.

Go to your JournalController class and modify it to look like Listing 2-11.

Listing 2-11. com.apress.spring.web.JournalController.java

```
package com.apress.spring.web;

import java.util.List;

import org.springframework.beans.factory.annotation.Autowired;
import org.springframework.http.MediaType;
import org.springframework.stereotype.Controller;
import org.springframework.ui.Model;
import org.springframework.web.bind.annotation.RequestMapping;
```

```
import org.springframework.web.bind.annotation.ResponseBody;

import com.apress.spring.domain.Journal;
import com.apress.spring.repository.JournalRepository;

@Controller
public class JournalController {

    @Autowired
    JournalRepository repo;

    @RequestMapping(value="/journal", produces = {MediaType.APPLICATION_JSON_UTF8_VALUE})
    public @ResponseBody List<Journal> getJournal(){
        return repo.findAll();
    }

    @RequestMapping("/")
    public String index(Model model){
        model.addAttribute("journal", repo.findAll());
        return "index";
    }
}
```

Listing 2-12 shows you the modified version of the JournalController class. Remember that at some point this will become a service, so by adding the getJournal method and using the @ResponseBody, it will automatically respond with JSON data. But how does Spring Boot know about transforming the objects into the JSON format? Well, this is not Spring Boot, it's the Spring MVC module. When you use the @ResponseBody annotation, Spring MVC will automatically use the correct HTTP message converters to transform your response into JSON data.

If you run the application again and point your browser to http://localhost:8080/journal, you should get something similar to Figure 2-13.

```
[
  ▼ {                                                                    RAW
      id: 1,
      title: "Get to know Spring Boot",
      created: 1451631600000,
      summary: "Today I will learn Spring Boot",
      createdAsShort: "01/01/2016"
  },
  ▼ {
      id: 2,
      title: "Simple Spring Boot Project",
      created: 1451718000000,
      summary: "I will do my first Spring Boot Project",
      createdAsShort: "01/02/2016"
  },
  ▼ {
      id: 3,
      title: "Spring Boot Reading",
      created: 1454310000000,
      summary: "Read more about Spring Boot",
      createdAsShort: "02/01/2016"
  },
  ▼ {
      id: 4,
      title: "Spring Boot in the Cloud",
      created: 1456815600000,
      summary: "Spring Boot using Cloud Foundry",
      createdAsShort: "03/01/2016"
  }
]
```

Figure 2-13. Added a JSON response at http://localhost:8080/journal

Now you can create better applications that actually use this data to be exposed as a nice web interface. My intention for the journal web interface was just as an example, and I bet you can create a better looking web interface.

How Spring Boot Works

I think now is time to see how Spring Boot does it; how it works internally to relieve the developer from the headache of a J2EE web application. If you are a Spring or J2EE developer, you saw that you didn't use a configuration file—no XML (web.xml), no @Configuration class, or any other Spring Beans definition file.

Maybe you are thinking that Spring Boot generated code—some classes to create all the necessary files to run this application—but that's not the case, Spring Boot never generates code and will never output any source code. Remember that I said that Spring Boot is an opinionated technology, which means that it follows the best practices to create a very robust application with minimum effort.

Let's see what is really happening when you run the SpringBootJournalApplication app. Listing 2-10 shows the main application. It is marked with the @SpringBootApplication annotation. This annotation looks like Listing 2-12.

Listing 2-12. org.springframework.boot.autoconfigure.SpringBootApplication.java

```
package org.springframework.boot.autoconfigure;

@Target(ElementType.TYPE)
@Retention(RetentionPolicy.RUNTIME)
@Documented
@Inherited
@Configuration
@EnableAutoConfiguration
@ComponentScan
public @interface SpringBootApplication {

    Class<?>[] exclude() default {};

    String[] excludeName() default {};

    @AliasFor(annotation = ComponentScan.class, attribute = "basePackages")
    String[] scanBasePackages() default {};

    @AliasFor(annotation = ComponentScan.class, attribute = "basePackageClasses")
    Class<?>[] scanBasePackageClasses() default {};

}
```

Listing 2-12 shows the @SpringBootApplication annotation. What is important to see is that this is a composed annotation because it contains the @Configuration, @EnableAutoConfiguration, and @ComponentScan annotations. Don't worry I will explain all these annotation in the following chapters. In version 1.0 of Spring Boot, you needed to use these three annotations to create a Spring Boot app. Since version 1.2.0, the Spring team created this enhanced @SpringBootApplication annotation. Remember, Spring Boot tries to simplify everything without having a configuration file.

The important key for Spring Boot to work is the @EnableAutoConfiguration annotation, because it contains the Auto-Configuration feature, and this is where it all starts to happen. Spring Boot will use auto-configuration based on your classpath, your annotations, and your configuration to add the right technology and create a suitable application. This means that all those annotations facilitate how Spring Boot will configure your app.

To sum up, in Listing 2-10 Spring Boot uses the @SpringBootApplication and the auto-configuration (based on the @EnableAutoConfiguration annotation) to try to identify all your components. First it will inspect your classpath, and because your dependency is a spring-boot-starter-web, it will try to configure the application as a web application. It will also identify that the JournalController class is a web controller because it is marked with the @Controller and because it contains the @RequestMapping annotations. And because the spring-boot-starter-web has the Tomcat server as a dependency, the Spring Boot will use it when you run your application.

Yes, a Tomcat server. Spring Boot has all these non-functional features that bring more to your application. You will learn more about this in later chapters, but for now you need to know that every time you create a web application, you will have a Tomcat server embedded. Note that you can exclude Tomcat and use another server like Jetty or Undertow.

You can also create a standalone application, by going to the command line and executing this:

```
$ mvn package
```

This command will create a JAR file in the target folder. Then you can execute the following command:

```
$ java -jar target/spring-boot-journal-0.0.1-SNAPSHOT.jar
```

You will have a running application (go to the http://localhost:8080). This technique helps to create and distribute the application to your clients.

Summary

This chapter showed you how to install and use Spring Boot with your first Spring Boot Journal application. You saw that there are many possibilities for using Spring Boot—by command line with the Spring Boot CLI; using the Spring Initializr web service with cURL; and by using the Spring Tool Suite (STS).

With your first application, you saw how easy it was to integrate different technologies and, with a few lines of code, have a good looking and functional web application. You also learned how Spring Boot works internally and how it creates your application based on your classpath and annotations.

The next chapter goes deeper into a configuration that you can use to extend Spring Boot even more.

CHAPTER 3

■ ■ ■

Spring Boot Auto-Configuration, Features, and More

This chapter talks about the Spring Boot features that involve configuration. First it shows you how Spring Boot works when it's using the auto-configuration feature (in detail) when you add the @EnableAutoConfiguration annotation. Then the chapter shows you some of Spring Boot's extra features, such as externalizing your configuration properties, its enable and disable features, and more.

Auto-Configuration

The previous chapter explained that auto-configuration is one of the important features in Spring Boot because it will try to do its best to configure your Spring Boot application according to your classpath (this will be according to your maven pom.xml or gradle build.gradle files), annotations, and any Java configuration declarations.

The example in Listing 3-1 is the same one from previous chapters, but in this case I want to use it to explain what happens behind the scenes when Spring Boot runs it.

Listing 3-1. app.groovy

```
@RestController
class WebApp{

    @RequestMapping("/")
    String greetings(){
        "Spring Boot Rocks"
    }
}
```

You can run this program using the Spring Boot CLI (Command Line Interface) with this command:

```
$ spring run app.groovy
```

Spring Boot won't generate any code (no output), but will add some on the fly. This is one of the advantages of Groovy, in that you can have access to the AST (Abstract Syntax Tree) at running time. For Java, this normally happens using proxy classes. Spring Boot will start by importing missing dependencies, like importing the org.springframework.web.bind.annotation.RestController annotation, among others.

© Felipe Gutierrez 2016
F. Gutierrez, *Pro Spring Boot*, DOI 10.1007/978-1-4842-1431-2_3

Next, it will identify that you need a Web Spring Boot Starter (I will talk more about it in the following sections) because you marked your class and your method with the @RestController and the @RequestMapping annotations, so it will add to the code the @Grab("spring-boot-web-starter") annotation.

Next, it will add the necessary annotation that will trigger some auto-configuration, the @EnableAutoConfiguration annotation, and last, it will add the main method that will be the entry point for the application. You can see the resultant code in Listing 3-2.

Listing 3-2. app.groovy modified by Spring Boot

```
import org.springframework.web.bind.annotation.RestController;
// Other Imports

@Grab("spring-boot-web-starter")
@EnableAutoConfiguration
@RestController
class WebApp{
   @RequestMapping("/")
    String greetings(){
        "Spring Boot Rocks"
   }

   public static void main(String[] args) {
        SpringApplication.run(WebApp.class, args);
   }
}
```

Listing 3-2 shows the actual modified program that Spring Boot will run. All this "build-up" is happening in memory. You can see in action how the auto-configuration works, by running Listing 3-1 with the --debug parameter. Take a look:

```
$ spring run app.groovy --debug
...
DEBUG 49009 --- [] autoConfigurationReportLoggingInitializer :
===========================
AUTO-CONFIGURATION REPORT
===========================

Positive matches:
-----------------
//You will see all the conditions that were met to enable a web application. And this is
because you have the //@RestController annotation.

Negative matches:
-----------------
//You will find all the conditions that failed. For example you will find that the
ActiveMQAutoConfiguration class did //not match, because you don't have any reference of the
ActiveMQConnectionFactory.
```

Review the output from the command in your terminal and you'll see all the positive and negative matches that Spring Boot did before running this simple application. Because you are running the Spring Boot CLI, it's doing a lot by trying to guess what kind of application you want to run. When you create a Maven or Gradle project and specify some dependencies (pom.xml or build.gradle), you are helping Spring Boot make decisions based on your dependencies.

Disabling a Specific Auto-Configuration

Recall that Chapter 2 covered the @SpringBootApplication annotation a bit. This annotation is equivalent to the @Configuration, @ComponentScan, and @EnableAutoConfiguration annotations. You can disable a specific auto-configuration by adding the @EnableAutoConfiguration annotation to your class with the exclude parameter. Listing 3-3 shows an example.

Listing 3-3. app.groovy

```
import org.springframework.boot.autoconfigure.jms.activemq.ActiveMQAutoConfiguration

@RestController
@EnableAutoConfiguration(exclude=[ActiveMQAutoConfiguration.class])
class WebApp{

    @RequestMapping("/")
        String greetings(){
            "Spring Boot Rocks"
        }
}
```

Listing 3-3 shows the @EnableAutoConfiguration annotation with the exclude parameter. This parameter receives an array of auto-configuration classes. If you run this again with the following command:

```
$ spring run app.groovy --debug
...
Exclusions:
-----------

    org.springframework.boot.autoconfigure.jms.activemq.ActiveMQAutoConfiguration
...
```

You will see the exclusion of the ActiveMQAutoConfiguration class. This is a very useful technique for Groovy scripts, when you want Spring Boot to skip certain and unnecessary auto-configurations. You might wonder why you would want to exclude a configuration. Well, sometimes you will have dependencies that work in two different types of applications—web and non-web for example—and you want to use the jackson-core library that handles JSON objects to create a non-web app. This library can work in web or non-web apps, but the auto-configuration will guess that, based on this dependency, your application is a web app. In that case, you can exclude the web auto-configuration from happening. This is one example of many where you might use the auto-configuration exclusion.

Listing 3-4 shows this exclusion on a Java Spring Boot app.

Listing 3-4. DemoApplication.java—Spring Boot snippet

```
package com.example;

import org.springframework.boot.SpringApplication;
import org.springframework.boot.autoconfigure.SpringBootApplication;
import org.springframework.boot.autoconfigure.jdbc.DataSourceAutoConfiguration;
import org.springframework.boot.autoconfigure.jms.activemq.ActiveMQAutoConfiguration;

@SpringBootApplication(exclude={ActiveMQAutoConfiguration.class,DataSourceAutoConfiguration.class})
public class DemoApplication {

        public static void main(String[] args) {
                SpringApplication.run(DemoApplication.class, args);
        }
}
```

Listing 3-4 shows you a Java version. In this example the main class is declaring only the @SpringBootApplication annotation, and within this annotation you can exclude the auto-configuration classes. Listing 3-4 shows two classes being excluded—the ActiveMQAutoConfiguration and DataSourceAutoConfiguration classes. Why is @EnableAutoConfiguration annotation not being used? Remember that the @SpringBootApplication annotation inherits @EnableAutoConfiguration, @Configuration, and @ComponentScan, which is why you can use the exclude parameter within the @SpringBootApplication.

If you run a Maven or Gradle project (using the example in Listing 3-4) with the debug option, you will see output like this:

```
$ spring run DemoApplication.java --debug
...
Exclusions:
-----------

    org.springframework.boot.autoconfigure.jms.activemq.ActiveMQAutoConfiguration
    org.springframework.boot.autoconfigure.jdbc.DataSourceAutoConfiguration
...
```

■ **Note**   Groovy handles the arrays in a different way from Java. The example in Listing 3-3 (app.groovy) uses in the exclude parameter [ ] (square brackets) to handle arrays, which is the Groovy way. Listing 3-4 (DemoApplication.java) uses in the exclude parameter and { } (curly braces) to handle the arrays, which is the Java way.

You can find all the book's source code at the Apress web site or by going to https://github.com/felipeg48/pro-spring-boot.

@EnableAutoConfiguration and @Enable<Technology> Annotations

You will find that the Spring Framework and some of its modules—like Spring Core, Spring Data, Spring AMQP, and Spring Integration—provide @Enable<Technology> annotations. For example, @EnableTransactionManagement, @EnableRabbit, and @EnableIntegration are part of the modules mentioned. Within Spring applications, you can use these annotations to follow the pattern "convention over configuration," thus making your apps even easier to develop and maintain without worrying too much about configuration.

Spring Boot can also take advantage of these annotations. These annotations are used in the @EnableAutoConfiguration annotation to do the auto-configuration. Let's take a closer look at the @EnableAutoConfiguration annotation and see the logic behind it. You'll see where the @Enable<Technology> annotations fit. It's worth mentioning that in other chapters you will be learning more about these annotations. See Listing 3-5.

Listing 3-5. Snippet of org.springframework.boot.autoconfigure.EnableAutoConfiguration.java

```
...
// More declarations here ...
...
@Import(EnableAutoConfigurationImportSelector.class)
public @interface EnableAutoConfiguration {

        Class<?>[] exclude() default {};

        String[] excludeName() default {};

}
```

Listing 3-5 shows you the @EnableAutoConfiguration annotation. As you already know, this class will attempt to guess and configure the beans that your application will need. The auto-configuration classes are applied based on the classpath and which beans your app has defined, but what this makes more powerful is the org.springframework.boot.autoconfigure.EnableAutoConfigurationImportSelector class that finds all the necessary configuration classes.

The EnableAutoConfigurationImportSelector class has a several methods, but one of the most important for the auto-configuration to happen is the getCandidateConfiguration method. See Listing 3-6.

Listing 3-6. Snippet of org.springframework.boot.autoconfigure.EnableAutoConfigurationImportSelector

```
...
protected List<String> getCandidateConfigurations(AnnotationMetadata metadata,
                        AnnotationAttributes attributes) {
  return SpringFactoriesLoader.loadFactoryNames(
                        getSpringFactoriesLoaderFactoryClass(), getBeanClassLoader());
}
...
```

Listing 3-6 shows you a snippet of the EnableAutoConfigurationImportSelector class, where the getCandidateConfigurations method returns SpringFactoriesLoader.loadFactoryNames. The SpringFactoriesLoader.loadFactories will look for the META-INF/spring.factories defined in the spring-boot-autoconfigure JAR. See Listing 3-7 for its contents.

Listing 3-7. Snippet of `spring-boot-autoconfigure-<version>.jar#META-INF/spring.factories`

```
# Initializers
org.springframework.context.ApplicationContextInitializer=\
org.springframework.boot.autoconfigure.logging.AutoConfigurationReportLoggingInitializer
...


# Application Listeners
org.springframework.context.ApplicationListener=\
org.springframework.boot.autoconfigure.BackgroundPreinitializer


# Auto Configure
org.springframework.boot.autoconfigure.EnableAutoConfiguration=\
org.springframework.boot.autoconfigure.admin.SpringApplicationAdminJmxAutoConfiguration,\
org.springframework.boot.autoconfigure.aop.AopAutoConfiguration,\
org.springframework.boot.autoconfigure.amqp.RabbitAutoConfiguration,\
org.springframework.boot.autoconfigure.MessageSourceAutoConfiguration,\
org.springframework.boot.autoconfigure.PropertyPlaceholderAutoConfiguration,\
org.springframework.boot.autoconfigure.batch.BatchAutoConfiguration,\
org.springframework.boot.autoconfigure.cache.CacheAutoConfiguration,\
org.springframework.boot.autoconfigure.cassandra.CassandraAutoConfiguration,\
org.springframework.boot.autoconfigure.cloud.CloudAutoConfiguration,\
....
....
```

As you can see from Listing 3-7, the `spring.factories` defined all the auto-configuration classes that will be used to guess what kind of application you are running. Let's take a look at the CloudAutoConfiguration class. See Listing 3-8.

Listing 3-8. `org.springframework.boot.autoconfigure.cloud.CloudAutoConfiguration.java`

```
package org.springframework.boot.autoconfigure.cloud;

import org.springframework.boot.autoconfigure.AutoConfigureOrder;
import org.springframework.boot.autoconfigure.EnableAutoConfiguration;
import org.springframework.boot.autoconfigure.condition.ConditionalOnClass;
import org.springframework.boot.autoconfigure.condition.ConditionalOnMissingBean;
import org.springframework.boot.autoconfigure.condition.ConditionalOnProperty;
import org.springframework.cloud.Cloud;
import org.springframework.cloud.app.ApplicationInstanceInfo;
import org.springframework.cloud.config.java.CloudScan;
import org.springframework.cloud.config.java.CloudScanConfiguration;
import org.springframework.context.annotation.Configuration;
import org.springframework.context.annotation.Import;
import org.springframework.context.annotation.Profile;
import org.springframework.core.Ordered;

@Configuration
@Profile("cloud")
@AutoConfigureOrder(CloudAutoConfiguration.ORDER)
@ConditionalOnClass(CloudScanConfiguration.class)
@ConditionalOnMissingBean(Cloud.class)
```

```
@ConditionalOnProperty(prefix = "spring.cloud", name = "enabled", havingValue = "true",
matchIfMissing = true)
@Import(CloudScanConfiguration.class)
public class CloudAutoConfiguration {

    // Cloud configuration needs to happen early (before data, mongo etc.)
    public static final int ORDER = Ordered.HIGHEST_PRECEDENCE + 20;

}
```

Listing 3-8 shows you the CloudAutoConfiguration class. As you can see, it's very short class, but it will configure a cloud application if it finds the spring-cloud classes. But how? It will use the @ConditionalOnClass and @ConditionalOnMissingBean annotations to decide if the application is a cloud app. Don't worry too much about this, because you are going to use these annotations when you create your own auto-configuration class in the last chapter of the book.

Another thing to note in Listing 3-8 is the use of the @ConditionalOnProperty, which applies only if the spring.cloud property is enabled. It's worth mentioning that this auto-configuration will be executed in a cloud profile, denoted by the @Profile annotation. The @Import annotation will be applied only if the other annotations met their conditions, meaning that the import of the CloudScanConfiguration class will be executed if the spring-cloud classes are in the classpath.

Spring Boot Features

This section shows you some of the Spring Boot features. Spring Boot is highly customizable, from the auto-configuration that guesses what kind of application you are trying to run (explained in the previous section), to customize how it starts, what to show, and what to enable or disable based on its own properties. So let's get started.

Let's create a Spring Boot Java project with the spring init command. (Make sure you have the Spring Boot installed on your system. If not, you can review the previous chapter on how to install it.) Execute the following command in a terminal window:

```
$ spring init -g=com.apres.spring -a=spring-boot-simple --package=com.apress.spring
-name=spring-boot-simple -x
```

This command will create a Maven Java project with a groupId=com.apress.spring, an artifactId=spring-boot-simple, and a package=com.apress.spring with a project's name=spring-boot-simple. It will be created in the current directory (-x). Don't worry too much about the parameters; you'll learn more about them in the next chapter. This command will generate the structure shown in Figure 3-1.

```
.
├── mvnw
├── mvnw.cmd
├── pom.xml
└── src
    ├── main
    │   ├── java
    │   │   └── com
    │   │       └── apress
    │   │           └── spring
    │   │               └── SpringBootSimpleApplication.java
    │   └── resources
    │       └── application.properties
    └── test
        └── java
            └── com
                └── apress
                    └── spring
                        └── SpringBootSimpleApplicationTests.java

12 directories, 6 files
```

Figure 3-1. *Spring Boot project—directory structure*

Figure 3-1 shows you the project structure after running the spring init command. Let's run the application and see what happens. You will see (in the next chapter in more detail) that the Spring Initializr includes a Maven wrapper that you can use. To run it, execute the following command in the same terminal window:

```
$ ./mvnw spring-boot:run
```

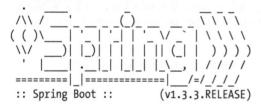

```
 .   ____          _            __ _ _
/\\ / ___'_ __ _ _(_)_ __  __ _ \ \ \ \
( ( )\___ | '_ | '_| | '_ \/ _` | \ \ \ \
 \\/  ___)| |_)| | | | | || (_| |  ) ) ) )
  '  |____| .__|_| |_|_| |_\__, | / / / /
 =========|_|==============|___/=/_/_/_/
 :: Spring Boot ::        (v1.3.3.RELEASE)
```

```
INFO[main] c.a.spring.SpringBootSimpleApplication    : Starting SpringBootSimpleApplication
on liukang.local with PID 75712 (/Books/pro-spring-boot/spring-boot-simple-java/target/
classes started by felipeg in /Books/pro-spring-boot/spring-boot-simple-java)
INFO[main] c.a.spring.SpringBootSimpleApplication    : No active profile set, falling back to
default profiles: default
INFO[main] s.c.a.AnnotationConfigApplicationContext : Refreshing org.springframework.
context.annotation.AnnotationConfigApplicationContext@203f6b5: startup date [Thu Feb 25
19:00:34 MST 2016]; root of context hierarchy
INFO[main] o.s.j.e.a.AnnotationMBeanExporter         : Registering beans for JMX exposure on startup
INFO[main] c.a.spring.SpringBootSimpleApplication    : Started SpringBootSimpleApplication in
0.789 seconds (JVM running for 4.295)
INFO[Th-1] s.c.a.AnnotationConfigApplicationContext : Closing org.springframework.context.
annotation.AnnotationConfigApplicationContext@203f6b5: startup date [Thu Feb 25 19:00:34
MST 2016]; root of context hierarchy
INFO[Th-1] o.s.j.e.a.AnnotationMBeanExporter         : Unregistering JMX-exposed beans on shutdown
```

You should see something similar to the output above. It will show you a banner ("Spring") and some logs. The main application is shown in Listing 3-9.

Listing 3-9. src/main/java/com/apress/spring/SpringBootSimpleApplication.java

```java
package com.apress.spring;

import org.springframework.boot.SpringApplication;
import org.springframework.boot.autoconfigure.SpringBootApplication;

@SpringBootApplication
public class SpringBootSimpleApplication {

    public static void main(String[] args) {
        SpringApplication.run(SpringBootSimpleApplication.class, args);
    }
}
```

Listing 3-9 shows you the main application. You already know about it from the previous chapters, but let's review it again:

- @SpringBootApplication. This annotation is actually the @ComponentScan, @Configuration, and @EnableAutoConfiguration annotations. You already know everything about @EnableAutoConfiguration from the previous sections.

- SpringApplication. This class provides the bootstrap for the Spring Boot application that is executed in the main method. You need to pass the class that will be executed.

Now, you are ready to start customizing the Spring Boot app.

SpringApplication Class

You can have a more advanced configuration using the Spring application, because you can create an instance out of it and do a lot more. See Listing 3-10.

Listing 3-10. Version 2 of src/main/java/com/apress/spring/SpringBootSimpleApplication.java

```java
package com.apress.spring;

import org.springframework.boot.SpringApplication;
import org.springframework.boot.autoconfigure.SpringBootApplication;

@SpringBootApplication
public class SpringBootSimpleApplication {

    public static void main(String[] args) {

        SpringApplication app = new SpringApplication(SpringBootSimpleApplication.class);
        //add more features here.
            app.run(args);

    }
}
```

Custom Banner

Every time you run your application, you can see a banner being displayed at the beginning of the application. That banner can be customized in different ways. Listing 3-11 shows how to implement the org.springframework.boot.Banner interface.

Listing 3-11. Version 3 of src/main/java/com/apress/spring/SpringBootSimpleApplication.java

```
package com.apress.spring;

import java.io.PrintStream;

import org.springframework.boot.Banner;
import org.springframework.boot.SpringApplication;
import org.springframework.boot.autoconfigure.SpringBootApplication;
import org.springframework.core.env.Environment;

@SpringBootApplication
public class SpringBootSimpleApplication {

    public static void main(String[] args) {

        SpringApplication app = new SpringApplication(SpringBootSimpleApplication.class);
        app.setBanner(new Banner() {
                @Override
                public void printBanner(Environment environment, Class<?> sourceClass,
                PrintStream out) {
                        out.print("\n\n\tThis is my own banner!\n\n".toUpperCase());
                }
        });
            app.run(args);
    }
}
```

When you run the application, you will see something like this:

```
$ ./mvnw spring-boot:run

        THIS IS MY OWN BANNER!

INFO[main] c.a.spring.SpringBootSimpleApplication    : Starting SpringBootSimpleApplication
on liukang.local with PID 75712 (/Books/pro-spring-boot/spring-boot-simple-java/target/
classes started by felipeg in /Books/pro-spring-boot/spring-boot-simple-java)
...
...
INFO[main] c.a.spring.SpringBootSimpleApplication    : Started SpringBootSimpleApplication in
0.789 seconds (JVM running for 4.295)
INFO[Th-1] s.c.a.AnnotationConfigApplicationContext : Closing org.springframework.context.
annotation.AnnotationConfigApplicationContext@203f6b5: startup date [Thu Feb 25 19:00:34 MST
2016]; root of context hierarchy
INFO[Th-1] o.s.j.e.a.AnnotationMBeanExporter         : Unregistering JMX-exposed beans on shutdown
```

You can also create your own ASCII banner and display it. There is a very cool site that creates ASCII art from text (http://patorjk.com). See Figure 3-2.

Apps	
Gradient Image Generator	For creating gradient images (an image that fades from one color to another). A very old app and there aren't many good reasons use it. But it's here just in case.
Gradient Image Generator	Creates a color palette from an image. I made it one afternoon on a lark a long time ago.
Keyboard Layout Analyzer	The default layout of the keys on your keyboard is not very good. There are actually several popular layouts you can set yourself up with. This app analyzes the text you type and lets you see what layout would benefit you most.
Text Color Fader	Create color faded text for your HTML documents, emails, profiles, message board posts, and whatever else you can think of.
Text to ASCII Art Generator	Create text art from words. Like this:
Typing Speed Test	How fast kind you type? This app is kind of old, but still serves its purposes and it gives you some nice stats and has some handy options.
Social Media Showdown	Whoâ€™s more popular on the web? Various APIs are used to pit websites against each other to see who is â€œLikedâ€ the most.
Years Spent Watching YouTube	An app that will tell you how many viewing years people have put into watching particular YouTube videos.

Figure 3-2. `http://patorjk.com`—*text to ASCII art generator*

Figure 3-2 shows you the http://patorjk.com site. You can click the "Text to ASCII Art Generator" link. Once you are there, add the text "Pro Spring Boot" in the text field (or whatever you want). Then click Test All to see all the different ASCII art. See Figure 3-3.

Figure 3-3. *ASCII art*

Figure 3-3 shows you all the ASCII art (around 314 different drawings). Select your favorite and click the button Select Text. Copy it (Ctrl+C Windows/Cmd+C Mac) and then create a file named banner.txt in the src/main/resources/ directory. See Figure 3-4.

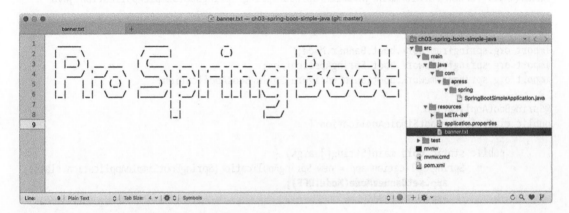

Figure 3-4. *The content of src/main/resource/banner.txt*

You can run your application again using this command:

```
$ ./mvnw spring-boot:run
```

You will see the ASCII art you added to the banner.txt file. If you run your app using Listing 3-11 (where you are setting the banner), it will override it and use the banner.txt file that is in your classpath. That's the default.

By default, Spring Boot will look for the banner.txt in the classpath. But you can change its location. Create another banner.txt file (or copy the one you have already) in the src/main/resources/META-INF/ directory. Then you can run the application by passing a -D parameter. Execute the following command:

```
$ ./mvnw spring-boot:run -Dbanner.location=classpath:/META-INF/banner.txt
```

This command is using the -D flag to pass the banner.location property that is pointing to the new classpath location: /META-INF/banner.txt. You can declare this property in the src/main/resources/ application.properties file, as follows:

```
banner.location=classpath:/META-INF/banner.txt
```

And run it like this:

```
$ ./mvnw spring-boot:run
```

You have several options for the setting up the banner.txt file. You can remove completely the banner. You can define it in src/main/resources/applications.property like this:

```
spring.main.banner-mode=off
```

CHAPTER 3 ■ SPRING BOOT AUTO-CONFIGURATION, FEATURES, AND MORE

This command has precedence over the default banner.txt located at the classpath:banner.txt location. You can also do this programmatically. See Listing 3-12.

Listing 3-12. Version 4 of src/main/java/com/apress/spring/SpringBootSimpleApplication.java

```java
package com.apress.spring;

import org.springframework.boot.Banner.Mode;
import org.springframework.boot.SpringApplication;
import org.springframework.boot.autoconfigure.SpringBootApplication;

@SpringBootApplication
public class SpringBootSimpleApplication {

        public static void main(String[] args) {
                SpringApplication app = new SpringApplication(SpringBootSimpleApplication.class);
                app.setBannerMode(Mode.OFF);
                app.run(args);
        }
}
```

SpringApplicationBuilder

The SpringApplicationBuilder class provides a fluent API and is a builder for the SpringApplication and ApplicationContext instances. It also provides hierarchy support. Everything that I showed you so far (with the SpringApplication) can be set with this builder. This is another way to configure your Spring Boot application. You use the other approach or maybe you are more comfortable with the fluent API where you can have more readable code. See Listing 3-13.

Listing 3-13. Version 5 of src/main/java/com/apress/spring/SpringBootSimpleApplication.java

```java
package com.apress.spring;

import org.springframework.boot.Banner;
import org.springframework.boot.autoconfigure.SpringBootApplication;
import org.springframework.boot.builder.SpringApplicationBuilder;

@SpringBootApplication
public class SpringBootSimpleApplication {

        public static void main(String[] args) {

                new SpringApplicationBuilder()
                .bannerMode(Banner.Mode.OFF)
                .sources(SpringBootSimpleApplication.class)
                .run(args);

        }
}
```

Listing 3-13 shows you the `SpringApplicationBuilder` fluent API. Next, let's consider more examples.

You can have a hierarchy when you're creating a Spring app (If you want to know more about application context in Spring, I recommend you read the Apress book called "Pro Spring 4ᵗʰ Edition") and you can create this with the `SpringApplicationBuilder`.

```
new SpringApplicationBuilder(SpringBootSimpleApplication.class)
        .child(MyConfig.class)
        .run(args);
```

If you have a web configuration, make sure it's being declared as a child. All the web configuration must depend on a main Spring context, which is why it needs to be declared as a child. Also parent and children must share the same `org.springframework.core.Environment` interface (this represents the environment in which the current application is running and is related to profiles and properties declarations).

You can log the info at startup or not; by default, this is set to true:

```
new SpringApplicationBuilder(SpringBootSimpleApplication.class)
        .logStartupInfo(false)
        .run(args);
```

You can activate profiles:

```
new SpringApplicationBuilder(SpringBootSimpleApplication.class)
        .profiles("prod","cloud")
        .run(args);
```

You'll learn more about profiles later, so you can make sense of the line above.

You can attach listeners for some of the `ApplicationEvent` events:

```
Logger log = LoggerFactory.getLogger(SpringBootSimpleApplication.class);
new SpringApplicationBuilder(SpringBootSimpleApplication.class)
        .listeners(new ApplicationListener<ApplicationEvent>() {

                @Override
                public void onApplicationEvent(ApplicationEvent event) {
                        log.info("#### > " + event.getClass().getCanonicalName());
                }

        })
        .run(args);
```

When you run your application, you should see at least the following output:

```
...
#### > org.springframework.boot.context.event.ApplicationPreparedEvent
...
#### > org.springframework.context.event.ContextRefreshedEvent
#### > org.springframework.boot.context.event.ApplicationReadyEvent
...
#### > org.springframework.context.event.ContextClosedEvent
...
```

Then your application can add the necessary logic to handle those events. In addition, you can have these events: ApplicationStartedEvent (sent at the start), ApplicationEnvironmentPreparedEvent (sent when the environment is known), ApplicationPreparedEvent (sent after the bean definitions), ApplicationReadyEvent (sent when the application is ready), ApplicationFailedEvent (sent in case of exception during the startup), and the other I showed you in the output (related to the Spring container). All these events can be useful when you want to set up your application (database, check up for some services, etc.) before it runs, or if your application fails during a start (ApplicationFailedEvent), because you'll probably want to send a notification somewhere.

You can remove any web environment auto-configuration. Remember that Spring Boot will try to guess what kind of app you are running based on the classpath, and for a web app, the algorithm is very simple. Imagine that you are using some libraries that actually can run without a web environment and your app is not a web app; however, Spring Boot tries to configure it as such:

```
new SpringApplicationBuilder(SpringBootSimpleApplication.class)
       .web(false)
       .run(args);
```

The previous section showed you how to you use @EnableAutoConfiguration and its parameter exclude, by passing the auto-configuration classes that you don't want to be checked on. The above code is where you set the web(false) and it's the same idea as the exclude parameter. As you can see, you have many options for configuring Spring Boot.

Application Arguments

Spring Boot allows you to get the arguments passed to the application. When you have this:

```
SpringApplication.run(SpringBootSimpleApplication.class, args);
```

You can access the args in your beans. See Listing 3-14.

Listing 3-14. Version 10 of src/main/java/com/apress/spring/SpringBootSimpleApplication.java

```
package com.apress.spring;

import java.io.IOException;
import java.util.List;

import org.slf4j.Logger;
import org.slf4j.LoggerFactory;
import org.springframework.beans.factory.annotation.Autowired;
import org.springframework.boot.ApplicationArguments;
import org.springframework.boot.SpringApplication;
import org.springframework.boot.autoconfigure.SpringBootApplication;
import org.springframework.stereotype.Component;

@SpringBootApplication
public class SpringBootSimpleApplication {

        public static void main(String[] args) throws IOException {
                SpringApplication.run(SpringBootSimpleApplication.class, args);
        }
}
```

```
@Component
class MyComponent {

        private static final Logger log = LoggerFactory.getLogger(MyComponent.class);

        @Autowired
        public MyComponent(ApplicationArguments args) {
                boolean enable = args.containsOption("enable");
                 if(enable)
                        log.info("## > You are enable!");

                List<String> _args = args.getNonOptionArgs();
                        log.info("## > extra args ...");
                if(!_args.isEmpty())
                        _args.forEach(file -> log.info(file));
        }
}
```

When you execute args.containsOption("enable"), it will expect the argument as --<arg>, so in Listing 3-14 it will be expecting --enable. The getNonOptionArgs will take other arguments. To test it, you can execute the following command:

$ ./mvnw spring-boot:run -Drun.arguments="--enable"

You should see the text: ## > You are enable. Also you can run it like this:

$ ./mvnw spring-boot:run -Drun.arguments="arg1,arg2"

Accessing Arguments with an Executable JAR

You have the option to create a standalone app, in the form of an executable JAR (you will see more about this). To create a executable JAR, simply execute the following command:

$ ./mvnw package

This command will create an executable JAR, meaning that you can run it like this:

$ java -jar target/spring-boot-simple-0.0.1-SNAPSHOT.jar

You can pass arguments like this:

$ java -jar target/spring-boot-simple-0.0.1-SNAPSHOT.jar --enable arg1 arg2

You should get the same text for the enable arg and a list of arg1 and arg2.

ApplicationRunner and CommandLineRunner

Spring Boot allows you to execute code before your application starts. Spring Boot has the
ApplicationRunner and the CommandLineRunner interfaces that expose the run methods. See Listing 3-15.

Listing 3-15. Version 11 of src/main/java/com/apress/spring/SpringBootSimpleApplication.java

```java
package com.apress.spring;

import java.io.IOException;

import org.slf4j.Logger;
import org.slf4j.LoggerFactory;
import org.springframework.beans.factory.annotation.Autowired;
import org.springframework.boot.ApplicationArguments;
import org.springframework.boot.ApplicationRunner;
import org.springframework.boot.CommandLineRunner;
import org.springframework.boot.SpringApplication;
import org.springframework.boot.autoconfigure.SpringBootApplication;
import org.springframework.context.annotation.Bean;

@SpringBootApplication
public class SpringBootSimpleApplication implements CommandLineRunner, ApplicationRunner{
        private static final Logger log = LoggerFactory.getLogger
        (SpringBootSimpleApplication.class);

        public static void main(String[] args) throws IOException {

                SpringApplication.run(SpringBootSimpleApplication.class, args);

        }

        @Bean
        String info(){
                return "Just a simple String bean";
        }

        @Autowired
        String info;

        @Override
        public void run(ApplicationArguments args) throws Exception {
                log.info("## > ApplicationRunner Implementation...");
                log.info("Accessing the Info bean: " + info);
                args.getNonOptionArgs().forEach(file -> log.info(file));
        }
```

```
    @Override
    public void run(String... args) throws Exception {
            log.info("## > CommandLineRunner Implementation...");
            log.info("Accessing the Info bean: " + info);
            for(String arg:args)
                    log.info(arg);
    }
}
```

Listing 3-15 shows you the CommandLineRunner and ApplicationRunner interfaces and their implementations. CommandLineRunner exposes the public void(String... args) method and ApplicationRunner exposes the public void run(ApplicationArguments args) method. These are practically the same. It's not necessary to implement both at the same time; if you want to have more control over the arguments, implement the ApplicationRunner interface. You can run Listing 3-15 with the following command:

```
$ ./mvnw spring-boot:run -Drun.arguments="arg1,arg2"
```

You should see the the logs for the info bean and the printout of the arguments passed. Listing 3-16 shows another way to use the CommandLineRunner interface.

Listing 3-16. Version 12 of src/main/java/com/apress/spring/SpringBootSimpleApplication.java

```
package com.apress.spring;

import java.io.IOException;

import org.slf4j.Logger;
import org.slf4j.LoggerFactory;
import org.springframework.beans.factory.annotation.Autowired;
import org.springframework.boot.CommandLineRunner;
import org.springframework.boot.SpringApplication;
import org.springframework.boot.autoconfigure.SpringBootApplication;
import org.springframework.context.annotation.Bean;

@SpringBootApplication
public class SpringBootSimpleApplication {
        private static final Logger log = LoggerFactory.getLogger
        (SpringBootSimpleApplication.class);

        public static void main(String[] args) throws IOException {

                SpringApplication.run(SpringBootSimpleApplication.class, args);

        }

        @Bean
        String info(){
                return "Just a simple String bean";
        }
```

```
@Autowired
String info;

@Bean
CommandLineRunner myMethod(){
        return args -> {
                log.info("## > CommandLineRunner Implementation...");
                log.info("Accessing the Info bean: " + info);
                for(String arg:args)
                        log.info(arg);
        };
    }
}
```

Listing 3-16 shows a method that's annotated with the @Bean annotation returning a CommandLineRunner implementation. This example uses the Java 8 syntax (lambda) to do the return. You can add as many methods that return a CommandLineRunner as you want. If you want to execute these in certain order, you can use the @Order annotation. If you want to run Listing 3-16 just execute the same command as before:

```
$ ./mvnw spring-boot:run -Drun.arguments="arg1,arg2"
```

Application Configuration

Developers know that they are never going to get rid of some application configuration. They will always be looking where they can persist URLs, IPs, credentials, and database information, for example. Basically any data that they normally use quite often in their applications. They know as a best practice that they need to avoid to hardcode this kind of configuration information. That's why they need to externalize it so it can be secure and easy to use and deploy.

With Spring you can use XML and the <context:property-placeholder/> tag, or you can use the @PropertySource annotation to declare your properties. You simply point to a file that has them declared. Spring Boot offers you the same mechanism but with improvements:

Spring Boot has different options for saving your application configuration:

- You can use a file named application.properties, which should be located in the root classpath of your application (there are more places where you can add this file that you'll learn about later).

- You can use a YAML notation file named application.yml that also needs to be located in the root classpath (there are more places where you can add this file that you'll learn about later).

- You can use environment variables. This is becoming the default practices for cloud scenarios.

- You can use command-line arguments.

Remember that Spring Boot is an opinionated technology, so most of its application configuration is based on a common application.properties or application.yml file. If none is specified, it already has those property's values as defaults. You can get the complete list of the common application properties here: https://docs.spring.io/spring-boot/docs/current/reference/html/common-application-properties.html.

One of the best features from Spring (and of course from Spring Boot as well) is that you can access the properties values by using the @Value annotation (with the name of the property) or from the org.springframework.core.env.Environment interface, which extends from the org.springframework. core.env.PropertyResolver interface. For example, if you have a src/main/resources/application. properties file with the following content:

```
data.server=remoteserver:3030
```

You can access the data.server property in your application by using the @Value annotation, as shown in the following snippet:

```
//...
@Service
public class MyService {

        @Value("${data.server}")
        private String server;

        //...
}
```

This code snippet shows you the usage of the @Value annotation. Spring Boot will inject the data.server property value from the application.properties file in the server variable with its value: remoteserver:3030.

If you don't want to use the application.properties, you can inject the properties via the command line:

```
$ java -jar target/myapp.jar --data.server=remoteserver:3030
```

You will get the same result. If you don't like the application.properties file or you hate the YAML syntax, you can also use a specialized environment variable named SPRING_APPLICATION_JSON to expose the same properties and its values. For example:

```
$ SPRING_APPLICATION_JSON='{ "data":{"server":"remoteserver:3030"}}' java -jar target/myapp.jar
```

(You must put the SRPING_APPLICATION_JSON variable before you execute the java -jar or the Maven command.) Again, you will get the same result. As you can see, Spring Boot gives you several ways to expose application properties.

Configuration Properties Examples

Let's create a simple project that will help you understand the application configuration:

```
$ spring init -g=com.apres.spring -a=spring-boot-config --package=com.apress.spring
-name=spring-boot-config -x
```

This command will create a simple Maven Java project. Before continuing with the project, you must know that Spring Boot uses an order if you want to override your application configuration properties:

- Command-line arguments
- SPRING_APPLICATION_JSON

- JNDI (java:comp/env)
- System.getProperties()
- OS environment variables
- RandomValuePropertySource (random.*)
- Profile-specific (application-{profile}.jar) outside of the package JAR
- Profile-specific (application-{profile}.jar) inside of the package JAR
- Application properties (application.properties) outside of the package JAR
- Application properties (application.properties) inside of the package JAR
- @PropertySource
- SpringApplication.setDefaultProperties

As you can see, that's the order for overriding the application properties. I'll clarify a little on the "outside" and "inside" package JAR. This means that if you have a JAR library dependency that has an application.properties (or YAML file) in it and it's being used in your application, then your application with its own application.properties file will have precedence over the application.properties that is in the JAR library.

Let's start with some examples.

Command-Line Arguments

Go to your project (that you did with the Spring init command) and edit the main class to look like Listing 3-17.

Listing 3-17. src/main/java/com/apress/spring/SpringBootConfigApplication.java

```java
package com.apress.spring;

import org.slf4j.Logger;
import org.slf4j.LoggerFactory;
import org.springframework.beans.factory.annotation.Value;
import org.springframework.boot.CommandLineRunner;
import org.springframework.boot.SpringApplication;
import org.springframework.boot.autoconfigure.SpringBootApplication;
import org.springframework.context.annotation.Bean;

@SpringBootApplication
public class SpringBootConfigApplication {

        private static Logger log = LoggerFactory.getLogger(SpringBootConfigApplication.class);

        public static void main(String[] args) {
                SpringApplication.run(SpringBootConfigApplication.class, args);
        }

        @Value("${server.ip}")
        String serverIp;
```

```
@Bean
CommandLineRunner values(){
        return args -> {
                log.info(" > The Server IP is: " + serverIp);
        };
}
}
```

Listing 3-17 shows you the main class. As you can see, it is using the @Value("${server.ip}") annotation. This annotation will translate the text "${server.ip}" and will look for this property and its value in the order mentioned earlier.

You can run this example by executing the following command in the root of your project:

```
$ ./mvnw spring-boot:run -Dserver.ip=192.168.12.1
```

If you package first your app (to create an executable JAR) and then run it with this:

```
$ ./mvnw package -DskipTests=true
$ java -jar target/spring-boot-config-0.0.1-SNAPSHOT.jar --server.ip=192.168.12.1
```

In either case, you will see something similar to the following output:

```
  .   ____          _            __ _ _
 /\\ / ___'_ __ _ _(_)_ __  __ _ \ \ \ \
( ( )\___ | '_ | '_| | '_ \/ _` | \ \ \ \
 \\/  ___)| |_)| | | | | || (_| |  ) ) ) )
  '  |____| .__|_| |_|_| |_\__, | / / / /
 =========|_|==============|___/=/_/_/_/
 :: Spring Boot ::        (v1.3.3.RELEASE)

INFO 97094 -[m] c.a.spring.SpringBootConfigApplication  : Starting
SpringBootConfigApplication v0.0.1-SNAPSHOT on liukang.local with PID 97094
INFO 97094 -[m] c.a.spring.SpringBootConfigApplication  : No active profile set, falling
back to default profiles: default
INFO 97094 -[m] s.c.a.AnnotationConfigApplicationContext : Refreshing startup date [Sat Feb
27 10:44:24 MST 2016]; root of context hierarchy
INFO 97094 -[m] o.s.j.e.a.AnnotationMBeanExporter        : Registering beans for JMX
exposure on startup
INFO 97094 -[m] c.a.spring.SpringBootConfigApplication  : > The Server IP is: 192.168.12.1
INFO 97094 -[m] c.a.spring.SpringBootConfigApplication  : Started
SpringBootConfigApplication in 1.624 seconds (JVM running for 2.255)
INFO 97094 -[t] s.c.a.AnnotationConfigApplicationContext : Closing startup date [Sat Feb 27
10:44:24 MST 2016]; root of context hierarchy
INFO 97094 -[t] o.s.j.e.a.AnnotationMBeanExporter        : Unregistering JMX-exposed beans
on shutdown
```

You can see from this output the text " > The Server IP is: 1921.68.12.1". Now, let's create the application.properties file. See Listing 3-18.

Listing 3-18. src/main/resources/application.properties

```
server.ip=192.168.23.4
```

If you run the application with the same command-line arguments, you will see that the arguments have precedence over the application.properties file. If you run it without the arguments, such as:

```
$ ./mvnw spring-boot:run
```

or

```
$ ./mvnw package
$ java -jar target/spring-boot-config-0.0.1-SNAPSHOT.jar
```

You get the text: "> The Server IP is: 192.168.3.4". If you are used to JSON formatting, perhaps you are interested in passing your properties in this format. You can use the spring.application.json property. You can run it like this:

```
$ ./mvnw spring-boot:run -Dspring.application.json='{"server":{"ip":"192.168.145.78"}}'
```

or

```
$ java -jar target/spring-boot-config-0.0.1-SNAPSHOT.jar --spring.application.json='{"server":{"ip":"192.168.145.78"}}'
```

Or you can also add it as environment variable:

```
$ SPRING_APPLICATION_JSON='{"server":{"ip":"192.168.145.78"}}' java -jar target/spring-boot-config-0.0.1-SNAPSHOT.jar
```

You will see the text: "> The Server IP is: 192.168.145.78". You can also add your environment variable that refers to your property like this:

```
$ SERVER_IP=192.168.150.46 ./mvnw spring-boot:run
```

or

```
$ SERVER_IP=192.168.150.46 java -jar target/spring-boot-config-0.0.1-SNAPSHOT.jar
```

You will see the text "> The Server IP is: 192.168.150.46". How does Spring Boot know that the environment variable is related to the server.ip property?

■ **Note** If you are using Windows OS, all the environment variables must have the keyword SET before the variable. For example: C:\> **SET** SERVER_IP=192.168.150.46 java -jar target/spring-boot-config-0.0.1-SNAPSHOT.jar

---

Relaxed Binding

Spring Boot uses relaxed rules for binding. See Table 3-1.

Table 3-1. *Spring Boot Relaxed Binding*

Property	Description
message.destinationName	Standard camel case.
message.destination-name	Dashed notation, which is the recommended way to add the application.properties or YML file.
MESSAGE_DESTINATION_NAME	Uppercase, which is the recommended way to denote OS environment variables.

Table 3-1 shows you the relaxed rules that apply to property names. That's why in the previous example, the server.ip property is recognized also as SERVER_IP. These relaxed rules help you avoid collision names. They have to do with the @ConfigurationProperties annotation and its prefix, which you see in a later section.

Changing Location and Name

Spring Boot has an order to find the application.properties or YAML file. It will look in:

- The /config subdirectory located in the current directory
- The current directory
- A classpath /config package
- The classpath root

You can test this by creating a /config subdirectory in your current directory and adding a new application.properties, and then test that the order is true. Remember that you should already have a application.properties file in the classpath root (src/main/resources).

Spring Boot allows you to change the name and location of the properties file. So for example, imagine that you will use the /config subdirectory and the name of the properties file is now mycfg.properties (its content is server.ip=127.0.0.1). Then you can run the app with the following command:

```
$./mvnw spring-boot:run -Dspring.config.name=mycfg
```

or

```
$ ./mvnw package -DskipTests=true
$ java -jar target/spring-boot-config-0.0.1-SNAPSHOT.jar --spring.config.name=mycfg
```

or

```
$ SPRING_CONFIG_NAME=mycfg java -jar target/spring-boot-config-0.0.1-SNAPSHOT.jar
```

You should see the text: "> The Server IP is: 127.0.0.1". It's not necessary to include the .properties with the name because it will automatically use it (same for a YAML file; you don't need to specify the extension). And as said before, you can also change its location. For example, create a subdirectory named app and add a mycfg.properties file (its content is server.ip=localhost). Then you can run or execute your app with the following:

```
$ ./mvnw spring-boot:run -Dspring.config.name=mycfg -Dspring.config.location=file:app/
```

or

```
$ java -jar target/spring-boot-config-0.0.1-SNAPSHOT.jar --spring.config.location=file:app/
--spring.config.name=mycfg
```

You can add the mycfg.properties file to the src/main/resources/META-INF/conf (you can create it) and execute this:

```
$ mkdir -p src/main/resources/META-INF/conf
$ cp config/mycfg.properties src/main/resources/META-INF/conf/
$ ./mvnw clean spring-boot:run -Dspring.config.name=mycfg -Dspring.config.
location=classpath:META-INF/conf/
```

You should see the text: "> The Server IP is: 127.0.0.1". Try to change the value of the property so you can see that it is looking in the classpath. (Normally it will print an error that says Resource or File not found in the classpath.) Spring Boot also has an order to search for the properties file:

- classpath
- classpath:/config
- file:
- file:config/

Unless you change the order with the spring.config.location property. To change the location of the properties file, you need to set the SPRING_CONFIG_LOCATION environment variable.

■ **Note** If you are using Windows OS, the slash is \ for creating directories or copying files.

Profile Based

Since version 3.1, the Spring Framework added a cool feature that allows developers to create custom properties and beans based on profiles. This is a useful way to separate environments without having to recompile or package a Spring app. You simply have to specify the active profile with the @ActiveProfiles annotation (when you are testing classes) or get the current environment and use the setActiveProfiles method. You can also use the SPRING_PROFILES_ACTIVE environment variable or the spring.profiles.active property.

You can use the properties file using this format: application-{profile}.properties. Create two files in your config/ subdirectory: application-qa.properties and application-prod.properties. Here are the contents of each one:

- application-qa.properties

  server.ip=localhost

- application-prod.properties

  server.ip=http://my-remote.server.com

Now you can run your example with the following:

```
$ ./mvnw clean spring-boot:run -Dspring.profiles.active=prod
```

When you execute this command, take a look at the beginning of the logs. You should see something similar to the following output:

```
  .   ____          _            __ _ _
 /\\ / ___'_ __ _ _(_)_ __  __ _ \ \ \ \
( ( )\___ | '_ | '_| | '_ \/ _` | \ \ \ \
 \\/  ___)| |_)| | | | | || (_| |  ) ) ) )
  '  |____| .__|_| |_|_| |_\__, | / / / /
 =========|_|==============|___/=/_/_/_/
 :: Spring Boot ::        (v1.3.3.RELEASE)

INFO 2242 -[m] ...ConfigApplication       : Starting SpringBootConfigApplication on liukang.
                                            local with PID 2242
INFO 2242 -[m] ...ConfigApplication       : The following profiles are active: prod
INFO 2242 -[m] ...gApplicationContext     : Refreshing AnnotationConfigApplicationContext
                                            @696a03a3y
INFO 2242 -[m] ...BeanExporter            : Registering beans for JMX exposure on startup
INFO 2242 -[m] ...ConfigApplication       : > The Server IP is: http://my-remote.server.com
INFO 2242 -[m] ...ConfigApplication       : Started SpringBootConfigApplication in 1.586 seconds
INFO 2242 -[ t] ...gApplicationContext    : Closing @696a03a3
INFO 2242 -[ t] ...BeanExporter           : Unregistering JMX-exposed beans on shutdown
```

You should see the legend that reads "The following profiles are active: prod" and of course the profile application properties active (application-prod.properties) value: "> The Server IP is: http://my-remote.server.com". As an exercise, try to change the name of the application-prod. properties to mycfg-prod.properties and the application-qa.properties to mycfg-qa.properties, and use the Spring properties that will get the new name. If you don't set any active profiles, it will get the default, which means that it will grab the application.properties.

Custom Properties Prefix

Spring Boot allows you to write and use your own custom property prefix for your properties. The only thing you need to do is annotate with the @ConfigurationProperties annotation a Java class that will have setters and getters as their properties.

If you are using the STS IDE, I recommend including a dependency in your pom.xml. This dependency will create a code insight and it will trigger the editor's code completion for the properties. So add the next dependency in your pom.xml:

```
<dependency>
        <groupId>org.springframework.boot</groupId>
        <artifactId>spring-boot-configuration-processor</artifactId>
        <optional>true</optional>
</dependency>
```

This dependency will allow you to process your custom properties and have a code completion. Now, let's see the example. Modify your src/main/resource/application.properties file to look like Listing 3-19.

Listing 3-19. src/main/resources/application.properties

```
server.ip=192.168.3.5

myapp.server-ip=192.168.34.56
myapp.name=My Config App
myapp.description=This is an example
```

Listing 3-19 shows you the application.properties file. What is new is the second block, where the custom properties with myapp as the prefix are defined. Next, open your main app class and edit it to look like Listing 3-20.

Listing 3-20. Version2 of src/main/java/com/apress/spring/SpringBootConfigApplication.java

```
package com.apress.spring;

import org.slf4j.Logger;
import org.slf4j.LoggerFactory;
import org.springframework.beans.factory.annotation.Autowired;
import org.springframework.beans.factory.annotation.Value;
import org.springframework.boot.CommandLineRunner;
import org.springframework.boot.SpringApplication;
import org.springframework.boot.autoconfigure.SpringBootApplication;
import org.springframework.boot.context.properties.ConfigurationProperties;
import org.springframework.context.annotation.Bean;
import org.springframework.stereotype.Component;

@SpringBootApplication
public class SpringBootConfigApplication {

        private static Logger log = LoggerFactory.getLogger(SpringBootConfigApplication.class);

        public static void main(String[] args) {
                SpringApplication.run(SpringBootConfigApplication.class, args);
        }

        @Value("${myapp.server-ip}")
        String serverIp;

        @Autowired
        MyAppProperties props;

        @Bean
        CommandLineRunner values(){
                return args -> {
                        log.info(" > The Server IP is: " + serverIp);
                        log.info(" > App Name: " + props.getName());
                        log.info(" > App Info: " + props.getDescription());
                };
        }
```

```
@Component
@ConfigurationProperties(prefix="myapp")
public static class MyAppProperties {
        private String name;
        private String description;
        private String serverIp;

        public String getName() {
                return name;
        }
        public void setName(String name) {
                this.name = name;
        }
        public String getDescription() {
                return description;
        }
        public void setDescription(String description) {
                this.description = description;
        }
        public String getServerIp() {
                return serverIp;
        }
        public void setServerIp(String serverIp) {
                this.serverIp = serverIp;
        }
    }

}
```

Listing 3-20 shows you the main app class. Let's examine it:

- @Value("${myapp.server-ip}"). The annotation now has a myapp.server-ip, which means that the value will be equal to 192.168.34.56.

- @Autowired MyAppProperties props. This is creating an instance of the MyAppProperties type.

- @Component @ConfigurationProperties(prefix="myapp"). The @ConfigurationProperties annotation tells Spring Boot that the class will be used for all the properties defined in the application.properties file that has the myapp prefix. Meaning that it will recognized when you have myapp.serverIp (or myapp.server-ip), myapp.name, and myapp.description. The @Component annotation is used to make sure that the class is picked up as a bean.

The Spring Boot uses relaxed rules to bind environment properties to the @ConfigurationProperties beans, so you don't have any collision names.

Now if you run your app, you should see all your myapp properties:

```
$ ./mvnw clean spring-boot:run
...
> The Server IP is: 192.168.34.56
> App Name: My Config App
> App Info: This is an example
...
```

As you can see, you have plenty of options for using your application configuration properties. You haven't seen any YAML examples though, and if you want to use the YAML syntax, refer to the Spring Boot documentation for examples.

Summary

This chapter gave you a tour of the Spring Boot insights by explaining the auto-configuration feature, including how the @EnableAutoConfiguration annotation works behind the scenes. You learned how to exclude some of the auto-configuration classes as well.

You learned about some of the Spring Boot features and how to use the application configuration properties. You also learned how to customize your application configuration properties by adding a prefix.

The next chapter covers the Spring CLI in more detail.

CHAPTER 4

Spring Boot CLI

This chapter discussed a Spring Boot tool that can help you create prototypes and production-ready applications. This tool is part of the Spring Boot installation you performed in the first chapters. This is not a Maven or Gradle plugin or dependency.

I'm talking about the Spring Boot Command Line Interface (CLI). Just to recap, in previous chapters, you learned that you can get the CLI from the binary installation at http://repo.spring.io/release/org/springframework/boot/spring-boot-cli/ or, if you are using a Mac/Linux, you can use homebrew (http://brew.sh/) with the following command:

```
$ brew tap pivotal/tap
$ brew install springboot
```

If you are using Linux, you can use the sdkman tool (http://sdkman.io/) and install it with the following command:

```
$ sdk install springboot
```

All the examples will be in Java and Groovy. There is no real distinction between one language or another in the sense of compile, run, or package. The only difference is some extra parameters that will pass to the command line, but don't worry too much; you'll see those in a moment.

Spring Boot CLI

The first time I started to learn Spring Boot, which was around three years ago, it was the first alpha release, and the only available command was the run. What else do you need, right? It was amazing that with a few lines of code you can have a web application written in Groovy up and running. It was simple and awesome.

Now in version 1.3.X-GA and 1.4.X-SNAPSHOT, it has more options and an interactive shell that you'll see soon. To see the CLI in detail, you need to consider some simple examples. Let's start with the one in Listing 4-1, which shows the Groovy example from previous chapters.

Listing 4-1. app.groovy

```groovy
@RestController
class WebApp{

    @RequestMapping("/")
    String greetings(){
        "Spring Boot Rocks"
    }
}
```

Listing 4-1 shows you the simplest Groovy web application you can have and that you can run with Spring Boot. Now, let's see the same web application but in Java. See Listing 4-2.

Listing 4-2. WebApp.java

```
package com.apress.spring;

import org.springframework.boot.SpringApplication;
import org.springframework.boot.autoconfigure.SpringBootApplication;
import org.springframework.web.bind.annotation.RequestMapping;
import org.springframework.web.bind.annotation.RestController;

@RestController
@SpringBootApplication
public class WebApp {

    @RequestMapping("/")
    public String greetings(){
        return "Spring Boot Rocks in Java too!";
    }

    public static void main(String[] args) {
        SpringApplication.run(WebApp.class, args);
    }

}
```

Listing 4-2 shows you the Java version of the simplest web application. As I mentioned, Spring Boot enables you to choose Java or Groovy in order to create enterprise and production-ready applications with ease.

Let's start using all the CLI commands.

The run Command

The run command will allow you to run Java or Groovy Spring Boot applications. Its syntax is the following:

```
spring run [options] <files> [--] [args]
```

The available options are:

Option	Description
--autoconfigure [Boolean]	Adds the auto-configuration compiler transformation. Remember the auto-configuration features and how everything works by adding the @EnableAutoConfiguration or the composed @SpringBootApplication annotations. This is the same idea (default is true).
--classpath, -cp	Adds the classpath entries, and it's useful when you have third-party libraries. As a recommendation, you can create a lib/ folder in the root of your program and add all the classes or JARs there.
--no-guess-dependencies	Does not attempt to guess the dependencies. This is useful when you already use the @Grab annotation in your application.

(continued)

Option	Description
--no-guess-imports	Does not attempt to guess the imports. This is useful when you have already included some of the imports in your Groovy application. For example, in a Java app you can use this option because you are importing the classes you need. There is more about this in Chapter 3 (in the auto-configuration section).
-q, --quiet	Quiets logging. In other words, it won't print anything to the console.
-v, --verbose	Logs everything. It is useful for seeing what's going on, because it shows you even the code introspection and what is adding to the program. See Chapter 3 for more information.
--watch	Sets a watch to the file(s) for changes. It is useful when you don't want to stop and run the app again.

To run the Groovy application (shown in Listing 4-1), you simply execute:

```
$ spring run app.groovy
```

Executing this command, you will have a web application up and running and listening to port 8080 by default, but you can override this by executing the following command:

```
$ spring run app.groovy -- --server.port=8888
```

This command will run the web application and it will be listening in port 8888. Now, if you want to add some third-party library and load the dependencies, you simply execute:

```
$ spring run -cp lib/mylib.jar app.groovy
```

If you want to run the Java application (Listing 4-2), you just execute:

```
$ spring run WebApp.java
```

■ **Note** You can stop your application by pressing Ctrl+C in your keyboard.

If you are running a Java application, it's important to add the package keyword. You don't need to have a hierarchy or create any directories. If you don't add a package to Spring Boot scanning it will be impossible to run your app because it needs to scan all the available dependencies of Spring. It will start scanning all the dependencies used and start from the root of every dependency, so be careful!

If you have several files, you can use the wildcard * to compile all of them. Just execute this command:

```
$ spring run *.groovy
```

If, for some reason, you need to tweak the JVM and its options, you can execute the following command:

```
$ JAVA_OPTS=-Xmx2g spring run app.groovy
```

This command will increase the memory heap up to 2GB for the app.groovy application.

The test Command

The test command runs a Spring Groovy script and Java tests. Its syntax is the following:

```
spring test [options] files [--] [args]
```

The available options are:

Option	Description
--autoconfigure [Boolean]	Adds the auto-configuration compiler transformation (default is true).
--classpath, -cp	Adds the classpath entries, which is useful when you have third-party libraries. As a recommendation, you can create a lib/ folder in the root of your program and add all the classes or JARs there.
--no-guess-dependencies	Does not attempt to guess the dependencies. This is useful when you already use the @Grab annotation in your application.
--no-guess-imports	Does not attempt to guess the imports. This is useful when you already include some of the imports in your Groovy application. For example, in a Java app you can use this option because you are importing the classes you need. See more in Chapter 3 (in the auto-configuration section).

To run a test, you need a test, right? Listings 4-3, 4-4, and 4-5 show examples using the well known JUnit and Spock frameworks.

Listing 4-3. test.groovy

```
class MyTest{
        @Test
        void simple() {
                String str= "JUnit works with Spring Boot"
                assertEquals "JUnit works with Spring Boot",str
        }
}
```

Listing 4-3 shows you the simplest unit test, and if you can see you don't need to use any imports, Spring Boot will take care of that. To run it, you execute:

```
$ spring test test.groovy
```

Take a look at the Spock unit test shown in Listing 4-4.

Listing 4-4. spock.groovy

```
@Grab('org.spockframework:spock-core:1.0-groovy-2.4')
import spock.lang.Specification
import org.springframework.boot.test.OutputCapture

class SimpleSpockTest extends Specification {

    @org.junit.Rule
    OutputCapture capture = new OutputCapture()
```

```
def "get output and capture it"() {
    when:
    print 'Spring Boot works with Spock'

    then:
    capture.toString() == 'Spring Boot works with Spock'
    }

}
```

Listing 4-4 shows you the use of the Spock Framework by extending the Specification class and defining the methods. In order to use the Spock Framework it's necessary to import the necessary dependencies and to include those dependencies by adding the @Grab annotation that will include the Spock dependency for Groovy. The intention of this section is to show the usage of Spock. But if you are looking for more information about it, you can go to http://spockframework.org/. All its documentation is found at http://spockframework.github.io/spock/docs/1.0/index.html.

Listing 4-4 also shows you one of the new features of Spring Boot, which is the OutputCapture class. It allows you to capture output from System.out and System.err. In order to run this test, you execute the same instruction but change the name of the file:

```
$ spring test spock.groovy
```

It's important to know that Spring Boot won't always figure it out when you are using third-party libraries, so you must use the @Grab annotation and the correct import.

Take a look at the unit test in Java, shown in Listing 4-5.

Listing 4-5. MyTest.java

```
import org.junit.Rule;
import org.junit.Test;
import org.springframework.boot.test.OutputCapture;

import static org.hamcrest.Matchers.*;
import static org.junit.Assert.*;

public class MyTest {

        @Rule
        public OutputCapture capture = new OutputCapture();

        @Test
        public void stringTest() throws Exception {
                System.out.println("Spring Boot Test works in Java too!");
                assertThat(capture.toString(), containsString("Spring Boot Test works in
                Java too!"));
        }

}
```

Listing 4-5 shows you a unit test written in Java. The assertThat statement belongs to the org.junit. Assert class that can be accessed as static. The containsString is a static method from the org.hamcrest. Matchers class, and it will match the capture string. This unit test also uses the OutputCapture class. To run it, you just execute this command:

```
$ spring test MyTest.java
```

If you want to test the web application (Listing 4-1—app.groovy), you can create the code in Listing 4-6.

Listing 4-6. test.groovy

```
class SimpleWebTest {

    @Test
    void greetingsTest() {
        assertEquals("Spring Boot Rocks", new WebApp().greetings())
    }

}
```

To test this, just execute the following command:

```
$ spring test app.groovy test.groovy
```

This command will use the previous class—the WebApp (from Listing 4-1—app.groovy)—and it will call the greetings method to get the string back.

Although these examples are extremely simple, it's important to see how easy is to create and run tests using the command-line interface. A special chapter includes a more elaborated unit and integration test using all the power of Spring Boot.

The grab Command

The grab command will download all the Spring Groovy scripts and Java dependencies to the ./repository directory. Its syntax is the following:

```
spring grab [options] files [--] [args]
```

The available options are:

Option	Description
--autoconfigure [Boolean]	Adds the auto-configuration compiler transformation (default is true).
--classpath, -cp	Adds the classpath entries, which is useful when you have third-party libraries. As a recommendation, you can create a lib/ folder in the root of your program and add all the classes or JARs there.
--no-guess-dependencies	Does not attempt to guess the dependencies. This is useful when you already use the @Grab annotation in your application.
--no-guess-imports	Does not attempt to guess the imports. This is useful when you already include some of the imports in your Groovy application. For example, in a Java app you can use this option because you are importing the classes you need. For more information, see Chapter 3 (in the auto-configuration section).

You can use any of the listings you've seen so far to execute the grab command. For Listing 4-4, you can execute:

```
$ spring grab MyTest.java
```

If you check out the current directory, you will see the repository subdirectory created with all the dependencies. The grab command is useful when you want to execute a Spring Boot application that doesn't have an Internet connection and the libraries are needed. The grab command is also used to prepare your application before you can deploy it to the cloud. (You'll see this useful command in Chapter 13, "Spring Boot in the Cloud.")

The jar Command

The jar command will create a self-contained executable JAR file from a Groovy or Java script. Its syntax is the following:

```
spring jar [options] <jar-name> <files>
```

The available options are:

Option	Description
--autoconfigure [Boolean]	Adds the auto-configuration compiler transformation (default is true).
--classpath, -cp	Adds the classpath entries, which is useful when you have third-party libraries. As a recommendation, you can create a lib/ folder in the root of your program and add all the classes or JARs there.
--exclude	A pattern to find the files and exclude them from the final JAR file.
--include	A pattern to find the files and include them in the final JAR file.
--no-guess-dependencies	Does not attempt to guess the dependencies. This is useful when you already use the @Grab annotation in your application.
--no-guess-imports	Does not attempt to guess the imports. This is useful when you already include some of the imports in your Groovy application. For example, in a Java app you can use this option because you are importing the classes you need. For more information, see Chapter 3 (the auto-configuration section).

You can use Listing 4-1 (app.groovy) and execute the following command:

```
$ spring jar app.jar app.groovy
```

Now you can check out your current directory and see that there are two files—one named app.jar.original and another named app.jar. The only difference between the files is that the app.jar.original is the one created by the dependency management (Maven) to create the app.jar. It's a fat JAR that can be executed with the following:

```
$ java -jar app.jar
```

By executing this command, you will have a web application up and running. The jar command enables application portability, because you can ship your application and run it in any system that has Java installed, without worrying about an application container. Remember that Spring Boot will embed the Tomcat application server in a Spring Boot web application.

The war Command

This is very similar to the previous command. The war command will create a self-contained executable WAR file from a Groovy or Java script. Its syntax is the following:

```
spring war [options]  <war-name>  <files>
```

The available options are:

Option	Description
--autoconfigure [Boolean]	Adds the auto-configuration compiler transformation (default is true).
--classpath, -cp	Adds the classpath entries, which is useful when you have third-party libraries. As a recommendation, you can create a lib/ folder in the root of your program and add all the classes or JARs there.
--exclude	A pattern to find the files and exclude them from the final JAR file.
--include	A pattern to find the files and include them in the final JAR file.
--no-guess-dependencies	Does not attempt to guess the dependencies. This is useful when you already use the @Grab annotation in your application.
--no-guess-imports	Does not attempt to guess the imports. This is useful when you already include some of the imports in your groovy application. For example, in a Java app you can use this option because you are importing the classes you need. For more information, see Chapter 3 (the auto-configuration section).

You can use Listing 4-1 (app.groovy) to run the war command by executing the following:

```
$ spring war app.war app.groovy
```

After executing this command, you will have in your current directory the app.war.original and the app.war files. You can run it with the following command:

```
$ java -jar app.war
```

In the previous command I mentioned the word portability, right? So what would be the case for a WAR file? Well, you can use the WAR file in existing application containers like Pivotal tcServer, Tomcat, WebSphere, Jetty, etc.

■ **Note** You can use either command to create a portable and executable application. The only difference is that when you use the war command, it will create a "transportable" WAR, which means that you can run your application as a standalone or you can deploy it to a J2EE-compliant container. You are going to see a complete example in the following chapters.

The install Command

The install command is very similar to the grab command; the only difference is that you need to specify the library you want to install (in a coordinate format groupId:artifactId:version; the same as the @Grab annotation). It will download it and the dependencies in a lib directory. Its syntax is the following:

```
spring install [options] <coordinates>
```

The available options are:

Option	Description
--autoconfigure [Boolean]	Adds the auto-configuration compiler transformation (default is true).
--classpath, -cp	Adds the classpath entries, which is useful when you have third-party libraries. As a recommendation, you can create a lib/ folder in the root of your program and add all the classes or JARs there.
--no-guess-dependencies	Does not attempt to guess the dependencies. This is useful when you already use the @Grab annotation in your application.
--no-guess-imports	Does not attempt to guess the imports. This is useful when you already include some of the imports in your groovy application. For example, in a Java app you can use this option because you are importing the classes you need. For more information, see Chapter 3 (the auto-configuration section).

Take for example Listing 4-4 (spock.groovy). If you execute the following command:

```
$ spring install org.spockframework:spock-core:1.0-groovy-2.4
```

You will have in the lib directory the Spock library and its dependencies.

■ **Note** If you are using the SDKMAN tool (http://sdkman.io/), it will download the libraries in the $HOME/.sdkman/candidates/springboot/1.3.X.RELEASE/lib directory.

The uninstall Command

The uninstall command will uninstall the dependencies from the lib directory. Its syntax is the following:

```
spring uninstall [options] <coordinates>
```

The available options are:

Option	Description
--autoconfigure [Boolean]	Adds the auto-configuration compiler transformation (default is true).
--classpath, -cp	Adds the classpath entries, which is useful when you have third-party libraries. As a recommendation, you can create a lib/ folder in the root of your program and add all the classes or JARs there.
--no-guess-dependencies	Does not attempt to guess the dependencies. This is useful when you already use the @Grab annotation in your application.
--no-guess-imports	Does not attempt to guess the imports. This is useful when you already include some of the imports in your groovy application. For example, in a Java app you can use this option because you are importing the classes you need. For more information, see Chapter 3 (the auto-configuration section).

You can test this command by executing the following command:

```
$ spring uninstall org.spockframework:spock-core:1.0-groovy-2.4
```

It will remove all the Spock dependencies from the lib directory.

The init Command

The init command will help you initialize a new project by using the Spring Initializr (http://start.spring.io/). Whether or not you are using an IDE, this command will help you get everything ready to start developing Spring Boot applications. Its syntax is the following:

```
spring init [options] [location]
```

The available options are:

Option	Description
-a, --artifactId	The project coordinate; if it's not provided it, the default name is demo.
-b, --boot-version	The Spring Boot version to use; if it's not provided it will get the latest, defined as the parent-pom.
--build	The build system to use; the possible values are maven or gradle. If it's not specified, the default value is maven.
-d, --dependencies	A comma-separated list of dependency identifiers that will be included. For example, -d=web or -d=web,jdbc,actuator.
--description	The project description.
-f, --force	Overwrites existing files.
--format	A format of the generated content. Useful when you want to import your projects into an IDE like STS. The possible values are build and project. If it's not provided, the default value is project.

(continued)

Option	Description
-g, --groupId	The project coordinates defining the group ID. If it's not provided, it defaults to com.example.
-j, --java-version	The language level. If it's not provided, it defaults to 1.8.
-l, --language	Specifies the programming language. The possible values are java and groovy. If it's not provided, it defaults to java.
-n, --name	The name of the application. If it's not provided, it defaults to demo.
-p, --packaging	The project packaging. The values are jar, war, and zip. If it's not provided, it will generate a ZIP file.
--package-name	The package name. If it's not provided, it defaults to demo.
-t, --type	The project type. The values are maven-project, maven-build, gradle-project, and gradle-build. If it's not provided, it defaults to maven-project.
--target	The URL of the service to use. It defaults to https://start.spring.io. This means that you can create your own reference service.
-v, --version	The project version. If it's not provided, it defaults to 0.0.1-SNAPSHOT.
-x, --extract	Extracts the content of the project created in the current directory if the location is not specified.

You will use this command very often (if you are not using an IDE such as the STS or IntelliJ), so you can get used to it with the following examples.

To create a default project, you just execute:

```
$ spring init
```

It will generate a demo.zip file. You can unzip it and take a look at the structure (a Maven project structure), as shown in Figure 4-1, but the most important part will be the pom.xml file. If you look at this file, you can see the minimal dependencies: spring-boot-starter and spring-boot-starter-test.

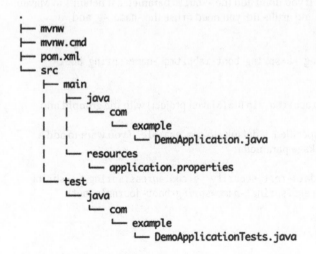

```
.
├── mvnw
├── mvnw.cmd
├── pom.xml
└── src
    ├── main
    │   ├── java
    │   │   └── com
    │   │       └── example
    │   │           └── DemoApplication.java
    │   └── resources
    │       └── application.properties
    └── test
        └── java
            └── com
                └── example
                    └── DemoApplicationTests.java

10 directories, 6 files
```

Figure 4-1. *The demo.zip contents*

Figure 4-1 shows the demo.zip structure. Take a look at the src folder, which contains the main/java/com/example/DemoApplication.java file and of course its unit test. Also you can see that it contains two additional files, mvnw (for UNIX) and mvnw.cmd (for Windows). These commands allow you to run a Maven project without actually having Maven installed on your system.

You can simply execute the following command:

```
$ ./mvnw spring-boot:run
```

This command will download the Maven tool (in the .mvn subdirectory) and run it. If you take a look at the DemoApplication.java class, you'll see that it's not doing much. It's simply running the Spring Boot application. With all this you have a template that you can use over and over. If you want to create a web application, the only thing you need to do is add the spring-boot-starter-web dependency.

init Examples

This section includes more examples using the init command. The following command will create a web application with JDBC Gradle project:

```
$ spring init -d=web,jdbc --build=gradle
```

This command will generate a demo.zip file, but with its contents using Gradle. It will include the Gradle wrapper so you don't have to install it.

If you want to generate only the pom.xml (for a Maven project) or build.gradle file (for a Gradle project), just add --format=build and --build=[gradle|maven]:

```
$ spring init -d=web,data-jpa,security --format=build --build=gradle
```

This command will create the build.gradle file with the web, JPA, and security dependencies.

```
$ spring init -d=jdbc,amqp --format=build
```

This command will create the pom.xml file. If you don't add the --build parameter, it defaults to Maven.

To create a project with the name, groupId and artifactId, you need to use the -name, -g, and -a parameters respectively:

```
$ spring init -d=amqp -g=com.apress.spring -a=spring-boot-rabbitmq -name=spring-boot-rabbitmq
```

This command will create a spring-boot-rabbitmq.zip file (Maven project) with the groupId and artifactId specified.

By default, when the package name is not specified, it defaults to com.example. If you want to add a package convention, you need to add the --package parameter:

```
$ spring init -d=web,thymeleaf,data-jpa,data-rest,security -g=com.apress.spring -a=spring-boot-journal-oauth --package-name=com.apress.spring -name=spring-boot-journal-oauth
```

It's fine to have a ZIP file for portability, but you can uncompress directly into the current directory. You simply add the -x parameter:

```
$ spring init -d=web,thymeleaf,data-jpa,data-rest,security,actuator,h2,mysql
-g=com.apress.spring -a=spring-boot-journal-cloud --package-name=com.apress.spring
-name=spring-boot-journal-cloud -x
```

This command will uncompress the ZIP file on the fly and the contents will be written to the current directory.

If you are curious and want to know more about the dependencies or other parameter values, you can execute the following command:

```
$ spring init --list
```

You will be using the spring init command throughout the entire book, so take a moment and review all its options.

An Alternative to the init Command

There will be times when you need just the pom.xml or build.gradle files, perhaps to check out the dependencies and declarations or to look at the plugins declarations. You execute the following command:

```
$ curl -s https://start.spring.io/pom.xml -d packaging=war -o pom.xml
```

Yes, you read it right! Remember that the init command calls the Spring Initializr service at https://start.spring.io, so you can use the UNIX cURL command. This command will generate only the pom.xml file. And if you are curious again to see what else you can do by using the UNIX cURL command, just execute the following:

```
$ curl start.spring.io
```

This command will print all the available options and some examples using cURL with the Spring Initializr. You learned in previous chapters that, within the STS (Spring Tool Suite) IDE, you can create a Spring Boot application by selecting Spring Starter Project. This wizard will connect to the Spring Initializr, so either you use an IDE or the command line to get a Spring Boot project structure.

The shell Command

The shell command will start an embedded shell. Execute the following command:

```
$ spring shell
Spring Boot (v1.3.X.RELEASE)
Hit TAB to complete. Type 'help' and hit RETURN for help, and 'exit' to quit.
$
```

As you can see from the output, you can type help to get more information about the shell. Actually the spring shell is the previous command, but just executed in an embedded shell. One of the benefits is that it has a TAB completion so you can get all the possible suggestions for the options.

The help Command

The help command will be your best friend. You can execute it as follows:

```
spring help
usage: spring [--help] [--version]
       <command> [<args>]

    Available commands are:

  run [options] <files> [--] [args]
    Run a spring groovy script

  test [options] <files> [--] [args]
    Run a spring groovy script test

  grab
    Download a spring groovy script's dependencies to ./repository

  jar [options] <jar-name> <files>
    Create a self-contained executable jar file from a Spring Groovy script

  war [options] <war-name> <files>
    Create a self-contained executable war file from a Spring Groovy script

  install [options] <coordinates>
    Install dependencies to the lib directory

  uninstall [options] <coordinates>
    Uninstall dependencies from the lib directory

  init [options] [location]
    Initialize a new project using Spring Initializr (start.spring.io)

  shell
    Start a nested shell

    Common options:

  -d, --debug Verbose mode
    Print additional status information for the command you are running

See 'spring help <command>' for more information on a specific command.
```

As you can see from this output, you can also execute the spring help <command>, which is very handy because you will get more information about the command and in some case some examples on how to use it. For example, if you want to know about the init command, just execute the following:

```
$ spring help init
```

Remember, the spring help command is your best friend.

Summary

The chapter showed you how to use the Spring Boot Command Line Interface. It explained all the different commands and their options.

You learned mentioned that one of the most important commands is the `init` command and it will be used in the entire book, either through a terminal in a command line or by using an IDE such as STS or IntelliJ.

In the next chapter, you are going to learn how to create Spring applications and then compare them side by side with Spring Boot applications.

CHAPTER 5

∎∎∎

Spring with Spring Boot

This chapter shows you how an old Spring developer used to do applications and compare them to Spring Boot. It also shows you how to use legacy Spring code with your Spring Boot applications.

Why this is important? I've been asked by several developers why Spring Boot is better than Spring or if Spring Boot will get rid of the Spring Framework. Remember that I said in the first chapters that Spring Boot is Spring, and you need to think of it as a new way to create the next generation of Spring applications.

Spring Web Applications

Let's start by creating the same simple web application from the other chapters that will print out "Spring Rocks!", this time using just Spring. First you need to know a little bit of background on the J2EE web and Spring MVC, because it's the base for all Spring web applications. If you already know about it, feel free to skip to the next sections.

J2EE Web Applications

Creating a Java web application hasn't been an easy task since the beginning. I explained in Chapter 1 that you need to get a lot going even before you can run your application, but let's get started. You are going to create a J2EE web application, a servlet application, in an "old-fashion" way, using Maven archetypes with a servlet 2.4 specification. If you recall, the servlet was the first attempt to use a server side request to produce some HTML content.

You are going to use Maven, so make sure you have it in your PATH. Let's start by creating the web project template by executing this command:

```
$ mvn archetype:create -DgroupId=com.apress.j2ee -DartifactId=simple-web-app
-DarchetypeArtifactId=maven-archetype-webapp
```

This command will create a simple-web-app folder with the structure shown in Figure 5-1.

© Felipe Gutierrez 2016
F. Gutierrez, *Pro Spring Boot*, DOI 10.1007/978-1-4842-1431-2_5

```
simple-web-app/
├── pom.xml
└── src
    └── main
        ├── resources
        └── webapp
            ├── WEB-INF
            │   └── web.xml
            └── index.jsp
```

5 directories, 3 files

Figure 5-1. *A simple-web-app structure*

Figure 5-1. shows you the result of executing the maven command. Let's start by adding a missing dependency in the pom.xml. Listing 5-1 shows you the final pom.xml.

Listing 5-1. simple-web-app/pom.xml

```xml
<project xmlns="http://maven.apache.org/POM/4.0.0"
xmlns:xsi="http://www.w3.org/2001/XMLSchema-instance"
    xsi:schemaLocation="http://maven.apache.org/POM/4.0.0
    http://maven.apache.org/maven-v4_0_0.xsd">
    <modelVersion>4.0.0</modelVersion>

    <groupId>com.apress.j2ee</groupId>
    <artifactId>simple-web-app</artifactId>
    <packaging>war</packaging>

    <version>1.0-SNAPSHOT</version>
    <name>simple-web-app Maven Webapp</name>
    <url>http://maven.apache.org</url>

    <dependencies>
        <dependency>
                <groupId>javax.servlet</groupId>
                <artifactId>servlet-api</artifactId>
                <version>2.4</version>
                <scope>provided</scope>
        </dependency>
        <dependency>
                <groupId>junit</groupId>
                <artifactId>junit</artifactId>
                <version>3.8.1</version>
                <scope>test</scope>
        </dependency>
    </dependencies>
```

```
        <build>
                <finalName>simple-web-app</finalName>
        </build>
</project>
```

The missing dependency was the `servlet-api artifactId`, and this is because you need to create a servlet class.

```
<dependency>
        <groupId>javax.servlet</groupId>
        <artifactId>servlet-api</artifactId>
        <version>2.4</version>
        <scope>provided</scope>
</dependency>
```

Another important part of the `pom.xml` file is the `<packaging>` tag. It tells Maven that this will be a Web ARchive or WAR. Next, let's create the servlet class. See Listing 5-2.

Listing 5-2. src/main/java/com/apress/j2ee/SimpleServlet.java

```java
package com.apress.j2ee;

import java.io.IOException;
import java.io.PrintWriter;

import javax.servlet.ServletException;
import javax.servlet.http.HttpServlet;
import javax.servlet.http.HttpServletRequest;
import javax.servlet.http.HttpServletResponse;

public class SimpleServlet extends HttpServlet {
        protected void service(HttpServletRequest request, HttpServletResponse response) throws
                                          ServletException, IOException {
            PrintWriter out = response.getWriter();
            out.println("<html>");
            out.println("<body>");
            out.println("<h1>Simple Web Application with Java</h1>");
            out.println("</body>");
            out.println("</html>");
        }

}
```

Listing 5-2 shows you the `SimpleServlet` class, which needs to be in the `src/main/java/com/apress/j2ee` path. The `SimpleServlet` is its method `service` and uses the `PrintWriter` class as a response for any request. Now you need to define the URL pattern that will use this servlet class. The URL pattern needs to be defined in the `web.xml` that is located in the `WEB-INF` folder. To be more specific, you need to edit the `src/webapp/WEB-INF/web.xml` file to declare the servlet class. See Listing 5-3.

Listing 5-3. src/webapp/WEB-INF/web.xml

```
<!DOCTYPE web-app PUBLIC
 "-//Sun Microsystems, Inc.//DTD Web Application 2.3//EN"
 "http://java.sun.com/dtd/web-app_2_3.dtd" >

<web-app>
  <display-name>Archetype Created Web Application</display-name>
  <servlet>
        <servlet-name>SimpleServlet</servlet-name>
        <display-name>SimpleServlet</display-name>
        <description>A simple Servlet</description>
        <servlet-class>com.apress.j2ee.SimpleServlet</servlet-class>
  </servlet>
  <servlet-mapping>
        <servlet-name>SimpleServlet</servlet-name>
        <url-pattern>/SimpleServlet</url-pattern>
  </servlet-mapping>
</web-app>
```

Listing 5-3 shows the web.xml file where you declare two sections—one is the name of the servlet, with the `<servlet>` tag. The other is the servlet mapping with the `<servlet-mapping>` tag where you add the URL that will be the endpoint of the request. In this case, it's the /SimpleServlet.

Now you can execute the following command to package your web application:

```
$ mvn clean package
```

This command will create the target/simple-web-app.war file. Now you need to look for an application server. You can use Pivotal tcServer (https://network.pivotal.io/products/pivotal-tcserver) or you can use Tomcat (http://tomcat.apache.org/). Or, if you are using a Mac/Linux, you can use brew (http://brew.sh/) by executing:

```
$ brew install tomcat
```

Place your WAR in your `<tomcat-installation>`/webapps/ directory and run your application server. To run your application server, you can go to the `<tomcat-installation>`/bin directory and execute the startup.sh script. Then you can go to your web browser and access http://localhost:8080/simple-web-app/SimpleServlet. You should see this text:

```
Simple Web Application with Java
```

Of course, you can use an IDE of your preference and import this Maven project to facilitate the creation of the servlet class and to edit the other files—you are more than welcome to do so. My point here is that either you choose and IDE or you do this manually like I showed you. It's still a hassle to create just a simple web application. This was the daily task for a web developer at least a decade ago.

After servlets, the JavaServer Pages (JSP) were born, but of course, J2EE evolved more and more. With its Servlet 3 specification, it provides a new configuration-less way for creating a web application by creating the @WebServlet that allows you to annotate your servlet class without a web.xml file.

Spring MVC Applications

The Spring Framework brought a new way to develop web applications by introducing a MVC (Model View Controller) pattern into the framework that is easy to set up and use. I know that the MVC was invented in the 70s and modeled by other frameworks and other programming languages even before the Spring Framework, but the Spring team did an excellent job using this pattern as a base model for every web application by simplifying its functionality.

Let's take a look at a Spring MVC application and its parts. You can use the previous Maven archetype:

```
$ mvn archetype:create -DgroupId=com.apress.spring -DartifactId=simple-web-spring-app
-DarchetypeArtifactId=maven-archetype-webapp
```

You are going to modify this because this particular Maven archetype is kind of old, but is useful just to create the files and directory structure. For example, you should change the web.xml version from 2.3 to 2.5, because you are going to use the Servlet 2.5 specification. This is one of the many hassles from J2EE. Now take a look at the final pom.xml in Listing 5-4.

Listing 5-4. pom.xml

```
<project xmlns="http://maven.apache.org/POM/4.0.0"
xmlns:xsi="http://www.w3.org/2001/XMLSchema-instance"
        xsi:schemaLocation="http://maven.apache.org/POM/4.0.0
        http://maven.apache.org/xsd/maven-4.0.0.xsd">
        <modelVersion>4.0.0</modelVersion>
        <groupId>org.springframework.samples.service.service</groupId>
        <artifactId>simple-web-spring-app</artifactId>
        <version>0.0.1-SNAPSHOT</version>
        <packaging>war</packaging>

        <properties>

                <!-- Generic properties -->
                <java.version>1.8</java.version>

                <!-- Web -->
                <jsp.version>2.2</jsp.version>
                <jstl.version>1.2</jstl.version>
                <servlet.version>2.5</servlet.version>

                <!-- Spring -->
                <spring-framework.version>3.2.3.RELEASE</spring-framework.version>

        </properties>

        <dependencies>

                <!-- Spring MVC -->
                <dependency>
                        <groupId>org.springframework</groupId>
                        <artifactId>spring-webmvc</artifactId>
                        <version>${spring-framework.version}</version>
                </dependency>
```

93

```
            <!-- Other Web dependencies -->
            <dependency>
                    <groupId>javax.servlet</groupId>
                    <artifactId>jstl</artifactId>
                    <version>${jstl.version}</version>
            </dependency>
            <dependency>
                    <groupId>javax.servlet</groupId>
                    <artifactId>servlet-api</artifactId>
                    <version>${servlet.version}</version>
                    <scope>provided</scope>
            </dependency>
            <dependency>
                    <groupId>javax.servlet.jsp</groupId>
                    <artifactId>jsp-api</artifactId>
                    <version>${jsp.version}</version>
                    <scope>provided</scope>
            </dependency>
        </dependencies>

        <build>
                <finalName>simple-web-spring-app</finalName>
        </build>

</project>
```

Listing 5-4 shows you the pom.xml that you will use for this application. Take a moment and analyze the differences from Listing 5-1. You will see that you are now using the Spring MVC version 3.2.3.RELEASE and some other dependencies like the tag libraries. Right now the Spring MVC is in its version 4.2 (it's simpler), but I wanted to show you how Spring developers used to do Spring web applications.

Next, let's look at web.xml. Modify it to look the same as the one in Listing 5-5.

Listing 5-5. src/main/webapp/WEB-INF/web.xml

```xml
<?xml version="1.0" encoding="ISO-8859-1"?>
<web-app xmlns:xsi="http://www.w3.org/2001/XMLSchema-instance"
        xmlns="http://java.sun.com/xml/ns/javaee"
        xsi:schemaLocation="http://java.sun.com/xml/ns/javaee
http://java.sun.com/xml/ns/javaee/web-app_2_5.xsd"
        id="WebApp_ID" version="2.5">

    <display-name>simple-web-spring-app</display-name>

    <servlet>
        <servlet-name>dispatcherServlet</servlet-name>
        <servlet-class>org.springframework.web.servlet.DispatcherServlet</servlet-class>
        <init-param>
            <param-name>contextConfigLocation</param-name>
            <param-value>/WEB-INF/mvc-config.xml</param-value>
        </init-param>
        <load-on-startup>1</load-on-startup>
    </servlet>
```

```
    <servlet-mapping>
        <servlet-name>dispatcherServlet</servlet-name>
        <url-pattern>/</url-pattern>
    </servlet-mapping>

</web-app>
```

Listing 5-5 shows you the web.xml. Remember that it must be exactly the same. Just take a look and compare it to Listing 5-3. First the version is now 2.5 (normally this was an indication of the servlet engine you will use), next there is the servlet declaration that adds the org.springframework.web.servlet.DispatcherServlet class that is the main dispatcher that will trigger the MVC pattern. As an additional declaration, the <init-param> tag will look for an XML configuration file, in this case WEB-INF/mvc-config.xml. This file is a Spring context configuration.

Next, take a look at the Spring configuration shown in Listing 5-6.

Listing 5-6. src/main/webapp/WEB-INF/mvc-config.xml

```
<?xml version="1.0" encoding="UTF-8"?>

<beans xmlns="http://www.springframework.org/schema/beans"
xmlns:xsi="http://www.w3.org/2001/XMLSchema-instance"
        xmlns:mvc="http://www.springframework.org/schema/mvc"
        xmlns:context="http://www.springframework.org/schema/context"
        xsi:schemaLocation="http://www.springframework.org/schema/mvc
        http://www.springframework.org/schema/mvc/spring-mvc.xsd
                http://www.springframework.org/schema/beans
                http://www.springframework.org/schema/beans/spring-beans.xsd
                http://www.springframework.org/schema/context
                http://www.springframework.org/schema/context/spring-context.xsd">

        <bean name="/showMessage.html"
                class="com.apress.spring.SimpleController" />

        <bean class="org.springframework.web.servlet.view.InternalResourceViewResolver">
                <property name="prefix" value="/WEB-INF/view/"/>
                <property name="suffix" value=".jsp"/>
        </bean>

</beans>
```

Listing 5-6 shows you the XML configuration. This is a typical Spring configuration where you define your bean (POJO-Plain Old Java Objects) classes that will be instantiate the Spring container. If you take a look at this XML, you will find that there is a bean and its name is /showMessage.html and it's pointing to the com.apress.spring.SimpleController Java class (you are going to see the code soon). This particular declaration is the URL that will map to the class to be executed when there is a request to the /showMessage.html URL. There is also another bean declaration that is mandatory, because this is where you define your views by declaring the InternalResourceViewResolver class. In this case, every view will be located at the /WEB-INF/view and every page will have the .jsp extension. This is very useful for security reasons, because you don't want to have access to the root folder and extract your pages.

Next look at the SimpleController class in Listing 5-7.

Listing 5-7. src/main/java/com/apress/spring/SimpleController.java

```java
package com.apress.spring;

import javax.servlet.http.HttpServletRequest;
import javax.servlet.http.HttpServletResponse;

import org.springframework.web.servlet.ModelAndView;
import org.springframework.web.servlet.mvc.AbstractController;

public class SimpleController extends AbstractController{

        @Override
        protected ModelAndView handleRequestInternal(HttpServletRequest request,
                HttpServletResponse response) throws Exception {

                ModelAndView model = new ModelAndView("showMessage");
                model.addObject("message", "Spring MVC Web Application");
                return model;
        }
}
```

Listing 5-7 shows you the `SimpleController` class. This class extends from the `AbstractController` class that has all the logic to manage your request (`/showMessage.html`). There is an override of the `handleRequestInternal` method that will respond by returning a `ModelAndView` instance that contains the information of what view to display. It carries some data in the `message` variable, in this case the text "Spring MVC Web Application".

Next, let's see the actual view that was declared in the controller with the code:

```java
ModelAndView model = new ModelAndView("showMessage");
```

This line tells the Spring MVC that the view will be the `showMessage`, which is actually located at `/WEB-INF/view/showMessage.jsp`. The page display will be handled by the `InternalResourceViewResolver` class, as shown in Listing 5-8

Listing 5-8. src/main/webapp/WEB-INF/view/showMessage.jsp

```jsp
<!DOCTYPE html>

<%@ page language="java" contentType="text/html; charset=UTF-8" pageEncoding="UTF-8"%>
<html>
        <head>
                <meta charset="utf-8">
                <title>Welcome</title>
        </head>
        <body>
                <h2>${message}</h2>
        </body>
</html>
```

Listing 5-8 shows you the showMessage.jsp file. What is interesting here is the <h2> tag that contains the ${message} declaration. This declaration will be executed and translated to the attribute that comes from the controller when you declare the following in Listing 5-7:

```
model.addObject("message", "Spring MVC Web Application");
```

So, Spring will render the "Spring MVC Web Application" message. Now, if you package your application with the following:

```
$ mvn clean package
```

You will have the target/simple-web-spring-app.war file. Now you can use the application server of your preference and deploy it. Once it's deployed you can access it in the web browser using the http://localhost:8080/simple-web-spring-app/showMessage.html URL and it will show the "Spring MVC Web Application" message. And that's it; it's a simple Spring MVC application!

If you already know Spring MVC, you may notice that I showed you a very old way to do it. Spring MVC versions 2.5, 3, and 4 allow you to add annotations to avoid extending from other classes and have more mapping in one single class. Take a look at Listing 5-9, which shows a better version of the controller using annotations.

Listing 5-9. src/main/java/com/apress/spring/SimpleController.java using annotations

```
package com.apress.spring;

import org.springframework.stereotype.Controller;
import org.springframework.web.bind.annotation.RequestMapping;
import org.springframework.web.bind.annotation.RequestMethod;
import org.springframework.web.servlet.ModelAndView;

@Controller
@RequestMapping("/showMessage.html")
public class HelloWorldController{

        @RequestMapping(method = RequestMethod.GET)
        public ModelAndView helloWorld(){

                ModelAndView model = new ModelAndView("showMessage");
                model.addObject("message", "Spring MVC Web App with annotations");

                return model;
        }
}
```

Listing 5-9 shows you a newer version of the Spring MVC where you can use annotations and remove extra configuration from the XML file. See Listing 5-10.

Listing 5-10. src/main/webapp/WEB-INF/mvc-config.xml

```xml
<?xml version="1.0" encoding="UTF-8"?>

<beans xmlns="http://www.springframework.org/schema/beans"
xmlns:xsi="http://www.w3.org/2001/XMLSchema-instance"
       xmlns:mvc="http://www.springframework.org/schema/mvc"
       xmlns:context="http://www.springframework.org/schema/context"
       xsi:schemaLocation="http://www.springframework.org/schema/mvc
http://www.springframework.org/schema/mvc/spring-mvc.xsd
            http://www.springframework.org/schema/beans
            http://www.springframework.org/schema/beans/spring-beans.xsd
            http://www.springframework.org/schema/context
            http://www.springframework.org/schema/context/spring-context.xsd">

    <context:component-scan base-package="com.apress.spring" />

    <bean class="org.springframework.web.servlet.view.InternalResourceViewResolver">
            <property name="prefix" value="/WEB-INF/view/"/>
            <property name="suffix" value=".jsp"/>
    </bean>

</beans>
```

Listing 5-10 shows you the `mvc-config.xml` file where now it's using the `<context:component-scan>` tag. Look at the `com.apress.spring` package level (sub-packages too) to find the marked classes. In this case it will find the `SimpleController` class because it's marked with the `@Controller` annotation. You can see that there is no more bean definitions about the request mapping; everything is now handled by the `SimpleController` class and its annotations, such as `@RequestMapping`.

As you can see, the Spring Framework and in this case the Spring MVC technology has evolved over the years, making it easier for developers to create Web applications.

Spring Boot Web Applications

Now it's Spring Boot's turn. You are going to use the same simple web application. You can use the minimal Spring Boot app in Groovy, as shown in Listing 5-11.

Listing 5-11. app.groovy

```groovy
@RestController
class WebApp{

    @RequestMapping("/showMessage.html")
    String greetings(){
        "Spring Boot MVC is easier"
    }
}
```

Listing 5-11 shows you the minimal Spring Boot web application. Just run it with the following command:

```
$ spring run app.groovy
```

Now you can open a browser and go to http://localhost:8080/showMessage.html. That was so easy! No Maven, no web.xml, no bean declarations, no configuration of any kind! That's the power of Spring Boot; it's an opinionated technology that allows you to create applications with ease.

But wait, let's do this simple web application using Maven. I mean, you are going to have at some point several classes and at least you need to have some structure, right?

In the previous chapter, you learned how to create a base template for Spring Boot using the Spring Boot CLI, remember? So open a terminal, create a folder (simple-web-spring-boot), and execute the following command:

```
$ mkdir simple-web-spring-boot
$ cd simple-web-spring-boot
$ spring init -d=web -g=com.apress.spring -a=simple-web-spring-boot --package-name=com.
apress.spring -name=simple-web-spring-boot -x
```

This command will create the base for your Spring Boot web application.

- The -d=web tells the CLI to include the web dependency (spring-boot-starter-web)

- The -g=com.apress.spring is the groupId

- The -a=simple-web-spring-boot-app is the artifactId

- The --package-name=com.apress.spring is the package name convention for the classes

- The -name=simple-web-spring-boot-app is the name of the application

- The -x will extract the template in the current directory; if you omit the extract option, you will find a simple-web-spring-boot-app.zip file

Your file structure should be similar to the one in Figure 5-2.

```
├── mvnw
├── mvnw.cmd
├── pom.xml
└── src
    ├── main
    │   ├── java
    │   │   └── com
    │   │       └── apress
    │   │           └── spring
    │   │               └── SimpleWebSpringBootApplication.java
    │   └── resources
    │       ├── application.properties
    │       ├── static
    │       └── templates
    └── test
        └── java
            └── com
                └── apress
                    └── spring
                        └── SimpleWebSpringBootApplicationTests.java

14 directories, 6 files
```

Figure 5-2. *Spring Boot structure after running the* spring init *command*

Now you can open `SimpleWebSpringBootApplication.java` and modify it to look the same as Listing 5-12.

Listing 5-12. src/main/java/com/apress/spring/SimpleWebSpringBootApplication.java

```java
package com.apress.spring;

import org.springframework.boot.SpringApplication;
import org.springframework.boot.autoconfigure.SpringBootApplication;
import org.springframework.web.bind.annotation.RestController;
import org.springframework.web.bind.annotation.RequestMapping;


@RestController
@SpringBootApplication
public class SimpleWebSpringBootApplication {

        @RequestMapping("/showMessage.html")
        public String index(){
                return "Spring Boot Rocks!";
        }

        public static void main(String[] args) {
                SpringApplication.run(SimpleWebSpringBootApplication.class, args);
        }
}
```

Listing 5-12 shows the modified `SimpleWebSpringBootApplication.java`, where it's marked as a web rest controller with the `@RestController` annotation and it defines an `index` method marked with `@RequestMapping`. This will accept all incoming requests to the `/showMessage.html` URL. You are familiar with `@SpringBootApplication`, which will trigger the auto-configuration. It's based on your classpath and the main method that will execute the application by calling the `SpringApplication.run` method. Remember, when you run the application it will lunch an embedded Tomcat and will start listening on port 8080.

To run it, just execute the following command:

```
$ ./mvnw spring-boot:run
```

This command will run the application, so open the browser and go to the `http://localhost:8080/showMessage.html`URL. You will see the message: "*Spring Boot Rocks!*". I showed you that when you use the CLI, it will access the `start.spring.io` URL and build and download your template. The cool thing is that it brings Maven or Gradle wrappers, so you don't need to install them. I know that in the previous examples I told you that you need to have Maven installed, right? So you are correct, you can run:

```
$ mvn spring-boot:run
```

Now you know more about old Java vs. Spring MVC vs. Spring Boot. Spring Boot still uses Spring MVC as the base for web applications, but in a very easy way. One of the major differences of Java/Spring MVC is that you get rid of the configuration files. No more XML files to deal with.

Of course, you will have some legacy Spring applications and you might want to incorporate some of these with your new Spring Boot applications. Let's see how you could use your existing Spring apps with Spring Boot.

Using Spring with Spring Boot

This section shows you how to use existing Spring apps in Spring Boot applications. Remember that Spring Boot is Spring, so this is an easy task, but let's start by considering the Spring container and the configurations and how you can use them in Spring Boot.

The Spring Framework in its first versions had a heavy dependency on XML configuration files. After Java 5 came into being, the Java configuration (annotations) was another mechanism used to configure the Spring container with the @Configuration (as marker for classes) and the @Bean annotations (for declaring the bean instances). Spring Boot follows the same pattern—you can use XML or annotation with Spring Boot.

XML with Spring Boot

If you have already several XML configuration files, you can integrate them with just one annotation in your main application. The org.springframework.context.annotation.ImportResource annotation accepts an array of string types to add the XML definitions.

If you are a Spring developer, you will recognize that this particular annotation was introduced in Spring version 3 and it hasn't changed. Your Spring Boot application will import your resources with ease. For example, you can declare the following in the main app or in a configuration class:

```
@ImportResource({"META-INF/spring/services-context.xml","META-INF/spring/repositories-
context.xml"})
@SpringBootApplication
public class SpringXmlApplication {

        @Autowired
        TaskRepository task;

        @Autowired
        ServiceFacade service;

        //More logic...
}
```

This code shows how you can use existing XML configuration files in your main Spring Boot application (or maybe you have already some Java config that you need to use):

```
@ImportResource("classpath:applicationContext.xml")
@Configuration
public class SimpleConfiguration {

        @Autowired
        Connection connection;  //This comes from the applicationContext.xml file.

        @Bean
        Database getDatabaseConnection(){
        return connection.getDBConnection();
            }

        // Mode code here....
}
```

This code shows how you can reuse your XML in an existing Java configuration class. You can also use a main class method to use your existing XML file:

```
public class Application {
    public static void main(String[] args) throws Exception {
        ConfigurableApplicationContext ctx = new SpringApplication("/META-INF/spring/
        integration.xml").run(args);
        System.out.println("Hit Enter to terminate");
        System.in.read();
        ctx.close();
    }
}
```

This example is related to the Spring Integration technology, where all the integration beans are working in the background.

Groovy Beans in Spring Boot

Another nice feature is that you can use the Groovy DSL (Domain Specific Language) for creating beans. This idea was taken from the Grails project, which is still very active and uses Spring as a base. In the upcoming version, it will include Spring Boot. With this Groovy beans DSL, you can create your Spring beans without the XML clutter. See Listing 5-13.

Listing 5-13. app.groovy

```
@RestController
class SimpleWebApp {

    @Autowired
    String text

    @RequestMapping("/")
    String index() {
        "You can do: ${text}!"
    }
}

beans {
    text String, "Spring Boot with Groovy beans"
}
```

Listing 5-13 shows you the beans DSL that you can use as well. In Chapter 18 of the book "Introducing Spring Framework" from Apress Publishing, I provided a small introduction to the Groovy DSL syntax. See that chapter if you want to get more familiar with it. You can run Listing 5-13 as usual:

```
$ spring run app.groovy
```

Point your browser at http://localhost:8080. You will get "You can do: Spring Boot with Groovy beans". So, you have ways to reuse Spring XML files or use the Groovy syntax to create some configurations.

Standalone Spring Apps vs. Spring Boot Apps

Not all applications are web apps; sometimes you need to run your Spring application in standalone mode without any server. You simply run it as a regular service or as a job and finish. To run a Spring application, you normally use the following code in your main method:

```
public static void main(final String[] args) {
    final ApplicationContext context = new ClassPathXmlApplicationContext("META-INF/spring/
    app-ctx.xml");
    final Service service = context.getBean(ServiceFacade.class);

        //Some process to run here
        //Extra work here
}
```

This code is using the ApplicationContext interface and the ClassPathXmlApplicationContext class to load the beans and initialize the container. After that you can use your beans by using the getBean method. Then you can do some process or call some functions and finish. In Spring Boot, it's a little different. In order to execute some code after the Spring Boot is initialized and running, you have some choices, as shown in Listing 5-14.

Listing 5-14. SpringBoot Example, Implementing the CommandLineRunner Interface

```
package com.apress.spring;
import org.springframework.boot.CommandLineRunner;
import org.springframework.boot.SpringApplication;
import org.springframework.boot.autoconfigure.SpringBootApplication;

@SpringBootApplication
public MyApplication implements CommandLineRunner {

    public void run(String... args) {
        // This will run after the SpringApplication.run(..)
        // Do something...
    }

    public static void main(String[] args) throws Exception {
            SpringApplication.run(MyApplication.class, args);
    }
}
```

Listing 5-14 shows you how you can run some processes or jobs after SpringApplication.run is called, by implementing the org.springframework.boot.CommandLineRunner interface and implementing the run(String... args) method. This is useful when you want to execute jobs or services, such as send a notification about the application or execute a SQL statement to update some rows before your application runs. This is not a web application; it is a standalone app.

Another alternative is to use the following code:

```
@Bean
public CommandLineRunner runner(){
    return new CommandLineRunner() {
        public void run(String... args){
            //Run some process here
        }
    };
}
```

This code shows you how to use the CommandLineRunner interface as a bean by marking the method with @Bean annotation. Or, if you are using Java 8, you can use the lambdas feature like this:

```
@Bean
public CommandLineRunner runner(Repository repo){
    return args -> {
        //Run some process here
    };
}
```

This code shows you how to use the CommandLineRunner interface using the Java 8 lambdas. In this case the method's parameter is a Repository, which is normally useful to do some database tasks.

Maybe you are wondering what you need to do if you need to run some code even before the CommandLineRunner. You can do this by returning an InitializingBean interface.

```
@Bean
InitializingBean saveData(Repository repo){
    return () -> {
        //Do some DB inserts
    };
}
```

This code shows you how to execute some code even before the CommandLineRunner. Perhaps you need to initialize a database before you run tasks on it. This can be helpful for testing purposes. Don't worry too much, I'll show you more detail and with some complete examples in the following chapters.

Using Spring Technologies in Spring Boot

I showed you in the previous sections of this chapter that Spring Boot is Spring, and you can use any Spring beans defined in a XML or a Java Configuration class. But what about some of the Spring technologies, such as Spring JMS, Spring AMQP, Spring Integration, Spring Caching, Spring Session, Spring Rest, etc.?

The following chapters show you how to use all these technologies in more detail, but I can tell you now that the auto-configuration is the base of this, which means all the new annotations that Spring Framework version 4 uses. The key here is to get used to some of the annotations that allow you to use these technologies very easily.

The only thing you need to know now is that there is an annotation called @Enable<Technology> for each of these technologies; see Table 5-1.

Table 5-1. *Spring Technologies Used in Spring Boot*

Annotation	Description
@EnableJms	Messaging with JMS technology
@EnableCaching	Caching abstraction
@EnableRabbit	Messaging for the AMQP with RabbitMQ
@EnableBatchProcessing	Spring batch
@EnableWebSecurity	Spring security
@EnableRedisHttpSession	Spring session
@EnableJpaRepositories	Spring data
@EnableIntegration	Spring integration

Table 5-1 shows you some of the @Enable<Technology> annotations that will be required when you want to create applications and use some of these Spring technologies. You'll learn more about these annotations during the course of this book.

Summary

This chapter explained the differences between old Java web apps, Spring MVC, and the new way, the Spring Boot way, to create web applications.

You learned how to use legacy or existing Spring apps along with Spring Boot, using either XML or Java configuration annotations. You also learned about multiple ways to run Spring Boot apps and execute code after the SpringApplication.run method executes and even before the CommandLineRunner interface with its run method executes.

You learned how to use all the Spring technologies by simply using the @Enable<Technology>. All these are covered in more detail in the following chapters.

In the next chapter, you are going to learn how to test your Spring Boot applications.

```
public class SprintBootApplicationTests {

    @Test
    public void contextLoads() {
    }

}
```

Listing 6-2 shows you the default test class. Let's examine it:

- @RunWith(SpringJUnit4ClassRunner.class). The @RunWith annotation
  belongs to the JUnit library and it will invoke the class it's referencing
  (SpringJUnit4ClassRunner.class) to run the tests instead of the runner built into
  JUnit. The SpringJUnit4ClassRunner class is a custom extension of the JUnit's
  BlockJUnit4ClassRunner. It provides all the functionality of the Spring Test Context
  Framework. The SpringJUnit4ClassRunner supports the following annotations:

  - @Test(expected=...)

  - @Test(timeout=...)

  - @Timed

  - @Repeat

  - @Ignore

  - @ProfileValueSourceConfiguration

  - @IfProfileValue

- You can also use the SpringClassRule and SpringMethodRule classes, both a custom
  JUnit TestRule interface that supports class-level features of the TestContext
  Framework. They are used together with the @ClassRule and @Rule annotations.

- @SpringApplicationConfiguration(classes = SprintBootApplication.class).
  This is a class-level annotation that knows how to load and configure an
  ApplicationContext, which means that you can have direct access to all the Spring
  container classes by just using the @Autowired annotation. In this case, the main
  SpringBootApplication class wires everything up.

- @Test. This is a JUnit test annotation that will execute the method when the tests
  start. You can have one or more methods. If you have several methods with this
  annotation, it won't execute them in order. For that you need to add the
  @FixMethodOrder(MethodSorters.NAME_ASCENDING) annotation to the class.

Web Testing

Let's create a web project. This section shows you how to test web applications using third-party libraries. You
can create a new directory (spring-boot-web) and execute the following commands in a terminal window:

```
$ mkdir spring-boot-web
$ cd spring-boot-web
$ spring init -d=web,thymeleaf --package=com.apress.spring -g=com.apress.spring
-a=spring-boot-web -name=sprint-boot-web -x
```

What is different about the previous project is that you are adding the -d=web,thymeleaf parameter, which will create a web project with the Thymeleaf technology as a view engine. The pom.xml file is shown in Listing 6-3.

Listing 6-3. pom.xml

```xml
<?xml version="1.0" encoding="UTF-8"?>
<project xmlns="http://maven.apache.org/POM/4.0.0"
xmlns:xsi="http://www.w3.org/2001/XMLSchema-instance"
        xsi:schemaLocation="http://maven.apache.org/POM/4.0.0
        http://maven.apache.org/xsd/maven-4.0.0.xsd">
        <modelVersion>4.0.0</modelVersion>

        <groupId>com.apress.spring</groupId>
        <artifactId>spring-boot-web</artifactId>
        <version>0.0.1-SNAPSHOT</version>
        <packaging>jar</packaging>

        <name>sprint-boot-web</name>
        <description>Demo project for Spring Boot</description>

        <parent>
                <groupId>org.springframework.boot</groupId>
                <artifactId>spring-boot-starter-parent</artifactId>
                <version>1.3.3.RELEASE</version>
                <relativePath/> <!-- lookup parent from repository -->
        </parent>

        <properties>
                <project.build.sourceEncoding>UTF-8</project.build.sourceEncoding>
                <java.version>1.8</java.version>
        </properties>

        <dependencies>

                <dependency>
                        <groupId>org.springframework.boot</groupId>
                        <artifactId>spring-boot-starter-web</artifactId>
                </dependency>
                <dependency>
                        <groupId>org.springframework.boot</groupId>
                        <artifactId>spring-boot-starter-thymeleaf</artifactId>
                </dependency>

                <dependency>
                        <groupId>org.springframework.boot</groupId>
                        <artifactId>spring-boot-starter-test</artifactId>
                        <scope>test</scope>
                </dependency>
        </dependencies>
```

```
<build>
        <plugins>
                <plugin>
                        <groupId>org.springframework.boot</groupId>
                        <artifactId>spring-boot-maven-plugin</artifactId>
                </plugin>
        </plugins>
</build>

</project>
```

Listing 6-3 shows you the pom.xml for a web project. As you can see, the dependencies are spring-boot-starter-web and spring-boot-starter-thymeleaf. Remember that by default the Spring Initializr will always bring the spring-boot-starter-test dependency. Next, take a look at the Java test-generated class shown in Listing 6-4.

Listing 6-4. src/test/java/com/apress/spring/SpringBootWebApplicationTests.java

```
package com.apress.spring;
import org.junit.Test;
import org.junit.runner.RunWith;
import org.springframework.test.context.web.WebAppConfiguration;
import org.springframework.boot.test.SpringApplicationConfiguration;
import org.springframework.test.context.junit4.SpringJUnit4ClassRunner;

@RunWith(SpringJUnit4ClassRunner.class)
@SpringApplicationConfiguration(classes = SprintBootWebApplication.class)
@WebAppConfiguration
public class SpringBootWebApplicationTests {

        @Test
        public void contextLoads() {
        }

}
```

Listing 6-4 shows you the test class. Because the project is a web app, the tests include a new annotation called @WebAppConfiguration. It's a class-level annotation that loads the org.springframework.web.context.WebApplicationContext implementation, which will ensure that all your files and beans related to the web app are accessible.

You are already familiar with the other annotations. Let's create an example application that you can use for the next chapters. In the next chapter, you will extend the Spring Boot journal (by using the Spring Data module) by creating a RESTful API. For now, you will use the domain class and create "hard-coded" data.

■ **Note**   I recommend this particular article if you want to know more about the REST maturity model by Dr. Leonard Richardson. You can find it at Martin Fowler's web site at http://martinfowler.com/articles/richardsonMaturityModel.html.

Let's start by identifying the journal domain class. See Listing 6-5.

Listing 6-5. src/main/java/com/apress/spring/domain/JournalEntry.java

```java
package com.apress.spring.domain;

import java.text.ParseException;
import java.text.SimpleDateFormat;
import java.util.Date;

public class JournalEntry {

    private String title;
    private Date created;
    private String summary;

    private final SimpleDateFormat format = new SimpleDateFormat("MM/dd/yyyy");

    public JournalEntry(String title, String summary, String date) throws
    ParseException{
        this.title = title;
        this.summary = summary;
        this.created = format.parse(date);
    }

    JournalEntry(){}

    public String getTitle() {
        return title;
    }

    public void setTitle(String title) {
        this.title = title;
    }

    public Date getCreated() {
        return created;
    }

    public void setCreated(String date) throws ParseException{
        Long _date = null;
        try{
            _date = Long.parseLong(date);
            this.created = new Date(_date);
            return;
        }catch(Exception ex){}
        this.created = format.parse(date);
    }

    public String getSummary() {
        return summary;
    }
```

```
        public void setSummary(String summary) {
                this.summary = summary;
        }

        public String toString(){
                StringBuilder value = new StringBuilder("* JournalEntry(");
                value.append("Title: ");
                value.append(title);
                value.append(",Summary: ");
                value.append(summary);
                value.append(",Created: ");
                value.append(format.format(created));
                value.append(")");
                return value.toString();
        }
}
```

Listing 6-5 shows you the domain class you will be using. I think the only thing to notice is that you will use a a small parsing process when you are setting the date (when you call setCreated) because you are passing the data as a string in a format of *MM/dd/yyyy*. If you pass a long type representing the timestamp, you can actually use the same setter. This is just for now; later in the book, you will see how this domain evolves.

Because you are going to test some RESTful endpoints, you need a controller. See Listing 6-6.

Listing 6-6. src/main/java/com/apress/spring/controller/JournalController.java

```java
package com.apress.spring.controller;

import java.text.ParseException;
import java.util.ArrayList;
import java.util.List;
import java.util.stream.Collectors;

import org.springframework.web.bind.annotation.PathVariable;
import org.springframework.web.bind.annotation.RequestBody;
import org.springframework.web.bind.annotation.RequestMapping;
import org.springframework.web.bind.annotation.RequestMethod;
import org.springframework.web.bind.annotation.RestController;

import com.apress.spring.domain.JournalEntry;

@RestController
public class JournalController {

  private static List<JournalEntry> entries = new ArrayList<JournalEntry>();
    static {
      try {
      entries.add(new JournalEntry("Get to know Spring Boot","Today I will learn Spring
      Boot","01/01/2016"));
      entries.add(new JournalEntry("Simple Spring Boot Project","I will do my first Spring
      Boot Project","01/02/2016"));
      entries.add(new JournalEntry("Spring Boot Reading","Read more about Spring
      Boot","02/01/2016"));
```

```
        entries.add(new JournalEntry("Spring Boot in the Cloud","Spring Boot using Cloud
        Foundry","03/01/2016"));
    } catch (ParseException e) {
                e.printStackTrace();
    }
}

@RequestMapping("/journal/all")
public List<JournalEntry> getAll() throws ParseException{
        return entries;
}

@RequestMapping("/journal/findBy/title/{title}")
public List<JournalEntry> findByTitleContains(@PathVariable String title) throws
ParseException{
        return entries
                .stream()
                    .filter(entry -> entry.getTitle().toLowerCase().contains(title.
                    toLowerCase()))
                    .collect(Collectors.toList());
}

@RequestMapping(value="/journal",method = RequestMethod.POST )
  public JournalEntry add(@RequestBody JournalEntry entry){
        entries.add(entry);
        return entry;
  }
}
```

Listing 6-6 shows you the controller class. As you can see, you are going to have some journal entries in memory, and you are defining some endpoints:

- /journal/all is where you will get all the journal entries in memory.

- /journal/findBy/title/{title} is where you can search for some part of the title to get some results that match.

- These two endpoints correspond to the HTTP GET methods.

- /journal – POST is where you will use the HTTP POST to add a new journal entry.

You already know about all the annotations used in this particular app, as they were discussed in the previous chapter. Next, you need to do your regular test and run the app to see if it works. You can run it with the following command:

```
$ ./mvnw spring-boot:run
```

Once it's running you can go to http://localhost:8080/journal/all. You should see the JSON results like the ones shown in Figure 6-1.

```
[
  ▼ {
        title: "Get to know Spring Boot",
        created: 1451628000000,
        summary: "Today I will learn Spring Boot"
  },
  ▼ {
        title: "Simple Spring Boot Project",
        created: 1451714400000,
        summary: "I will do my first Spring Boot Project"
  },
  ▼ {
        title: "Spring Boot Reading",
        created: 1454306400000,
        summary: "Read more about Spring Boot"
  },
  ▼ {
        title: "Spring Boot in the Cloud",
        created: 1456812000000,
        summary: "Spring Boot using Cloud Foundry"
  }
]
```

Figure 6-1. *http://localhost:8080/journal/all*

Figure 6-1 shows you the response you get by going to the /journal/all endpoint. Now, try the find endpoint. Look for the word "cloud". The URL to visit will be http://localhost:8080/journal/findBy/title/cloud. You should see the results shown in Figure 6-2.

```
[
  ▼ {
        title: "Spring Boot in the Cloud",
        created: 1456812000000,
        summary: "Spring Boot using Cloud Foundry"
  }
]
```

Figure 6-2. *http://localhost:8080/journal/findBy/title/cloud*

Figure 6-2 shows you the result of going to the /journal/findBy/title/{title} endpoint. Next let's try to post a new journal entry to the /journal endpoint. You can do that with the following command:

```
$ curl -X POST -d '{"title":"Test Spring Boot","created":"06/18/2016","summary":"Create Unit
Test for Spring Boot"}' -H "Content-Type: application/json" http://localhost:8080/journal
```

This command shows you how to use the cURL UNIX command where you are posting a new journal entry in a JSON format to the /journal endpoint. Now you can go to /journal/all to see the new entry. See Figure 6-3.

```
[
  ▼ {
        title: "Get to know Spring Boot",
        created: 1451628000000,
        summary: "Today I will learn Spring Boot"
    },
  ▼ {
        title: "Simple Spring Boot Project",
        created: 1451714400000,
        summary: "I will do my first Spring Boot Project"
    },
  ▼ {
        title: "Spring Boot Reading",
        created: 1454306400000,
        summary: "Read more about Spring Boot"
    },
  ▼ {
        title: "Spring Boot in the Cloud",
        created: 1456812000000,
        summary: "Spring Boot using Cloud Foundry"
    },
  ▼ {
        title: "Test Spring Boot",
        created: 1466226000000,
        summary: "Create Unit Test for Spring Boot"
    }
]
```

Figure 6-3. *The /journal/all endpoint after inserting a new journal entry*

Figure 6-3 shows you the new entry added by posting the JSON data to the /journal endpoint. Of course, this won't cover testing. This was just an attempt to partially test. Although it might not make too much sense right now, imagine if you needed to add 1,000 records and you have even more endpoints to cover or you have different domain apps that need to go through all kinds of test.

Testing manually like you just did won't work for the volume or for the application. That's where unit and integration testing come in.

Before I talk about the unit test, you are going to use a library that is useful to test JSON objects. It's called JsonPath by the company Jayway. So what you need to do is add the following dependency to your pom.xml:

```
<dependency>
        <groupId>com.jayway.jsonpath</groupId>
        <artifactId>json-path</artifactId>
        <scope>test</scope>
</dependency>
```

Because you are using the spring-boot-starter-test pom, you don't need to specify the version. Now, let's jump right into the new test you will be doing. See Listing 6-7.

Listing 6-7. src/test/java/com/apress/spring/SprintBootWebApplicationTests.java

```java
package com.apress.spring;

import static org.hamcrest.Matchers.containsString;
import static org.hamcrest.Matchers.iterableWithSize;
import static org.springframework.test.web.servlet.request.MockMvcRequestBuilders.get;
import static org.springframework.test.web.servlet.request.MockMvcRequestBuilders.post;
import static org.springframework.test.web.servlet.result.MockMvcResultMatchers.content;
import static org.springframework.test.web.servlet.result.MockMvcResultMatchers.jsonPath;
import static org.springframework.test.web.servlet.result.MockMvcResultMatchers.status;
import static org.springframework.test.web.servlet.setup.MockMvcBuilders.webAppContextSetup;

import java.io.IOException;
import java.nio.charset.Charset;
import java.util.Arrays;

import org.junit.Before;
import org.junit.FixMethodOrder;
import org.junit.Test;
import org.junit.runner.RunWith;
import org.junit.runners.MethodSorters;
import org.springframework.beans.factory.annotation.Autowired;
import org.springframework.boot.test.SpringApplicationConfiguration;
import org.springframework.http.MediaType;
import org.springframework.http.converter.HttpMessageConverter;
import org.springframework.http.converter.json.MappingJackson2HttpMessageConverter;
import org.springframework.mock.http.MockHttpOutputMessage;
import org.springframework.test.context.junit4.SpringJUnit4ClassRunner;
import org.springframework.test.context.web.WebAppConfiguration;
import org.springframework.test.web.servlet.MockMvc;
import org.springframework.web.context.WebApplicationContext;

import com.apress.spring.domain.JournalEntry;

@RunWith(SpringJUnit4ClassRunner.class)
@SpringApplicationConfiguration(classes = SprintBootWebApplication.class)
@WebAppConfiguration
@FixMethodOrder(MethodSorters.NAME_ASCENDING)
public class SprintBootWebApplicationTests {

        private final String SPRING_BOOT_MATCH = "Spring Boot";
        private final String CLOUD_MATCH = "Cloud";
        @SuppressWarnings("rawtypes")
        private HttpMessageConverter mappingJackson2HttpMessageConverter;
        private MediaType contentType = new MediaType(MediaType.APPLICATION_JSON.getType(),
            MediaType.APPLICATION_JSON.getSubtype(),
            Charset.forName("utf8"));
        private MockMvc mockMvc;
```

```java
    @Autowired
    private WebApplicationContext webApplicationContext;

    @Autowired
    void setConverters(HttpMessageConverter<?>[] converters) {
        this.mappingJackson2HttpMessageConverter = Arrays.asList(converters).stream().
        filter(
                converter -> converter instanceof MappingJackson2HttpMessageConverter).
                findAny().get();
    }

    @Before
    public void setup() throws Exception {
        this.mockMvc = webAppContextSetup(webApplicationContext).build();
    }

    @Test
    public void getAll() throws Exception {
            mockMvc.perform(get("/journal/all"))
            .andExpect(status().isOk())
            .andExpect(content().contentType(contentType))
            .andExpect(jsonPath("$",iterableWithSize(5)))
            .andExpect(jsonPath("$[0]['title']",containsString(SPRING_BOOT_MATCH)));
    }

    @Test
    public void findByTitle() throws Exception {
            mockMvc.perform(get("/journal/findBy/title/" + CLOUD_MATCH))
            .andExpect(status().isOk())
            .andExpect(content().contentType(contentType))
            .andExpect(jsonPath("$",iterableWithSize(1)))
            .andExpect(jsonPath("$[0]['title']",containsString(CLOUD_MATCH)));
    }

    @Test
    public void add() throws Exception {
            mockMvc.perform(post("/journal")
            .content(this.toJsonString(new JournalEntry("Spring Boot Testing","Create
            Spring Boot Tests","05/09/2016")))
            .contentType(contentType)).andExpect(status().isOk());
    }

    @SuppressWarnings("unchecked")
    protected String toJsonString(Object obj) throws IOException {
    MockHttpOutputMessage mockHttpOutputMessage = new MockHttpOutputMessage();
    this.mappingJackson2HttpMessageConverter.write(obj, MediaType.APPLICATION_JSON,
    mockHttpOutputMessage);
    return mockHttpOutputMessage.getBodyAsString();
    }
}
}
```

Listing 6-7 shows you the unit test you will execute. Let's examine it:

- `HttpMessageConverter<T>`, `MediaType`, `MockMvc`, `WebApplicationContext`. The `HttpMessageConverter<T>` is an interface that helps to convert from and to HTTP requests and responses. You are going to use it to create a JSON format to post when you test. The `MediaType` instance specifies that the actual call will be a JSON object. The `MockMvc` is a helper class provided by the Spring MVC test module; you can get more information at `http://docs.spring.io/spring-framework/docs/current/spring-framework-reference/html/integration-testing.html#spring-mvc-test-framework`. The `WebApplicationContext` will provide the configuration for a web application and it will be necessary to create the `MockMvc` instance.

- `setConverters(HttpMessageConverter)`. This will set up the `HttpMessageConverter<T>` instance that is being used to convert the request, which in this example is when you post to the `/journal` endpoint to add a new entry. `HttpMessageConverter<T>` works for every HTTP method.

- `toJsonString(Object)`. This is a helper method that will write the actual journal entry to a JSON object.

- `setup()`. This method is marked by the JUnit's `@Before` annotation, which means that it will call the setup method for every test. In this case, it's setting up the `MockMvc` instance to do some assertions on the code later.

- `getAll()`. This method will test the `/journal/all` endpoint. As you can see, it's using `mockMvc` to perform a HTTP GET method and it will assert that the status returned is the 200 CODE, that the response is a JSON object, and that the size returned of the collections is 5. You might wonder why this is 5 when there is only 4 in memory? I'll show why next.

- `findByTitle()`. This method will test the `/journal/findBy/title/{title}` endpoint. It will use the `mockMvc` instance to perform a get and it will assert that you have only one recurrence of a journal entry that includes the word "cloud".

- `add()`. This method will test the `/journal` endpoint by performing a POST using the `mockMvc` instance. It will assert that the content type is a JSON object (remember that you return the same object being posted) and that the status code is 200.

Why did you assert in the getAll method the size returned to 5? By default, the JUnit test methods are not running in sequence, which means that the getAll method can start first, then the add method, and so on. By default you don't control that order. If you need to run your test in order, you can use the `@FixMethodOrder(MethodSorters.NAME_ASCENDING)` annotation, which tells the JUnit to run the test based on the method's name in ascending order. This means that the add method will run first, then the getAll method, and finally the findByTitle method.

JsonPath together with the Hamcrest (`http://hamcrest.org/`) libraries give you the flexibility to test RESTful APIs. You can get more information at `https://github.com/jayway/JsonPath` and learn what else you can do with this library.

If you export this project into the STS IDE, you can run the unit test and visualize it like in Figure 6-4.

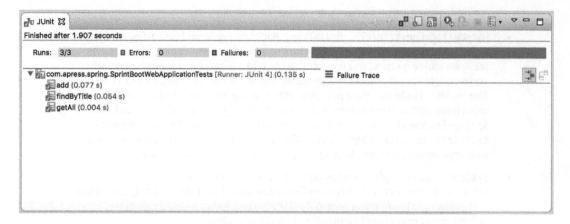

Figure 6-4. *Running the tests using the STS IDE*

You can create your unit tests using any framework you like. There is another project that makes testing your REST endpoint even easier. Go to https://github.com/jayway/rest-assured to find out more. The name of the library is Rest-Assured and it provides a fluent API to test RESTful APIs.

Summary

This chapter showed you how to test Spring and Spring Boot applications using the JUnit, using the provided MockMvc, and using other test libraries like Hamcrest and JsonPath.

In the following chapter, you learn about the persistence mechanism in Spring Boot and you will continue working with the journal app.

CHAPTER 7

■ ■ ■

Data Access with Spring Boot

Data has become the most important part of the IT world, from trying to access, persist, and analyze it, to using a few bytes to petabytes of information. There have been many attempts to create frameworks and libraries to facilitate a way for developers to interact with the data, but sometimes this becomes too complicated.

The Spring Framework after version 3.0 created different teams that specialized in the different technologies, and the Spring-Data project team was born. This particular project's goal is to make easier uses of data access technologies, from relational and non-relational databases, to map-reduce frameworks and cloud-based data services. This Spring-Data project is a collection of subprojects specific to a given database.

This chapter covers data access with Spring Boot using the simple application from Chapter 2—the Spring Boot journal app. You are going to make this simple app work with SQL and NoSQL databases. From the journal app, you are going to use only the model—nothing about the web, just pure data. Let's get started.

SQL Databases

Do you remember those days when (in the Java world) you needed to deal with all the JDBC (Java Database Connectivity) tasks? You had to download the correct drivers and connection strings, open and close connections, SQL statements, result sets, and transactions, and convert from result sets to objects. In my opinion, these are all very manual tasks. Then a lot of ORM (Object Relational Mapping) frameworks started to emerge to manage these tasks—frameworks like Castor XML, Object-Store, and Hibernate to mention a few. They allowed you to identify the domain classes and create XML that was related to the database's tables. At some point you also needed to be an expert to manage those kind of frameworks.

The Spring Framework helped a lot with those frameworks by following the template design pattern. It allowed you create an abstract class that defined ways to execute the methods and created the database abstractions that allowed you to focus only on your business logic. It left all the hard lifting to the Spring Framework, including handling connections (open, close, and pooling), transactions, and the way you interact with the frameworks.

It's worth mentioning that the Spring Framework relies on several interfaces and classes (like the `javax.sql.DataSource` interface) to get information about the database you are going to use, how to connect to it (by providing a connection string), and its credentials. Now, if you have some kind of transaction management to do, `DataSource` is essential. Normally `DataSource` requires the `Driver` class, the JDBC URL, the username, and password to connect to the database.

© Felipe Gutierrez 2016

F. Gutierrez, *Pro Spring Boot*, DOI 10.1007/978-1-4842-1431-2_7

Data Access Using the JDBC Template with Spring Boot

This section shows you the basics involved in data access by using only the JDBC abstraction from the Spring Framework using Spring Boot. You will be using the `spring-boot-starter-jdbc` pom. In the example, you are going to use the H2 in-memory database, which is a very effective engine for testing purposes.

Start by executing the Spring Boot CLI and using the `init` command:

```
$ spring init -d=jdbc,h2 -g=com.apress.spring -a=simple-jdbc-app --package-name=com.apress.
spring -name=simple-jdbc-app -x
```

As you can see, this command will create a simple application that depends on the `spring-boot-starter-jdbc` pom and the H2 (the H2 is an in-memory database engine) dependency. See Listing 7-1.

Listing 7-1. pom.xml

```xml
<?xml version="1.0" encoding="UTF-8"?>
<project xmlns="http://maven.apache.org/POM/4.0.0"
xmlns:xsi="http://www.w3.org/2001/XMLSchema-instance"
        xsi:schemaLocation="http://maven.apache.org/POM/4.0.0
        http://maven.apache.org/xsd/maven-4.0.0.xsd">
        <modelVersion>4.0.0</modelVersion>

        <groupId>com.apress.spring</groupId>
        <artifactId>simple-jdbc-app</artifactId>
        <version>0.0.1-SNAPSHOT</version>
        <packaging>jar</packaging>

        <name>simple-jdbc-app</name>
        <description>Demo project for Spring Boot</description>

        <parent>
                <groupId>org.springframework.boot</groupId>
                <artifactId>spring-boot-starter-parent</artifactId>
                <version>1.3.2.RELEASE</version>
                <relativePath/> <!-- lookup parent from repository -->
        </parent>

        <properties>
                <project.build.sourceEncoding>UTF-8</project.build.sourceEncoding>
                <java.version>1.8</java.version>
        </properties>

        <dependencies>
                <dependency>
                        <groupId>org.springframework.boot</groupId>
                        <artifactId>spring-boot-starter-jdbc</artifactId>
                </dependency>

                <dependency>
                                <groupId>com.h2database</groupId>
                                <artifactId>h2</artifactId>
                        <scope>runtime</scope>
                </dependency>
```

```
                <dependency>
                        <groupId>org.springframework.boot</groupId>
                        <artifactId>spring-boot-starter-test</artifactId>
                        <scope>test</scope>
                </dependency>
        </dependencies>

        <build>
                <plugins>
                        <plugin>
                                <groupId>org.springframework.boot</groupId>
                                <artifactId>spring-boot-maven-plugin</artifactId>
                        </plugin>
                </plugins>
        </build>

</project>
```

Listing 7-1 shows you the pom.xml file. You can see that the spring-boot-starter-jdbc pom and the H2 dependency are included. Next, let's reuse the Journal Java class from Chapter 2 as the main domain class. You need to create the directory structure. This class must be in the src/main/java/com/apress/spring/domain folder. See Listing 7-2.

Listing 7-2. src/main/java/com/apress/spring/domain/Journal.java

```java
package com.apress.spring.domain;

import java.text.SimpleDateFormat;
import java.util.Date;

public class Journal {

        private Long id;
        private String title;
        private Date created;
        private String summary;

        private SimpleDateFormat format = new SimpleDateFormat("MM/dd/yyyy");

        public Journal(Long id, String title, String summary, Date date){
                this.id = id;
                this.title = title;
                this.summary = summary;
                this.created = date;
        }

        Journal(){}

        public Long getId() {
                return id;
        }
```

```java
        public void setId(Long id) {
                this.id = id;
        }

        public String getTitle() {
                return title;
        }

        public void setTitle(String title) {
                this.title = title;
        }

        public Date getCreated() {
                return created;
        }

        public void setCreated(Date created) {
                this.created = created;
        }

        public String getSummary() {
                return summary;
        }

        public void setSummary(String summary) {
                this.summary = summary;
        }

        public String getCreatedAsShort(){
                return format.format(created);
        }

        public String toString(){
                StringBuilder value = new StringBuilder("* JournalEntry(");
                value.append("Id: ");
                value.append(id);
                value.append(",Title: ");
                value.append(title);
                value.append(",Summary: ");
                value.append(summary);
                value.append(",Created: ");
                value.append(getCreatedAsShort());
                value.append(")");
                return value.toString();
        }
}
```

Listing 7-2 shows you the Journal.java class. If you copied this class from Chapter 2, you need to remove all the annotations, because you don't need them now. This class is a simple POJO (plain old Java object). Next you will create a service in the src/main/java/com/apress/spring/service directory, which is the JournalService.java class. The actions of this service are to insert data into the database and get all the information from the database. See Listing 7-3 and analyze its contents.

Listing 7-3. src/main/java/com/apress/spring/service/JournalService.java

```java
package com.apress.spring.service;

import java.util.ArrayList;
import java.util.Date;
import java.util.List;

import org.slf4j.Logger;
import org.slf4j.LoggerFactory;
import org.springframework.beans.factory.annotation.Autowired;
import org.springframework.jdbc.core.JdbcTemplate;
import org.springframework.stereotype.Service;

import com.apress.spring.domain.Journal;

@Service
public class JournalService {
        private static final Logger log = LoggerFactory.getLogger(JournalService.class);

        @Autowired
        JdbcTemplate jdbcTemplate;

        public void insertData(){
                log.info("> Table creation");
                jdbcTemplate.execute("DROP TABLE JOURNAL IF EXISTS");
                jdbcTemplate.execute("CREATE TABLE JOURNAL(id SERIAL, title VARCHAR(255),
                summary VARCHAR(255), created TIMESTAMP)");
                log.info("> Inserting data...");
                jdbcTemplate.execute("INSERT INTO JOURNAL(title,summary,created)
                VALUES('Get to know Spring Boot','Today I will learn Spring Boot',
                '2016-01-01 00:00:00.00')");
                jdbcTemplate.execute("INSERT INTO JOURNAL(title,summary,created)
                VALUES('Simple Spring Boot Project','I will do my first Spring Boot
                project','2016-01-02 00:00:00.00')");
                jdbcTemplate.execute("INSERT INTO JOURNAL(title,summary,created)
                VALUES('Spring Boot Reading','Read more about Spring Boot',
                '2016-02-01 00:00:00.00')");
                jdbcTemplate.execute("INSERT INTO JOURNAL(title,summary,created)
                VALUES('Spring Boot in the Cloud','Learn Spring Boot using Cloud
                Foundry','2016-01-01 00:00:00.00')");
                log.info("> Done.");
        }

        public List<Journal> findAll(){
                List<Journal> entries = new ArrayList<>();
                jdbcTemplate.query("SELECT * FROM JOURNAL",
                                        new Object[]{},
                                        (rs,row) -> new Journal(rs.getLong("id"),
                                        rs.getString("title"), rs.getString("summary"),
                                        new Date(rs.getTimestamp("created").getTime())))
```

```
                        .forEach(entry -> entries.add(entry));
            return entries;
        }
}
```

Listing 7-3 shows you the JournalService.java class. Let's take a look at its contents:

- JdbcTemplate. It auto-wires a JdbcTemplate class that will be the responsible for executing tasks against the database. This particular class is based on the template design pattern that I mentioned that allows developers to focus only on the data and leave all the database tasks (insert, delete, etc.) to the template. How it knows which database to connect to is discussed shortly.

- insertData. This method will first try to drop a Journal table if it exists, then it will create the Journal table with its fields and, finally, it will insert the data into the database. All these actions will be through the jdbcTemplate instance by executing its method execute (this execute method accepts the SQL query syntax).

- findAll. This method will use the jdbcTemplate instance and the query method (that accepts a SQL syntax) to get all the data; it will return a collection of Journal instances.

- Logger. A log instance that prints out what is going on in the method calls.

Next, modify the SimpleJdbcAppApplication.java class to look like Listing 7-4.

Listing 7-4. src/main/java/com/apress/spring/SimpleJdbcAppAplication.java

```java
package com.apress.spring;

import org.slf4j.Logger;
import org.slf4j.LoggerFactory;
import org.springframework.beans.factory.annotation.Autowired;
import org.springframework.boot.CommandLineRunner;
import org.springframework.boot.SpringApplication;
import org.springframework.boot.autoconfigure.SpringBootApplication;

import com.apress.spring.service.JournalService;

@SpringBootApplication
public class SimpleJdbcAppApplication implements CommandLineRunner{
        private static final Logger log = LoggerFactory.getLogger(SimpleJdbcAppApplication.
        class);

        @Autowired
        JournalService service;

        public static void main(String[] args) {
                SpringApplication.run(SimpleJdbcAppApplication.class, args);
        }
```

```
@Override
public void run(String... arg0) throws Exception {
        log.info("@@ Inserting Data....");
        service.insertData();
        log.info("@@ findAll() call...");
        service.findAll().forEach(entry -> log.info(entry.toString()));
    }
}
```

Listing 7-4 shows you the SimpleJdbcAppApplication.java class. As you already know, this is the main class that will be executed:

- It declares the auto-wired version of the JournalService, making it available when the run method executes.

- It implements the CommandLineRunner interface, and of course you need to implement its method as well, called public void run(String... args). Just remember that this run method will be executed after the Spring Boot has started. This is a good place to call the JournalService instance and execute the data insertion and to call the findAll method.

- The Logger log instance prints out what is going on in the execution of the class.

To run the application, execute the following command:

```
$ ./mvnw spring-boot:run
```

This command will run the app using the Maven wrapper that comes with the Spring Initializr. If you have Maven as a global tool, just run this command:

```
$ mvn spring-boot:run
```

■ **Note**   If you are using the Maven wrapper (mvnw) command and you are getting the following error—
Error: Could not find or load main class org.apache.maven.wrapper.MavenWrapperMain—this
means that you don't have the .mvn folder and its JAR files in the current directory. So, you need to install them
manually. I know this sound redundant, but for this, you need to use Maven (a global installation and available in
your PATH environment variable) and execute $ mvn -N io.takari:maven:wrapper. Remember that the idea
of the Maven wrapper is portability, so if you want to send your code to somebody, just make sure to include the
.mvn folder and its content. That way, that person doesn't need to have/install Maven.

After executing either of these commands, you should see the following output:

```
INFO - [main] c.a.spring.SimpleJdbcAppApplication        : @@ Inserting Data....
INFO - [main] c.apress.spring.service.JournalService     : > Table creation
INFO - [main] c.apress.spring.service.JournalService     : > Inserting data...
INFO - [main] c.apress.spring.service.JournalService     : > Done.
INFO - [main] c.a.spring.SimpleJdbcAppApplication        : @@ findAll() call...
INFO - [main] c.a.spring.SimpleJdbcAppApplication        : * JournalEntry(Id: 1,Title: Get to
know Spring Boot,Summary: Today I will learn Spring Boot,Created: 01/01/2016)
```

```
INFO - [main] c.a.spring.SimpleJdbcAppApplication    : * JournalEntry(Id: 2,Title: Simple
Spring Boot Project,Summary: I will do my first Spring Boot project,Created: 01/02/2016)
INFO - [main] c.a.spring.SimpleJdbcAppApplication    : * JournalEntry(Id: 3,Title: Spring
Boot Reading,Summary: Read more about Spring Boot,Created: 02/01/2016)
INFO - [main] c.a.spring.SimpleJdbcAppApplication    : * JournalEntry(Id: 4,Title: Spring
Boot in the Cloud,Summary: Learn Spring Boot using Cloud Foundry,Created: 01/01/2016)
INFO - [main] c.a.spring.SimpleJdbcAppApplication    : Started SimpleJdbcAppApplication in
1.736 seconds (JVM running for 6.581)
```

As you can see from this output, the app is creating the table, inserting the data, and then finding all the data persisted into the database. But how? You didn't install any database engine or something to persist the data and you didn't create any DataSource or add any URL string connections. Remember that this simple app is using the H2 in-memory database. The magic happens within Spring Boot for all related actions against the database, like connection, query execution, and transactions (if you use the @Transactional annotation as a marker in the class). But again, how does Spring Boot know about it?

Remember that everything starts with the auto-configuration (provided by the @SpringBootApplication annotation). It will detect that you have a H2 in-memory database dependency and it will create the right javax.sql.DataSource implementation. This means that by default it will have the org.h2.Driver driver class, which is the connection URL as jdbc:h2:mem:testdb and the username: sa and password: empty to connect to the H2 engine.

The H2 engine offers a console where you can see all the tables and its data; however, this console is a web application. So, what do you think you will need to get access to the H2 console? You are correct! You need to include the spring-boot-starter-web pom dependency to your pom.xml.

```
<dependency>
      <groupId>org.springframework.boot</groupId>
      <artifactId>spring-boot-starter-web</artifactId>
</dependency>
```

You also need to add the following property to the src/main/resources/application.properties file. See Listing 7-5.

Listing 7-5. src/main/resources/application.properties.

```
spring.h2.console.enabled=true
```

Listing 7-5 shows you the contents of the application properties. This property will enable the H2 web console. Now, you can run your application again and the first thing you will notice is that it no longer stops; it keeps running. You can see the logs that the Tomcat embedded server started. Now go to your browser and go to http://localhost:8080/h2-console. You should see something similar to Figure 7-1.

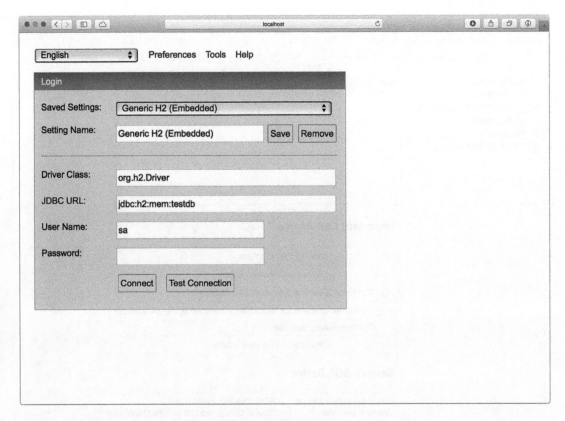

Figure 7-1. *H2 web console (http://localhost:8080/h2-console)*

Figure 7-1 shows you the H2 web console. You should see the Driver class, the JDBC URL, and the credentials. If by some reason the JDBC URL is not the same, modify its value to jdbc:h2:mem:testdb. If you then click the Connect button, you should see something similar to Figure 7-2.

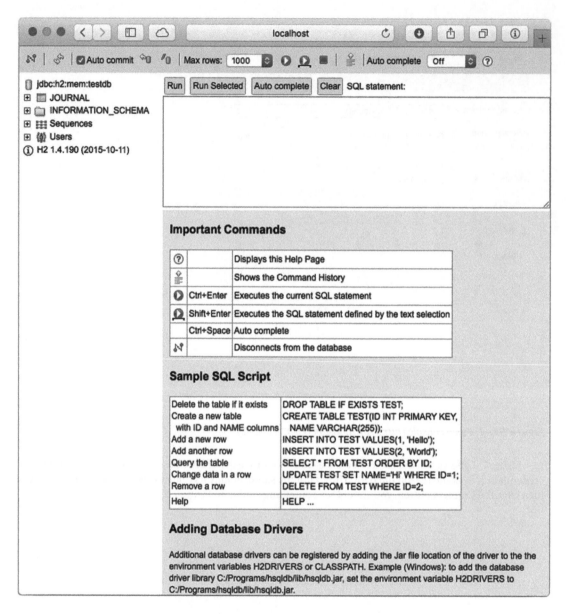

Figure 7-2. *H2 web console in-memory testdb connection*

Figure 7-2 shows you the in-memory database, including the testdb and the Journal table. You can expand it and see its definition. You can also execute some SQL queries. For example, you can run the SELECT * FROM JOURNAL to see all the data that the application inserted. See Figure 7-3.

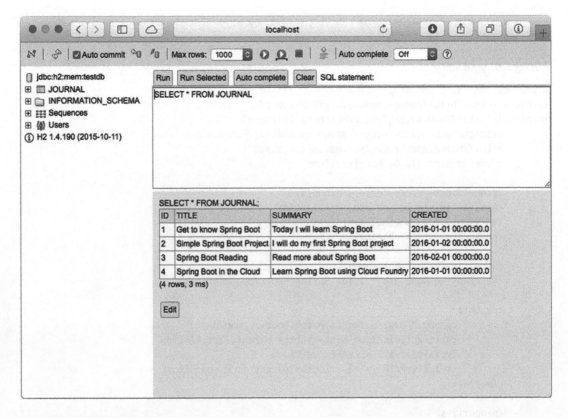

Figure 7-3. *SQL statements*

Figure 7-3 shows you the query result—all the data from the application. The H2 in-memory database is a very good option for creating applications that need a persistence mechanism, which is normally used for developing and testing purposes.

Don't forget to terminate your application by pressing Ctrl+C.

You can expose and persist data by using the JdbcTemplate, but there are easier ways. Let's take a look at another option, something that is familiar to you from Chapter 2, which is to use the JPA technology.

Data Access Using JPA with Spring Boot

The JPA (Java Persistence API, a J2EE specification. There is a nice article about JPA at http://www.oracle.com/technetwork/articles/java/jpa-137156.html) is another alternative to using lightweight persistence objects. Hibernate and Eclipse TopLink are the primary implementations of the JPA. The Spring Framework has been part since its inception and played a very important role by providing helpers and abstraction classes to make life easier for developers.

You are going to continue to use the same journal app and make it work using the JPA technology. So, to start, you can open a terminal and execute the Spring Initializr.

```
$ spring init -d=data-jpa,h2 -g=com.apress.spring -a=simple-jpa-app --package-name=com.
apress.spring -name=simple-jpa-app -x
```

Now, let's take a look at the pom.xml file. As you likely know, you'll need the spring-boot-starter-data-jpa starter pom. See Listing 7-6.

Listing 7-6. pom.xml

```xml
<?xml version="1.0" encoding="UTF-8"?>
<project xmlns="http://maven.apache.org/POM/4.0.0"
xmlns:xsi="http://www.w3.org/2001/XMLSchema-instance"
        xsi:schemaLocation="http://maven.apache.org/POM/4.0.0
        http://maven.apache.org/xsd/maven-4.0.0.xsd">
        <modelVersion>4.0.0</modelVersion>

        <groupId>com.apress.spring</groupId>
        <artifactId>simple-jpa-app</artifactId>
        <version>0.0.1-SNAPSHOT</version>
        <packaging>jar</packaging>

        <name>simple-jpa-app</name>
        <description>Demo project for Spring Boot</description>

        <parent>
                <groupId>org.springframework.boot</groupId>
                <artifactId>spring-boot-starter-parent</artifactId>
                <version>1.3.2.RELEASE</version>
                <relativePath /> <!-- lookup parent from repository -->
        </parent>

        <properties>
                <project.build.sourceEncoding>UTF-8</project.build.sourceEncoding>
                <java.version>1.8</java.version>
        </properties>

        <dependencies>
                <dependency>
                        <groupId>org.springframework.boot</groupId>
                        <artifactId>spring-boot-starter-data-jpa</artifactId>
                </dependency>

                <dependency>
                        <groupId>com.h2database</groupId>
                        <artifactId>h2</artifactId>
                        <scope>runtime</scope>
                </dependency>

                <dependency>
                        <groupId>org.springframework.boot</groupId>
                        <artifactId>spring-boot-starter-test</artifactId>
                        <scope>test</scope>
                </dependency>
        </dependencies>
```

```
<build>
        <plugins>
                <plugin>
                        <groupId>org.springframework.boot</groupId>
                        <artifactId>spring-boot-maven-plugin</artifactId>
                </plugin>
        </plugins>
</build>

</project>
```

Listing 7-6 shows you the pom.xml, and as you guessed, it required the spring-boot-starter-data-jpa and the h2 dependencies. Next, you are going to keep using the domain class, so let's take a look at the src/main/java/com/apress/spring/domain/Journal.java class. See Listing 7-7.

Listing 7-7. src/main/java/com/apress/spring/domain/Journal.java

```
package com.apress.spring.domain;

import java.text.ParseException;
import java.text.SimpleDateFormat;
import java.util.Date;

import javax.persistence.Entity;
import javax.persistence.GeneratedValue;
import javax.persistence.GenerationType;
import javax.persistence.Id;
import javax.persistence.Transient;

@Entity
public class Journal {

        @Id
        @GeneratedValue(strategy=GenerationType.AUTO)
        private Long id;
        private String title;
        private Date created;
        private String summary;

        @Transient
        private SimpleDateFormat format = new SimpleDateFormat("MM/dd/yyyy");

        public Journal(String title, String summary, String date) throws ParseException{
                this.title = title;
                this.summary = summary;
                this.created = format.parse(date);
        }
```

```java
        Journal(){}

        public Long getId() {
                return id;
        }

        public void setId(Long id) {
                this.id = id;
        }

        public String getTitle() {
                return title;
        }

        public void setTitle(String title) {
                this.title = title;
        }

        public Date getCreated() {
                return created;
        }

        public void setCreated(Date created) {
                this.created = created;
        }

        public String getSummary() {
                return summary;
        }

        public void setSummary(String summary) {
                this.summary = summary;
        }

        public String getCreatedAsShort(){
                return format.format(created);
        }

        public String toString(){
                StringBuilder value = new StringBuilder("* JournalEntry(");
                value.append("Id: ");
                value.append(id);
                value.append(",Title: ");
                value.append(title);
                value.append(",Summary: ");
                value.append(summary);
                value.append(",Created: ");
                value.append(getCreatedAsShort());
                value.append(")");
                return value.toString();
        }
}
```

Listing 7-7 shows the Journal.java class where it's using the javax.persistence package classes and interfaces, including the @Entity, @Id, and @Transient annotations. All these annotations belong to the JPA specification and are going to be used to denote an entity (the class marked with @Entity annotation) that will be mapped to a table (in this case to a Journal table) and to its fields (all private fields with setters and getters, except for the one annotated with the @Transient annotation, which won't be persistent to the database). The Long id property is marked with the @Id and @GeneratedValue annotations, making this field the primary key of the Journal table.

Next let's see the service; you are still going to use a service that will insert data and find all the data in the database. See Listing 7-8.

Listing 7-8. src/main/java/com/apress/spring/service/JournalService.java

```
package com.apress.spring.service;

import java.text.ParseException;
import java.util.List;

import org.slf4j.Logger;
import org.slf4j.LoggerFactory;
import org.springframework.beans.factory.annotation.Autowired;
import org.springframework.stereotype.Service;

import com.apress.spring.domain.Journal;
import com.apress.spring.repository.JournalRepository;

@Service
public class JournalService {
    private static final Logger log = LoggerFactory.getLogger(JournalService.class);

    @Autowired
    JournalRepository repo;

    public void insertData() throws ParseException{
        log.info("> Inserting data...");
        repo.save(new Journal("Get to know Spring Boot","Today I will learn Spring
        Boot","01/01/2016"));
        repo.save(new Journal("Simple Spring Boot Project","I will do my first Spring Boot
        Project","01/02/2016"));
        repo.save(new Journal("Spring Boot Reading","Read more about Spring
        Boot","02/01/2016"));
        repo.save(new Journal("Spring Boot in the Cloud","Spring Boot using Cloud
        Foundry","03/01/2016"));
        log.info("> Done.");
    }

    public List<Journal> findAll(){
        return repo.findAll();
    }

}
```

Listing 7-8 shows you the service you will be using, so let's examine its code:

- @Service. This annotation marks the class as a stereotype that will be recognized as a bean by the Spring container, so it can be used, for example, with the @Autowired annotation.

- JournalRepository. This instance is being auto-wired, but where is this JournalRepository interface? Don't worry, you are going to see it in the next segment. For now, you need to think of it as an instance that has the knowledge of how to use the data, from connecting to the database, to accessing it for its usage.

- insertData. This method will insert the data into the database. Note that there is no database or table creation; everything will be done by the abstraction of the JournalRepository.

- findAll. This method will call the JournalRepository instance to get all the data from the database, returning a list of Journal instances.

Next, let's see the JournalRepository interface. See Listing 7-9.

Listing 7-9. src/main/java/com/apress/spring/repository/JournalRepository.java

```
package com.apress.spring.repository;

import org.springframework.data.jpa.repository.JpaRepository;

import com.apress.spring.domain.Journal;

public interface JournalRepository extends JpaRepository<Journal, Long> { }
```

Listing 7-9 shows you the JournalRepository interface, but let's dig into it. The JournalRepository interface extends from another interface, the JpaRepository. The JpaRepository uses generics and requires a marked class by the @Entity annotation and the Id as a java.io.Serializable object. In this case the entity is the Journal.java class and the ID is a Long class.

The JpaRepository interface looks like Listing 7-10.

Listing 7-10. <spring-data-jpa>/org/springframework/data/jpa/repository/JpaRepository.java

```
public interface JpaRepository<T, ID extends Serializable> extends
PagingAndSortingRepository<T, ID> {

    List<T> findAll();

    List<T> findAll(Sort sort);

    List<T> findAll(Iterable<ID> ids);

    <S extends T> List<S> save(Iterable<S> entities);

    void flush();

    <S extends T> S saveAndFlush(S entity);
```

```
        void deleteInBatch(Iterable<T> entities);

        void deleteAllInBatch();

        T getOne(ID id);
}
```

Listing 7-10 shows you the JpaRepository that belongs to the spring-data-jpa JAR, and it provides
all those action methods that will run against the provided database. It's important to note that you don't
need to implement any of these methods, you only need to extend from this interface. But if you take a closer
look, you have additional behavior because it also extends from the PagingAndSortingRepository interface,
giving you out-of-the-box extra features when you need them.

The Spring Framework and in this case the spring-data technology will be in charge of creating
dynamic proxies that will implement these methods for you. This is because all these actions are very
generic and repetitive, so you don't have to implement them—you can let the spring-data do it on your
behalf.

Now, let's take a look at the main application. See Listing 7-11.

Listing 7-11. src/main/java/com/apress/spring/SimpleJpaAppApplication.java

```
package com.apress.spring;

import org.slf4j.Logger;
import org.slf4j.LoggerFactory;
import org.springframework.beans.factory.annotation.Autowired;
import org.springframework.boot.CommandLineRunner;
import org.springframework.boot.SpringApplication;
import org.springframework.boot.autoconfigure.SpringBootApplication;
import org.springframework.context.annotation.Bean;

import com.apress.spring.repository.JournalRepository;
import com.apress.spring.service.JournalService;

@SpringBootApplication
public class SimpleJpaAppApplication {
        private static final Logger log = LoggerFactory.getLogger(SimpleJpaAppApplication.
        class);

        public static void main(String[] args) {
                SpringApplication.run(SimpleJpaAppApplication.class, args);
        }

        @Bean
        CommandLineRunner start(JournalService service){
                return args -> {
                        log.info("@@ Inserting Data....");
                        service.insertData();
                        log.info("@@ findAll() call...");
                        service.findAll().forEach(entry -> log.info(entry.toString()));
                };
        }
}
```

Listing 7-11 shows you the main application, the `SimpleJpaAppApplication.java` class. Let's examine its code:

- `@SpringBootApplication`. This is the main annotation that will trigger the auto-configuration and will identify that you are using the `spring-boot-starter-data-jpa`. It will treat your application as a JPA app. It will also identify that you have declared the H2 in-memory database and will create the `javax.sql.DataSource` for you. It will be implemented with the H2 drivers and use the `testdb` database with the default credentials.

- `start`. This method is marked as a `Bean` and will return a `CommandLineRunner` interface. This is another way to tell the Spring Boot app to run this method after the Spring application is started. In this example it's using the Java 8 features to return a lambda where it's using the `JournalService` instance (the `start` method's parameter) to insert the data and then call the `findAll` method to get all the data from the database.

It's cool to see that you don't need to write any code for common database tasks—insert, update, and delete are covered—but what happens if you need to perform a very particular find? What if you need to find the journals that are after certain date, or you want to create a custom query with joins or stored procedures?

By extending to the `JpaRepository`, you can create "query" methods using the following a property naming convention. This provides extensibility in the behavior of the class. So for example, taking the `Journal.java` class, it contains the `title` property, so if you want to find all the titles that contain the word `Spring`, you can write a method like this:

```
public List<Journal> findByTitleContaining(String word);
```

This method will be translated to the SQL query: `select * from JOURNAL where title like %?1%`. Where the `?1` parameter will be the word `Spring`. So it would be something like this:

```
select * from journal where title like %Spring%
```

What if you need to look for all the journal entries after certain date? It is easy as create a method like so:

```
public List<Journal> findByCreatedAfter(Date date);
```

This method will be translated to the SQL query: `select * from JOURNAL where created > ?1`. Very easy. But what if you needed to run a particular query? For example, you can modify the `findByTitleContaining` method and write something equivalent like this:

```
@Query("select j from Journal j where j.title like %?1%")
List<Journal> findByCustomQuery(String word);
```

As you can see, you have many options. See Listing 7-12, which is a modified version of `JournalRepository.java`.

Listing 7-12. Modified Version of src/main/java/com/apress/spring/repository/JournalRepository.java

```java
package com.apress.spring.repository;

import java.util.Date;
import java.util.List;

import org.springframework.data.jpa.repository.JpaRepository;
import org.springframework.data.jpa.repository.Query;

import com.apress.spring.domain.Journal;

public interface JournalRepository extends JpaRepository<Journal, Long> {

        List<Journal> findByCreatedAfter(Date date);

        @Query("select j from Journal j where j.title like %?1%")
        List<Journal> findByCustomQuery(String word);
}
```

Listing 7-12 shows you another version of the JpaRepository, which contains the "query" method declarations based on its properties (the journal class properties) and marks a method (with any name) with the @Query annotation. The @Query annotation accepts the JPQL syntax.

If you want to know more about the options for naming the "query" methods and the keywords that you can use, I recommend you look at the spring-data reference at http://docs.spring.io/spring-data/jpa/docs/current/reference/html/#jpa.query-methods.query-creation.

Another Spring Boot feature using the spring-data enables you to use the schema.sql and data.sql files (in the root of the classpath) to create the database and insert data. This feature is useful when you have a dump of data and must initialize the database. So instead of using a service to insert the data, you can write data.sql and remove the insertData call from your service. See Listing 7-13.

Listing 7-13. src/main/resources/data.sql

```sql
INSERT INTO JOURNAL(title,summary,created) VALUES('Get to know Spring Boot','Today I will learn Spring Boot','2016-01-02 00:00:00.00');
INSERT INTO JOURNAL(title,summary,created) VALUES('Simple Spring Boot Project','I will do my first Spring Boot project','2016-01-03 00:00:00.00');
INSERT INTO JOURNAL(title,summary,created) VALUES('Spring Boot Reading','Read more about Spring Boot','2016-02-02 00:00:00.00');
INSERT INTO JOURNAL(title,summary,created) VALUES('Spring Boot in the Cloud','Learn Spring Boot using Cloud Foundry','2016-02-05 00:00:00.00');
```

Listing 7-13 shows the SQL statements that will be detected by Spring Boot. Now you can remove insertData from your JournalService.java class and see the same effect.

■ **Note** If you want to see the SQL statements that the JPA/Hibernate engine is executing, you can use the following property in the src/main/resources/application.properties file: spring.jpa.show-sql=true.

You can test this code as usual:

```
$ ./mvnw spring-boot:run
```

If you want to learn more about JPA, I recommend the Apress book entitled *Pro JPA 2, Second Edition* as well as the *Pro Spring Fourth Edition* and *Spring Recipes Third Edition.*

NoSQL Databases

NoSQL databases are another way to persist data, but in different way from the tabular relationships of the relational databases. There is already a classification system for these emergent NoSQL databases. You can find it based on its data model:

- Column (Cassandra, HBase, etc.)

- Document (CouchDB, MongoDB, etc.)

- Key-Value (Redis, Riak, etc.)

- Graph (Neo4J, Virtuoso, etc.)

- Multi-Model (OrientDB, ArangoDB, etc.)

As you can see, you have many options. I think the most important kind of feature here nowadays is to find a database that is scalable and can handle millions of records easily.

This section covers the MongoDB, a NoSQL document database. You are going to use the previous journal application, but before you start, you need to make sure that you have the MongoDB server installed on your computer.

If you are using Mac/Linux with the brew command (`http://brew.sh/`), execute the following command:

```
$ brew install mongodb
```

You can run it with this command:

```
$ mongod
```

Or you can install MongoDB by downloading it from the web site at `https://www.mongodb.org/downloads#production` and following the instructions.

Next, let's start by creating a new folder and a new application:

```
$ mkdir simple-mongo-app
$ cd simple-mongo-app
$ spring init -d=data-mongodb -g=com.apress.spring -a=simple-mongo-app --package-name=com.apress.spring -name=simple-mongo-app -x
```

The mandatory question is which starter pom will you need for this example? The `spring-boot-starter-data-mongodb` pom will be required for this example. See Listing 7-14.

Listing 7-14. pom.xml

```xml
<?xml version="1.0" encoding="UTF-8"?>
<project xmlns="http://maven.apache.org/POM/4.0.0"
xmlns:xsi="http://www.w3.org/2001/XMLSchema-instance"
        xsi:schemaLocation="http://maven.apache.org/POM/4.0.0
        http://maven.apache.org/xsd/maven-4.0.0.xsd">
        <modelVersion>4.0.0</modelVersion>

        <groupId>com.apress.spring</groupId>
        <artifactId>simple-mongo-app</artifactId>
        <version>0.0.1-SNAPSHOT</version>
        <packaging>jar</packaging>

        <name>simple-mongo-app</name>
        <description>Demo project for Spring Boot</description>

        <parent>
                <groupId>org.springframework.boot</groupId>
                <artifactId>spring-boot-starter-parent</artifactId>
                <version>1.3.2.RELEASE</version>
                <relativePath/> <!-- lookup parent from repository -->
        </parent>

        <properties>
                <project.build.sourceEncoding>UTF-8</project.build.sourceEncoding>
                <java.version>1.8</java.version>
        </properties>

        <dependencies>
                <dependency>
                        <groupId>org.springframework.boot</groupId>
                        <artifactId>spring-boot-starter-data-mongodb</artifactId>
                </dependency>

                <dependency>
                        <groupId>org.springframework.boot</groupId>
                        <artifactId>spring-boot-starter-test</artifactId>
                        <scope>test</scope>
                </dependency>
        </dependencies>

        <build>
                <plugins>
                        <plugin>
                                <groupId>org.springframework.boot</groupId>
                                <artifactId>spring-boot-maven-plugin</artifactId>
                        </plugin>
                </plugins>
        </build>

</project>
```

Listing 7-14 shows you the pom.xml file with the spring-boot-starter-data-mongodb pom as a dependency. Next let's look at the src/main/java/com/apress/spring/domain/Journal.java class. See Listing 7-15.

Listing 7-15. src/main/java/com/apress/spring/domain/Journal.java

```java
package com.apress.spring.domain;

import java.text.ParseException;
import java.text.SimpleDateFormat;
import java.util.Date;

import org.springframework.data.annotation.Id;
import org.springframework.data.annotation.Transient;

public class Journal {

        @Id
        private String id;
        private String title;
        private Date created;
        private String summary;

        @Transient
        private SimpleDateFormat format = new SimpleDateFormat("MM/dd/yyyy");

        public Journal(String title, String summary, String date) throws ParseException{
                this.title = title;
                this.summary = summary;
                this.created = format.parse(date);
        }

        Journal(){}

        public String getId() {
                return id;
        }

        public void setId(String id) {
                this.id = id;
        }

        public String getTitle() {
                return title;
        }

        public void setTitle(String title) {
                this.title = title;
        }
```

```java
    public Date getCreated() {
            return created;
    }

    public void setCreated(Date created) {
            this.created = created;
    }

    public String getSummary() {
            return summary;
    }

    public void setSummary(String summary) {
            this.summary = summary;
    }

    public String getCreatedAsShort(){
            return format.format(created);
    }

    public String toString(){
            StringBuilder value = new StringBuilder("* JournalEntry(");
            value.append("Id: ");
            value.append(id);
            value.append(",Title: ");
            value.append(title);
            value.append(",Summary: ");
            value.append(summary);
            value.append(",Created: ");
            value.append(getCreatedAsShort());
            value.append(")");
            return value.toString();
    }
}
```

Listing 7-15 shows you the Journal.java class. Let's review it:

- This time it uses the org.springframework.data.annotation.Id and the org.springframework.data.annotation.Transient annotations, which are different from the javax.persistence package (because they belong to the JPA specification). They allow you to have unique key (with the @Id annotation) and the @Transient marked property won't be persisted to the database.

- Another important difference is the ID. In the previous code, it was a Long type, but now it's String, which is required for the MongoDB. The rest of the code remains the same with its getters and setters.

Next, let's take a look at the src/main/java/com/apress/spring/repository/JournalRepository. java interface, as shown in Listing 7-16.

Listing 7-16. src/main/java/com/apress/spring/repository/JournalRepository.java

```java
package com.apress.spring.repository;

import java.util.List;

import org.springframework.data.mongodb.repository.MongoRepository;

import com.apress.spring.domain.Journal;

public interface JournalRepository extends MongoRepository<Journal, String> {

        public List<Journal> findByTitleLike(String word);
}
```

Listing 7-16 shows you the `JournalRepository.java` interface. Let's review it:

- Because this application is using the `spring-data` project and the `spring-data-mongodb` subproject libraries, you can extend it from the `MongoRepository` interface. This interface has common actions that run against the MongoDB. This interface needs a `Document` (in this case, the `Journal` class) that will contain an `id` and a `String`.

- Again, because you are using the `spring-data` and `spring-data-mongodb` abstractions, you can have "query" methods. In this example it will find a `title` that contains a word. The "query" method `findByTitleLike` will be translated to MongoDB query syntax. Something like `db.journal.find({"title": /.*?1*/})` or similar.

Now let's take a look at the main application. See Listing 7-17.

Listing 7-17. src/main/java/com/apress/spring/SimpleMongoAppApplication.java

```java
package com.apress.spring;

import org.slf4j.Logger;
import org.slf4j.LoggerFactory;
import org.springframework.boot.CommandLineRunner;
import org.springframework.boot.SpringApplication;
import org.springframework.boot.autoconfigure.SpringBootApplication;
import org.springframework.context.annotation.Bean;

import com.apress.spring.domain.Journal;
import com.apress.spring.repository.JournalRepository;

@SpringBootApplication
public class SimpleMongoAppApplication {
    private static final Logger log = LoggerFactory.getLogger(SimpleMongoAppApplication.
    class);

    public static void main(String[] args) {
      SpringApplication.run(SimpleMongoAppApplication.class, args);
    }
```

```
@Bean
CommandLineRunner start(JournalRepository repo){
    return args -> {
        log.info("> Deleting existing data...");
        repo.deleteAll();

        log.info("> Inserting new data...");
        repo.save(new Journal("Get to know Spring Boot","Today I will learn Spring
        Boot","01/02/2016"));
            repo.save(new Journal("Simple Spring Boot Project","I will do my
            first Spring Boot Project","01/03/2016"));
            repo.save(new Journal("Spring Boot Reading","Read more about Spring
            Boot","02/02/2016"));
            repo.save(new Journal("Spring Boot in the Cloud","Spring Boot using
            Cloud Foundry","03/01/2016"));

        log.info("> Getting all data...");
        repo.findAll().forEach(entry -> log.info(entry.toString()));

        log.info("> Getting data using like...");
        repo.findByTitleLike("Cloud").forEach(entry -> log.info(entry.toString()));

    };
}
}
```

Listing 7-17 shows you the main application. Does this app look familiar? It's not that different from its previous "relatives". Here, it's using the start method, which will be called after the Spring Boot app starts. It will delete all existing data, it will insert them, and then it will use some of the finder methods.

You can run it as usual, using the Maven wrapper or the global Maven installation:

```
$ ./mvnw spring-boot:run
```

You should see the following output:

```
> Deleting existing data...
> Inserting new data...
> Getting all data...
* JournalEntry(Id: 56b192d377c83f89cae51f5f,Title: Get to know Spring Boot,Summary: Today I
will learn Spring Boot,Created: 01/02/2016)
* JournalEntry(Id: 56b192d377c83f89cae51f60,Title: Simple Spring Boot Project,Summary:
I will do my first Spring Boot Project,Created: 01/03/2016)
* JournalEntry(Id: 56b192d377c83f89cae51f61,Title: Spring Boot Reading,Summary: Read more
about Spring Boot,Created: 02/02/2016)
* JournalEntry(Id: 56b192d377c83f89cae51f62,Title: Spring Boot in the Cloud,Summary:
Spring Boot using Cloud Foundry,Created: 03/01/2016)
> Getting data using like...
* JournalEntry(Id: 56b192d377c83f89cae51f62,Title: Spring Boot in the Cloud,Summary:
Spring Boot using Cloud Foundry,Created: 03/01/2016)
```

If you want to see the actual data in your MongoDB server, you can open a terminal and execute the following commands:

```
$ mongo
MongoDB shell version: 3.2.1
connecting to: test
> show collections
blog
journal
system.indexes
> db.journal.find()
{ "_id" : ObjectId("56b192d377c83f89cae51f5f"), "_class" : "com.apress.spring.domain.
Journal", "title" : "Get to know Spring Boot", "created" : ISODate("2016-01-02T07:00:00Z"),
"summary" : "Today I will learn Spring Boot" }
{ "_id" : ObjectId("56b192d377c83f89cae51f60"), "_class" : "com.apress.spring.domain.
Journal", "title" : "Simple Spring Boot Project", "created" : ISODate("2016-01-
03T07:00:00Z"), "summary" : "I will do my first Spring Boot Project" }
{ "_id" : ObjectId("56b192d377c83f89cae51f61"), "_class" : "com.apress.spring.domain.
Journal", "title" : "Spring Boot Reading", "created" : ISODate("2016-02-02T07:00:00Z"),
"summary" : "Read more about Spring Boot" }
{ "_id" : ObjectId("56b192d377c83f89cae51f62"), "_class" : "com.apress.spring.domain.
Journal", "title" : "Spring Boot in the Cloud", "created" : ISODate("2016-03-01T07:00:00Z"),
"summary" : "Spring Boot using Cloud Foundry" }
```

When you use the mongo client shell, you will be connected directly to the test database, which is what Spring Boot will use as main database to create the document collection. In this case, it's the name of the Java class: journal. Then you can use the db.journal.find() query to get all the data.

Spring Boot allows you to define the name of your database if you don't want to use the default one. You only need to add the following property to the src/main/resources/application.properties file:

```
spring.data.mongodb.database=myjournal
```

Then the MongoRepository will create the database using the myjournal name and will create the journal collection as well.

You can take a peek at the MongoDB server by using its client. You can see the database, the collection, and the data with the following commands:

```
$ mongo
MongoDB shell version: 3.2.3
connecting to: test
> show databases;
local       0.078GB
myjournal   0.078GB
test        0.203GB
> use myjournal
switched to db myjournal
> show collections
journal
system.indexes
> db.journal.find()
```

```
{ "_id" : ObjectId("56b0ef2d77c8a628197f0aa4"), "_class" : "com.apress.spring.domain.
Journal", "title" : "Get to know Spring Boot", "created" : ISODate("2016-01-02T07:00:00Z"),
"summary" : "Today I will learn Spring Boot" }
{ "_id" : ObjectId("56b0ef2d77c8a628197f0aa5"), "_class" : "com.apress.spring.domain.
Journal", "title" : "Simple Spring Boot Project", "created" : ISODate("2016-01-
03T07:00:00Z"), "summary" : "I will do my first Spring Boot Project" }
{ "_id" : ObjectId("56b0ef2d77c8a628197f0aa6"), "_class" : "com.apress.spring.domain.
Journal", "title" : "Spring Boot Reading", "created" : ISODate("2016-02-02T07:00:00Z"),
"summary" : "Read more about Spring Boot" }
{ "_id" : ObjectId("56b0ef2d77c8a628197f0aa7"), "_class" : "com.apress.spring.domain.
Journal", "title" : "Spring Boot in the Cloud", "created" : ISODate("2016-03-01T07:00:00Z"),
"summary" : "Spring Boot using Cloud Foundry" }
>
```

This feature (the properties specified in the application.properties file) works not only for Mongo but for every spring-data application. You can get more info about the right property setting at https://docs.spring.io/spring-boot/docs/current/reference/html/common-application-properties.html.

Summary

This chapter discussed relational and NoSQL databases and explained how the Spring Data project and subprojects define several helpers and abstraction classes that will help you have data access regardless of the database engine you use.

I started by showing you the JdbcTemplate that is based on the template design pattern. You saw execute methods that allow you to interact with the relational database. The relational database examples used the H2 in-memory database, which is a very good technology for prototyping and testing purposes.

The chapter showed you the H2 web console by adding the spring-boot-starter-web pom and setting the spring.h2.console.enabled=true property to true. The chapter showed you the JPA and explained how you can avoid writing common CRUD (Create, Read, Update, and Delete) tasks by creating an interface that extends from the JpaRepository. You also learned that you can have "query" methods to support more tasks for your data applications.

You saw the NoSQL document database, the MongoDB, and learned how you can use the MongoRepository, which is very similar to the regular JPA.

In the next chapter, you are going to start using all the data code from this chapter because you are going to create web applications with Spring Boot.

CHAPTER 8

■ ■ ■

Web Development with Spring Boot

Nowadays the web is the main channel for any type of application—from desktop to mobile devices, from social and business applications to games, and from simple content to streaming data. With this is mind, Spring Boot can help you easily develop the next generation of web applications.

This chapter shows you how to create Spring Boot web applications. You have already learned, with some examples in earlier chapters, what you can do with the web. You learned that Spring Boot makes it easier to create web apps with a few lines of code and that you don't need to worry about configuration files or look for an application server to deploy your web application. By using Spring Boot and its auto-configuration, you can have an embedded application server like Tomcat or Jetty, which makes your app very distributable and portable.

Spring MVC

Let's start talking about the Spring MVC technology and some of its features. Remember that the Spring Framework consists of about 20 modules or technologies, and the web technology is one of them. For the web technology, the Spring Framework has the spring-web, `spring-webmvc`, `spring-websocket`, and `spring-webmvc-portlet` modules.

The `spring-web` module has basic web integration features such as multipart file upload functionality, initialization of the Spring container (by using servlet listeners), and a web-oriented application context. The `spring-mvc` module (aka, the web server module) contains all the Spring MVC (Model-View-Controller) and REST services implementations for web applications. These modules provide many features, such as very powerful JSP tag libraries, customizable binding and validation, flexible model transfer, customizable handler and view resolution, and so on.

The Spring MVC is designed around the `org.springframework.web.servlet.DispatcherServlet` class. This servlet is very flexible and has a very robust functionality that you won't find in any other MVC web frameworks out there. With the `DispatcherServlet` you have out-of-the-box several resolutions strategies, including View resolvers, Locale resolvers, Theme resolvers, and Exception handlers. In other words, the `DispatcherServlet` will take a HTTP request and redirect it to the right handler (the class marked with the `@Controller` and the methods that use the `@RequestMapping` annotations) and the right view (your JSPs).

© Felipe Gutierrez 2016

F. Gutierrez, *Pro Spring Boot*, DOI 10.1007/978-1-4842-1431-2_8

Spring Boot Web Applications

You are going to continue using the Spring Boot Journal application, but with some modifications, so you can see the power of using the Spring MVC with Spring Boot. Let's start by creating the journal app.

Open a terminal and execute the following commands:

```
$ mkdir spring-boot-journal
$ cd spring-boot-journal
$ spring init -d=web,thymeleaf,data-jpa,data-rest -g=com.apress.spring -a=spring-boot-
journal --package-name=com.apress.spring -name=spring-boot-journal -x
```

These commands will be the initial template for the Spring Boot journal. Now you are getting familiar with the Spring Initializr. In this case you already know that you are going create a web application that will use the Thymeleaf templating engine for the views, the JPA for all the data access, and a new starter, the data-rest, which will allow to expose the data repositories as RESTful API.

Take a look at the pom.xml file, shown in Listing 8-1.

Listing 8-1. pom.xml

```xml
<?xml version="1.0" encoding="UTF-8"?>
<project xmlns="http://maven.apache.org/POM/4.0.0"
xmlns:xsi="http://www.w3.org/2001/XMLSchema-instance"
        xsi:schemaLocation="http://maven.apache.org/POM/4.0.0
        http://maven.apache.org/xsd/maven-4.0.0.xsd">
        <modelVersion>4.0.0</modelVersion>

        <groupId>com.apress.spring</groupId>
        <artifactId>spring-boot-journal</artifactId>
        <version>0.0.1-SNAPSHOT</version>
        <packaging>jar</packaging>

        <name>spring-boot-journal</name>
        <description>Demo project for Spring Boot</description>

        <parent>
                <groupId>org.springframework.boot</groupId>
                <artifactId>spring-boot-starter-parent</artifactId>
                <version>1.3.2.RELEASE</version>
                <relativePath/> <!-- lookup parent from repository -->
        </parent>

        <properties>
                <project.build.sourceEncoding>UTF-8</project.build.sourceEncoding>
                <java.version>1.8</java.version>
        </properties>

        <dependencies>
                <dependency>
                        <groupId>org.springframework.boot</groupId>
                        <artifactId>spring-boot-starter-data-jpa</artifactId>
                </dependency>
```

```
                <dependency>
                        <groupId>org.springframework.boot</groupId>
                        <artifactId>spring-boot-starter-data-rest</artifactId>
                </dependency>
                <dependency>
                        <groupId>org.springframework.boot</groupId>
                        <artifactId>spring-boot-starter-thymeleaf</artifactId>
                </dependency>
                <dependency>
                        <groupId>org.springframework.boot</groupId>
                        <artifactId>spring-boot-starter-web</artifactId>
                </dependency>

                        <!-- MYSQL -->
                <dependency>
                        <groupId>mysql</groupId>
                        <artifactId>mysql-connector-java</artifactId>
                </dependency>

                <dependency>
                        <groupId>org.springframework.boot</groupId>
                        <artifactId>spring-boot-starter-test</artifactId>
                        <scope>test</scope>
                </dependency>
        </dependencies>

        <build>
                <plugins>
                        <plugin>
                                <groupId>org.springframework.boot</groupId>
                                <artifactId>spring-boot-maven-plugin</artifactId>
                        </plugin>
                </plugins>
        </build>

</project>
```

Listing 8-1 shows you the pom.xml file that you are going to be using for the Spring Boot journal app. Do you notice something different? You already know that spring-boot-starter-data-jpa, spring-boot-starter-data-rest, spring-boot-starter-data-web, and spring-boot-starter-data-thymeleaf are the starter poms because they were added as dependencies in the Spring Initializr. But note that there is now a MySQL dependency, which means that you need to have the MySQL server up and running in your system. If you want to install it, you can use brew for OS X/Linux:

```
$ brew install mysql
```

Or if you are using Windows you can find a version on the MySQL web site at http://dev.mysql.com/downloads/mysql/.

Did you notice that in Listing 8-1, there is no <version> tag in the MySQL dependency? This is because the spring-boot-starter-parent pom has a dependency on the spring-boot-dependencies, where all the versions that work with Spring are declared—in this case the MySQL driver library. That's why working with Spring Boot is so easy—you just add the right starter pom and don't have to worry about third-party dependencies.

Let's start by configuring the MySQL properties in the application. You can open and edit src/main/resources/application.properties to look like Listing 8-2.

Listing 8-2. src/main/resources/application.properties

```
#Spring DataSource
spring.datasource.url = jdbc:mysql://localhost:3306/journal
spring.datasource.username = springboot
spring.datasource.password = springboot
spring.datasource.testWhileIdle = true
spring.datasource.validationQuery = SELECT 1
#JPA-Hibernate
spring.jpa.show-sql = true
spring.jpa.hibernate.ddl-auto = create-drop
spring.jpa.hibernate.naming-strategy = org.hibernate.cfg.ImprovedNamingStrategy
spring.jpa.properties.hibernate.dialect = org.hibernate.dialect.MySQL5Dialect
```

Listing 8-2 shows you the application.properties file that the journal app will use. As you can see, it's very straightforward. You have two sections. The first section declares the values that the javax.sql. DataSource will use, such as the JDBC URL, the credentials, and testWhileIdle and validationQuery. These are useful for keeping the connection if it's been idle for a long time. The second section declares all dependencies related to JPA and Hibernate. The show-sql will log all the SQL (you can turn this on and off). The hibernate.ddl-auto property will create the table (based on your declared entities annotated with @Entity) and when the app finishes, it will drop it. The other possible values are create and update (the update value is recommended for production environments). hibernate.name-strategy will use the best naming for your tables and fields in your database, and hibernate.dialect is useful for generating the SQL optimized for the database engine—in this case MySQL.

■ **Note**   In order to use the MySQL database and the credentials from Listing 8-2, don't forget to create the journal database and add user privileges to the MySQL server. If you prefer, feel free to use your own credentials.

Next let's add the domain src/main/java/com/apress/spring/domain/JournalEntry.java class; see Listing 8-3.

Listing 8-3. src/main/java/com/apress/spring/domain/JournalEntry.java

```
package com.apress.spring.domain;

import java.text.ParseException;
import java.text.SimpleDateFormat;
import java.util.Date;

import javax.persistence.Entity;
import javax.persistence.GeneratedValue;
import javax.persistence.GenerationType;
```

```java
import javax.persistence.Id;
import javax.persistence.Table;
import javax.persistence.Transient;

import com.apress.spring.utils.JsonDateSerializer;
import com.fasterxml.jackson.annotation.JsonIgnore;
import com.fasterxml.jackson.databind.annotation.JsonSerialize;

@Entity
@Table(name="entry")
public class JournalEntry {

        @Id
        @GeneratedValue(strategy=GenerationType.AUTO)
        private Long id;
        private String title;
        private Date created;
        private String summary;

        @Transient
        private final SimpleDateFormat format = new SimpleDateFormat("yyyy-MM-dd");

        public JournalEntry(String title, String summary, String date) throws
        ParseException{
                this.title = title;
                this.summary = summary;
                this.created = format.parse(date);
        }

        JournalEntry(){}

        public Long getId() {
                return id;
        }

        public void setId(Long id) {
                this.id = id;
        }

        public String getTitle() {
                return title;
        }

        public void setTitle(String title) {
                this.title = title;
        }

        @JsonSerialize(using=JsonDateSerializer.class)
        public Date getCreated() {
                return created;
        }
```

```
        public void setCreated(Date created) {
                this.created = created;
        }

        public String getSummary() {
                return summary;
        }

        public void setSummary(String summary) {
                this.summary = summary;
        }

        @JsonIgnore
        public String getCreatedAsShort(){
                return format.format(created);
        }

        public String toString(){
                StringBuilder value = new StringBuilder("* JournalEntry(");
                value.append("Id: ");
                value.append(id);
                value.append(",Title: ");
                value.append(title);
                value.append(",Summary: ");
                value.append(summary);
                value.append(",Created: ");
                value.append(format.format(created));
                value.append(")");
                return value.toString();
        }
}
```

Listing 8-3 shows you the JournalEntry.java class. This class is a little different from the previous chapters. One of the differences is that the JournalEntry class is marked with the @Table(name="entry") annotation and with an attribute of name and value of entry. This will tell JPA/Hibernate that the table to generate will be named entry. The next difference is that the getDateMethod is marked with the @JsonSerialize(using=JsonDateSerializer.class) annotation.

The @JsonSerialize annotation has defined a JsonDateSerializer.class that will be used to serialize the data. This is a customized class that you will see soon. This is useful for printing out the date in a particular format, and this time you are going to use the standard ISO.DATE format that corresponds with this pattern: yyyy-MM-dd.

Also in Listing 8-3 you can see that the getCreatedAsShort() method is marked with @JsonIgnore, which will ignore the property when the JSON printout of the class is called. Next, consider the src/main/java/com/apress/spring/utils/JsonDateSerializer.java class. Remember that this class will serialize the date into a JSON object with a particular date format (ISO.DATE). See Listing 8-4.

Listing 8-4. src/main/java/com/apress/spring/utils/JsonDateSerializer.java

```java
package com.apress.spring.utils;

import java.io.IOException;
import java.text.SimpleDateFormat;
import java.util.Date;

import com.fasterxml.jackson.core.JsonGenerator;
import com.fasterxml.jackson.core.JsonProcessingException;
import com.fasterxml.jackson.databind.JsonSerializer;
import com.fasterxml.jackson.databind.SerializerProvider;

public class JsonDateSerializer extends JsonSerializer<Date>{

    private static final SimpleDateFormat dateFormat = new SimpleDateFormat("yyyy-MM-dd");

    @Override
    public void serialize(Date date, JsonGenerator gen, SerializerProvider provider)
            throws IOException, JsonProcessingException {
        String formattedDate = dateFormat.format(date);
        gen.writeString(formattedDate);
    }
}
```

Listing 8-4 shows you the JsonDateSerializer class that will be called by the JSON converter when needed. This will happen automatically inside the HttpMessaConverter<T> class handled by the Spring MVC. This class extends from the JsonSerializer class; it's necessary to override the serialize method that will be called when the serialization happens. This serializer is based on the JSON Jackson library. This dependency is already included in the spring-boot-starter-web pom.

Next, let's look at the src/main/java/com/apress/spring/repository/JournalRepository.java interface, which is the same one from previous chapters. See Listing 8-5.

Listing 8-5. src/main/java/com/apress/spring/repository/JournalRepository.java

```java
package com.apress.spring.repository;

import org.springframework.data.jpa.repository.JpaRepository;
import com.apress.spring.domain.JournalEntry;

public interface JournalRepository extends JpaRepository<JournalEntry, Long> { }
```

Listing 8-5 shows you the JournalRepository.java interface, which is the one that has all the JPA actions and all the CRUD (Create-Read-Update-Delete) actions. Of course, you are going to need to modify it to add some finders, but you will do that later in this chapter.

Let's run the app and see what happens:

```
$ ./mvnw spring-boot:run
```

After you run this command and then open a browser and go to http://localhost:8080, you will get some kind of message. Most likely an error about opening a type: application/hal+json or a Save File As window because the browser doesn't know how to handle this particular type of response.

What you are getting from the application is a HAL+JSON response. The HAL (Hypertext Application Language) is a representation of media, such as links. This is used by the HATEOAS (Hypermedia as the Engine of Application State) as a way to manage REST endpoints through media links, but how does the HATEOAS/HAL get here? Well, very simple. Remember that in the pom.xml file there is the spring-boot-starter-data-rest dependency. This dependency will include the JPA models as a way to expose through the HATEOAS media links for your REST API. This journal app is now an operational REST API web application.

Returning to the browser problem—how can you see the result of the application/hal+json format? If you want to see it right away, you can open a terminal and execute the following command:

```
$ curl -i http://localhost:8080
HTTP/1.1 200 OK
Server: Apache-Coyote/1.1
Content-Type: application/hal+json;charset=UTF-8
Transfer-Encoding: chunked
Date: Fri, 05 Feb 2016 00:12:29 GMT

{
  "_links" : {
    "journalEntries" : {
      "href" : "http://localhost:8080/journalEntries{?page,size,sort}",
      "templated" : true
    },
    "profile" : {
      "href" : "http://localhost:8080/profile"
    }
  }
}
```

After executing the cURL command, you should get the same output, which shows the HAL+JSON type format. If you want to use the browser, I suggest that you use Google Chrome and install the JSONView add-on. If you do so, you can see the HAL+JSON type in your browser. Safari and Firefox have the same plugin/add-on, but it doesn't work properly all the time. See Figure 8-1.

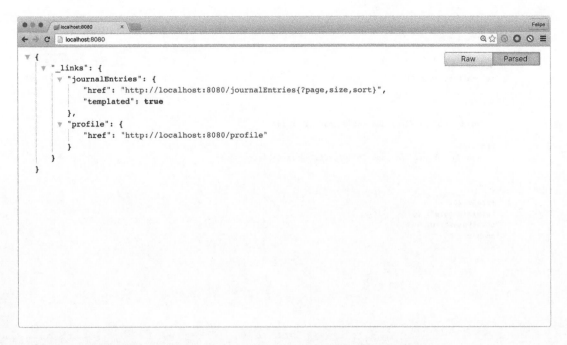

Figure 8-1. *Google Chrome and the JSONView add-on at* `http://localhost:8080`

Figure 8-1 shows you the browser view of the HAL+JSON type response. See that it defines several links, such as `http://localhost:8080/journalEntries`. You will see a JSON format that exposes the `_links` key with two additional entries: `journalEntries` (this is the plural of your `JournalEntry` domain class) and `profile`. You can click on those links, but if you click in the first reference—`journalEntries` (`http://localhost:8080/journalEntries{?page,size,sort}`)—you will get an error, so you must adjust the URL to be only `http://localhost:8080/journalEntries`. You can actually add default values to the actual link but in this project we are not going to do that.

If you click on the `http://localhost:8080/profile` you will be redirected to the ALPS metadata. The ALPS is a data format for defining simple descriptions of application-level semantics. If you want to know more about ALPS you can go here to `http://alps.io/`. See Figure 8-2.

Figure 8-2. `http://localhost:8080/journalEntries`

Figure 8-2 shows the result of going to one of the URLs defined; in this case the `http://localhost:8080/journalEntries` URL. This is the result of using `spring-boot-starter-data-rest` and `spring-boot-starter-data-jpa`, where you defined your interface that extends from the `JpaRepository` interface (Listing 8-5).

Another thing to notice is the `_embedded/journalEntries`, which is actually the data that is pulled from MySQL server. By default the Spring Data REST will create the plural of the entity, so the `JournalEntry` class will become the `journalEntries` collection. Now, if you take a look at the MySQL server with the `mysql` shell, you will notice that table create was `entry` due the `@Table` annotation in the `JournalEntry` class. So far you don't have any data.

You can stop the app by pressing Ctrl+C on your keyboard. Now, let's add some data. Create the `src/main/resources/data.sql` file. See Listing 8-6.

Listing 8-6. src/main/resources/data.sql

```
INSERT INTO ENTRY(title,summary,created) VALUES('Get to know Spring Boot','Today I will
learn Spring Boot','2016-01-02 00:00:00.00');
INSERT INTO ENTRY(title,summary,created) VALUES('Simple Spring Boot Project','I will do my
first Spring Boot project','2016-01-03 00:00:00.00');
INSERT INTO ENTRY(title,summary,created) VALUES('Spring Boot Reading','Read more about
Spring Boot','2016-02-02 00:00:00.00');
INSERT INTO ENTRY(title,summary,created) VALUES('Spring Boot in the Cloud','Learn Spring
Boot using Cloud Foundry','2016-02-05 00:00:00.00');
```

You can run this application as usual:

```
$ ./mvnw spring-boot:run
```

And you can execute via the cURL command:

```
$ curl -i http://localhost:8080/journalEntries
HTTP/1.1 200 OK
Server: Apache-Coyote/1.1
Content-Type: application/hal+json;charset=UTF-8
Transfer-Encoding: chunked
Date: Fri, 05 Feb 2016 02:22:54 GMT


{
  "_embedded" : {
    "entry" : [ {
      "title" : "Get to know Spring Boot",
      "created" : "2016-01-02",
      "summary" : "Today I will learn Spring Boot",
      "_links" : {
        "self" : {
          "href" : "http://localhost:8080/api/journal/1"
        },
        "journalEntry" : {
          "href" : "http://localhost:8080/api/journal/1"
        }
      }
    }, {
      "title" : "Simple Spring Boot Project",
      "created" : "2016-01-03",
      "summary" : "I will do my first Spring Boot project",
      "_links" : {
        "self" : {
          "href" : "http://localhost:8080/api/journal/2"
        },
        "journalEntry" : {
          "href" : "http://localhost:8080/api/journal/2"
        }
      }
    }, {
      "title" : "Spring Boot Reading",
      "created" : "2016-02-02",
      "summary" : "Read more about Spring Boot",
      "_links" : {
        "self" : {
          "href" : "http://localhost:8080/api/journal/3"
        },
        "journalEntry" : {
          "href" : "http://localhost:8080/api/journal/3"
        }
      }
    }, {
      "title" : "Spring Boot in the Cloud",
      "created" : "2016-02-05",
```

```
      "summary" : "Learn Spring Boot using Cloud Foundry",
      "_links" : {
        "self" : {
          "href" : "http://localhost:8080/api/journal/4"
        },
        "journalEntry" : {
          "href" : "http://localhost:8080/api/journal/4"
        }
      }
    } ]
  },
  "_links" : {
    "self" : {
      "href" : "http://localhost:8080/api/journal"
    },
    "profile" : {
      "href" : "http://localhost:8080/api/profile/journal"
    },
    "search" : {
      "href" : "http://localhost:8080/api/journal/search"
    }
  },
  "page" : {
    "size" : 20,
    "totalElements" : 4,
    "totalPages" : 1,
    "number" : 0
  }
}
```

You will see something similar to the previous output. Or if you are using Google Chrome with the JSONView add-on, you should see something like Figure 8-3.

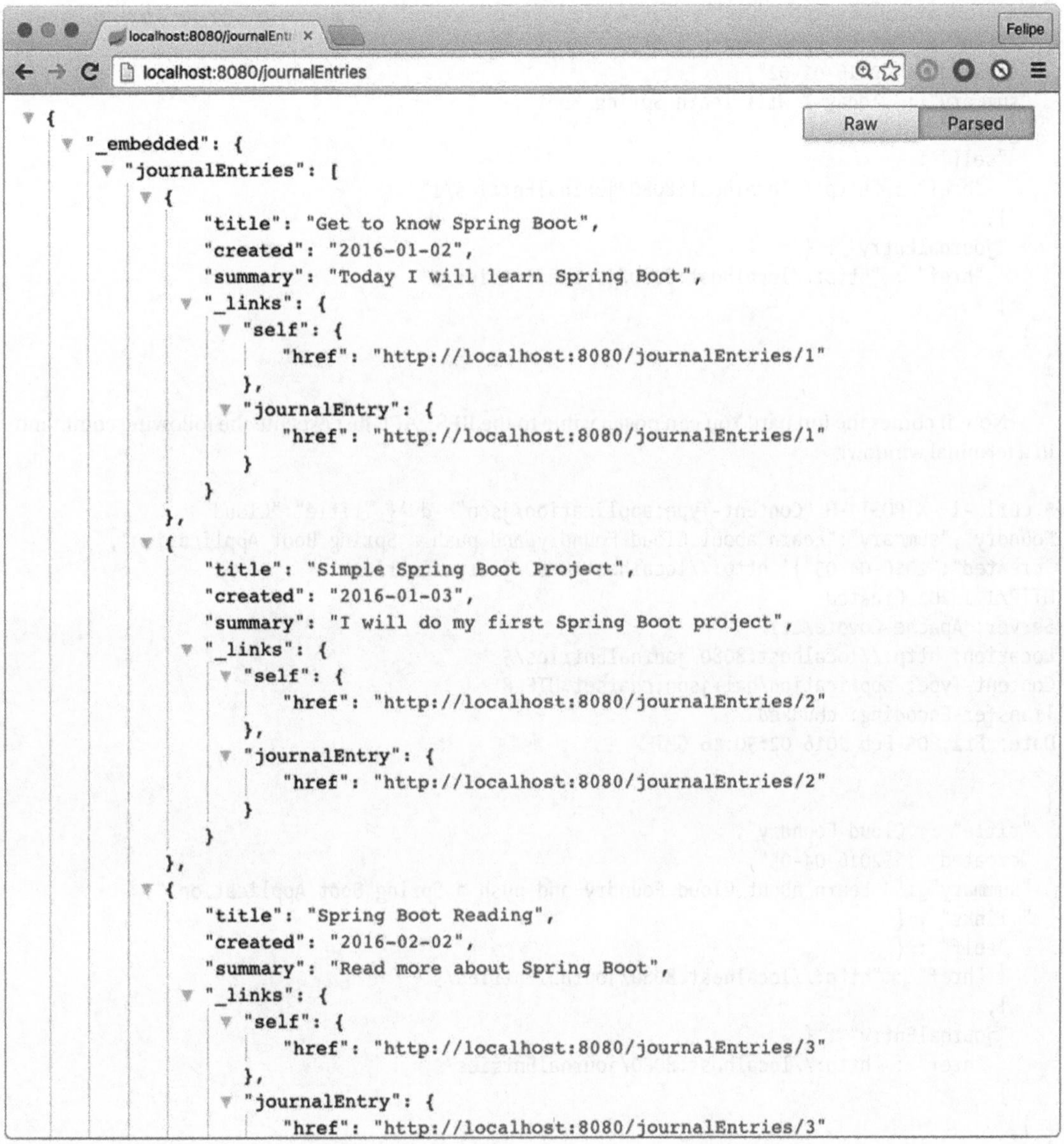

Figure 8-3. `http://localhost:8080/journalEntries`

Click one of the links from any entry. For example, click `http://localhost:8080/journalEntries/1` or use the cURL command:

```
$ curl -i http://localhost:8080/journalEntries/1
HTTP/1.1 200 OK
Server: Apache-Coyote/1.1
Content-Type: application/hal+json;charset=UTF-8
Transfer-Encoding: chunked
Date: Fri, 05 Feb 2016 02:33:26 GMT
```

```
{
  "title" : "Get to know Spring Boot",
  "created" : "2016-01-02",
  "summary" : "Today I will learn Spring Boot",
  "_links" : {
    "self" : {
      "href" : "http://localhost:8080/journalEntries/1"
    },
    "journalEntry" : {
      "href" : "http://localhost:8080/journalEntries/1"
    }
  }
}
```

Now, it comes the fun part! You can post a value to the REST API. Just execute the following command in a terminal window:

```
$ curl -i -X POST -H "Content-Type:application/json" -d '{ "title":"Cloud
Foundry","summary":"Learn about Cloud Foundry and push a Spring Boot Application",
"created":"2016-04-05"}' http://localhost:8080/journalEntries
HTTP/1.1 201 Created
Server: Apache-Coyote/1.1
Location: http://localhost:8080/journalEntries/5
Content-Type: application/hal+json;charset=UTF-8
Transfer-Encoding: chunked
Date: Fri, 05 Feb 2016 02:50:16 GMT

{
  "title" : "Cloud Foundry",
  "created" : "2016-04-05",
  "summary" : " Learn about Cloud Foundry and push a Spring Boot Application ",
  "_links" : {
    "self" : {
      "href" : "http://localhost:8080/journalEntries/5"
    },
    "journalEntry" : {
      "href" : "http://localhost:8080/journalEntries/5"
    }
  }
}
```

Yes! You have the GET, POST, PUT, PATCH, and DELETE HTTP methods, which you can run against the http://localhost:8080/journalEntries URL.

Now stop your application (Ctrl+C). What about searching? Maybe you need to pass some parameters. Let's modify the JournalRepository and add the method queries. See Listing 8-7.

Listing 8-7. src/main/java/com/apress/spring/repository/JournalRepository.java

```java
package com.apress.spring.repository;

import java.util.Date;
import java.util.List;

import org.springframework.data.jpa.repository.JpaRepository;
import org.springframework.data.repository.query.Param;
import org.springframework.format.annotation.DateTimeFormat;
import org.springframework.format.annotation.DateTimeFormat.ISO;

import com.apress.spring.domain.JournalEntry;

public interface JournalRepository extends JpaRepository<JournalEntry, Long> {

        List<JournalEntry> findByCreatedAfter(@Param("after") @DateTimeFormat(iso =
        ISO.DATE) Date date);
        List<JournalEntry> findByCreatedBetween(@Param("after") @DateTimeFormat(iso =
        ISO.DATE) Date after,@Param("before") @DateTimeFormat(iso = ISO.DATE) Date before);
        List<JournalEntry> findByTitleContaining(@Param("word") String word);
        List<JournalEntry> findBySummaryContaining(@Param("word") String word);

}
```

Listing 8-7 shows you the new version of the JournalRepository.java interface. There are four query methods with parameters marked by the @Param and @DateTimeFormat annotations. @Param has a value that will define the parameter name to use for the URL. @DateTimeFormat is a helper for that parameter when the type is the date value, meaning that you will need to pass a date in the form of yyyy-mm-dd, which is the ISO date format.

Now you can run your application:

```
$ ./mvnw spring-boot:run
```

And execute the following command in a different terminal window:

```
$ curl -i http://localhost:8080/journalEntries
```

When you execute this command, you will see at the end of the response a new URL in the _links section:

```
...
"_links" : {
    "self" : {
      "href" : "http://localhost:8080/journalEntries"
    },
    "profile" : {
      "href" : "http://localhost:8080/profile/journalEntries"
    },
    "search" : {
      "href" : "http://localhost:8080/journalEntries/search"
    }
  },
```

```
  "page" : {
    "size" : 20,
    "totalElements" : 4,
    "totalPages" : 1,
    "number" : 0
  }
}
```

You will find the search element pointing to http://localhost:8080/journalEntries/search. You can query that URL with cURL or the browser:

```
$ curl -i http://localhost:8080/journalEntries/search
HTTP/1.1 200 OK
Server: Apache-Coyote/1.1
Content-Type: application/hal+json;charset=UTF-8
Transfer-Encoding: chunked
Date: Fri, 05 Feb 2016 03:05:31 GMT

{
  "_links" : {
    "findByCreatedAfter" : {
      "href" : "http://localhost:8080/journalEntries/search/findByCreatedAfter{?after}",
      "templated" : true
    },
    "findByTitleContaining" : {
      "href" : "http://localhost:8080/journalEntries/search/findByTitleContaining{?word}",
      "templated" : true
    },
    "findByCreatedBetween" : {
      "href" : "http://localhost:8080/journalEntries/search/findByCreatedBetween
      {?after,before}",
      "templated" : true
    },
    "findBySummaryContaining" : {
      "href" : "http://localhost:8080/journalEntries/search/findBySummaryContaining{?word}",
      "templated" : true
    },
    "self" : {
      "href" : "http://localhost:8080/journalEntries/search"
    }
  }
}
```

You can search using the GET HTTP method. After you added the methods, they were converted into an endpoint—that is, into RESTful API! So, by using the findByTitleContaining method, you can execute the following command:

```
$ curl -i http://localhost:8080/journalEntries/search/findByTitleContaining?word=Cloud
HTTP/1.1 200 OK
Server: Apache-Coyote/1.1
Content-Type: application/hal+json;charset=UTF-8
```

```
Transfer-Encoding: chunked
Date: Fri, 05 Feb 2016 03:07:12 GMT

{
  "_embedded" : {
    "journalEntries" : [ {
      "title" : "Spring Boot in the Cloud",
      "created" : "2016-02-05",
      "summary" : "Learn Spring Boot using Cloud Foundry",
      "_links" : {
        "self" : {
          "href" : "http://localhost:8080/journalEntries/4"
        },
        "journalEntry" : {
          "href" : "http://localhost:8080/journalEntries/4"
        }
      }
    } ]
  },
  "_links" : {
    "self" : {
      "href" : "http://localhost:8080/journalEntries/search/findByTitleContaining?word=Cloud"
    }
  }
}
```

What about the dates? You added several methods to look for a date. Let's get all the entries after 2016-02-01 (assuming you are using the data.sql as in Listing 8-6):

```
$ curl -i http://localhost:8080/journalEntries/search/findByCreatedAfter?after=2016-02-01
HTTP/1.1 200 OK
Server: Apache-Coyote/1.1
Content-Type: application/hal+json;charset=UTF-8
Transfer-Encoding: chunked
Date: Fri, 05 Feb 2016 03:20:25 GMT

{
  "_embedded" : {
    "journalEntries" : [ {
      "title" : "Spring Boot Reading",
      "created" : "2016-02-02",
      "summary" : "Read more about Spring Boot",
      "_links" : {
        "self" : {
          "href" : "http://localhost:8080/journalEntries/3"
        },
        "journalEntry" : {
          "href" : "http://localhost:8080/journalEntries/3"
        }
      }
```

```
    }, {
      "title" : "Spring Boot in the Cloud",
      "created" : "2016-02-05",
      "summary" : "Learn Spring Boot using Cloud Foundry",
      "_links" : {
        "self" : {
          "href" : "http://localhost:8080/journalEntries/4"
        },
        "journalEntry" : {
          "href" : "http://localhost:8080/journalEntries/4"
        }
      }
    } ]
  },
  "_links" : {
    "self" : {
      "href" : "http://localhost:8080/journalEntries/search/findByCreatedAfter?
      after=2016-02-01"
    }
  }
}
```

If you want to try findByCreatedBetween, you can execute the following command (the URL is now enclosed with double quotes for the two parameters—after and before):

```
$ curl -i "http://localhost:8080/journalEntries/search/findByCreatedBetween?
after=2016-02-01&before=2016-03-01"
HTTP/1.1 200 OK
Server: Apache-Coyote/1.1
Content-Type: application/hal+json;charset=UTF-8
Transfer-Encoding: chunked
Date: Fri, 05 Feb 2016 03:24:07 GMT

{
  "_embedded" : {
    "journalEntries" : [ {
      "title" : "Spring Boot Reading",
      "created" : "2016-02-02",
      "summary" : "Read more about Spring Boot",
      "_links" : {
        "self" : {
          "href" : "http://localhost:8080/journalEntries/3"
        },
        "journalEntry" : {
          "href" : "http://localhost:8080/journalEntries/3"
        }
      }
    }, {
      "title" : "Spring Boot in the Cloud",
      "created" : "2016-02-05",
      "summary" : "Learn Spring Boot using Cloud Foundry",
```

```
    "_links" : {
      "self" : {
        "href" : "http://localhost:8080/journalEntries/4"
      },
      "journalEntry" : {
        "href" : "http://localhost:8080/journalEntries/4"
      }
    }
  } ]
  },
  "_links" : {
    "self" : {
      "href" : "http://localhost:8080/journalEntries/search/findByCreatedBetween?
      after=2016-02-01&before=2016-03-01"
    }
  }
}
```

This is amazing. By adding only a query method, you have all this functionality. As an exercise, you can test the findBySummaryContaining search.

You can the application by pressing Ctrl+C on your keyboard. Next, let's create a web controller to show the entries journal in a nice way. See Listing 8-8.

Listing 8-8. src/main/java/com/apress/spring/web/JournalController.java

```java
package com.apress.spring.web;

import org.springframework.beans.factory.annotation.Autowired;
import org.springframework.web.bind.annotation.RequestMapping;
import org.springframework.web.bind.annotation.RequestMethod;
import org.springframework.web.bind.annotation.RestController;
import org.springframework.web.servlet.ModelAndView;

import com.apress.spring.repository.JournalRepository;

@RestController
public class JournalController {

        private static final String VIEW_INDEX = "index";

        @Autowired
        JournalRepository repo;

        @RequestMapping(value="/", method = RequestMethod.GET)
        public ModelAndView index(ModelAndView modelAndView){
                modelAndView.setViewName(VIEW_INDEX);
                modelAndView.addObject("journal", repo.findAll());
                return modelAndView;
        }
}
```

Listing 8-8 shows you the `JournalController.java` class. Let's examine it:

- **@RestController.** This class is marked with the @RestController annotation, making it available as a web controller for the DispatcherServlet.

- **@RequestMapping.** This annotation is used over the index method that will become the request handler for all incoming requests at the root level. The index method has a modelAndView parameter that will be instantiated in the request. Inside the method, the modelAndView instance will set the view (index.html) and the model (journal) with all the elements found by calling the repo.findAll method. The index method will return the modelAndView instance.

- **@Autowired.** The JournalRepository interface will be instantiated and used here by the index method. Remember that this class extends from the JpaRepository, which means that it will generate all the CRUD and search logic needed.

Before you run the application, make sure you have the same files as in Chapter 2. You need the following:

- src/main/resources/static/css folder with all the CSS files (bootstrap-glyphicons.css, bootstrap.min.css, and style.css)

- src/main/resources/templates folder with the index.html file, which is shown in Listing 8-9

Listing 8-9. src/main/resources/templates/index.html

```
<!doctype html>
<html lang="en-US" xmlns:th="http://www.thymeleaf.org">
<head>
  <meta charset="utf-8"></meta>
  <meta http-equiv="Content-Type" content="text/html"></meta>
  <title>Spring Boot Journal</title>
  <link rel="stylesheet" type="text/css" media="all" href="css/bootstrap.min.css"></link>
  <link rel="stylesheet" type="text/css" media="all" href="css/bootstrap-glyphicons.css">
  </link>
  <link rel="stylesheet" type="text/css" media="all" href="css/styles.css"></link>
</head>

<body>
<div class="container">
  <h1>Spring Boot Journal</h1>
  <ul class="timeline">
   <div th:each="entry,status : ${journal}">
    <li th:attr="class=${status.odd}?'timeline-inverted':''">
      <div class="tl-circ"></div>
      <div class="timeline-panel">
        <div class="tl-heading">
          <h4><span th:text="${entry.title}">TITLE</span></h4>
          <p><small class="text-muted"><i class="glyphicon glyphicon-time"></i>
          <span th:text="${entry.createdAsShort}">CREATED</span></small></p>
        </div>
        <div class="tl-body">
          <p><span th:text="${entry.summary}">SUMMARY</span></p>
        </div>
```

```
        </div>
      </li>
    </div>
  </ul>
</div>
</body>
</html>
```

Listing 8-9 shows you the index.html file. Remember that this file is using the Thymeleaf view engine. If you want to know more about the Thymeleaf engine, visit http://www.thymeleaf.org/.

Now, if you rerun your application and point to the browser to http://localhost:8080, you will see something similar to Figure 8-4.

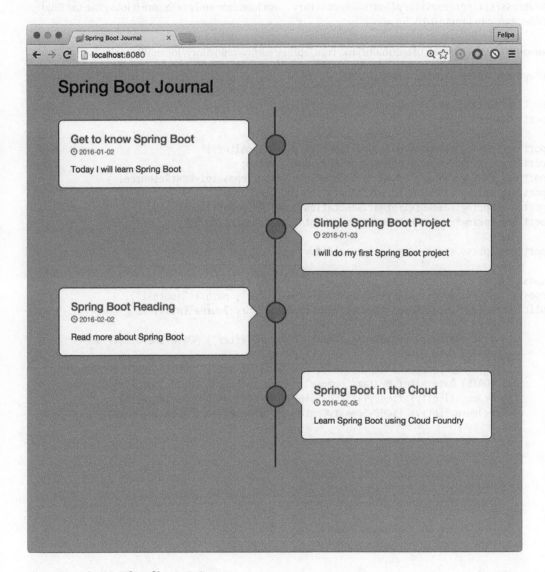

Figure 8-4. *http://localhost:8080*

Figure 8-4 shows the result of having a web controller. You can still point to http://localhost:8080/journalEntries and see the HAL+JSON response, but I think it would be nice if you had a separate path for your REST calls, something like /api path. That's one of the benefits of using Spring Boot; it's so configurable. Go to the src/main/resources/application.properties file and add the following line to the end:

```
spring.data.rest.basePath=/api
```

If you are running you application, terminate it by pressing Ctrl+C. Then you can rerun your application. You should now have the HAL+JSON response in the http://localhost:8080/api URL. If you want to add more entries, you need to post to the http://localhost:8080/api/journalEntries URL.

After testing the new endpoint, you can stop your application.

That journalEntries path is too long, but it can be modified!. Let's change it. Go to the src/main/java/com/apress/spring/repository/JournalRepository.java interface and make sure it looks like the final version shown in Listing 8-10.

Listing 8-10. Final Version of src/main/java/com/apress/spring/repository/JournalRepository.java

```java
package com.apress.spring.repository;

import java.util.Date;
import java.util.List;

import org.springframework.data.jpa.repository.JpaRepository;
import org.springframework.data.repository.query.Param;
import org.springframework.data.rest.core.annotation.RepositoryRestResource;
import org.springframework.format.annotation.DateTimeFormat;
import org.springframework.format.annotation.DateTimeFormat.ISO;
import org.springframework.transaction.annotation.Transactional;

import com.apress.spring.domain.JournalEntry;

@Transactional
@RepositoryRestResource(collectionResourceRel = "entry", path = "journal")
public interface JournalRepository extends JpaRepository<JournalEntry, Long> {

        List<JournalEntry> findByCreatedAfter(@Param("after") @DateTimeFormat(iso =
        ISO.DATE) Date date);
        List<JournalEntry> findByCreatedBetween(@Param("after") @DateTimeFormat(iso =
        ISO.DATE) Date after,@Param("before") @DateTimeFormat(iso = ISO.DATE) Date before);
        List<JournalEntry> findByTitleContaining(@Param("word") String word);
        List<JournalEntry> findBySummaryContaining(@Param("word") String word);

}
```

Listing 8-10 shows you the final version of the JournalRepository interface. Two annotations were added. @Transactional makes all the REST calls transactional, which protects the data where there are concurrent calls to the REST API. The @RepositoryRestResource annotation modifies the path to journal and, instead of grabbing the plural names, it will call entry.

If you rerun your application, you will have a better URL to get to the REST API: http://localhost:8080/api/journal. Feel free to inspect the URL and search. It will now be the http://localhost:8080/api/journal/search URL.

How about that! You have a very cool journal application! Did you notice that you didn't do anything in the web controller? In the past, you needed to create the save, delete, find, and update methods. But not any more; you have spring-data-rest and very good solution for a web application.

Now, you can stop your application by pressing Ctrl+C.

Playing with the HAL Browser

One of the newest features of spring-data-rest and the web components is that you can install a HAL browser that works out of the box. The only thing you need to do is add the following dependency to your pom.xml file.

```
<dependency>
        <groupId>org.springframework.data</groupId>
        <artifactId>spring-data-rest-hal-browser</artifactId>
</dependency>
```

If you rerun your application, go to the http://localhost:8080/api/browser. You should get something similar to Figure 8-5.

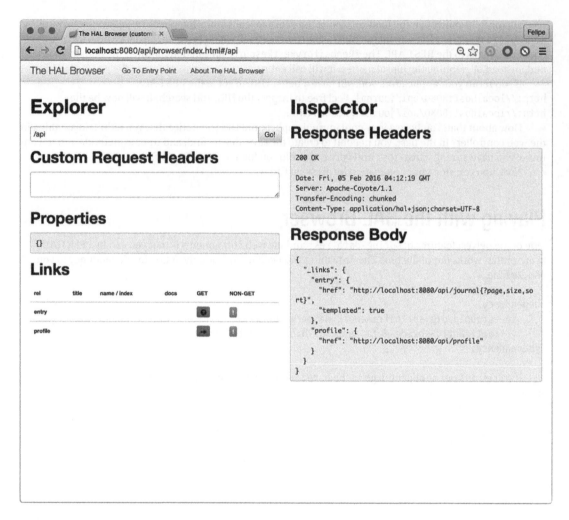

Figure 8-5. `http://localhost:8080/api/browser`

Figure 8-5 shows you the HAL browser, which is a very nice tool to inspect your REST API. Add /api/journal to the Explorer field and click the Go button. You should see all the journal entries. See Figure 8-6.

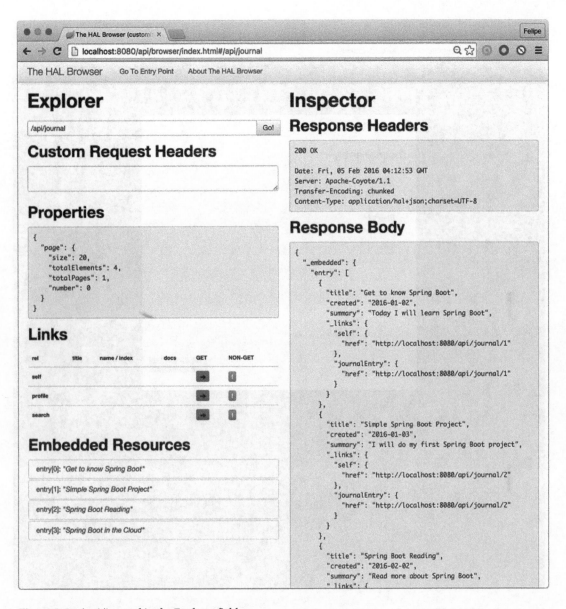

Figure 8-6. */api/journal in the Explorer field*

Figure 8-6 shows you the result of exploring the /api/journal. Inserting data is also easy. Note the Links section in Figure 8-5. Click the yellow icon belonging to the entry caption (in its NON-GET column). This will bring up the window you'll use to input the data. See Figure 8-7.

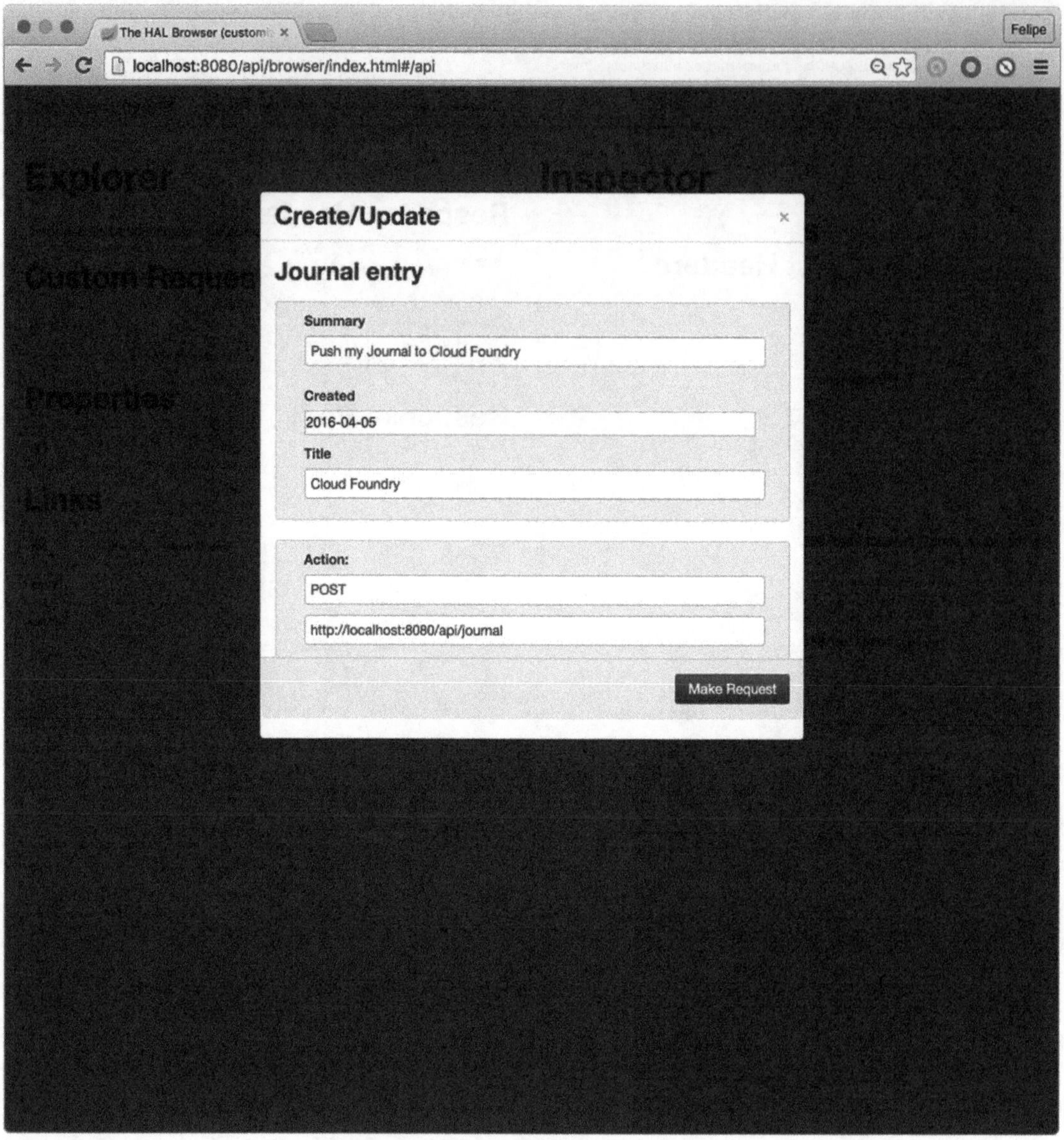

Figure 8-7. *NON-GET action in journal entry form*

Figure 8-7 shows you the journal entry form. As you can see, you have options. Feel free to click the links and go back to your home and see all the data. Nice work! You created a Spring Boot web application with a REST API.

Summary

This chapter showed you how to create a more robust journal application by using `spring-data-rest` and all its features. Earlier chapters showed you how to extend the `AbstractController` class to get the Spring MVC working, but since version 2.5 of the Spring Framework, in the web module (`spring-web-mvc`), you can use annotations instead, such as `@Controller`, `@RestController`, `@RequestMapping`, `@ResponseBody`, and so on.

It's important to note that Spring Boot simplifies web development by removing all XML (Spring app context and `web.xml`) configuration files.

The next chapter discusses how to use security, and of course you are going to learn how to secure your journal application.

CHAPTER 9

Security with Spring Boot

This chapter shows you how to use security in your Spring Boot applications in order to secure your web application. You learn everything from using basic security to using OAuth. Security has become a primary and important factor for desktop, web, and mobile applications in the last decade. But security is a little hard to implement because you need to think about everything—cross-site scripting, authorization, and authentication, secure sessions, identification, encryption, and lot more. There is still a lot to do just to implement simple security in your applications.

The Spring security team has being working hard to make it easier for developers to bring security to their applications, from securing service methods to entire web applications. Spring security is centered around `AuthenticationProvider` and specialized `UserDetailsService`; it also provides integration with identity provider systems, such as LDAP, Active Directory, Kerberos, PAM, AOuth, and so on. You are going to see and review a few of them in the examples in this chapter.

Simple Security for Spring Boot

The starter pom you need is `spring-boot-starter-security`, as you probably knew. The examples in this chapter are based on Chapter 8's examples. Let's start by creating the project. Open a terminal window and execute the following commands:

```
$ mkdir spring-boot-journal-secure
$ cd spring-boot-journal-secure
$ spring init -d=web,thymeleaf,data-jpa,data-rest,mysql,security -g=com.apress.spring
-a=spring-boot-journal-secure --package-name=com.apress.spring -name=spring-boot-journal-
secure -x
```

Start by reviewing the pom.xml. See Listing 9-1.

Listing 9-1. pom.xml

```xml
<?xml version="1.0" encoding="UTF-8"?>
<project xmlns="http://maven.apache.org/POM/4.0.0" xmlns:xsi="http://www.w3.org/2001/
XMLSchema-instance"
        xsi:schemaLocation="http://maven.apache.org/POM/4.0.0 http://maven.apache.org/xsd/
        maven-4.0.0.xsd">
        <modelVersion>4.0.0</modelVersion>

        <groupId>com.apress.spring</groupId>
        <artifactId>spring-boot-journal-secure</artifactId>
```

© Felipe Gutierrez 2016
F. Gutierrez, *Pro Spring Boot*, DOI 10.1007/978-1-4842-1431-2_9

```
<version>0.0.1-SNAPSHOT</version>
<packaging>jar</packaging>

<name>spring-boot-journal-secure</name>
<description>Demo project for Spring Boot</description>

<parent>
        <groupId>org.springframework.boot</groupId>
        <artifactId>spring-boot-starter-parent</artifactId>
        <version>1.3.2.RELEASE</version>
        <relativePath/> <!-- lookup parent from repository -->
</parent>

<properties>
        <project.build.sourceEncoding>UTF-8</project.build.sourceEncoding>
        <java.version>1.8</java.version>
</properties>

<dependencies>
        <dependency>
                <groupId>org.springframework.boot</groupId>
                <artifactId>spring-boot-starter-data-jpa</artifactId>
        </dependency>
        <dependency>
                <groupId>org.springframework.boot</groupId>
                <artifactId>spring-boot-starter-data-rest</artifactId>
        </dependency>

        <dependency>
                <groupId>org.springframework.boot</groupId>
                <artifactId>spring-boot-starter-security</artifactId>
        </dependency>

        <dependency>
                <groupId>org.springframework.boot</groupId>
                <artifactId>spring-boot-starter-thymeleaf</artifactId>
        </dependency>
        <dependency>
                <groupId>org.springframework.boot</groupId>
                <artifactId>spring-boot-starter-web</artifactId>
        </dependency>
        <dependency>
                <groupId>mysql</groupId>
                <artifactId>mysql-connector-java</artifactId>
        </dependency>
        <dependency>
                <groupId>org.springframework.boot</groupId>
                <artifactId>spring-boot-starter-test</artifactId>
                <scope>test</scope>
        </dependency>
</dependencies>
```

```
    <build>
        <plugins>
            <plugin>
                <groupId>org.springframework.boot</groupId>
                <artifactId>spring-boot-maven-plugin</artifactId>
            </plugin>
        </plugins>
    </build>
</project>
```

Listing 9-1 shows the pom.xml, and the new addition is spring-boot-starter-security. Remember, because this app is the same one as in the previous chapter (the journal app), you need still the mysql-connector-java dependency driver.

Next, copy all the journal classes (src/main/java) and all the web, SQL, and property files (src/main/resources) from the previous chapter; you should end up with something similar to Figure 9-1.

```
.
├── mvnw
├── mvnw.cmd
├── pom.xml
└── src
    ├── main
    │   ├── java
    │   │   └── com
    │   │       └── apress
    │   │           └── spring
    │   │               ├── SpringBootJournalSecureApplication.java
    │   │               ├── domain
    │   │               │   └── JournalEntry.java
    │   │               ├── repository
    │   │               │   └── JournalRepository.java
    │   │               ├── utils
    │   │               │   └── JsonDateSerializer.java
    │   │               └── web
    │   │                   └── JournalController.java
    │   └── resources
    │       ├── application.properties
    │       ├── data.sql
    │       ├── static
    │       │   └── css
    │       │       ├── bootstrap-glyphicons.css
    │       │       ├── bootstrap.min.css
    │       │       └── styles.css
    │       └── templates
    │           └── index.html
    └── test
        └── java
            └── com
                └── apress
                    └── spring
                        └── SpringBootJournalSecureApplicationTests.java

19 directories, 15 files
```

Figure 9-1. *The spring-boot-journal-secure project structure*

Next, let's run it with the usual command:

```
$ ./mvnw spring-boot:run
```

After executing this command, you should be able to see a new line about the
AuthenticationManagerConfiguration class. Something like the following output:

```
...
INFO 29387 --- [] .e.DelegatingFilterProxyRegistrationBean : Mapping filter:
'springSecurityFilterChain' to: [/*]
INFO 29387 --- [] o.s.b.c.e.ServletRegistrationBean        : Mapping servlet:
'dispatcherServlet' to [/]
INFO 29387 --- [] b.a.s.AuthenticationManagerConfiguration :
```

Using default security password: f3f818e9-a36f-48ca-9b44-5ed4b3224384

```
INFO 29387 --- [] o.s.s.web.DefaultSecurityFilterChain     : Creating filter chain:
Ant [pattern='/css/**'], []
INFO 29387 --- [] o.s.s.web.DefaultSecurityFilterChain     : Creating filter chain:
Ant [pattern='/js/**'], []
...
```

In the console, you should see the text: "Using default security password: xxx-xxxx-xxx ..."
with a GUID (Global Unique ID) that you will use to authenticate. If you go to your browser and visit
http://localhost:8080, you should see something similar to Figure 9-2.

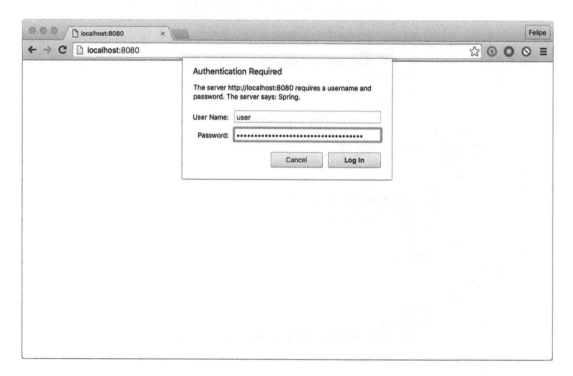

Figure 9-2. *Basic security authentication on* http://localhost:8080

Figure 9-2 shows the basic security window, and of course the fields are going to be empty in the beginning. I've just put the values that you will need to enter. By default, the AuthenticationManager interface implementation has a single username, called user. So, in the User Name box, you enter the value user. The password is the GUID that you saw on the logs—a random password. This example uses the f3f818e9-a36f-48ca-9b44-5ed4b3224384 GUID. This GUID changes every time you run the application.

That's it! That's the easiest and most basic security you can add to your web application, and the only thing you did was add the spring-boot-starter-security pom. When the Spring Boot app starts, the auto-configuration will identify that you have the web and the security dependencies and it will create the basic security authentication. Of course, this is not very useful with production apps.

Security Using the application.properties File

Remember that with Spring Boot you can configure the security of your web app by using the application.properties file. First stop your application by pressing Ctrl+C on your keyboard; then go to src/main/resources/application.properties and add the security section to the end of the file. You'll have something similar to Listing 9-2.

Listing 9-2. src/main/resources/application.properties

```
spring.datasource.url = jdbc:mysql://localhost:3306/journal
spring.datasource.username = springboot
spring.datasource.password = springboot
spring.datasource.testWhileIdle = true
spring.datasource.validationQuery = SELECT 1

spring.jpa.show-sql = true
spring.jpa.hibernate.ddl-auto = create-drop
spring.jpa.hibernate.naming-strategy = org.hibernate.cfg.ImprovedNamingStrategy
spring.jpa.properties.hibernate.dialect = org.hibernate.dialect.MySQL5Dialect

spring.data.rest.basePath=/api

# Security
security.user.name = springboot
security.user.password = isawesome
```

Listing 9-2 shows the application.properties file and all its sections. At the very end of the file is the security section where you can specify the username and password for the basic authentication. Now if you run the journal app with the command:

```
$ ./mvnw spring-boot:run
```

And then go to the http://localhost:8080 URL, you can test your new username (springboot) and password (isawesome) and see the result. You can use cURL to access your /api and make sure it's also secured with:

```
$ curl -i http://springboot:isawesome@localhost:8080/api
HTTP/1.1 200 OK
Server: Apache-Coyote/1.1
X-Content-Type-Options: nosniff
X-XSS-Protection: 1; mode=block
Cache-Control: no-cache, no-store, max-age=0, must-revalidate
```

```
Pragma: no-cache
Expires: 0
X-Frame-Options: DENY
Strict-Transport-Security: max-age=31536000 ; includeSubDomains
Content-Type: application/hal+json;charset=UTF-8
Transfer-Encoding: chunked
Date: Sat, 06 Feb 2016 23:00:29 GMT

{
  "_links" : {
    "entry" : {
      "href" : "http://localhost:8080/api/journal{?page,size,sort}",
      "templated" : true
    },
    "profile" : {
      "href" : "http://localhost:8080/api/profile"
    }
  }
}
```

Using this command, you can see that passing the username:password gives you access to the REST API. You can stop your application now.

In-Memory Security

Using the application.properties file isn't a real solution. Let's see how you can use in-memory security. You are going to create a new src/main/java/com/apress/spring/config/InMemorySecurityConfiguration.java file, as shown in Listing 9-3.

Listing 9-3. src/main/java/com/apress/spring/config/InMemorySecurityConfiguration.java

```java
package com.apress.spring.config;

import org.springframework.beans.factory.annotation.Autowired;
import org.springframework.context.annotation.Configuration;
import org.springframework.security.config.annotation.authentication.builders.
AuthenticationManagerBuilder;
import org.springframework.security.config.annotation.authentication.configuration.
EnableGlobalAuthentication;

@Configuration
@EnableGlobalAuthentication
public class InMemorySecurityConfiguration {

    @Autowired
    public void configureGlobal(AuthenticationManagerBuilder auth) throws Exception {
        auth.inMemoryAuthentication().withUser("user").password("password").
        roles("USER")
                        .and().withUser("admin").password("password").
                        roles("USER", "ADMIN");
    }
}
```

Listing 9-3 shows the InMemorySecurityConfiguration.java class. Let's dig into it:

- @Configuration. This annotation tells the Spring Boot to use it as part of the configuration; it's similar to using XML files.

- @EnableGlobalAuthentication. This annotation marks the class and configures all the necessary beans to activate the security on the application; it signals that the annotated class can be used to configure a global instance of the AuthenticationManagerBuilder.

- @Autowired/configureGlobal(AuthenticationManagerBuilder auth). This method is called to auto-wire the AuthenticationManagerBuilder. The AuthenticationManagerBuilder allows you to easily build your authentication by adding UserDetailsService and the authentication providers. You are going to learn more about the options in the following sections. In this case, it will use in-memory because it's calling the inMemoryAuthentication method and setting up two users with their passwords and roles.

Before you run the application, comment out the security.user.name and security.user.password properties from the src/main/resources/application.properties file. Just add a # sign in front of them, like this:

```
#security.user.name=springboot
#security.user.password=isawesome
```

Now you can run the journal app as usual:

```
$ ./mvnw spring-boot:run
```

After execute this command, go to http://localhost:8080. You should be prompted for the username and password. Use the ones in the code—for example, user as username and password as password. After testing this code, you can stop your application.

Security Using a Database

Using the in-memory isn't a real solution either, but there are alternatives. How about using a database? Normally this is one of the most common approaches to saving users. Let's see what you need to modify in order to use a database as a security mechanism.

You are using MySQL as a database engine, so let's continue using that. First, you are going to create a security configuration. Create the src/main/java/apress/spring/config/JdbcSecurityConfiguration.java file. See Listing 9-4.

Listing 9-4. src/main/java/apress/spring/config/JdbcSecurityConfiguration.java

```java
package com.apress.spring.config;

import java.sql.ResultSet;

import org.springframework.beans.factory.annotation.Autowired;
import org.springframework.context.annotation.Bean;
import org.springframework.context.annotation.Configuration;
import org.springframework.jdbc.core.JdbcTemplate;
import org.springframework.jdbc.core.RowMapper;
```

```
import org.springframework.security.config.annotation.authentication.builders.
AuthenticationManagerBuilder;
import org.springframework.security.config.annotation.authentication.configuration.
EnableGlobalAuthentication;
import org.springframework.security.config.annotation.authentication.configurers.
GlobalAuthenticationConfigurerAdapter;
import org.springframework.security.core.authority.AuthorityUtils;
import org.springframework.security.core.userdetails.User;
import org.springframework.security.core.userdetails.UserDetailsService;

@Configuration
@EnableGlobalAuthentication
public class JdbcSecurityConfiguration extends GlobalAuthenticationConfigurerAdapter{

        @Bean
        public UserDetailsService userDetailsService(JdbcTemplate jdbcTemplate) {
                RowMapper<User> userRowMapper = (ResultSet rs, int i) ->
                    new User(
                        rs.getString("ACCOUNT_NAME"),
                        rs.getString("PASSWORD"),
                        rs.getBoolean("ENABLED"),
                        rs.getBoolean("ENABLED"),
                        rs.getBoolean("ENABLED"),
                        rs.getBoolean("ENABLED"),
                        AuthorityUtils.createAuthorityList("ROLE_USER", "ROLE_ADMIN"));
                return username ->
                jdbcTemplate.queryForObject("SELECT * from ACCOUNT where ACCOUNT_NAME = ?",
                                    userRowMapper, username);
        }

        @Autowired
        private UserDetailsService userDetailsService;

        @Override
        public void init(AuthenticationManagerBuilder auth) throws Exception {
                auth.userDetailsService(this.userDetailsService);
        }
}
```

Listing 9-4 shows the JdbcSecurityConfiguration.java class. Let's examine it:

- @Configuration. The JdbcSecurityConfiguration.java class is marked with the @Configuration, which allows Spring Boot to recognize this class as another configuration file where normally you declare your beans. It's the same as using an XML file.

- @EnableGlobalAuthentication. This annotation marks the class and configures all the necessary beans to activate the security on the application.

- GlobalAuthenticationConfigurerAdapter. The JdbcSecurityConfiguration.java class extends from the GlobalAuthenticationConfigurerAdapter abstract class. This class also implements the SecurityConfigurer interface and exposes an init method that will be overridden in the JdbcSecurityConfiguration.java class.

- init(AuthenticationManagerBuilder). Overrides the
  GlobalAuthenticationConfigurerAdapter init method. In this method, the
  AuthenticationManagerBuilder instance is used to build in-memory, LDAP, or
  JDBC-based authentication by setting up a UserDetailsService instance.

- @Bean/userDetailsService(JdbcTemplate). This method will set up a
  JdbcTemplate instance that will create a new org.springframework.security.
  core.userdetails.User instance after a ResultSet is returned by using
  RowMapper that will match its constructor (User). This User instance accepts the
  username, password, enabled, accountNonExpired, credentialsNonExpired,
  accountNonLocked, and authorities collections as the constructor's parameters.
  How the ResultSet will match the RowMapper? Well, the Spring Security team
  provides a SQL schema that will work by adding the users. Don't worry, as you are
  going to see the SQL schema in just a moment. If you wonder where this is, you can
  go to https://docs.spring.io/spring-security/site/docs/current/reference/
  html/appendix-schema.html.

- @Autowired/userDetailsService. This instance is retrieved from the
  userDetailsService method because it's declared as a bean.

Remember that you have the InMemorySecurityConfiguration class, so this means that only one can
be used, not both. So you can leave it and the JdbcSecurityConfiguration will take precedence and all
the users will be in the MySQL database. Another option is that you can comment out the main annotation
(@Configuration and @EnableGlobalAuthentication) and it will be the same. The best solution is to use
profiles, by using the @Profile annotation and activating the profiles at run time with -Dspring.active.
profiles=memory or whatever name you give to the profile.

Because this is a JDBC security, you need to add the table with its data to the src/main/resources/
schema.sql file. Here it will be for the table description and for the src/main/resources/data.sql.
See Listings 9-5 and 9-6.

Listing 9-5. src/main/resources/schema.sql

```
-- SECURITY: USER ACCOUNT
DROP TABLE IF EXISTS account;
CREATE TABLE account ( ACCOUNT_NAME VARCHAR(255) NOT NULL,
                       PASSWORD VARCHAR(255 ) NOT NULL,
                       ID SERIAL,
                       ENABLED BOOL DEFAULT true) ;

-- JOURNAL TABLE: ENTRY
DROP TABLE IF EXISTS entry;
CREATE TABLE entry (
  ID BIGINT(20) NOT NULL AUTO_INCREMENT,
  CREATED DATETIME DEFAULT NULL,
  SUMMARY VARCHAR(255) DEFAULT NULL,
  TITLE VARCHAR(255) DEFAULT NULL,
  PRIMARY KEY (ID)
);
```

Listing 9-5 shows the schema.sql, which contains the mandatory account table for the security.
This table is mandatory and is an adaptation from the Spring Security documents: https://docs.spring.
io/spring-security/site/docs/current/reference/html/appendix-schema.html. Also notice that the

journal table entry is defined, because when you create schema.sql the property (spring.jpa.hibernate. ddl-auto = create-drop) from the application.properties file will drop the table recently created. That means that you need to comment out the property spring.jpa.hibernate.ddl-auto=create-drop (from the application.properties) so it won't affect the behavior. If you leave this property in, you'll get something like: "Can't find journal.entry table error".

Listing 9-6. src/main/resources/data.sql

```
-- USERS IN JOURNAL
INSERT INTO ACCOUNT(account_name , password) VALUES('springboot', 'isawesome');
INSERT INTO ACCOUNT(account_name , password) VALUES('springsecurity', 'isawesometoo');

-- JOURNAL DATA
INSERT INTO ENTRY(title,summary,created) VALUES('Get to know Spring Boot','Today I will
learn Spring Boot','2016-01-02 00:00:00.00');
INSERT INTO ENTRY(title,summary,created) VALUES('Simple Spring Boot Project','I will do my
first Spring Boot project','2016-01-03 00:00:00.00');
INSERT INTO ENTRY(title,summary,created) VALUES('Spring Boot Reading','Read more about
Spring Boot','2016-02-02 00:00:00.00');
INSERT INTO ENTRY(title,summary,created) VALUES('Spring Boot in the Cloud','Learn Spring
Boot using Cloud Foundry','2016-02-05 00:00:00.00');
```

Listing 9-6 shows data.sql. You will add the two account users and the journal data to this file. Now you are ready to run the journal app. Remember before you run it to comment out the spring.jpa. hibernate.ddl-auto = create-drop property from the application.properties.

To run it, use the normal command:

```
$ ./mvnw spring-boot:run
```

After executing the command, you can go to http://localhost:8080 and use the springsecurity username and the isawesometoo password. That's it; it's very easy to implement JDBC security.

Now stop your application. Let's continue.

Securing Resources

Now you know how to secure the entire journal app, but sometimes you will required to secure just some parts of your application. In this section you will secure the /api endpoint, because you are exposing POST, PUT, and DELETE actions and you don't want anybody to access it without credentials.

You are going to create the src/main/java/com/apress/spring/config/ ResourceSecurityConfiguration.java class. This class will have all that you need for securing your resources. See Listing 9-7 (version 1).

Listing 9-7. src/main/java/com/apress/spring/config/ResourceSecurityConfiguration.java (Version 1)

```java
package com.apress.spring.config;

import org.springframework.context.annotation.Configuration;
import org.springframework.security.config.annotation.authentication.configuration.
EnableGlobalAuthentication;
import org.springframework.security.config.annotation.web.builders.HttpSecurity;
import org.springframework.security.config.annotation.web.configuration.
WebSecurityConfigurerAdapter;
```

```
@Configuration
@EnableGlobalAuthentication
public class ResourceSecurityConfiguration extends WebSecurityConfigurerAdapter{

    @Override
    protected void configure(HttpSecurity http) throws Exception {
        http.authorizeRequests()
            .antMatchers("/").permitAll()
            .antMatchers("/api/**").authenticated()
            .and()
            .httpBasic();

    }

}
```

Listing 9-7 shows the ResourceSecurityConfiguration class. Let's review it:

- **@Configuration.** This annotation is picked up by Spring as part of the context configuration. Here is where you declare beans or in this case configure part of the security.

- **WebSecurityConfigurerAdapter.** There are different ways to configure the resources of your web application and extending from the abstract WebSecurityConfigurerAdapter class is one of them. One of the common patterns is to override the configure(HttpSecurity) and configure(AuthenticationManagerBuilder) methods, but because you have the init(AuthenticationManagerBuilder) method overridden from the GlobalAuthenticationConfigurerAdapter of the JdbcSecurityConfiguration class, it's not necessary to do it here. That's why the only method you need to override is the one with the HttpSecurity instance as a parameter.

- **configure(HttpSecurity).** This method is overridden from the abstract class WebSecurityConfigurerAdapter, and here is where you specify which resources to secure. In this case, the HttpSecurity instance class allows you to configure web-based security for specific HTTP requests. By default it will be applied to all requests, but you can restrict it by using its fluent API. In the example, you get into the root (http://localhost:8080) of your web app with the .antMatchers("/").permitAll() call and restrict the endpoint /api with .antMatchers("/api/**").authenticated() call by making this restricting as HttpBasicConfigurer security.

Let's test it. Run you journal app by executing the following command:

```
$ ./mvnw spring-boot:run
```

If you go to your browser and point to the http://localhost:8080 URL, you will see the journal entries right away; you don't have to enter the username and password anymore. Now, if you go to the http://localhost:8080/api URL, you will be prompted for the username and password! Excellent—you have secured your REST API endpoints.

Let's test the same app using the command line. Open another terminal windows and execute the following command:

```
$ curl -i http://localhost:8080/api
HTTP/1.1 401 Unauthorized
Server: Apache-Coyote/1.1
X-Content-Type-Options: nosniff
X-XSS-Protection: 1; mode=block
Cache-Control: no-cache, no-store, max-age=0, must-revalidate
Pragma: no-cache
Expires: 0
X-Frame-Options: DENY
Set-Cookie: JSESSIONID=CEE76CAE303F0A7819357DBF5CD017D7; Path=/; HttpOnly
WWW-Authenticate: Basic realm="Realm"
Content-Type: application/json;charset=UTF-8
Transfer-Encoding: chunked
Date: Tue, 09 Feb 2016 17:32:20 GMT

{"timestamp":1455039140053,"status":401,"error":"Unauthorized","message":"Full
authentication is required to access this resource","path":"/api"}
```

You will see that calling directly to the /api endpoint gives you the JSON message with some errors, like the status 401 and the unauthorized errors. This means that you need to pass the username and password. You can execute either of these two commands:

```
$ curl -i http://springboot:isawesome@localhost:8080/api
```

Or:

```
$ curl -i -u springboot:isawesome http://localhost:8080/api
HTTP/1.1 200 OK
Server: Apache-Coyote/1.1
X-Content-Type-Options: nosniff
X-XSS-Protection: 1; mode=block
Cache-Control: no-cache, no-store, max-age=0, must-revalidate
Pragma: no-cache
Expires: 0
X-Frame-Options: DENY
Set-Cookie: JSESSIONID=2E8653866CBBBBB7070A715E404A4C72; Path=/; HttpOnly
Content-Type: application/hal+json;charset=UTF-8
Transfer-Encoding: chunked
Date: Tue, 09 Feb 2016 17:36:23 GMT

{
  "_links" : {
    "entry" : {
      "href" : "http://localhost:8080/api/journal{?page,size,sort}",
      "templated" : true
    },
```

```
    "profile" : {
      "href" : "http://localhost:8080/api/profile"
    }
  }
}
```

Both commands are passing the username and password, so now you have full access to the /api endpoint. Of course, this offers a way to secure resources, but users are used to seeing a login form to access some restricted area. Remember that the HttpSecurity class has a fluent API (a builder), so it already has an integrated login form! Next, stop the app so you can modify some code. See Listing 9-8, which is version 2 of the ResourceSecurityConfiguration.java class.

Listing 9-8. src/main/java/com/apress/spring/config/ResourceSecurityConfiguration.java (Version 2)

```
package com.apress.spring.config;

import org.springframework.context.annotation.Configuration;
import org.springframework.security.config.annotation.web.builders.HttpSecurity;
import org.springframework.security.config.annotation.web.configuration.
WebSecurityConfigurerAdapter;

@Configuration
public class ResourceSecurityConfiguration extends WebSecurityConfigurerAdapter{

        @Override
        protected void configure(HttpSecurity http) throws Exception {
                http.authorizeRequests()
                    .antMatchers("/").permitAll()
                    .antMatchers("/api/**").authenticated()
                    .and()
                    .formLogin();
        }

}
```

Listing 9-8 shows version 2 of the ResourceSecurityConfiguration.java class. Let's examine it:

- and().formLogin(). This is the only change. You removed the and().httpBasic() call and replaced it with the and().formLogin() call. When you try to access the /api endpoint it will redirect you to a basic web form (http://localhost:8080/login). After entering the username and password, you will be redirected to the /api endpoint.

You can run your application as usual. You can go to http://localhost:8080/api, where you will see something similar to Figure 9-3.

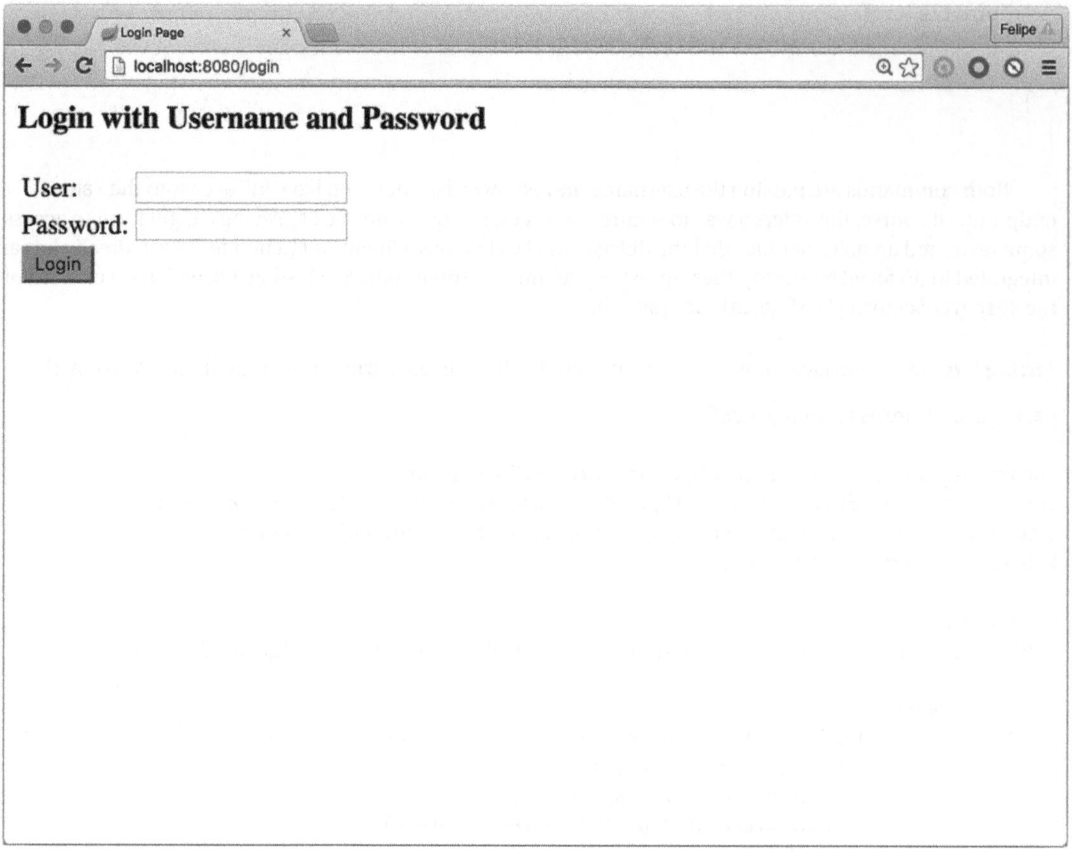

Figure 9-3. `http://localhost:8080/api` ➤ *redirects to* ➤ `http://localhost:8080/login url`

Figure 9-3 shows the result of accessing the `http://localhost:8080/api`. It will redirect to the `http://localhost:8080/login` page. After you provide the correct credentials, it will redirect to the URL you were looking for, which is `http://localhost:8080/api`, because now you are authenticated. As you can see, it's very easy to add a login form. Now you can stop your application.

Maybe you are wondering whether you can have custom login and logout forms. Yes, you can, and it's very easy to implement them. See Listing 9-9, which shows version 3 of the `ResourceSecurityConfiguration.java` class.

Listing 9-9. src/main/java/com/apress/spring/config/ResourceSecurityConfiguration.java (Version 3)

```
package com.apress.spring.config;

import org.springframework.context.annotation.Configuration;
import org.springframework.security.config.annotation.web.builders.HttpSecurity;
import org.springframework.security.config.annotation.web.configuration.
WebSecurityConfigurerAdapter;
```

```
@Configuration
public class ResourceSecurityConfiguration extends WebSecurityConfigurerAdapter{

        @Override
        protected void configure(HttpSecurity http) throws Exception {
                http.authorizeRequests()
                    .antMatchers("/").permitAll()
                    .antMatchers("/api/**").authenticated()
                    .and()
                    .formLogin().loginPage("/login").permitAll()
                    .and()
                    .logout().permitAll();

        }

}
```

Listing 9-9 shows version 3 of the ResourceSecurityConfiguration.java class. Let's examine it:

- formLogin().loginPage("/login").permitAll(). This call uses a login page. This page is your custom page. You are going to see its contents in a few more lines.

- logout().permitAll(). This call has a logout endpoint that you can access to clear all credentials.

Both lines, for the login and logout, end with the permitAll() method call. This makes them accessible with any authorization, which is what you want. You don't want to secure the login and logout endpoint, right?

Next, let's create the src/main/resources/templates/login.html page. See Listing 9-10.

Listing 9-10. src/main/resources/templates/login.html

```html
<!DOCTYPE html>
<html xmlns:th="http://www.thymeleaf.org">
<head>
        <title>Login</title>
        <link rel="stylesheet" type="text/css" media="all" href="css/bootstrap.min.css">
        </link>
        <link rel="stylesheet" type="text/css" media="all" href="css/bootstrap-glyphicons.
        css"></link>
        <link rel="stylesheet" type="text/css" media="all" href="css/styles.css"></link>
</head>
<body>
    <div class="container">
        <div class="content">
            <p th:if="${param.logout}" class="alert">You have been logged out</p>
            <p th:if="${param.error}" class="alert alert-error">There was an error, please
            try again</p>
            <h2>Login to Spring Boot Journal</h2>
            <form name="form" th:action="@{/login}" action="/login" method="POST">
                <input type="text" name="username" value="" placeholder="Username" />
                <input type="password" name="password" placeholder="Password" />
```

```
                <input type="submit" id="login" value="Login" class="btn btn-primary" />
            </form>
        </div>
    </div>
</body>
</html>
```

Listing 9-10 shows the login.html page. You're using the Thymeleaf to get access to the correct post endpoint (with the th:action and th:if) and using some parameters, but let's consider it in more detail:

- th:if="${param.logout}" / th:if="${param.error}". These are Thymeleaf conditionals, and they are asking for the parameter logout and error. So if the endpoint is /login?logout it will trigger the /logout endpoint (clearing all credentials) and it will show the message: You have been logged out. If the endpoint is /login?error it will display the message: There was an error, please try again. The error will be triggered when you enter a bad password or username.

- th:action="@{/login}" / method="POST" will post the username and password to the /login endpoint. If it succeeds, it will redirect to the /api endpoint; if not, it will trigger an error message.

- <input>. The input tags for the username and password must be named username and password. This is mandatory, but you can override them by providing the parameter names in the UsernamePasswordAuthenticationFilter class.

To activate the /logout, the protected endpoint is the /api and the response is always a HAL+JSON, so you can click a button to log out from the main page, the index.html page. See Listing 9-11.

Listing 9-11. src/main/resources/templates/index.html (Version 2)

```
<!doctype html>
<html lang="en-US" xmlns:th="http://www.thymeleaf.org" xmlns:sec="http://www.thymeleaf.org/
extras/spring-security">
<head>
  <meta charset="utf-8"></meta>
  <meta http-equiv="Content-Type" content="text/html"></meta>
  <title>Spring Boot Journal</title>
  <link rel="stylesheet" type="text/css" media="all" href="css/bootstrap.min.css"></link>
  <link rel="stylesheet" type="text/css" media="all" href="css/bootstrap-glyphicons.css">
  </link>
  <link rel="stylesheet" type="text/css" media="all" href="css/styles.css"></link>
</head>

<body>
<div class="container">
  <h1>Spring Boot Journal</h1>
  <p sec:authorize="isAuthenticated()">
        <form th:action="@{/logout}" method="post">
            <input type="submit" value="Sign Out"/>
        </form>
  </p>
  <ul class="timeline">
   <div th:each="entry,status : ${journal}">
```

```
        <li th:attr="class=${status.odd}?'timeline-inverted':''">
          <div class="tl-circ"></div>
          <div class="timeline-panel">
            <div class="tl-heading">
              <h4><span th:text="${entry.title}">TITLE</span></h4>
              <p><small class="text-muted">
                    <i class="glyphicon glyphicon-time"></i>
                    <span th:text="${entry.createdAsShort}">CREATED</span>
                    </small></p>
            </div>
            <div class="tl-body">
              <p><span th:text="${entry.summary}">SUMMARY</span></p>
            </div>
          </div>
        </li>
      </div>
    </ul>
  </div>
</body>
</html>
```

Listing 9-11 shows version 2 of the index.html page, but what is different from version 1? Let's examine it:

- xmlns:sec. There is a new namespace, xmlns:sec, that points to the Thymeleaf extras and the Spring security tags/attributes. This means that you are going to use this namespace for something.

- sec:authorized. This attribute is part of the Thymeleaf library and it will execute the isAuthenticated() method. This method is a global method of the main web security, so this attribute knows how to access the global security and execute the method. If the current user is authenticated, it will show a small form that contains the post to the /logout endpoint.

- th:action="@{/logout}" method="post". Here the endpoint is the /logout and *must* be a POST in order to work. If the user is authenticated the Sign Out button will appear. If you click it, it will go to the /logout endpoint (clearing all credentials) and will redirect to the /login?logout endpoint automatically.

You are almost there! Don't run your journal app yet! Are you missing something? Yes, there are two things to do. First you need to modify your web JournalController. In the login.html you declared the /login, and the ResourceSecurityConfiguration is also declaring the /login endpoint. So, right now the controller doesn't know where to locate the /login endpoint. See Listing 9-12.

Listing 9-12. src/main/java/com/apress/spring/web/JournalController.java

```java
package com.apress.spring.web;

import org.springframework.beans.factory.annotation.Autowired;
import org.springframework.web.bind.annotation.RequestMapping;
import org.springframework.web.bind.annotation.RequestMethod;
import org.springframework.web.bind.annotation.RestController;
import org.springframework.web.servlet.ModelAndView;
```

```
import com.apress.spring.repository.JournalRepository;

@RestController
public class JournalController {

        private static final String VIEW_INDEX = "index";
        private static final String VIEW_LOGIN = "login";

        @Autowired
        JournalRepository repo;

        @RequestMapping(value="/", method = RequestMethod.GET)
        public ModelAndView index(ModelAndView modelAndView){
                modelAndView.setViewName(VIEW_INDEX);
                modelAndView.addObject("journal", repo.findAll());
                return modelAndView;
        }

        @RequestMapping(value="/login")
        public ModelAndView login(ModelAndView modelAndView){
                modelAndView.setViewName(VIEW_LOGIN);
                return modelAndView;
        }
}
```

Listing 9-12 shows the web JournalController.java class. Remember that you need to specify the /login endpoint mapping. The login(ModelAndView) method is mapped to the /login endpoint (by using the @RequestMapping annotation). It only sets the view name to login, and remember that it will find the page (login.html) in the templates folder.

If you don't want to modify your web controller, you can create a class, extend from the WebMvcConfigurerAdapter, and override the addViewControllers(ViewControllerRegistry) method. You can then set the controller and view for the login page. For example, instead of creating a new class, you can add this declaration to any class that has the @Configuration annotation. See this code:

```
@Configuration
static protected class LoginController extends WebMvcConfigurerAdapter{
        @Override
        public void addViewControllers(ViewControllerRegistry registry) {
                registry.addViewController("/login").setViewName("login");
        }
}
```

Again, this code is necessary only if you didn't want to modify your web JournalController class. This code will configure the web controller and set the view.

Now the second and last part before you run the journal app. Remember that you used the namespace xmlns:sec from the Thymeleaf library in the index.html page. This is a particular tag library that is not included, so you need to add it to the pom.xml. See Listing 9-13.

Listing 9-13. pom.xml (Version 2, Including spring-security-taglibs and thymeleaf-extras-springsecurity4)

```xml
<?xml version="1.0" encoding="UTF-8"?>
<project xmlns="http://maven.apache.org/POM/4.0.0" xmlns:xsi="http://www.w3.org/2001/
XMLSchema-instance"
        xsi:schemaLocation="http://maven.apache.org/POM/4.0.0 http://maven.apache.org/xsd/
        maven-4.0.0.xsd">
        <modelVersion>4.0.0</modelVersion>

        <groupId>com.apress.spring</groupId>
        <artifactId>spring-boot-journal-secure</artifactId>
        <version>0.0.1-SNAPSHOT</version>
        <packaging>jar</packaging>

        <name>spring-boot-journal-secure</name>
        <description>Demo project for Spring Boot</description>

        <parent>
                <groupId>org.springframework.boot</groupId>
                <artifactId>spring-boot-starter-parent</artifactId>
                <version>1.3.2.RELEASE</version>
                <relativePath /> <!-- lookup parent from repository -->
        </parent>

        <properties>
                <project.build.sourceEncoding>UTF-8</project.build.sourceEncoding>
                <java.version>1.8</java.version>
        </properties>

        <dependencies>
                <dependency>
                        <groupId>org.springframework.boot</groupId>
                        <artifactId>spring-boot-starter-data-jpa</artifactId>
                </dependency>
                <dependency>
                        <groupId>org.springframework.boot</groupId>
                        <artifactId>spring-boot-starter-data-rest</artifactId>
                </dependency>
                <dependency>
                        <groupId>org.springframework.boot</groupId>
                        <artifactId>spring-boot-starter-thymeleaf</artifactId>
                </dependency>
                <dependency>
                        <groupId>org.springframework.boot</groupId>
                        <artifactId>spring-boot-starter-web</artifactId>
                </dependency>

                <!-- SECURITY -->
                <dependency>
                        <groupId>org.springframework.boot</groupId>
                        <artifactId>spring-boot-starter-security</artifactId>
                </dependency>
```

```
        <dependency>
                <groupId>org.springframework.security</groupId>
                <artifactId>spring-security-taglibs</artifactId>
        </dependency>

        <dependency>
                <groupId>org.thymeleaf.extras</groupId>
                <artifactId>thymeleaf-extras-springsecurity4</artifactId>
        </dependency>

        <dependency>
                <groupId>mysql</groupId>
                <artifactId>mysql-connector-java</artifactId>
        </dependency>
        <dependency>
                <groupId>org.springframework.boot</groupId>
                <artifactId>spring-boot-starter-test</artifactId>
                <scope>test</scope>
        </dependency>
    </dependencies>

    <build>
        <plugins>
            <plugin>
                    <groupId>org.springframework.boot</groupId>
                    <artifactId>spring-boot-maven-plugin</artifactId>
            </plugin>
        </plugins>
    </build>
</project>
```

Listing 9-13 shows the new pom.xml. What is the difference from the previous version (Listing 9-1)? You are adding the spring-security-taglibs and thymeleaf-extras-springsecurity4 dependencies, which are necessary for the index.html page.

Now you are ready to run your journal app. As usual, execute the following command:

```
$ ./mvnw spring-boot:run
```

After executing this command, make sure that you don't see the Sign Out button from the main page (http://localhost:8080). Next, go to http://localhost:8080/api; you will see something similar to Figure 9-4.

Figure 9-4. *http://localhost:8080/api ➤ redirects to the http://localhost:8080/login page*

Figure 9-4 shows the custom login.html page. A different look from the default one, don't you think? Now test your credentials and you should see the HAL+JSON result (remember that in Google Chrome you can see the HAL+JSON response better). After logging in and seeing the /api endpoint, you can go to http://localhost:8080 to see that the main page is now showing the Sign Out button. See Figure 9-5.

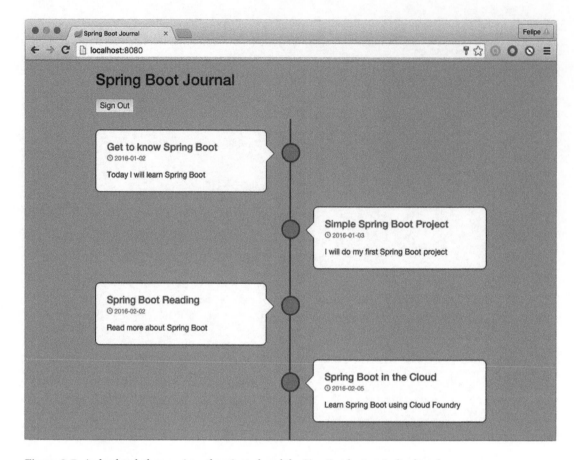

Figure 9-5. *index.html: the user is authenticated and the Sign Out button is displayed*

Figure 9-5 shows the result of the xmlns:sec namespace (the sec:authorize attribute in the <p/> tag), which will call the isAuthenticated() method and then display the button. If you click the button you will be redirected to the /login?logout url. See Figure 9-6.

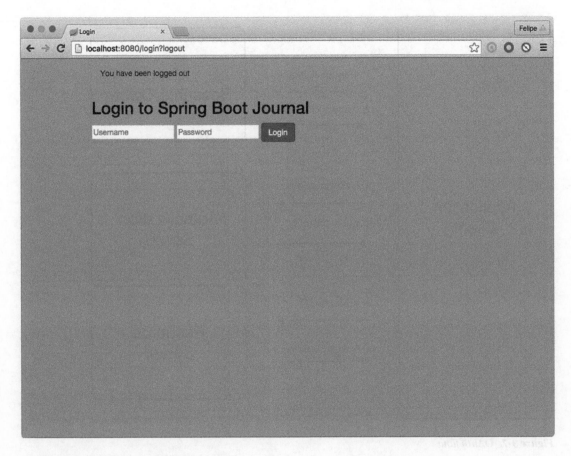

Figure 9-6. *After clicking the Sign Out button*

Figure 9-6 shows the result of clicking the Sign Out button from the main page. You are redirected to the /login?logout page. Remember that the Sign Out button has the /logout as its action and it will clear out all credentials and redirect to the /login page with the ?logout parameter. It will show the message: "You have been logged out".

Wow! Very impressive. Even though there are a few steps involved, setting up security for your resources is very easy with Spring and Spring Boot.

Spring Boot with OAuth2

OAuth2 is an open standard, and it's used by companies like Pivotal, Google, Amazon, Facebook, Twitter, and much more. These companies provide access to services by providing access tokens that are based on credentials (client IDs and secret keys). The best way to describe it is with an image; see Figure 9-7.

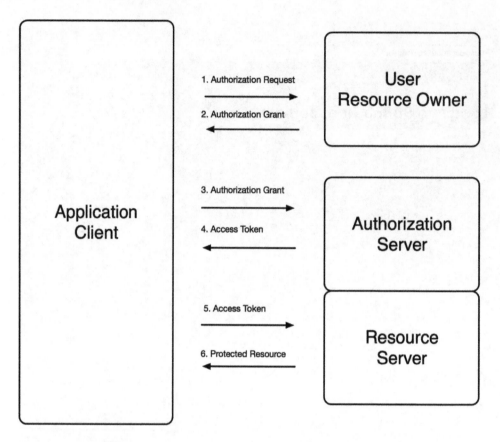

Figure 9-7. *OAuth flow*

Figure 9-7 shows the OAuth flow. The Resource Owner (user) authorizes an application to access the account. This is limited to the scope (read or write) of the authorization granted. Here the Resource Owner will be the journal application because it's the one that will use OAuth as a security mechanism. The Authorization Server verifies the identity of the user and it is in charge of issuing access tokens to the application client. The Resource Server secures the resources and will allow its access only through the access token. The Application Client wants access, so it must be authorized by a username, password, and keys. The authorization must be validated by an API.

You are going to add OAuth to your journal app, and you are going to use only a few classes and the same directory structure. You will no longer use the login page, so some of those classes will be removed. You can start fresh form the command line and execute the following commands:

```
$ mkdir spring-boot-journal-oauth
$ cd spring-boot-journal-oauth
$ spring init -d=web,thymeleaf,data-jpa,data-rest,security -g=com.apress.spring -a=spring-boot-journal-oauth --package-name=com.apress.spring -name=spring-boot-journal-oauth -x
```

The pom.xml file is almost identical to Listing 9-1; the only new dependency is spring-security-oauth2. See Listing 9-14.

Listing 9-14. pom.xml for OAuth

```
<?xml version="1.0" encoding="UTF-8"?>
<project xmlns="http://maven.apache.org/POM/4.0.0" xmlns:xsi="http://www.w3.org/2001/
XMLSchema-instance"
        xsi:schemaLocation="http://maven.apache.org/POM/4.0.0 http://maven.apache.org/xsd/
maven-4.0.0.xsd">
        <modelVersion>4.0.0</modelVersion>

        <groupId>com.apress.spring</groupId>
        <artifactId>spring-boot-journal-oauth</artifactId>
        <version>0.0.1-SNAPSHOT</version>
        <packaging>jar</packaging>

        <name>spring-boot-journal-oauth</name>
        <description>Demo project for Spring Boot</description>

        <parent>
                <groupId>org.springframework.boot</groupId>
                <artifactId>spring-boot-starter-parent</artifactId>
                <version>1.3.2.RELEASE</version>
                <relativePath/> <!-- lookup parent from repository -->
        </parent>

        <properties>
                <project.build.sourceEncoding>UTF-8</project.build.sourceEncoding>
                <java.version>1.8</java.version>
        </properties>

        <dependencies>
                <dependency>
                        <groupId>org.springframework.boot</groupId>
                        <artifactId>spring-boot-starter-data-jpa</artifactId>
                </dependency>
                <dependency>
                        <groupId>org.springframework.boot</groupId>
                        <artifactId>spring-boot-starter-data-rest</artifactId>
                </dependency>
                <dependency>
                        <groupId>org.springframework.boot</groupId>
                        <artifactId>spring-boot-starter-security</artifactId>
                </dependency>
                <dependency>
                        <groupId>org.springframework.boot</groupId>
                        <artifactId>spring-boot-starter-thymeleaf</artifactId>
                </dependency>
                <dependency>
                        <groupId>org.springframework.boot</groupId>
                        <artifactId>spring-boot-starter-web</artifactId>
                </dependency>
```

```
        <dependency>
                <groupId>org.springframework.security.oauth</groupId>
                <artifactId>spring-security-oauth2</artifactId>
        </dependency>

        <dependency>
                <groupId>mysql</groupId>
                <artifactId>mysql-connector-java</artifactId>
        </dependency>
        <dependency>
                <groupId>org.springframework.boot</groupId>
                <artifactId>spring-boot-starter-test</artifactId>
                <scope>test</scope>
        </dependency>
    </dependencies>

    <build>
        <plugins>
            <plugin>
                    <groupId>org.springframework.boot</groupId>
                    <artifactId>spring-boot-maven-plugin</artifactId>
            </plugin>
        </plugins>
    </build>

</project>
```

Listing 9-14 shows the pom.xml file and the new dependency called spring-security-oauth2.
Don't forget your MySQL dependency. Now you need to copy the same structure from the previous project.
See Figure 9-8.

```
.
├── mvnw
├── mvnw.cmd
├── pom.xml
└── src
    ├── main
    │   ├── java
    │   │   └── com
    │   │       └── apress
    │   │           └── spring
    │   │               ├── SpringBootJournalOauthApplication.java
    │   │               ├── config
    │   │               │   ├── JdbcSecurityConfiguration.java
    │   │               │   └── ResourceOAuthSecurityConfiguration.java
    │   │               ├── domain
    │   │               │   └── JournalEntry.java
    │   │               ├── repository
    │   │               │   └── JournalRepository.java
    │   │               ├── utils
    │   │               │   └── JsonDateSerializer.java
    │   │               └── web
    │   │                   └── JournalController.java
    │   └── resources
    │       ├── application.properties
    │       ├── data.sql
    │       ├── schema.sql
    │       ├── static
    │       │   └── css
    │       │       ├── bootstrap-glyphicons.css
    │       │       ├── bootstrap.min.css
    │       │       └── styles.css
    │       └── templates
    │           └── index.html
    └── test
        └── java
            └── com
                └── apress
                    └── spring
                        └── SpringBootJournalOauthApplicationTests.java

20 directories, 18 files
```

Figure 9-8. *The spring-boot-journal-oauth directory structure*

Figure 9-8 shows the final structure of the spring-boot-journal-oauth project. One of the new classes is ResourceOAuthSecurityConfiguration.java. The class defines everything about OAuth; you will see that later in this section.

In the web JournalController.java remove the login method. The end class will look like Listing 9-15.

Listing 9-15. src/main/java/com/apress/spring/web/JournalController.java

```java
package com.apress.spring.web;

import org.springframework.beans.factory.annotation.Autowired;
import org.springframework.web.bind.annotation.RequestMapping;
import org.springframework.web.bind.annotation.RequestMethod;
import org.springframework.web.bind.annotation.RestController;
import org.springframework.web.servlet.ModelAndView;
```

```java
import com.apress.spring.repository.JournalRepository;

@RestController
public class JournalController {

        private static final String VIEW_INDEX = "index";

        @Autowired
        JournalRepository repo;

        @RequestMapping(value="/", method = RequestMethod.GET)
        public ModelAndView index(ModelAndView modelAndView){
                modelAndView.setViewName(VIEW_INDEX);
                modelAndView.addObject("journal", repo.findAll());
                return modelAndView;
        }
}
```

Listing 9-15 shows theJournalController.java class; this is the same as in previous chapters. The index.html file remains the same; you just remove the xmlns:sec namespace. See Listing 9-16.

Listing 9-16. src/main/resources/templates/index.html

```html
<!doctype html>
<html lang="en-US" xmlns:th="http://www.thymeleaf.org">
<head>
  <meta charset="utf-8"></meta>
  <meta http-equiv="Content-Type" content="text/html"></meta>
  <title>Spring Boot Journal</title>
  <link rel="stylesheet" type="text/css" media="all" href="css/bootstrap.min.css"></link>
  <link rel="stylesheet" type="text/css" media="all" href="css/bootstrap-glyphicons.css">
  </link>
  <link rel="stylesheet" type="text/css" media="all" href="css/styles.css"></link>
</head>

<body>
<div class="container">
  <h1>Spring Boot Journal</h1>
  <ul class="timeline">
   <div th:each="entry,status : ${journal}">
    <li th:attr="class=${status.odd}?'timeline-inverted':''">
      <div class="tl-circ"></div>
      <div class="timeline-panel">
        <div class="tl-heading">
          <h4><span th:text="${entry.title}">TITLE</span></h4>
          <p>
                        <small class="text-muted">
                                <i class="glyphicon glyphicon-time"></i>
                                <span th:text="${entry.createdAsShort}">CREATED</span>
                        </small>
                </p>
        </div>
```

```
    <div class="tl-body">
      <p><span th:text="${entry.summary}">SUMMARY</span></p>
    </div>
  </div>
  </li>
  </div>
  </ul>
</div>
</body>
</html>
```

Listing 9-16 shows the index.html page. You just removed the xmlns:sec namespace. Remember all the other classes and files remain the same; nothing will change.

Next, create the src/main/java/com/apress/spring/config/ResourceOAuthSecurityConfiguration. java class. See Listing 9-17.

Listing 9-17. src/main/java/com/apress/spring/config/ResourceOAuthSecurityConfiguration.java

```
package com.apress.spring.config;

import org.springframework.context.annotation.Configuration;
import org.springframework.security.config.annotation.web.builders.HttpSecurity;
import org.springframework.security.oauth2.config.annotation.web.configuration.
EnableAuthorizationServer;
import org.springframework.security.oauth2.config.annotation.web.configuration.
EnableResourceServer;
import org.springframework.security.oauth2.config.annotation.web.configuration.
ResourceServerConfigurerAdapter;

@Configuration
@EnableAuthorizationServer
@EnableResourceServer
public class ResourceOAuthSecurityConfiguration extends ResourceServerConfigurerAdapter{

        @Override
        public void configure(HttpSecurity http) throws Exception {
                http.authorizeRequests()
                    .antMatchers("/").permitAll()
                    .antMatchers("/api/**").authenticated();
        }

}
```

Listing 9-17 shows the ResourceOAuthSecurityConfiguration.java class. Let's examine it:

- @Configuration. This annotation is used as a marker to configure any existing beans or any other configuration before the application starts.

- @EnableAuthorizationServer. This annotation enables the authorization /oauth/ authorize and the token /oauth/token endpoints. The user is responsible for securing the authorization endpoint. The token endpoint will be automatically secured using HTTP basic authentication on the client's credentials.—in this case by using the username and password from the database.

- @EnableResourceServer. This annotation enables the Spring security filter that authenticates requests via an incoming OAuth2 token.

- ResourceServerConfigurerAdapter. The ResourceOAuthSecurityConfiguration class extends this class ResourceServerConfigurerAdapter, which is just a interface marker because it implements the ResourceServerConfigurer interface, allowing the program to override the configure(ResourceServerSecurityConfigurer) and configure(HttpSecurity) methods. In this case the class is overriding configure(HttpSecurity) to add security to some resources.

- configure(HttpSecurity). This is an override method and it's using the HttpSecurity instance to call the authorizeRequests() method builder. Remember that this instance has a fluent API, so it's easy to configure the requests and secure them.

- .antMatchers("/").permitAll(). Allows you to see the main page, the index.html page.

- .antMatchers("/api/**").authenticated(). Secures the REST API /api endpoint with OAuth2.

Now, let's run it. As usual, you can use the following command:

```
$ ./mvnw spring-boot:run
```

After executing this command, you can go to http://localhost:8080. You should see the home page with all the journal entries. Now, if you go to http://localhost:8080/api, you should see something similar to Figure 9-9.

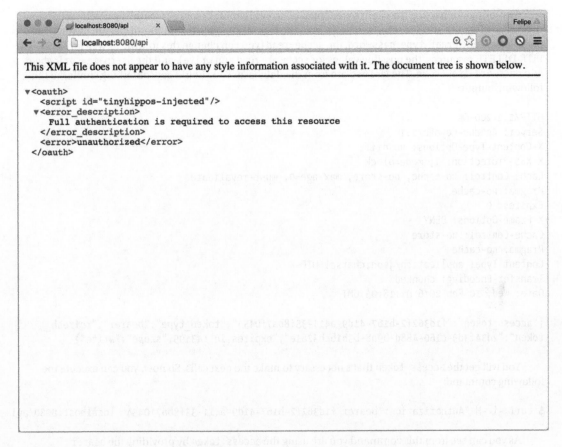

Figure 9-9. http://localhost:8080/api is now protected by the OAuth2 security

Figure 9-9 shows the result of going to the /api endpoint. Now it's secured by the OAuth2 security. In order to access it, go to the terminal and use the flow you saw earlier (Figure 9-7). However, before that take note of the two GUIDs that were printed out in the logs:

...

```
security.oauth2.client.clientId = acd167f6-04f8-4306-a118-03e2356f73aa
security.oauth2.client.secret = 2dd4bec5-fe62-4568-94a1-c31ac3c4eb4e
```

...

Remember that OAuth2 needs a client ID and secret keys and these values change every time you start the application. Now, go to the terminal and execute:

```
$ curl -i localhost:8080/oauth/token -d "grant_type=password&scope=read&username=springb
oot&password=isawesome" -u acd167f6-04f8-4306-a118-03e2356f73aa:2dd4bec5-fe62-4568-94a1-
c31ac3c4eb4e
```

The format for passing the client's credential is -u <clientId>:<secret>. Note the colon : separating them. The clientId and secret are the keys from the logs. Also notice that in the -d you are passing these parameters—the grant_type=password, the scope=read (you can change this to write as well for POST, PUT, DELETE resources, the possible values for scope are read and write), and the username=springboot and password=isawesome. The last two are from the database. You should get something similar to the following output:

```
HTTP/1.1 200 OK
Server: Apache-Coyote/1.1
X-Content-Type-Options: nosniff
X-XSS-Protection: 1; mode=block
Cache-Control: no-cache, no-store, max-age=0, must-revalidate
Pragma: no-cache
Expires: 0
X-Frame-Options: DENY
Cache-Control: no-store
Pragma: no-cache
Content-Type: application/json;charset=UTF-8
Transfer-Encoding: chunked
Date: Wed, 10 Feb 2016 01:18:05 GMT
```

{"access_token":"f1d362f2-b167-41d9-a411-35f8ba7f0454","token_type":"bearer","refresh_token":"2d34f3d9-c160-488d-b9a8-b3b1bcb3281e","expires_in":43199,"scope":"write"}

You will get the access_token that's necessary to make the next calls. So now, you can execute the following command:

```
$ curl -i -H "Authorization: bearer f1d362f2-b167-41d9-a411-35f8ba7f0454" localhost:8080/api
```

As you can see from this command you are using the access_token by providing the bearer declaration. After you execute this command, you should get the following:

```
HTTP/1.1 200 OK
Server: Apache-Coyote/1.1
X-Content-Type-Options: nosniff
X-XSS-Protection: 1; mode=block
Cache-Control: no-cache, no-store, max-age=0, must-revalidate
Pragma: no-cache
Expires: 0
X-Frame-Options: DENY
Content-Type: application/hal+json;charset=UTF-8
Transfer-Encoding: chunked
Date: Wed, 10 Feb 2016 01:19:57 GMT
```

```
{
  "_links" : {
    "entry" : {
      "href" : "http://localhost:8080/api/journal{?page,size,sort}",
      "templated" : true
    },
    "profile" : {
      "href" : "http://localhost:8080/api/profile"
    }
  }
}
```

As you can see, you still need to add the client ID and secret keys from the logs. Of course, you need a way to use the database and save those keys, as well as get the correct access_token by providing the keys and your credentials, but this will be your homework. This process will be very similar to the JDBC security example.

End users would never use the cURL command to access secure application with OAuth2. They normally use a web interface to do that. There is a guide that talks about Spring Boot and OAuth2 that uses AngularJS as a client, and I recommend you read it: https://spring.io/guides/tutorials/spring-boot-oauth2/.

■ **Note**   I know this chapter has a lot of code, but don't worry too much, as you can download it from the Apress site or go to GitHub at http://github.com/felipeg48/pro-spring-boot.

Summary

This chapter showed you how you can use security in your web apps, from a simple HTTP to using in-memory and JDBC. It also showed you how to implement OAuth authentication. As you can see, adding security is now simpler than ever. With a few commands, you can secure your applications with ease. I know that there are more ways to secure application, such as using SSL and TLS, and enabling these technologies is also very simple in Spring Boot.

The following chapter discusses messaging with Spring Boot.

CHAPTER 10

■ ■ ■

Messaging with Spring Boot

This chapter is all about messaging. It explains, with examples, how to use HornetQ for implementing the JMS (Java Message Service), RabbitMQ for implementing AMQP (Advanced Message Queuing Protocol), Redis for Pub/Sub, and WebSockets for implementing STOMP (Simple or Streaming Text Oriented Message Protocol) with Spring Boot.

What Is Messaging?

Messaging is a way of communicating between one or more entities and it is everywhere.

Computer messaging in one form or another has been around since the invention of the computer, and it is defined as a method of communication between hardware and/or software components or applications. There is always a sender and one or more receivers. Messaging can be synchronous and asynchronous, pub-sub and peer-to-peer, RPC and enterprise-based, Message Broker, ESB (Enterprise Service Bus), MOM (Message Oriented Middleware), etc.

From all of this, we can say for certain that messaging enables distributed communication that must be loosely coupled, meaning that it doesn't matter how or what message the sender is publishing, the receiver consumes the message without telling the sender.

Of course, there is a lot we could say about messaging, from the old techniques and technologies to new protocols and messaging patterns, but the intention of this chapter is to work with examples that illustrate how Spring Boot can do messaging.

With this in mind, let's start creating some examples using some of the technologies and message brokers out there.

JMS with Spring Boot

Let's start by using JMS (Java Message Service). This is an old technology that is still being used by some companies that have legacy applications. JMS was created by Sun Microsystems to create a way to send messages synchronously and asynchronously, and it defines interfaces that need to be implemented by message brokers such as WebLogic, IBM MQ, ActiveMQ, HornetQ, etc.

JMS is a Java-only technology, and even so there have been some attempts to create message bridges to combine JMS with other programming languages. Still it's difficult or very expensive to mix different technologies. I know that you are thinking that this is not true, because you can use Spring integration, Google Protobuffers, Apache Thrift, and another technologies to integrate JMS, but it's still a lot of work, because you need to know and maintain code from all these technologies.

Let's start by creating an example using JMS with Spring Boot. The Spring Boot team has a HornetQ starter pom available, so that's the one you are going to use. HornetQ is an open source asynchronous messaging project from JBoss.

© Felipe Gutierrez 2016
F. Gutierrez, *Pro Spring Boot*, DOI 10.1007/978-1-4842-1431-2_10

You can execute the Spring Initializr command:

```
$ mkdir spring-boot-jms
$ cd spring-boot-jms
$ spring init -d=hornetq -g=com.apress.spring -a=spring-boot-jms
--package-name=com.apress.spring -name=spring-boot-jms -x
```

This command will create the project structure and generate the pom.xml that you need. Let's take a look at it. See Listing 10-1.

Listing 10-1. pom.xml

```xml
<?xml version="1.0" encoding="UTF-8"?>
<project xmlns="http://maven.apache.org/POM/4.0.0" xmlns:xsi="http://www.w3.org/2001/
XMLSchema-instance"
        xsi:schemaLocation="http://maven.apache.org/POM/4.0.0 http://maven.apache.org/xsd/
        maven-4.0.0.xsd">
        <modelVersion>4.0.0</modelVersion>

        <groupId>com.apress.spring</groupId>
        <artifactId>spring-boot-jms</artifactId>
        <version>0.0.1-SNAPSHOT</version>
        <packaging>jar</packaging>

        <name>spring-boot-jms</name>
        <description>Demo project for Spring Boot</description>

        <parent>
                <groupId>org.springframework.boot</groupId>
                <artifactId>spring-boot-starter-parent</artifactId>
                <version>1.3.2.RELEASE</version>
                <relativePath/> <!-- lookup parent from repository -->
        </parent>

        <properties>
                <project.build.sourceEncoding>UTF-8</project.build.sourceEncoding>
                <java.version>1.8</java.version>
        </properties>

        <dependencies>
                <dependency>
                        <groupId>org.springframework.boot</groupId>
                        <artifactId>spring-boot-starter-hornetq</artifactId>
                </dependency>

                <dependency>
                        <groupId>org.hornetq</groupId>
                        <artifactId>hornetq-jms-server</artifactId>
                </dependency>
```

```xml
            <dependency>
                    <groupId>org.springframework.boot</groupId>
                    <artifactId>spring-boot-starter-test</artifactId>
                    <scope>test</scope>
            </dependency>
        </dependencies>

        <build>
            <plugins>
                    <plugin>
                            <groupId>org.springframework.boot</groupId>
                            <artifactId>spring-boot-maven-plugin</artifactId>
                    </plugin>
            </plugins>
        </build>

</project>
```

Listing 10-1 shows the pom.xml file you are going to use in this example. When you execute the Spring Initializr command you put the hornetq as the dependency, which adds the spring-boot-starter-hornetq starter pom. This starter pom will have all the hornetq client dependencies, and in this example you also need the hornetq-jms-server dependency because you are going to use the embedded hornetq broker.

Next let's see how to configure the hornetq server. The configuration will take place in the application. properties file. See Listing 10-2.

Listing 10-2. src/main/resources/application. properties

```
spring.hornetq.mode=embedded
spring.hornetq.embedded.enabled=true
spring.hornetq.embedded.queues=springbootQueue,pivotalQueue

myqueue=springbootQueue
```

Listing 10-2 shows the application.properties file that you need to configure the hornetq server. As you can see, you will use the embedded mode to declare the queues that are going to be created by the hornetq server (the queue: pivotalQueue is not being used, but I wanted you to see that you can create as many queues as you want separated by commas). Also you have another property named myqueue=springbootQueue, which is one of the queues you declared first. It's the one that you will reference in your code.

Now let's look at the producer that will send the messages to the broker's queue. See Listing 10-3.

Listing 10-3. src/main/java/com/apress/spring/message/Producer.java

```java
package com.apress.spring.message;

import org.slf4j.Logger;
import org.slf4j.LoggerFactory;
import org.springframework.jms.core.JmsTemplate;

public class Producer {
        private static final Logger log = LoggerFactory.getLogger(Producer.class);
        private JmsTemplate jmsTemplate;
```

```
        public Producer(JmsTemplate jmsTemplate){
                this.jmsTemplate = jmsTemplate;
        }

        public void sendTo(String queue, String message) {
                this.jmsTemplate.convertAndSend(queue, message);
                log.info("Producer> Message Sent");
        }
}
```

Listing 10-3 shows the Producer.java class. Let's examine it:

- JmsTemplate. The JmsTemplate instance is a helper class that simplifies synchronous JMS access code. This template uses the DynamicDestinationResolver and SimpleMessageConverter classes as default strategies for resolving a destination name (queue names) or converting a message.

- Producer(jmsTemplate). The constructor will use the JmsTemplate as a parameter.

- sendTo(queue, message). This method has two parameters—the name of queue (destination) and the message, both as type String. This method uses the jmsTemplate to use the convertAndSend method call to send the message and pass the name of the queue and the actual message. The convertAndSend method will try to use the best available message converter, and by default it will use the SimpleMessageConverter class. The SimpleMessageConverter will identify if the message is a String, Map, byte[] array, or Serializable object.

Next, let's look at the Consumer.java class. See Listing 10-4.

Listing 10-4. src/main/java/com/apress/spring/message/Consumer.java

```
package com.apress.spring.message;

import javax.jms.JMSException;
import javax.jms.Message;
import javax.jms.MessageListener;

import org.slf4j.Logger;
import org.slf4j.LoggerFactory;

public class Consumer implements MessageListener{
        private Logger log = LoggerFactory.getLogger(Consumer.class);

        @Override
        public void onMessage(Message message) {
                try {
                        log.info("Consumer> " + message.getBody(Object.class));
                }catch (JMSException ex) {
                        ex.printStackTrace();
                }
        }
}
```

Listing 10-4 shows the Consumer. java class. Let's examine it:

- MessageListener. In, it's necessary to implement from the MessageListener interface and implement the onMessage(Message) method. The MessageListener interface receives asynchronously delivered messages.

- onMessage(Message). The method onMessage has as parameter called the Message interface, which is the root interface of all JMS messages. It defines the message header and contains a lot of methods (that you can look up in the JMS API docs), but the important one here is getBody. This method is based on Java generics that get a Class type.

Every time the producer sends a message to the queue, this consumer will be listening to that queue and will consume the message. Then you can process it or do your business logic around the message. In this example you are printing out the message.

Next, you need to do some extra configuration involving how to connect to the HornetQ server. So far you have the producer and consumer, but how do these two classes know how to connect to the broker? See Listing 10-5.

Listing 10-5. src/main/java/com/apress/spring/config/MessagingConfig.java

```java
package com.apress.spring.config;

import javax.jms.ConnectionFactory;

import org.springframework.beans.factory.annotation.Autowired;
import org.springframework.beans.factory.annotation.Value;
import org.springframework.context.annotation.Bean;
import org.springframework.context.annotation.Configuration;
import org.springframework.jms.listener.DefaultMessageListenerContainer;

import com.apress.spring.message.Consumer;

@Configuration
public class MessagingConfig {

        @Autowired
        private ConnectionFactory connectionFactory;

        @Value("${myqueue}")
        private String queue;

        @Bean
        public DefaultMessageListenerContainer messageListener() {
                DefaultMessageListenerContainer container = new
                DefaultMessageListenerContainer();
                container.setConnectionFactory(this.connectionFactory);
                container.setDestinationName(queue);
                container.setMessageListener(new Consumer());
                return container;
        }
}
```

Listing 10-5 shows the `MessagingConfig.java` class. Let's examine it:

- `@Configuration`. You already know about this annotation. It tells the Spring container to configure any declared methods annotated with the `@Bean` annotations.

- `@Autowired ConnectionFactory`. The `ConnectionFactory` is an interface. The Spring container will configure this by implementing this interface creating a connection with the default user identity to the broker. In this case it will create the connection to the HornetQ server with the default credentials. The `connectionFactory` is useful for both consumer and producer.

- `@Bean messageListener`. This method defines a bean that will return a `DefaultMessageListenerContainer` instance. The `DefaultMessageListenerContainer` class needs the `connectionFactory`, the `destinationName` (queue = `springbootQueue`), and the `messageListener` that in this case is the `Consumer`. The `DefaultMessageListenerContainer` will be responsible for connecting to the queue and listening through the consumer's `MessageListener` interface implementation.

- `@Value queue`. The `@Value` annotation will look into the `application.properties` file and will retrieve the value associated with it, in this case the `myqueue`. So the queue instance will be `springbootQueue` as its value.

That's how you configure the connection to the HornetQ server, but Listing 10-5 only uses the `connectionFactory` instance to declare and use the consumer. What about the producer? As you remember in Listing 10-3 the `Producer` class constructor needs the `JmsTemplate`, and the `JmsTemplate` class needs the `connectionFactory` instance to know where to send the message. Listing 10-6 is the main application and it shows where you send a message.

Listing 10-6. src/main/java/com/apress/spring/SpringBootJmsApplication.java

```
package com.apress.spring;

import org.springframework.beans.factory.annotation.Value;
import org.springframework.boot.CommandLineRunner;
import org.springframework.boot.SpringApplication;
import org.springframework.boot.autoconfigure.SpringBootApplication;
import org.springframework.context.annotation.Bean;
import org.springframework.jms.core.JmsTemplate;

import com.apress.spring.message.Producer;

@SpringBootApplication
public class SpringBootJmsApplication {

        public static void main(String[] args) {
                SpringApplication.run(SpringBootJmsApplication.class, args);
        }

        @Value("${myqueue}")
        String queue;
```

```
    @Bean
    CommandLineRunner sendMessage(JmsTemplate jmsTemplate){
        return args -> {
            Producer producer = new Producer(jmsTemplate);
            producer.sendTo(queue, "Spring Boot Rocks!");
        };
    }
}
```

Listing 10-6 shows the main app, the SpringBootJmsApplication class. As you can see, it's declaring a @Bean CommandLineRunner method. (This means that it will be executed after the Spring Boot finishes its pre-configuration. Also, this method has the JmsTemplate instance, which will be autowired automatically.) The JmsTemplate is one of its constructors and it has a ConnectionFactory as parameter. Spring Boot is intelligent enough to auto-wire the JmsTemplate instance by using the ConnectionFactory that you configured in the MessagingConfig class (Listing 10-5) when you declared the @Autowired ConnectionFactory instance. The method then will instantiate the Producer class by passing the jmsTemplate instance, and then it will use the sendTo method to send the message to the queue, in this case the springbootQueue queue.

Let's run it as usual:

```
$ ./mvnw spring-boot:run
```

After running the program you should have the logs from the consumer and producer, something similar to this:

```
...
INFO 96581 --- [ssageListener-1] com.apress.spring.message.Consumer  : Consumer> Spring Boot Rocks!
INFO 96581 --- [main] com.apress.spring.message.Producer    : Producer> Message Sent
...
```

If you run your application several times, you will notice that the Consumer prints out its message before the Producer. When Spring Boot starts doing the auto-configuration and properly wiring the beans, the messageListener bean is part of that wiring, so it automatically starts to listen to the Queue for messages. Remember that the Producer is declared in the sendMessage method. This method happens last because it returns the CommandLineRunner interface. That's why you see the Consumer print out before the Producer.

Congratulations, you created a Spring Boot application with JMS!

A Simpler JMS Consumer

I will show you a simpler consumer. This is possible thanks to the Spring Messaging team that created some annotations to simplify everything.

Start by creating another jms version project: spring-boot-jms-v2. Execute the following command:

```
$ mkdir spring-boot-jms-v2
$ cd spring-boot-jms-v2
$ spring init -d=hornetq -g=com.apress.spring -a=spring-boot-jms-v2 --package-name=com.
apress.spring -name=spring-boot-jms-v2 -x
```

This command will create the same structure as the previous example, but here you only will modify the main application and the application properties. The pom.xml is the same in both examples (of course, don't forget to include the hornetq-jms-server dependency), so there's no need to review it. Now, let's see the application.properties file. See Listing 10-7.

Listing 10-7. src/main/resources/application.properties

```
spring.hornetq.mode=embedded
spring.hornetq.embedded.enabled=true
spring.hornetq.embedded.queues=springbootQueue,springQueue

myqueue=springbootQueue
myotherqueue=springQueue
```

Listing 10-7 shows the application.properties; now it has the myqueue and myotherqueue properties and you will be using these keys in the main application. Next, let's see the main application. See Listing 10-8.

Listing 10-8. src/main/java/com/apress/spring/SpringBootJmsV2Application.java

```java
package com.apress.spring;

import org.slf4j.Logger;
import org.slf4j.LoggerFactory;
import org.springframework.beans.factory.annotation.Value;
import org.springframework.boot.CommandLineRunner;
import org.springframework.boot.SpringApplication;
import org.springframework.boot.autoconfigure.SpringBootApplication;
import org.springframework.context.annotation.Bean;
import org.springframework.jms.annotation.JmsListener;
import org.springframework.jms.core.JmsTemplate;

@SpringBootApplication
public class SpringBootJmsV2Application {
        private static final Logger log = LoggerFactory.getLogger(SpringBootJmsV2
        Application.class);

        public static void main(String[] args) {
                SpringApplication.run(SpringBootJmsV2Application.class, args);
        }

        @JmsListener(destination="${myqueue}")
        public void simplerConsumer(String message){
                log.info("Simpler Consumer> " + message);
        }

        @Value("${myqueue}")
        String queue;

        @Bean
        CommandLineRunner start(JmsTemplate template){
                return args -> {
                        log.info("Sending> ...");
```

```
                        template.convertAndSend(queue, "SpringBoot Rocks!");
               };
       }
}
```

Listing 10-8 shows the SpringBootJmsV2Application app. You know most of the code, but there is a new annotation called @JmsListener(destination). This annotation will create a consumer listener and the message will be handled by the method. You only need to pass the destination parameter (the name of the queue) and that's it. Spring will take care of the rest.

Run this application as usual:

```
$ ./mvnw spring-boot:run
```

After running it, you should get the following output:

```
...
INFO 99889 --- [           main] c.a.spring.SpringBootJmsV2Application    : Sending> ...
INFO 99889 --- [enerContainer-1] c.a.spring.SpringBootJmsV2Application    : Simpler
Consumer> SpringBoot Rocks!
...
```

That's your simpler Consumer. This is awesome—with just a simple annotation you have a functional consumer—but there is more! First stop your application by pressing Ctrl+C.

Spring JMS allows you to reply from the same method where the @JmsListener annotation is. Listing 10-9 shows a new version of the SpringBootJmsV2Application app.

Listing 10-9. The src/main/java/com/apress/spring/SpringBootJmsV2Application.java Version with Reply

```
package com.apress.spring;

import org.slf4j.Logger;
import org.slf4j.LoggerFactory;
import org.springframework.beans.factory.annotation.Value;
import org.springframework.boot.CommandLineRunner;
import org.springframework.boot.SpringApplication;
import org.springframework.boot.autoconfigure.SpringBootApplication;
import org.springframework.context.annotation.Bean;
import org.springframework.jms.annotation.JmsListener;
import org.springframework.jms.core.JmsTemplate;
import org.springframework.messaging.handler.annotation.SendTo;

@SpringBootApplication
public class SpringBootJmsV2Application {
        private static final Logger log = LoggerFactory.getLogger(SpringBootJmsV2Applicati
on.class);

        public static void main(String[] args) {
                SpringApplication.run(SpringBootJmsV2Application.class, args);
        }
```

```
        @JmsListener(destination="${myqueue}")
        @SendTo("${myotherqueue}")
        public String simplerConsumer(String message){
                log.info("Simpler Consumer> " + message);
                return message + " and Spring Messaging too!";
        }

        @JmsListener(destination="${myotherqueue}")
        public void anotherSimplerConsumer(String message){
                log.info("Another Simpler Consumer> " + message);
        }

        @Value("${myqueue}")
        String queue;

        @Bean
        CommandLineRunner start(JmsTemplate template){
                return args -> {
                        log.info("Sending> ...");
                        template.convertAndSend(queue, "SpringBoot Rocks!");
                };
        }
}
```

Listing 10-9 shows a new version of the main app. Let's examine it:

- @JmsListener. Now you have two methods as consumers, one
  with the destination="${myqueue}" (springbootQueue) and the
  destination="${myotherqueue}" (springQueue).

- @SendTo. This annotation will reply to the destination specified, in this case
  "${myotherqueue}" (springQueue), but take a look at the method simplerConsumer.
  It now has a return type, a string, which will allow @SendTo to send the message to the
  destination.

This scenario is best used when you process your message and then need to have a reply queue.
Now, if you run the application, you should have the following output:

```
...
INFO 224 --- [m] c.a.spring.SpringBootJmsV2Application : Sending> ...
INFO 224 --- [c ] c.a.spring.SpringBootJmsV2Application   : Simpler Consumer> SpringBoot Rocks!
INFO 224 --- [c ] c.a.spring.SpringBootJmsV2Application : Another Simpler Consumer>
SpringBoot Rocks! and Spring Messaging too!
...
```

Now you know that there are more ways to do consumers with Spring Messaging and Spring Boot.

Connect to Remote JMS Server

Now you know how to write a Spring Boot JMS applications. These were simple examples where you are using an embedded broker, but you can also use a remote broker. You simply need to change the application.properties. For example:

```
spring.hornetq.mode=native
spring.hornetq.host=192.168.1.10
spring.hornetq.port=9876
```

You can read about all the properties for HornetQ in the Spring Boot reference at https://docs. spring.io/spring-boot/docs/current/reference/html/common-application-properties.html.

RabbitMQ with Spring Boot

Since the first attempts from companies like Sun/Oracle/IBM with JMS and Microsoft with MSMQ, the protocols they used were proprietary. I know that JMS just defines an Interface API, but trying to mix technologies or programming languages is a hassle. Gratefully and thanks to the team of JPMorgan, the AMQP (Advance Message Queuing Protocol) was created. It's an open standard application layer for MOM. In other words, AMQP is a wire-level protocol, meaning that you can use any technology or programming language with this protocol.

Messaging brokers are competing with each other to prove that they are robust, reliable, and scalable, but the most important issue is how fast they are. I've been working with a lot of brokers, and so far one of the easiest to use, easiest to scale and fastest is RabbitMQ. RabbitMQ implements the AMQP protocol.

It would take an entire book to describe each part of RabbitMQ and all the concepts around it, but I'll try to explain some of them based on this section's example.

Installing RabbitMQ

Before I talk about RabbitMQ let's install it. If you are using Mac OSX/Linux, you can use the brew command:

```
$ brew upgrade
$ brew install rabbitmq
```

If you are using another UNIX or a Windows system, you can go to the RabbitMQ web site and use the installers (http://www.rabbitmq.com/download.html). RabbitMQ is written in Erlang, so its major dependency is to install the Erlang runtime in your system. Nowadays all the RabbitMQ installers come with all the Erlang dependencies. Make sure to have the executables in your PATH variable. If you are using brew, you don't need to worry about setting the PATH variable.

RabbitMQ/AMQP: Exchanges, Bindings, and Queues

The AMQP defines three concepts that are a little different from the JMS world, but very easy to understand. AMQP defines *exchanges*, which are entities where the messages are sent. Every *exchange* takes a message and routes it to a zero or more *queues*. This routing involves an algorithm that is based on the exchange type and some rules, called *bindings*.

The AMPQ protocol defines four exchange types: *Direct, Fanout, Topic,* and *Headers*. Figure 10-1 shows these different exchange types.

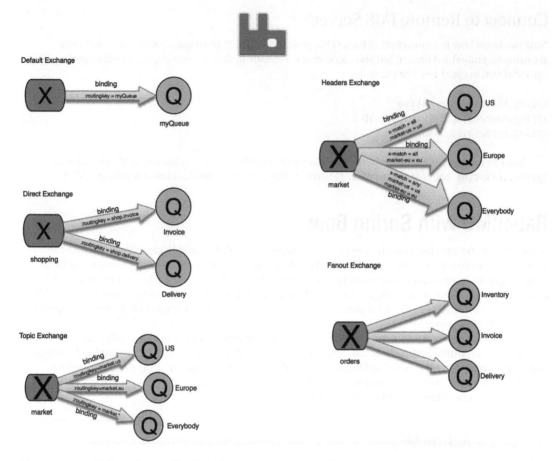

Figure 10-1. *AMQP exchanges/bindings/queues*

Figure 10-1 shows the possible exchange types. So, the main idea is to send a message to an exchange including a routing key, then the exchange based on its type will deliver the message to the queue (or it won't if the routing key doesn't match).

The *default exchange* will be bound automatically to every queue created. The direct exchange is bound to a queue by a routing key; you can see this exchange type as one-to-one binding. The *topic exchange* is similar to the Direct Exchange; the only difference is that in its binding you can add a wildcard into its routing key. The *headers exchange* is similar to the topic exchange; the only difference is that the binding is based on the message headers (this is a very powerful exchange, and you can do *all* and *any* expressions for its headers). The *fanout exchange* will copy the message to all the bound queues; you can see this exchange as a message broadcast.

You can get more information about these topics at `https://www.rabbitmq.com/tutorials/amqp-concepts.html`.

The example in this section will use the default exchange type, which means that the routing key will be equal to the name of the queue. Every time you create a queue, RabbitMQ will create a binding from the default exchange (that the actual name is just an empty string) to the queue using the queue's name.

Get started by creating your project. Execute the following commands:

```
$ mkdir spring-boot-rabbitmq
$ cd spring-boot-rabbitmq
$ spring init -d=amqp -g=com.apress.spring -a=spring-boot-rabbitmq --package-name=com.
apress.spring -name=spring-boot-rabbitmq -x
```

Now, let's take a look a the pom.xml. See Listing 10-10.

Listing 10-10. pom.xml

```xml
<?xml version="1.0" encoding="UTF-8"?>
<project xmlns="http://maven.apache.org/POM/4.0.0" xmlns:xsi="http://www.w3.org/2001/
XMLSchema-instance"
        xsi:schemaLocation="http://maven.apache.org/POM/4.0.0 http://maven.apache.org/xsd/
        maven-4.0.0.xsd">
        <modelVersion>4.0.0</modelVersion>

        <groupId>com.apress.spring</groupId>
        <artifactId>spring-boot-rabbitmq</artifactId>
        <version>0.0.1-SNAPSHOT</version>
        <packaging>jar</packaging>

        <name>spring-boot-rabbitmq</name>
        <description>Demo project for Spring Boot</description>

        <parent>
                <groupId>org.springframework.boot</groupId>
                <artifactId>spring-boot-starter-parent</artifactId>
                <version>1.3.2.RELEASE</version>
                <relativePath/> <!-- lookup parent from repository -->
        </parent>

        <properties>
                <project.build.sourceEncoding>UTF-8</project.build.sourceEncoding>
                <java.version>1.8</java.version>
        </properties>

        <dependencies>
                <dependency>
                        <groupId>org.springframework.boot</groupId>
                        <artifactId>spring-boot-starter-amqp</artifactId>
                </dependency>

                <dependency>
                        <groupId>org.springframework.boot</groupId>
                        <artifactId>spring-boot-starter-test</artifactId>
                        <scope>test</scope>
                </dependency>
        </dependencies>
```

```
        <build>
                <plugins>
                        <plugin>
                                <groupId>org.springframework.boot</groupId>
                                <artifactId>spring-boot-maven-plugin</artifactId>
                        </plugin>
                </plugins>
        </build>

</project>
```

Listing 10-10 shows the pom.xml file. As you can see, it includes the spring-boot-starter-amqp starter pom. This pom will include all the spring-amqp and rabbitmq-client libraries needed for connecting to the RabbitMQ Broker.

Next let's create the Producer and Consumer. See Listings 10-11 and 10-12.

Listing 10-11. src/main/java/com/apress/spring/rabbitmq/Producer.java

```java
package com.apress.spring.rabbitmq;

import org.slf4j.Logger;
import org.slf4j.LoggerFactory;
import org.springframework.amqp.rabbit.core.RabbitTemplate;
import org.springframework.beans.factory.annotation.Autowired;
import org.springframework.stereotype.Component;

@Component
public class Producer {
        private static final Logger log = LoggerFactory.getLogger(Producer.class);

        @Autowired
        RabbitTemplate rabbitTemplate;

        public void sendTo(String routingkey,String message){
                log.info("Sending> ...");
                this.rabbitTemplate.convertAndSend(routingkey,message);
        }
}
```

Listing 10-11 shows the Producer.java class. Let's examine it:

- @Component. This annotation marks the class to be picked up by the Spring container.

- @Autowired RabbitTemplate. The RabbitTemplate is a helper class that simplifies synchronous access to RabbitMQ for sending and receiving messages. This is very similar to the JmsTemplate you saw earlier.

- sendTo(routingKey,message). This method has as parameters the routing key and the message. In this case the routing key will be the name of the queue. This method is using the rabbitTemplate instance to call the convertAndSend method that accepts the routing key and the message. Remember that the message will be sent to the exchange (the default exchange) and the exchange will route the message to the right queue.

Next, the Consumer class is shown in Listing 10-12.

Listing 10-12. src/main/java/com/apress/spring/rabbitmq/Consumer.java

```java
package com.apress.spring.rabbitmq;

import org.slf4j.Logger;
import org.slf4j.LoggerFactory;
import org.springframework.amqp.rabbit.annotation.RabbitListener;
import org.springframework.stereotype.Component;

@Component
public class Consumer {

        private static final Logger log = LoggerFactory.getLogger(Consumer.class);

        @RabbitListener(queues="${myqueue}")
        public void handler(String message){
                log.info("Consumer> " + message);
        }
}
```

Listing 10-12 shows the Consumer.java class. Let's examine it:

- @Component. You already know this annotation. It will mark the class to be picked up by the Spring container.

- @RabbitListener. This annotation will mark the method (because you can use this annotation in a class as well) for creating a handler for any incoming messages, meaning that it will create a listener that is connected to the RabbitMQ's queue and will pass that message to the method. Behind the scenes, the listener will do its best to convert the message to the appropriate type by using the right message converter (an implementation of the org.springframework.amqp.support.converter. MessageConverter interface).

As you can see from the Producer and Consumer, the code is very simple. If you created this by only using the RabbitMQ Java client (https://www.rabbitmq.com/java-client.html), at least you need more lines of code, for creating a connection, a channel, a message and send the message, or if you are writing a consumer, then you need to open a connection, create a channel, create a basic consumer, and get into a loop for processing every incoming message. This is a lot for simple producers or consumers. That's why the Spring AMQP team created this, a simple way to do a heavy task in a few lines of code.

For this project, you will also depend on the src/main/resources/application.properties file and it contains only one line:

```
myqueue=spring-boot
```

That's the name of the queue that you are going to be using in RabbitMQ. Next, let's take a look at the main application. See Listing 10-13.

Listing 10-13. src/main/java/com/apress/spring/SpringBootRabbitmqApplication.java

```java
package com.apress.spring;

import org.springframework.amqp.core.Queue;
import org.springframework.beans.factory.annotation.Value;
import org.springframework.boot.CommandLineRunner;
import org.springframework.boot.SpringApplication;
import org.springframework.boot.autoconfigure.SpringBootApplication;
import org.springframework.context.annotation.Bean;

import com.apress.spring.rabbitmq.Producer;

@SpringBootApplication
public class SpringBootRabbitmqApplication {

        public static void main(String[] args) {
                SpringApplication.run(SpringBootRabbitmqApplication.class, args);
        }

        @Value("${myqueue}")
        String queue;

        @Bean
        Queue queue(){
                return new Queue(queue,false);
        }

        @Bean
        CommandLineRunner sender(Producer producer){
                return args -> {
                        producer.sendTo(queue, "Hello World");
                };
        }
}
```

Listing 10-13 shows the `main` app. Let's examine it:

- `@Value String`. You are familiar with this annotation, It will get the value from the `application.properties`.

- `@Bean Queue`. This will instantiate a bean of type Queue and will create a Queue with the name provided by the queue string (spring-boot). The Queue class in its constructor accepts the name of the queue and if that queue will be durable or not to a server restart, meaning that if your restart your server the queue will be gone.

- `@Bean CommandLineRunner`. You are also familiar with this annotation and what it means. It will be executed after all the configuration is done in Spring Boot, and as you can see it's using the `Producer` instance that calls the `sendTo` method that accepts the name of the queue as the routing key and the message. (Remember that the `Producer` class is annotated with the @Component annotation, so that's why it can be recognized as a parameter through the @Bean annotation.)

Remember that in the AMQP protocol you need an exchange that is bound to a queue, so this particular example will create at runtime a *queue* named spring-boot, and by default all the queues are bound to a default exchange. That's why you didn't provide any information about a exchange. So, when the producer sends the message it will be sent first to the default exchange then routed to the queue (spring-boot).

Before you run your example, make sure your RabbitMQ server is up and running. You can start it by opening a terminal and executing the following command:

```
$ rabbitmq-server
```

```
                  RabbitMQ 3.6.0. Copyright (C) 2007-2015 Pivotal Software, Inc.
  ##  ##      Licensed under the MPL.  See http://www.rabbitmq.com/
  ##  ##
  ##########  Logs: /usr/local/var/log/rabbitmq/rabbit@localhost.log
  ######  ##        /usr/local/var/log/rabbitmq/rabbit@localhost-sasl.log
  ##########
              Starting broker... completed with 12 plugins.
```

This output shows the RabbitMQ server with 12 plugins installed. I forgot to mention that sometimes the RabbitMQ server doesn't come up with the web console manager installed, so you need to enable it by executing the following:

```
$ rabbitmq-plugins enable rabbitmq_management
```

This will enable the web console and open port 15672. You can go to your browser at http://localhost:15672 and it will prompt for a username and password. The default credentials are guest:guest. You should then see the web console similar to Figure 10-2.

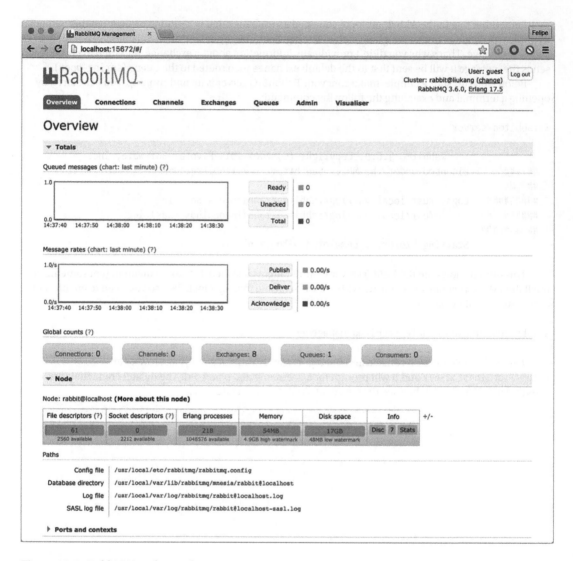

Figure 10-2. *RabbitMQ web console management*

Figure 10-2 shows the RabbitMQ web console. Now you can run the project as usual:

```
$ ./mvnw spring-boot:run
```

After you execute this command, you should have something similar to the following output:

```
...
INFO 80961 --- [          main] com.apress.spring.rabbitmq.Producer : Sending> ...
INFO 80961 --- [cTaskExecutor-1] com.apress.spring.rabbitmq.Consumer       : Consumer> Hello World
...
```

If you take a look at the RabbitMQ web console in the Queues tab, you should have defined the spring-boot queue. See Figure 10-3.

Figure 10-3. *RabbitMQ web console Queues tab*

Figure 10-3 shows the Queues tab from the RabbitMQ web console. The message you just sent was delivered right away. If you want to play a little more and see some part of the throughput, you can modify the main app as shown in Listing 10-14, but don't forget to stop your app by pressing Ctrl+C.

Listing 10-14. Version 2 of src/main/java/com/apress/spring/SpringBootRabbitmqApplication.java

```java
package com.apress.spring;

import java.util.Date;

import org.springframework.amqp.core.Queue;
import org.springframework.beans.factory.annotation.Autowired;
import org.springframework.beans.factory.annotation.Value;
import org.springframework.boot.SpringApplication;
import org.springframework.boot.autoconfigure.SpringBootApplication;
import org.springframework.context.annotation.Bean;
import org.springframework.scheduling.annotation.EnableScheduling;
import org.springframework.scheduling.annotation.Scheduled;

import com.apress.spring.rabbitmq.Producer;

@EnableScheduling
@SpringBootApplication
public class SpringBootRabbitmqApplication {

        public static void main(String[] args) {
                SpringApplication.run(SpringBootRabbitmqApplication.class, args);
        }

        @Value("${myqueue}")
        String queue;

        @Bean
        Queue queue(){
                return new Queue(queue,false);
        }

        @Autowired
        Producer producer;

        @Scheduled(fixedDelay = 500L)
        public void sendMessages(){
                producer.sendTo(queue, "Hello World at " + new Date());
        }

}
```

Listing 10-14 shows a modified version of the main app. Let's examine this new version:

- @EnableScheduling. This annotation will tell (via auto-configuration) the Spring container that the org.springframework.scheduling.annotation. ScheduleAnnotationBeanPostProcessor class needs to be created. It will register all the methods annotated with @Scheduled to be invoked by a org.springframework. scheduling.TaskScheduler interface implementation according to the fixedRate, fixedDelay, or cron expression in the @Scheduled annotation.

- `@Scheduled(fixedDelay = 500L)`. This annotation will tell the `TaskScheduler` interface implementation to execute the `sendMessages` method with a fixed delay of 500 milliseconds. This means that every half of a second you will send a message to the queue.

The other part of the app you already know. So if you execute the project again, you should see endless messaging. While this is running take a look at the RabbitMQ console and see the output. You can put a `for` loop to send even more messages in a half of a second.

Remote RabbitMQ

If you want to access a remote RabbitMQ, you add the following properties to the `application.properties` file:

```
spring.rabbitmq.host=mydomain.com
spring.rabbitmq.username=rabbituser
spring.rabbitmq.password=thisissecured
spring.rabbitmq.port=5672
spring.rabbitmq.virtual-host=/production
```

You can always read about all the properties for RabbitMQ in the Spring Boot reference at `https://docs.spring.io/spring-boot/docs/current/reference/html/common-application-properties.html`.

Now you know how easy is to use RabbitMQ with Spring Boot. If you want to learn more about RabbitMQ and the Spring AMQP technology, you can get more info at the main projects web site at `http://projects.spring.io/spring-amqp/`.

You can stop RabbitMQ by pressing Ctrl+C where you start the broker. There are more options on how to use RabbitMQ, like creating a cluster or having high availability. You can find more information about this at `http://www.rabbitmq.com/`.

Redis Messaging with Spring Boot

Now it's Redis' turn. Redis (REmote DIctionary Server) is a NoSQL key-value store database. It's written in C and even though has a small footprint in its core, it's very reliable, scalable, powerful, and super fast. Its primary function is to store data structures like Lists, hashes, strings, sets, and sorted sets. One of the other main features is that it provides a publish/subscribe messaging system, which is why you are going to use Redis only as message broker.

Installing Redis

Installing Redis is very simple. If you are using Mac OSX/Linux, you can use `brew` and execute the following:

```
$ brew update && brew install redis
```

If you are using a different flavor of UNIX or Windows, you can go to the Redis web site and download the Redis installers at `http://redis.io/download`. Or if you want to compile it according to your system, you can do that as well by downloading the source code.

Let's start the project by executing the following commands:

```
$ mkdir spring-boot-redis
$ cd spring-boot-redis
$ spring init -d=redis -g=com.apress.spring -a=spring-boot-redis --package-name=com.apress.
spring -name=spring-boot-redis -x
```

Now, let's review the pom.xml. See Listing 10-15.

Listing 10-15. pom.xml

```
<?xml version="1.0" encoding="UTF-8"?>
<project xmlns="http://maven.apache.org/POM/4.0.0" xmlns:xsi="http://www.w3.org/2001/
XMLSchema-instance"
        xsi:schemaLocation="http://maven.apache.org/POM/4.0.0 http://maven.apache.org/xsd/
        maven-4.0.0.xsd">
        <modelVersion>4.0.0</modelVersion>

        <groupId>com.apress.spring</groupId>
        <artifactId>spring-boot-redis</artifactId>
        <version>0.0.1-SNAPSHOT</version>
        <packaging>jar</packaging>

        <name>spring-boot-redis</name>
        <description>Demo project for Spring Boot</description>

        <parent>
                <groupId>org.springframework.boot</groupId>
                <artifactId>spring-boot-starter-parent</artifactId>
                <version>1.3.2.RELEASE</version>
                <relativePath/> <!-- lookup parent from repository -->
        </parent>

        <properties>
                <project.build.sourceEncoding>UTF-8</project.build.sourceEncoding>
                <java.version>1.8</java.version>
        </properties>

        <dependencies>
                <dependency>
                        <groupId>org.springframework.boot</groupId>
                        <artifactId>spring-boot-starter-redis</artifactId>
                </dependency>

                <dependency>
                        <groupId>org.springframework.boot</groupId>
                        <artifactId>spring-boot-starter-test</artifactId>
                        <scope>test</scope>
                </dependency>
        </dependencies>
```

```
        <build>
                <plugins>
                        <plugin>
                                <groupId>org.springframework.boot</groupId>
                                <artifactId>spring-boot-maven-plugin</artifactId>
                        </plugin>
                </plugins>
        </build>

</project>
```

Listing 10-15 shows the pom.xml. You probably already know what start pom you need in order to use Redis, it's spring-boot-redis-starter. This pom will include all the spring-data-redis libraries and its dependencies.

Next, let's see the Producer and Consumer. See Listings 10-16 and 10-17.

Listing 10-16. src/main/java/com/apress/spring/redis/Producer.java

```
package com.apress.spring.redis;

import org.slf4j.Logger;
import org.slf4j.LoggerFactory;
import org.springframework.beans.factory.annotation.Autowired;
import org.springframework.data.redis.core.StringRedisTemplate;
import org.springframework.stereotype.Component;

@Component
public class Producer {
        private static final Logger log = LoggerFactory.getLogger(Producer.class);
        private StringRedisTemplate template;

        @Autowired
        public Producer(StringRedisTemplate template){
                this.template = template;
        }

        public void sendTo(String topic, String message){
                log.info("Sending> ...");
                this.template.convertAndSend(topic, message);
        }
}
```

Listing 10-16 shows the Producer.java class. Let's examine it:

- @Component. This annotation will mark the Producer class to be considered a bean for the Spring container.

- @Autowired *Producer*. This is the first time I showed you this annotation in a constructor. This will resolve the parameter StringRedisTemplate first, before the Spring container creates this class. The StringRedisTemplate class is a String-focused extension of the RedisTemplate class, which is a helper that simplifies Redis data access code.

- sendTo. This method sends a message using the template's method called convertAndSend, passing the channel/topic and the message.

233

As you can see, it's a very simple Producer. Now, let's take a look at the Consumer. See Listing 10-17.

Listing 10-17. src/main/java/com/apress/spring/redis/Consumer.java

```
package com.apress.spring.redis;

import org.slf4j.Logger;
import org.slf4j.LoggerFactory;
import org.springframework.stereotype.Component;

@Component
public class Consumer {
        private static final Logger log = LoggerFactory.getLogger(Consumer.class);

        public void messageHandler(String message) {
                        log.info("Consumer> " + message);
                }
}
```

Listing 10-17 show you the Consumer.java class. This class only uses the @Component annotation, which you already know. For this project, you will need also the src/main/resources/application.properties file with its contents:

```
topic=spring-boot
```

The spring-boot value will be used in the following file. Next, let's see the configuration. You need to connect to Redis, as shown in Listing 10-18.

Listing 10-18. src/main/java/com/apress/spring/config/RedisConfig.java

```
package com.apress.spring.config;

import org.springframework.beans.factory.annotation.Value;
import org.springframework.context.annotation.Bean;
import org.springframework.context.annotation.Configuration;
import org.springframework.data.redis.connection.RedisConnectionFactory;
import org.springframework.data.redis.listener.PatternTopic;
import org.springframework.data.redis.listener.RedisMessageListenerContainer;
import org.springframework.data.redis.listener.adapter.MessageListenerAdapter;

import com.apress.spring.redis.Consumer;

@Configuration
public class RedisConfig {

        @Value("${topic}")
        String topic;

        @Bean
        RedisMessageListenerContainer container(RedisConnectionFactory connectionFactory,
                        MessageListenerAdapter listenerAdapter) {
```

```
            RedisMessageListenerContainer container = new
            RedisMessageListenerContainer();
            container.setConnectionFactory(connectionFactory);
            container.addMessageListener(listenerAdapter, new PatternTopic(topic));

            return container;
    }

    @Bean
    MessageListenerAdapter listenerAdapter(Consumer consumer) {
            return new MessageListenerAdapter(consumer, "messageHandler");
    }

}
```

Listing 10-18 shows the RedisConfig.java class. In order to connect to Redis, you must have declared a RedisMessageListenerContainer that will connect to Redis and subscribe to a channel or topic using a MessageListenerAdapter. Let's examine the class:

- @Bean RedisMessageListenerContainer. This container is very similar to the other message containers (JMS, Rabbit). This container needs a ConnectionFactory implementation (RedisConnectionFactory) based on the default credentials, host, and port will connect to Redis (unless you override them in the application. properties—more about this later). It also needs a MessageListenerAdapter and a channel/topic to subscribe. As you can see the message listener is the call of the listenerAdapter method that is resolved through the @Bean annotation and the channel/topic is the PatternTopic class with the value of the String topic (topic=spring-boot from the application.properties).

- @Bean MessageListenerAdapter. This method returns a new MessageListenerAdapter that is the Consumer class (it will use Consumer because is marked with the @Component annotation) and the method (messageHandler) that will handle the message once it is delivered.

Take your time to analyze it. MessageListenerAdapter is very similar to the JMS and Rabbit adapters. This adapter pattern will simplify the way you consume your message, regardless of its type, because under the covers it will do its best to do serialization and deserialization to get the right type of message to the method handler.

Next, let's see the main application. See Listing 10-19.

Listing 10-19. src/main/java/com/apress/spring/SpringBootRedisApplication. java

```
package com.apress.spring;

import org.springframework.beans.factory.annotation.Value;
import org.springframework.boot.CommandLineRunner;
import org.springframework.boot.SpringApplication;
import org.springframework.boot.autoconfigure.SpringBootApplication;
import org.springframework.context.annotation.Bean;

import com.apress.spring.redis.Producer;
```

```
@SpringBootApplication
public class SpringBootRedisApplication {

        public static void main(String[] args) {
                SpringApplication.run(SpringBootRedisApplication.class, args);
        }

        @Value("${topic}")
        String topic;

        @Bean
        CommandLineRunner sendMessage(Producer producer){
                return args -> {
                        producer.sendTo(topic, "Spring Boot rocks with Redis messaging!");
                };
        }
}
```

Listing 10-19 shows the main app; you are already familiar with everything here.

Before you run the project, make sure you have the Redis server up and running. To start it, execute the following command in a terminal:

```
$ redis-server
89887:C 11 Feb 20:17:55.320 # Warning: no config file specified, using the default config.
In order to specify a config file use redis-server /path/to/redis.conf
89887:M 11 Feb 20:17:55.321 * Increased maximum number of open files to 10032 (it was
originally set to 256).
```

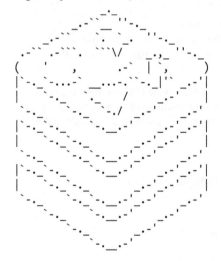

```
Redis 3.0.7 (00000000/0) 64 bit

Running in standalone mode
    Port: 6379
PID: 89887


http://redis.io
```

```
89887:M 11 Feb 20:17:55.323 # Server started, Redis version 3.0.7
89887:M 11 Feb 20:17:55.323 * The server is now ready to accept connections on port 6379
```

This output indicates that Redis is ready and listening in the port 6379. Now you can run the project as usual:

```
$ ./mvnw spring-boot:run
```

After executing this command, you should have in your logs something similar to the following output:

```
...
INFO 90211 --- [main] com.apress.spring.redis.Producer    : Sending> ...
INFO 90211 --- [c-2] com.apress.spring.redis.Consumer  : Consumer> Spring Boot rocks with
Redis messaging!
...
```

Well done! You have created a Spring Bot messaging app using Redis. You can shut down Redis by pressing Ctrl+C.

Remote Redis

If you want to access Redis remotely, you need to add the following properties to the application.properties file:

```
spring.redis.database=0
spring.redis.host=localhost
spring.redis.password=mysecurepassword
spring.redis.port=6379
```

You can always read about all the properties for Redis in the Spring Boot reference: https://docs.spring.io/spring-boot/docs/current/reference/html/common-application-properties.html.

You saw what you need to use Redis as a messaging broker, but if you want to know more about the key-value store with Spring, you can check out the Spring Data Redis project at http://projects.spring.io/spring-data-redis/.

WebSockets with Spring Boot

It might seem logical that a topic about WebSockets should be in the web chapter instead, but I consider WebSockets more related to messaging, and that's why this section is in this chapter.

WebSockets is a new way of communication, and it's replacing the client/server web technology. It allows long-held single TCP socket connections between the client and server. It's also called *push* technology, and it's where the server can send data to the web without the client do long polling to request a new change.

This section shows you an example where you will send a message through a REST endpoint (Producer) and receive the messages (Consumer) using a web page and some JavaScript libraries. So, let's get started. Open a terminal and execute the following commands:

```
$ mkdir spring-boot-websockets
$ cd spring-boot-websockets
$ spring init -d=websocket -g=com.apress.spring -a=spring-boot-websockets --package-
name=com.apress.spring -name=spring-boot-websockets -x
```

Let's take a look at the pom.xml file. See Listing 10-20.

Listing 10-20. pom.xml

```xml
<?xml version="1.0" encoding="UTF-8"?>
<project xmlns="http://maven.apache.org/POM/4.0.0" xmlns:xsi="http://www.w3.org/2001/
XMLSchema-instance"
        xsi:schemaLocation="http://maven.apache.org/POM/4.0.0 http://maven.apache.org/xsd/
        maven-4.0.0.xsd">
        <modelVersion>4.0.0</modelVersion>

        <groupId>com.apress.spring</groupId>
        <artifactId>spring-boot-websockets</artifactId>
        <version>0.0.1-SNAPSHOT</version>
        <packaging>jar</packaging>

        <name>spring-boot-websockets</name>
        <description>Demo project for Spring Boot</description>

        <parent>
                <groupId>org.springframework.boot</groupId>
                <artifactId>spring-boot-starter-parent</artifactId>
                <version>1.3.2.RELEASE</version>
                <relativePath/> <!-- lookup parent from repository -->
        </parent>

        <properties>
                <project.build.sourceEncoding>UTF-8</project.build.sourceEncoding>
                <java.version>1.8</java.version>
        </properties>

        <dependencies>
                <dependency>
                        <groupId>org.springframework.boot</groupId>
                        <artifactId>spring-boot-starter-websocket</artifactId>
                </dependency>

                <dependency>
                        <groupId>org.springframework.boot</groupId>
                        <artifactId>spring-boot-starter-test</artifactId>
                        <scope>test</scope>
                </dependency>
        </dependencies>

        <build>
                <plugins>
                        <plugin>
                                <groupId>org.springframework.boot</groupId>
                                <artifactId>spring-boot-maven-plugin</artifactId>
                        </plugin>
                </plugins>
        </build>

</project>
```

The spring-boot-starter-websocket is the pom that will bring all the dependencies that you need for creating a WebSockets messaging application. Between the dependencies you will have all the spring-webmvc, spring-messaging, spring-websocket, and tomcat-embedded you need, so there is no need to include the spring-boot-starter-web dependency. The WebSockets starter pom will use them automatically.

Next, let's see the Producer that will send the message to the HTML page. See Listing 10-21.

Listing 10-21. src/main/java/com/apress/spring/websocket/Producer.java

```java
package com.apress.spring.websocket;

import java.text.SimpleDateFormat;
import java.util.Date;

import org.springframework.beans.factory.annotation.Autowired;
import org.springframework.messaging.simp.SimpMessagingTemplate;
import org.springframework.stereotype.Component;

@Component
public class Producer {

    private static final SimpleDateFormat dateFormatter = new SimpleDateFormat("MM/dd/
    yyyy HH:mm:ss");

    @Autowired
    private SimpMessagingTemplate template;

    public void sendMessageTo(String topic, String message) {
        StringBuilder builder = new StringBuilder();
        builder.append("[");
        builder.append(dateFormatter.format(new Date()));
        builder.append("] ");
        builder.append(message);

        this.template.convertAndSend("/topic/" + topic, builder.toString());
    }
}
```

Listing 10-21 shows the Producer.java class that will be sending messages to the HTML page. Let's examine it:

- @Component. This annotation will register the Producer class as the bean for the Spring container.

- @Autowired SimpMessagingTemplate. This class is an implementation of the SimpMessagesSendingOperations class that provides methods for sending message to users.

- sendMessageTo. This method uses the SimpleMessagingTemplate instance to call the convertAndSend method (a familiar method from other technologies). The convertAndSend method requires a destination, in this case the topic where the message will be sent, and the message itself. You may have noticed that there is a / topic path before the topic's name. This is the way WebSockets will identify the topic name, by adding the /topic prefix.

This results in a very simple `Producer` class. This class will be used in the REST endpoint, as shown in Listing 10-22.

Listing 10-22. src/main/java/com/apress/spring/web/WebSocketController.java

```java
package com.apress.spring.web;

import org.springframework.beans.factory.annotation.Autowired;
import org.springframework.web.bind.annotation.PathVariable;
import org.springframework.web.bind.annotation.RequestMapping;
import org.springframework.web.bind.annotation.RequestParam;
import org.springframework.web.bind.annotation.RestController;

import com.apress.spring.websocket.Producer;

@RestController
public class WebSocketController {

        @Autowired
        Producer producer;

        @RequestMapping("/send/{topic}")
        public String sender(@PathVariable String topic, @RequestParam String message){
                producer.sendMessageTo(topic, message);
                return "OK-Sent";
        }

}
```

Listing 10-22 shows the REST endpoint. Let's examine it:

- `@RestController`. This annotation marks the class as a REST controller. This will register endpoints marked with the `@RequestMapping` annotation.

- `@RequestMapping("/send/{topic}")`. This annotation is the REST endpoint. In this case, it requires the topic path variable. The method sender accepts two parameters—the topic that is marked as `@PathVariable` that matches the endpoint signature (from the `@RequestMapping` annotation) and the message that is annotated with `@RequestParameter`, meaning that this value will be passed as an `url` param. The sender method uses the `Producer` instance to send the message to the specified topic.

Now you have your REST endpoint and your producer ready to send messages to a particular topic. Next, let's configure the endpoints necessary to create the WebSockets connections. See Listing 10-23.

Listing 10-23. src/main/java/com/apress/spring/config/WebSocketConfig.java

```java
package com.apress.spring.config;

import org.springframework.context.annotation.Configuration;
import org.springframework.messaging.simp.config.MessageBrokerRegistry;
import org.springframework.web.socket.config.annotation.
AbstractWebSocketMessageBrokerConfigurer;
```

```
import org.springframework.web.socket.config.annotation.EnableWebSocketMessageBroker;
import org.springframework.web.socket.config.annotation.StompEndpointRegistry;

@Configuration
@EnableWebSocketMessageBroker
public class WebSocketConfig extends AbstractWebSocketMessageBrokerConfigurer{

    @Override
    public void registerStompEndpoints(StompEndpointRegistry registry) {
        registry.addEndpoint("/stomp").withSockJS();
    }

    @Override
    public void configureMessageBroker(MessageBrokerRegistry config) {
        config.enableSimpleBroker("/topic");
        config.setApplicationDestinationPrefixes("/app");
    }
}
```

Listing 10-23 shows the WebSocketConfig class. Let's examine it:

- @Configuration. You know that this will mark the class as configuration for the Spring container.

- @EnableWebSocketMessageBroker. This annotation will use the auto-configuration to create all the necessary artifacts to enable broker-backed messaging over WebSockets using a very high-level messaging sub-protocol. If you need to customize the endpoints you need to override the methods from the AbstractWebSocketMessageBrokerConfigurer class.

- AbstractWebSocketMessageBrokerConfigurer. The WebSocketConfig is extending from this class. It will override methods to customize the protocols and endpoints.

- registerStompEndpoints(StompEndpointRegistry registry). This method will register the Stomp (https://stomp.github.io/) endpoint; in this case it will register the /stomp endpoint and use the JavaScript library SockJS (https://github.com/sockjs).

- configureMessageBroker(MessageBrokerRegistry config). This method will configure the message broker options. In this case, it will enable the broker in the /topic endpoint. This means that the clients who want to use the WebSockets broker need to use the /topic to connect.

Now, let's see the actual consumer, which is the web page that will connect to the WebSockets broker. Create the folder called static in src/main/resources/static and create index.html. See Listing 10-24.

Listing 10-24. src/main/resources/static/index.html

```
<!DOCTYPE html>
<html>
<head>
    <title>Spring Boot WebSocket Messaging</title>
    <script type="text/javascript" src="//cdn.jsdelivr.net/jquery/2.2.0/jquery.min.js">
    </script>
```

```html
<script type="text/javascript" src="//cdn.jsdelivr.net/sockjs/1.0.3/sockjs.min.js">
</script>
<script type="text/javascript" src="//cdnjs.cloudflare.com/ajax/libs/stomp.js/2.3.3/
stomp.min.js"></script>
</head>
<body>
    <div>
        <h3>Messages:</h3>
        <ol id="messages"></ol>
    </div>

    <script type="text/javascript">
        $(document).ready(function() {
            var messageList = $("#messages");
            var socket = new SockJS('/stomp');
            var stompClient = Stomp.over(socket);

            stompClient.connect({ }, function(frame) {
                stompClient.subscribe("/topic/message", function(data) {
                    var message = data.body;
                    messageList.append("<li>" + message + "</li>");
                });
            });
        });
    </script>
</body>
</html>
```

Listing 10-24 shows the index.html web page. Notice that this page is in the src/main/resources/ static path, not in the templates. This is because you are not using any particular view engine like before. So static files like this web page should be in the static folder. The index.html page uses several JavaScript libraries. You can find always the latest at http://cdn.jsdelivr.net and http://cdnjs.cloudflare.com. It uses the jQuery that will be use for append the messages to an HTML list. It will use the sockjs library to connect to the /stomp endpoint, and it will use Stomp library to subscribe to the broker's /topic/message endpoint. The final topic will be /topic/message (or topic = message), so that's where the producer needs to send the message.

Now you are ready to start testing your Spring Boot WebSockets project. You can run the application as usual:

```
$ ./mvnw spring-boot:run
```

Open the a browser and go to http://localhost:8080. You should see the messages text. Next, open a terminal and execute the following commands:

```
$ curl localhost:8080/send/message -d "message=Spring Boot Rocks"
OK-Sent
$ curl localhost:8080/send/message -d "message=Spring Boot with WebSocket is awesome"
OK-Sent
$ curl localhost:8080/send/message -d "message=Hello World"
OK-Sent
```

After using the first command you should see the messages appear in the browser. Verify that you are using the path variable /message, and that it is the WebSockets topic. Also you are passing a parameter message? It's equivalent to use:

```
$ curl "http://ocalhost:8080/send/message?message=Hi There"
```

See Figure 10-4 for the results of these commands.

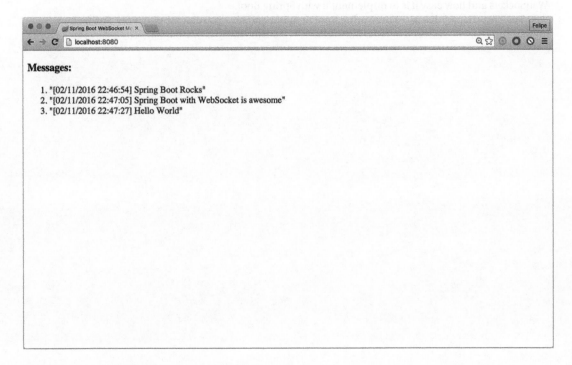

Figure 10-4. *SockJS and Stomp messages*

Figure 10-4 shows the result of posting messages through WebSockets. Now imagine the possibilities for new applications that require some notification in real-time (such as creating real-time chat rooms or updating stocks on the fly for your customers or updating your web site without preview or restart). With Spring Boot and WebSockets you are covered.

■ **Note**   All the code is available from the Apress site. You can also get the latest at
https://github.com/felipeg48/pro-spring-boot repository.

Summary

This chapter discussed all the technologies that are used for messaging, including JMS (Java Message Service) and HornetQ. It also discussed how to connect to a remote server by providing the server name and port in the `application.properties` file.

You learned about AMQP and RabbitMQ and how you can send and receive messages using Spring Boot. You also learned about Redis and how to use its Pub/Sub messaging, and finally you learned about WebSockets and how easy it is to implement it with Spring Boot.

The next chapter discusses the Spring Boot Actuator and how you can monitor your Spring Boot application.

CHAPTER 11

Spring Boot Actuator

This chapter discusses the Spring Actuator module and explains how you can use all its features to monitor your Spring Boot applications.

A common task during and after development that every developer does is to start checking out the logs. Developers check to see if the business logic works as it supposed to, or check out the processing time of some services, and so on. Even though they should have their unit, integration, and regression tests in place, they are not exempt from externals failures like network (connections, speed, etc.), disk (space, permissions, etc.), and more.

When you deploy to production, it's even more critical. You must pay attention to your applications and sometimes to the whole system. When you start depending on some non-functional requirements like monitoring systems that check for the health of the different applications, or maybe that set alerts when your application gets to a certain threshold or even worse, when your application crashes, you need to act ASAP.

Developers depend on many third-party technologies to do their job, and I'm not saying that this is bad, but this means that all the heavy lifting is in the dev-ops teams. They must monitor every single application and the entire system as a whole.

Spring Boot Actuator

Spring Boot includes an Actuator module, which introduces production-ready non-functional requirements to your application. The Spring Boot Actuator module provides monitoring, metrics, and auditing right out of box.

What makes the Actuator module more attractive is that you can expose data through different technologies, like HTTP (endpoints), JMX, and SSH (using CRaSH at http://www.crashub.org/).

Let's start with a basic web application. Open a terminal and execute the following commands:

```
$ mkdir spring-boot-web-actuator
$ cd spring-boot-actuator
$ spring init -d=web,actuator -g=com.apress.spring -a=spring-boot-web-actuator
--package-name=com.apress.spring -name=spring-boot-web-actuator -x
```

As you can see, the dependencies are web and actuator, and this will include the spring-boot-starter-web and the spring-boot-starter-actuator poms. See Listing 11-1.

Listing 11-1. pom.xml

```xml
<?xml version="1.0" encoding="UTF-8"?>
<project xmlns="http://maven.apache.org/POM/4.0.0"
xmlns:xsi="http://www.w3.org/2001/XMLSchema-instance"
      xsi:schemaLocation="http://maven.apache.org/POM/4.0.0
      http://maven.apache.org/xsd/maven-4.0.0.xsd">
      <modelVersion>4.0.0</modelVersion>

      <groupId>com.apress.spring</groupId>
      <artifactId>spring-boot-web-actuator</artifactId>
      <version>0.0.1-SNAPSHOT</version>
      <packaging>jar</packaging>

      <name>spring-boot-web-actuator</name>
      <description>Demo project for Spring Boot</description>

      <parent>
            <groupId>org.springframework.boot</groupId>
            <artifactId>spring-boot-starter-parent</artifactId>
            <version>1.3.2.RELEASE</version>
            <relativePath/> <!-- lookup parent from repository -->
      </parent>

      <properties>
            <project.build.sourceEncoding>UTF-8</project.build.sourceEncoding>
            <java.version>1.8</java.version>
      </properties>

      <dependencies>
            <dependency>
                  <groupId>org.springframework.boot</groupId>
                  <artifactId>spring-boot-starter-web</artifactId>
            </dependency>

            <dependency>
                  <groupId>org.springframework.boot</groupId>
                  <artifactId>spring-boot-starter-actuator</artifactId>
            </dependency>

            <dependency>
                  <groupId>org.springframework.boot</groupId>
                  <artifactId>spring-boot-starter-test</artifactId>
                  <scope>test</scope>
            </dependency>
      </dependencies>
```

```
        <build>
                <plugins>
                        <plugin>
                                <groupId>org.springframework.boot</groupId>
                                <artifactId>spring-boot-maven-plugin</artifactId>
                        </plugin>
                </plugins>
        </build>
</project>
```

Listing 11-1 shows the pom.xml file with the web and actuator starter poms. Now, let's open the main app and create a basic web controller and endpoint. See Listing 11-2.

Listing 11-2. src/main/java/com/apress/spring/SpringBootWebActuatorApplication.java

```java
package com.apress.spring;

import org.springframework.boot.SpringApplication;
import org.springframework.boot.autoconfigure.SpringBootApplication;
import org.springframework.web.bind.annotation.RequestMapping;
import org.springframework.web.bind.annotation.RestController;


@RestController
@SpringBootApplication
public class SpringBootWebActuatorApplication {

        public static void main(String[] args) {
                SpringApplication.run(SpringBootWebActuatorApplication.class, args);
        }

        @RequestMapping("/")
        public String index(){
                return "Spring Boot Actuator";
        }
}
```

Listing 11-2 shows the main application. As you can see, there is nothing new. It's just a simple web application that maps to the root and returns the string "Spring Boot Actuator". It's based on what you already know about the @RestController and the @RequestMapping annotations.

Let's start the application by executing the following:

```
$ ./mvnw spring-boot:run
```

After running the application, you should see these mappings in your logs:

```
...
INFO - [m] o.s...M: Mapped "{[/]}"
...
INFO - [m] o.s...E: Mapped "{[/health || /health.json],produces=[application/json]}"
INFO - [m] o.s...E: Mapped "{[/beans || /beans.json],methods=[GET],produces=[application/json]}"
INFO - [m] o.s...E: Mapped "{[/info || /info.json],methods=[GET],produces=[application/json]}"
```

```
INFO - [m] o.s...E: Mapped "{[/mappings || /mappings.json],methods=[GET],
produces=[application/json]}"
INFO - [m] o.s...E: Mapped "{[/env/{name:.*}],methods=[GET],produces=[application/json]}"
INFO - [m] o.s...E: Mapped "{[/env || /env.json],methods=[GET],produces=[application/json]}"
INFO - [m] o.s...E: Mapped "{[/metrics/{name:.*}],methods=[GET],produces=[application/json]}"
INFO - [m] o.s...E: Mapped "{[/metrics || /metrics.json],methods=[GET],produces=
[application/json]}"
INFO - [m] o.s...E: Mapped "{[/autoconfig || /autoconfig.json],methods=[GET],produces=
[application/json]}"
INFO - [m] o.s...E: Mapped "{[/trace || /trace.json],methods=[GET],produces=[application/json]}"
INFO - [m] o.s...E: Mapped "{[/configprops || /configprops.json],methods=[GET],
produces=[application/json]}"
INFO - [m] o.s...E: Mapped "{[/dump || /dump.json],methods=[GET],produces=[application/json]}"
...
```

First, you should see the RequestMappingHandlerMapping class mapped to the endpoint / from the @RequestMapping annotation you have in the index method. Also you will see, the EndpointHandlerMapping class mapped to several endpoints that belong to the Actuator module. Let's see each endpoint in detail.

/actuator

This endpoint is not listed by the EndpointHandlerMapping class, but let's see what it does and how to activate it. You can stop your application by pressing Ctrl+C on your keyboard.

The /actuator endpoint will provide a hypermedia-based discovery page for all the other endpoints, but it will require the Spring HATEOAS in the classpath, so if you include this in your pom.xml:

```
<dependency>
        <groupId>org.springframework.hateoas</groupId>
        <artifactId>spring-hateoas</artifactId>
</dependency>
```

You can rerun your application and you will see that now is listed by the EndpointHandlerMapping class logs and you can access it through the URL /actuator. So, if you go to http://localhost:8080/actuator, you should see something similar to Figure 11-1.

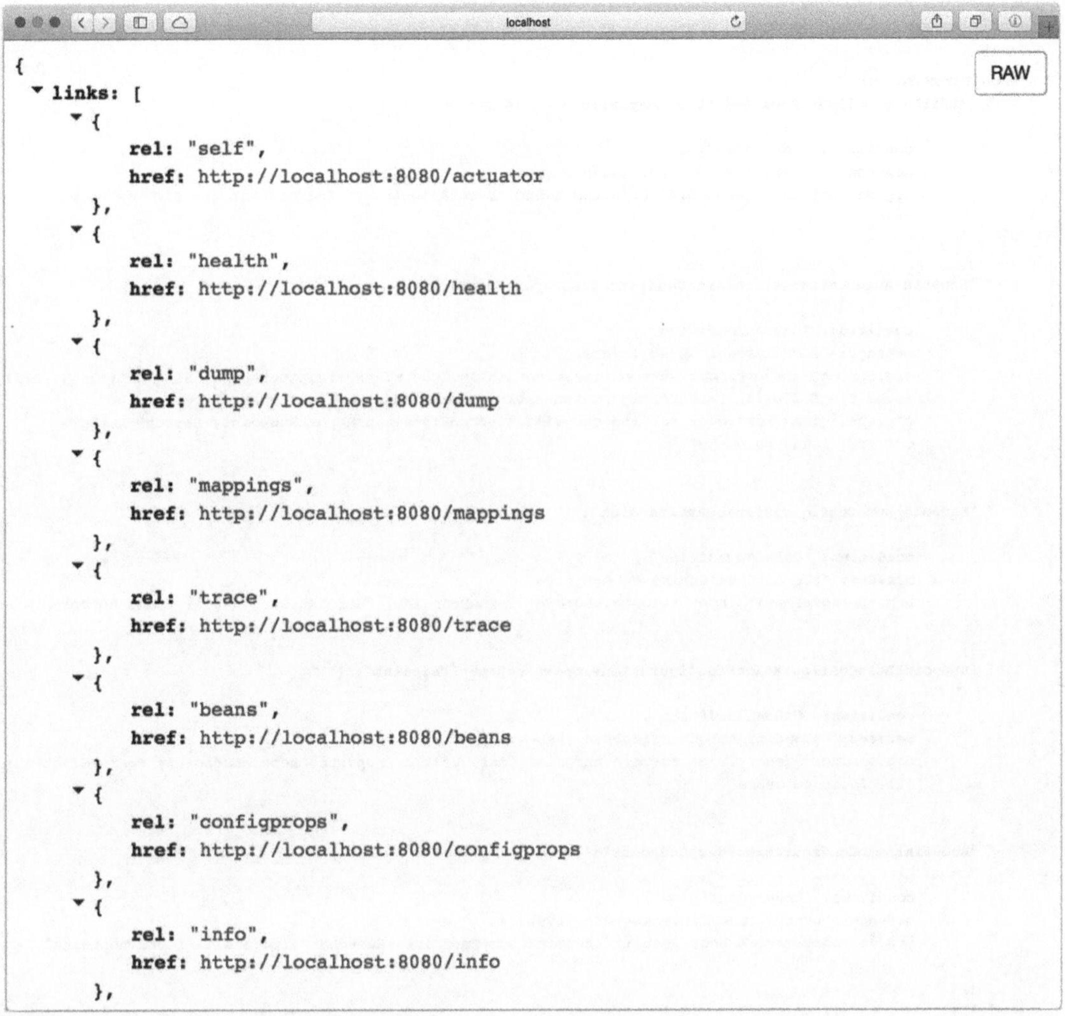

```
{                                                                                    RAW
  ▼ links: [
    ▼ {
        rel: "self",
        href: http://localhost:8080/actuator
      },
    ▼ {
        rel: "health",
        href: http://localhost:8080/health
      },
    ▼ {
        rel: "dump",
        href: http://localhost:8080/dump
      },
    ▼ {
        rel: "mappings",
        href: http://localhost:8080/mappings
      },
    ▼ {
        rel: "trace",
        href: http://localhost:8080/trace
      },
    ▼ {
        rel: "beans",
        href: http://localhost:8080/beans
      },
    ▼ {
        rel: "configprops",
        href: http://localhost:8080/configprops
      },
    ▼ {
        rel: "info",
        href: http://localhost:8080/info
      },
```

Figure 11-1. http://localhost:8080/actuator

Figure 11-1 shows all the links that you can access through the Actuator module. The Actuator gives you all the possible endpoints that you can access. Remember, you need to add the Spring HATEOAS dependency to your pom.xml file as well.

/autoconfig

This endpoint will display the auto-configuration report. It will give you two groups: positiveMatches and negativeMatches. Remember that the main feature of Spring Boot is that it will auto-configure your application by seeing the classpath and dependencies. This has everything to do with the starter poms and extra dependencies that you add to your pom.xml file. If you go to http://localhost:8080/autoconfig, you should see something similar to Figure 11-2.

Figure 11-2. `http://localhost:8080/autoconfig`

/beans

This endpoint will display all the Spring beans that are used in your application. Remember that even though you add a few lines of code to create a simple web application, behind the scenes Spring starts to create all the necessary beans to run your app. If you go to `http://localhost:8080/beans`, you should see something similar to Figure 11-3.

Figure 11-3. `http://localhost:8080/beans`

/configprops

This endpoint will list all the configuration properties that are defined by the @ConfigurationProperties beans, which is something that I showed you in earlier chapters. Remember that you can add your own configuration properties prefix and that they can be defined and accessed in the application.properties or YAML files. Figure 11-4 shows an example of this endpoint.

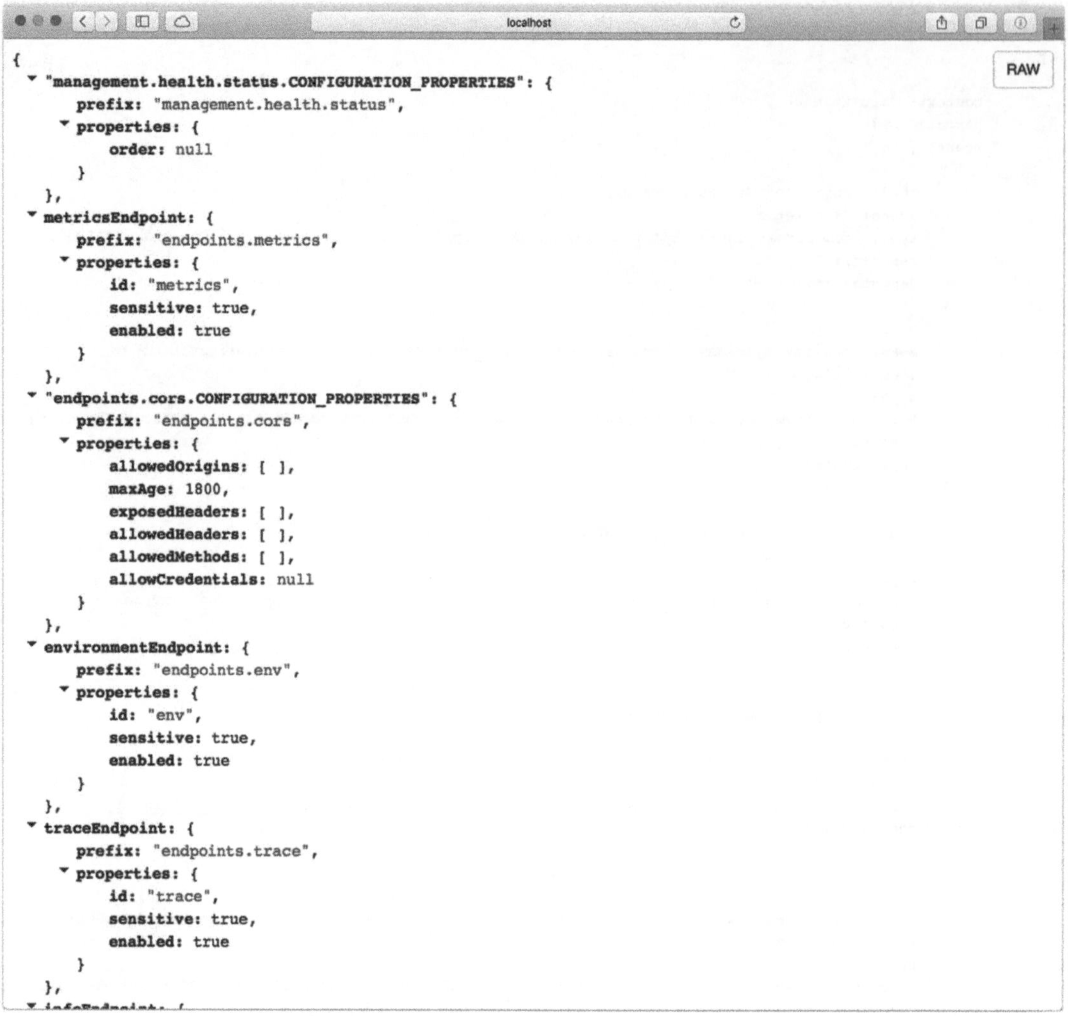

```
{
    ▼ "management.health.status.CONFIGURATION_PROPERTIES": {
          prefix: "management.health.status",
        ▼ properties: {
              order: null
          }
    },
    ▼ metricsEndpoint: {
          prefix: "endpoints.metrics",
        ▼ properties: {
              id: "metrics",
              sensitive: true,
              enabled: true
          }
    },
    ▼ "endpoints.cors.CONFIGURATION_PROPERTIES": {
          prefix: "endpoints.cors",
        ▼ properties: {
              allowedOrigins: [ ],
              maxAge: 1800,
              exposedHeaders: [ ],
              allowedHeaders: [ ],
              allowedMethods: [ ],
              allowCredentials: null
          }
    },
    ▼ environmentEndpoint: {
          prefix: "endpoints.env",
        ▼ properties: {
              id: "env",
              sensitive: true,
              enabled: true
          }
    },
    ▼ traceEndpoint: {
          prefix: "endpoints.trace",
        ▼ properties: {
              id: "trace",
              sensitive: true,
              enabled: true
          }
    },
```

Figure 11-4. `http://localhost:8080/configprops`

You can stop you application by pressing Ctrl+C.

/docs

This endpoint will show HTML pages with all the documentation for all the Actuator module endpoints. This endpoint can be activated by including the spring-boot-actuator-docs dependency in pom.xml:

```xml
<dependency>
        <groupId>org.springframework.boot</groupId>
        <artifactId>spring-boot-actuator-docs</artifactId>
</dependency>
```

After adding this dependency to your application, you can rerun it and see in the logs that the /docs endpoint is listed. See Figure 11-5 as the result of including the spring-boot-actuator-docs (http://localhost:8080/docs). Very useful!

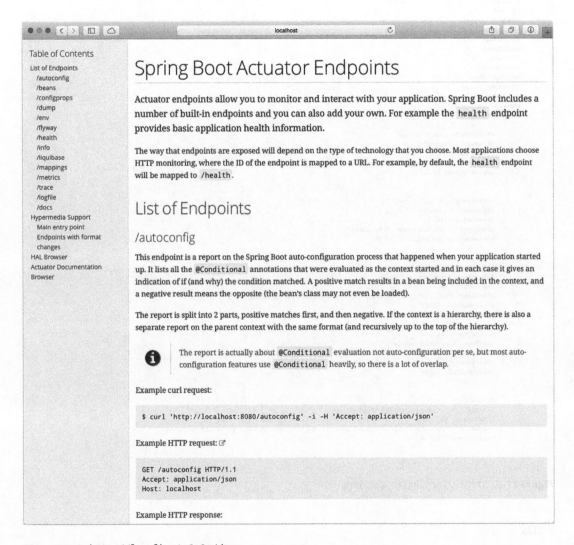

Figure 11-5. http://localhost:8080/docs

/dump

This endpoint will perform a thread dump of your application. It shows all the threads running and their stack trace of the JVM that is running your app. Go to http://localhost:8080/dump endpoint. See Figure 11-6.

```
[
  ▾ {
      threadName: "http-nio-8080-exec-10",
      threadId: 34,
      blockedTime: -1,
      blockedCount: 0,
      waitedTime: -1,
      waitedCount: 0,
      lockName: null,
      lockOwnerId: -1,
      lockOwnerName: null,
      inNative: false,
      suspended: false,
      threadState: "RUNNABLE",
    ▾ stackTrace: [
        ▾ {
            methodName: "dumpThreads0",
            fileName: "ThreadImpl.java",
            lineNumber: -2,
            className: "sun.management.ThreadImpl",
            nativeMethod: true
          },
        ▾ {
            methodName: "dumpAllThreads",
            fileName: "ThreadImpl.java",
            lineNumber: 446,
            className: "sun.management.ThreadImpl",
            nativeMethod: false
          },
        ▾ {
            methodName: "invoke",
            fileName: "DumpEndpoint.java",
            lineNumber: 44,
            className: "org.springframework.boot.actuate.endpoint.DumpEndpoint",
            nativeMethod: false
          },
        ▾ {
            methodName: "invoke",
            fileName: "DumpEndpoint.java",
            lineNumber: 31,
            className: "org.springframework.boot.actuate.endpoint.DumpEndpoint",
            nativeMethod: false
          },
        ▾ {
            methodName: "invoke",
            fileName: "AbstractEndpointMvcAdapter.java",
            lineNumber: 53,
            className: "org.springframework.boot.actuate.endpoint.mvc.AbstractEndpointMvcAdapter",
            nativeMethod: false
          },
        ▾ {
```

Figure 11-6. `http://localhost:8080/dump`

/env

This endpoint will expose all the properties from the Spring's ConfigurableEnvironment interface. This will show any active profiles and system environment variables and all application properties, including the Spring Boot properties. Go to `http://localhost:8080/env`. See Figure 11-7.

```
{
    profiles: [ ],
  ▼ "server.ports": {
        "local.server.port": 8080
    },
    servletContextInitParams: { },
  ▼ systemProperties: {
        "com.sun.management.jmxremote.authenticate": "false",
        "java.runtime.name": "Java(TM) SE Runtime Environment",
        "sun.boot.library.path": "/Library/Java/JavaVirtualMachines/jdk1.8.0_66.jdk/Contents/Home/jre/lib",
        "java.vm.version": "25.66-b17",
        gopherProxySet: "false",
        "java.vm.vendor": "Oracle Corporation",
        "java.vendor.url": "http://java.oracle.com/,
        "java.rmi.server.randomIDs": "true",
        "path.separator": ":",
        "java.vm.name": "Java HotSpot(TM) 64-Bit Server VM",
        "file.encoding.pkg": "sun.io",
        "user.country": "US",
        "sun.java.launcher": "SUN_STANDARD",
        "sun.os.patch.level": "unknown",
        PID: "81757",
        "com.sun.management.jmxremote.port": "64142",
        "java.vm.specification.name": "Java Virtual Machine Specification",
        "user.dir": "/Users/felipeg/Progs/Books/pro-spring-boot/ch11-spring-boot-web-actuator",
        "java.runtime.version": "1.8.0_66-b17",
        "java.awt.graphicsenv": "sun.awt.CGraphicsEnvironment",
        "org.jboss.logging.provider": "slf4j",
        "java.endorsed.dirs": "/Library/Java/JavaVirtualMachines/jdk1.8.0_66.jdk/Contents/Home/jre/lib/endorsed",
        "os.arch": "x86_64",
        "java.io.tmpdir": "/var/folders/t1/sl1893vx63v_p116c9tsbg340000gn/T/",
        "line.separator": "\n",
        "java.vm.specification.vendor": "Oracle Corporation",
        "os.name": "Mac OS X",
        "sun.jnu.encoding": "UTF-8",
        "spring.beaninfo.ignore": "true",
        "java.library.path":
"/Users/felipeg/Library/Java/Extensions:/Library/Java/Extensions:/Network/Library/Java/Extensions:/System/Library/Java/Extensio
        "java.specification.name": "Java Platform API Specification",
        "java.class.version": "52.0",
        "sun.management.compiler": "HotSpot 64-Bit Tiered Compilers",
        "spring.liveBeansView.mbeanDomain": "",
        "os.version": "10.11.3",
        "http.nonProxyHosts": "local|*.local|169.254/16|*.169.254/16",
        "user.home": "/Users/felipeg",
        "catalina.useNaming": "false",
        "user.timezone": "America/Denver",
        "java.awt.printerjob": "sun.lwawt.macosx.CPrinterJob",
        "file.encoding": "UTF-8",
        "java.specification.version": "1.8",
        "catalina.home": "/private/var/folders/t1/sl1893vx63v_p116c9tsbg340000gn/T/tomcat.1193775557036903923.8080".
```

Figure 11-7. `http://localhost:8080/`

/flyway

This endpoint will provide all the information about your database migration scripts; it's based on the
Flyway project (`https://flywaydb.org/`). This is very useful when you want to have full control of your
database by versioning your schemas. If you are familiar with Ruby on Rails, this is very similar to the active
record migrations.

Before you continue, you can stop your application. To activate this endpoint you need to include the
following dependencies:

```
<dependency>
        <groupId>org.springframework.boot</groupId>
        <artifactId>spring-boot-starter-data-jpa</artifactId>
</dependency>
```

255

```
<dependency>
        <groupId>org.flywaydb</groupId>
        <artifactId>flyway-core</artifactId>
</dependency>
<dependency>
        <groupId>com.h2database</groupId>
        <artifactId>h2</artifactId>
        <scope>runtime</scope>
</dependency>
```

Because this is related to the database app, you need to include the previous dependencies, but let's use the main app to add simple code to enable a database application. Create a Person domain class. See Listing 11-3.

Listing 11-3. src/main/java/com/apress/spring/domain/Person.java

```java
package com.apress.spring.domain;

import javax.persistence.Entity;
import javax.persistence.GeneratedValue;
import javax.persistence.Id;

@Entity
public class Person {

        @Id
        @GeneratedValue
        private Long id;
        private String firstName;
        private String lastName;

        public String getFirstName() {
                return this.firstName;
        }

        public void setFirstName(String firstName) {
                this.firstName = firstName;
        }

        public String getLastName() {
                return this.lastName;
        }

        public void setLastName(String lastname) {
                this.lastName = lastname;
        }

        @Override
        public String toString() {
                return "Person (firstName=" + this.firstName + ", lastName=" +
                this.lastName + ")";
        }
}
```

Listing 11-3 shows a basic class annotated with the @Entity, @Id, and @GeneratedValue annotations, something that you already know and that I showed you in earlier chapters. Next, let's create the repository interface. See Listing 11-4.

Listing 11-4. src/main/java/com/apress/spring/repository/PersonRepository.java

```
package com.apress.spring.repository;

import org.springframework.data.repository.CrudRepository;

import com.apress.spring.domain.Person;

public interface PersonRepository extends CrudRepository<Person, Long> { }
```

Listing 11-4 shows the PersonRepository.java interface. This time, instead of extending from JpaRepository, you are extending from the CrudRepository interface. This interface doesn't have the paging and sorting functionality, but for this example with basic CRUD operation it's more than enough.

Next, let's add the following properties to the application.properties. See Listing 11-5.

Listing 11-5. src/main/resources/application.properties

```
spring.jpa.hibernate.ddl-auto=validate
spring.h2.console.enabled=true
```

Listing 11-5 shows the two properties you are going to use—the first one validates the schemas/data you are going to use and the second enables the /h2-console endpoint for you to see the table structure and the queries.

Next, modify the main app to look like Listing 11-6.

Listing 11-6. src/main/java/com/apress/spring/SpringBootWebActuatorApplication.java

```
package com.apress.spring;

import org.slf4j.Logger;
import org.slf4j.LoggerFactory;
import org.springframework.boot.CommandLineRunner;
import org.springframework.boot.SpringApplication;
import org.springframework.boot.autoconfigure.SpringBootApplication;
import org.springframework.context.annotation.Bean;
import org.springframework.web.bind.annotation.RequestMapping;
import org.springframework.web.bind.annotation.RestController;

import com.apress.spring.repository.PersonRepository;

@RestController
@SpringBootApplication
public class SpringBootWebActuatorApplication {

        public static void main(String[] args) {
                SpringApplication.run(SpringBootWebActuatorApplication.class, args);
        }
```

257

```
@RequestMapping("/")
public String index(){
        return "Spring Boot Actuator";
}

private static final Logger log = LoggerFactory.getLogger(SpringBootWebActuator
Application.class);

@Bean
CommandLineRunner findAll(PersonRepository repo){
        return args ->{
                log.info("> Persons in Database: ");
                repo.findAll().forEach(person -> log.info(person.toString()));
        };
}
}
```

Listing 11-6 shows the SpringBootWebActuatorApplication.java class. Note the last few lines, where you are defining a log (to print out the database records) and the @Bean CommandLineRunner, where it will run after Spring Boot finalizes its auto-configuration and executes the findAll method. It receives the PersonRepository that will be auto-wired and will return the output of calling the repo.findAll from the database.

Now, before you run the application, you need to create the db/migration structure under src/main/resources and add two versions of an init SQL scripts. This structure (db/migration) is required for this application to work. See Figure 11-8.

```
.
├── mvnw
├── mvnw.cmd
├── pom.xml
└── src
    ├── main
    │   ├── java
    │   │   └── com
    │   │       └── apress
    │   │           └── spring
    │   │               ├── SpringBootWebActuatorApplication.java
    │   │               ├── domain
    │   │               │   └── Person.java
    │   │               └── repository
    │   │                   └── PersonRepository.java
    │   └── resources
    │       ├── application.properties
    │       ├── db
    │       │   └── migration
    │       │       ├── V1__init.sql
    │       │       └── V2__init.sql
    │       ├── static
    │       └── templates
    └── test
        └── java
            └── com
                └── apress
                    └── spring
                        └── SpringBootWebActuatorApplicationTests.java

18 directories, 10 files
```

Figure 11-8. *The directory structure with the db/migration SQL scripts*

Figure 11-8 shows the final structure for your current application and it's important to notice the two SQL scripts used to initialize the database. Note that they have versions V1 and V2. The naming convention of using versions is required for this to work. See Listings 11-7 (V1) and 11-8 (V2).

Listing 11-7. src/main/resources/db/migration/V1__init.sql

```sql
DROP TABLE IF EXISTS PERSON;

CREATE TABLE PERSON (
        id BIGINT GENERATED BY DEFAULT AS IDENTITY,
        first_name varchar(255) not null,
        last_name varchar(255) not null
);

insert into PERSON (first_name, last_name) values ('Red', 'Lobster');
```

Listing 11-7 shows very simple SQL that will define the table and one record.

Listing 11-8. src/main/resources/db/migration/V2__init.sql

```
insert into PERSON (first_name, last_name) values ('Ronald', 'McDonald');
insert into PERSON (first_name, last_name) values ('Jack', 'InTheBox');
insert into PERSON (first_name, last_name) values ('Carl', 'Jr');
```

Listing 11-8 shows version 2 of the init SQL script. As you can see, the only difference is that V2 has more records to add. Now, if you run your application as usual:

```
$ ./mvnw spring-boot:run
```

You will find the following output in the logs:

```
...
INFO 87925 --- [m] o.f.. : Flyway 3.2.1 by Boxfuse
INFO 87925 --- [m] o.f.. : Database: jdbc:h2:mem:testdb (H2 1.4)
INFO 87925 --- [m] o.f.. : Validated 2 migrations (execution time 00:00.013s)
INFO 87925 --- [m] o.f.. : Creating Metadata table: "PUBLIC"."schema_version"
INFO 87925 --- [m] o.f.. : Current version of schema "PUBLIC": << Empty Schema >>
INFO 87925 --- [m] o.f.. : Migrating schema "PUBLIC" to version 1 - init
INFO 87925 --- [m] o.f.. : Migrating schema "PUBLIC" to version 2 - init
INFO 87925 --- [m] o.f.. : Successfully applied 2 migrations to schema "PUBLIC" (execution
                           time 00:00.090s).
INFO 87925 --- [m] .... : Building JPA container EntityManagerFactory for persistence unit
                          'default'
...
INFO 87925 --- [m] ...E : Mapped "{[/flyway || /flyway.json]
...
INFO 87925 --- [m] ...App: > Persons in Database:
INFO 87925 --- [m] ...App: Person (firstName=Red, lastName=Lobster)
INFO 87925 --- [m] ...App: Person (firstName=Ronald, lastName=McDonald)
INFO 87925 --- [m] ...App: Person (firstName=Jack, lastName=InTheBox)
INFO 87925 --- [m] ...App: Person (firstName=Carl, lastName=Jr)
...
```

As you can see from this output, the Flyway will kick in and execute the migration script in order based on its version, so it will execute the V1__init.sql first, then the V2__init.sql. That's why at the end you will see the four persons in the output. Also it's been mapped to the /flyway endpoint, so if you go to http://localhost:8080/flyway, you will see the information about the scripts executed and its state after its execution. See Figure 11-9.

```
[
    {
        type: "SQL",
        checksum: 385338629,
        version: "1",
        description: "init",
        script: "V1__init.sql",
        state: "SUCCESS",
        installedOn: 1455652053477,
        executionTime: 14
    },
    {
        type: "SQL",
        checksum: -2099332614,
        version: "2",
        description: "init",
        script: "V2__init.sql",
        state: "SUCCESS",
        installedOn: 1455652053499,
        executionTime: 8
    }
]
```
RAW

Figure 11-9. `http://localhost:8080/flyway`

As you can see, you have now the power of using database migrations by adding the flyway-core dependency together with the Actuator module. As an exercise, consider what you would need to do to enable the flyway in your Spring Boot journal application.

/health

This endpoint will show the health of the application. If you are doing a database app like in the previous section (/flyway) you will see the DB status and by default you will see also the diskSpace from your system. If you are running your app, you can go to http://localhost:8080/health. See Figure 11-10.

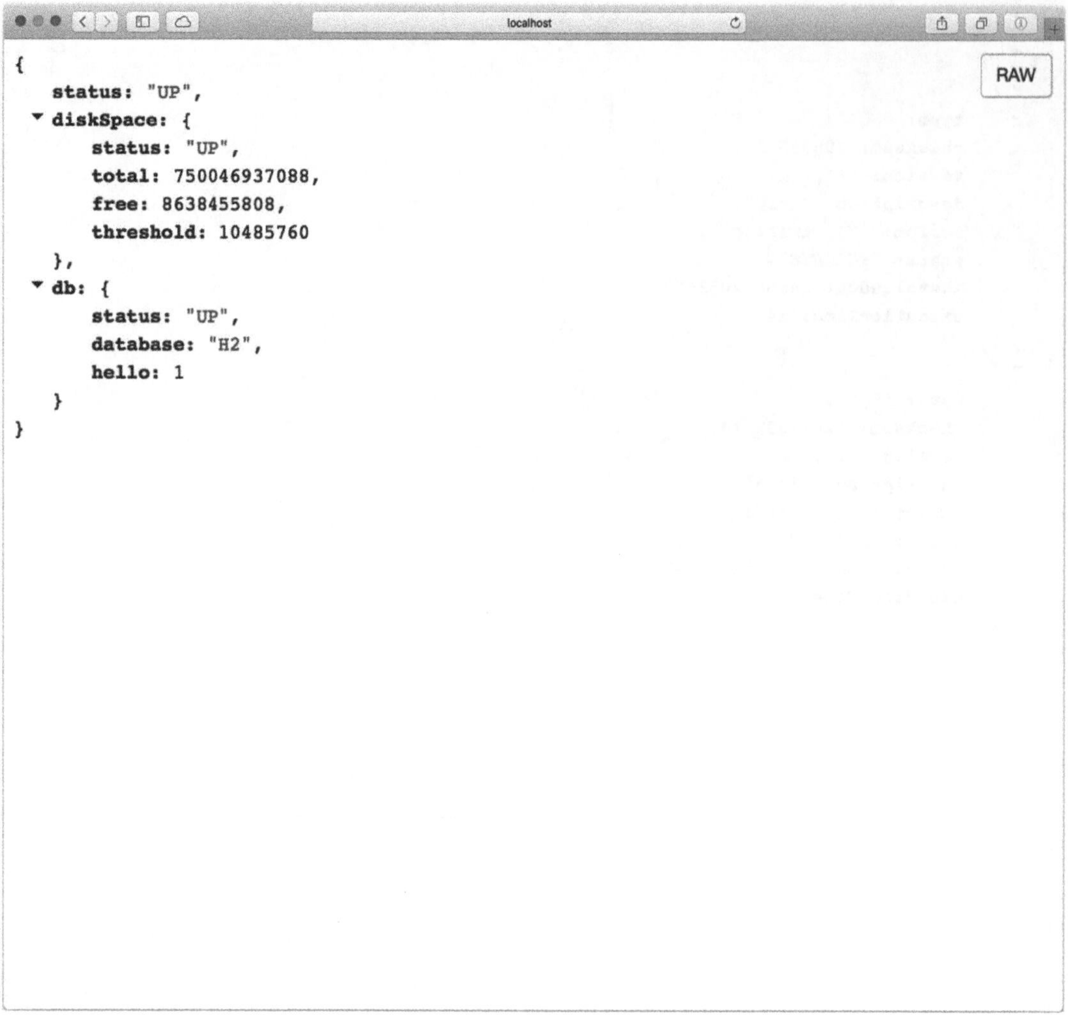

```
{
    status: "UP",
  ▼ diskSpace: {
        status: "UP",
        total: 750046937088,
        free: 8638455808,
        threshold: 10485760
    },
  ▼ db: {
        status: "UP",
        database: "H2",
        hello: 1
    }
}
```

RAW

Figure 11-10. `http://localhost:8080/health`

Figure 11-10 shows the result of the health not only of your app but of the database connectivity. This is very useful if you want to find about external services, such as in this example the database.

/info

This endpoint will display the public application info. This means that you need to add this information to `application.properties`. It's recommended that you add it if you have multiple Spring Boot applications. So, before you continue, stop your application. Next, modify your `application.properties` file so that it looks like Listing 11-9.

Listing 11-9. src/main/resources/appplication.properties

```
info.app.name=Spring Boot Web Actuator Application
info.app.description=This is an example of the Actuator module
info.app.version=1.0.0

spring.jpa.hibernate.ddl-auto=validate
spring.h2.console.enabled=true
```

After adding the properties to your application.properties file, go to http://localhost:8080/info. You should see something similar to Figure 11-11.

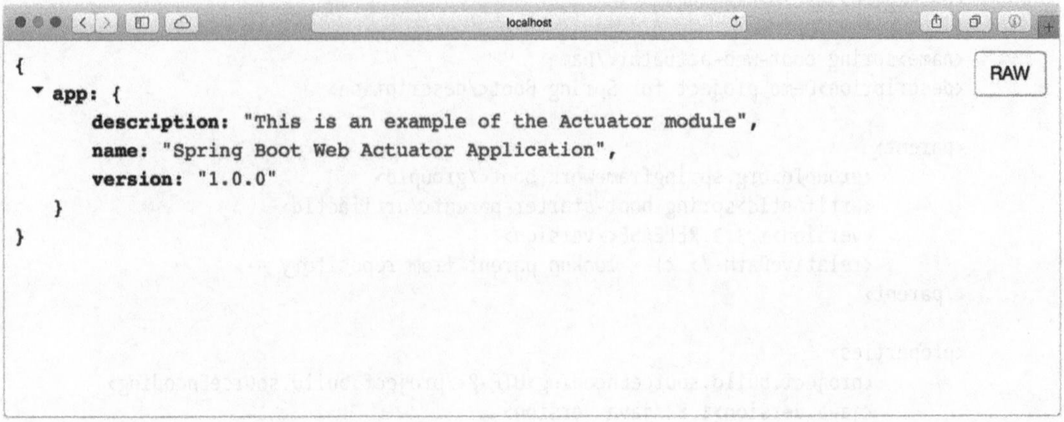

Figure 11-11. http://localhost:8080/info

Figure 11-11 shows the information about your application, but it's necessary to modify the application.properties with the info.app properties.

/liquibase

This endpoint will show all the Liquibase (http://www.liquibase.org/) database migrations that have been applied. This is very similar to Flyway. If you are running your application, you can stop it now.

You need to add the liquibase-core pom in order to enable the /liquibase endpoint:

```
<dependency>
        <groupId>org.liquibase</groupId>
        <artifactId>liquibase-core</artifactId>
</dependency>
```

Modify your pom.xml to look like Listing 11-10.

Listing 11-10. pom.xml

```xml
<?xml version="1.0" encoding="UTF-8"?>
<project xmlns="http://maven.apache.org/POM/4.0.0"
xmlns:xsi="http://www.w3.org/2001/XMLSchema-instance"
        xsi:schemaLocation="http://maven.apache.org/POM/4.0.0
        http://maven.apache.org/xsd/maven-4.0.0.xsd">
        <modelVersion>4.0.0</modelVersion>

        <groupId>com.apress.spring</groupId>
        <artifactId>spring-boot-web-actuator</artifactId>
        <version>0.0.1-SNAPSHOT</version>
        <packaging>jar</packaging>

        <name>spring-boot-web-actuator</name>
        <description>Demo project for Spring Boot</description>

        <parent>
                <groupId>org.springframework.boot</groupId>
                <artifactId>spring-boot-starter-parent</artifactId>
                <version>1.3.2.RELEASE</version>
                <relativePath /> <!-- lookup parent from repository -->
        </parent>

        <properties>
                <project.build.sourceEncoding>UTF-8</project.build.sourceEncoding>
                <java.version>1.8</java.version>
        </properties>

        <dependencies>
                <dependency>
                        <groupId>org.springframework.boot</groupId>
                        <artifactId>spring-boot-starter-web</artifactId>
                </dependency>
                <dependency>
                        <groupId>org.springframework.boot</groupId>
                        <artifactId>spring-boot-starter-actuator</artifactId>
                </dependency>
                <dependency>
                        <groupId>org.springframework.hateoas</groupId>
                        <artifactId>spring-hateoas</artifactId>
                </dependency>
                <dependency>
                        <groupId>org.springframework.boot</groupId>
                        <artifactId>spring-boot-actuator-docs</artifactId>
                </dependency>

                <dependency>
                        <groupId>org.springframework.boot</groupId>
                        <artifactId>spring-boot-starter-data-jpa</artifactId>
                </dependency>
```

```
        <dependency>
                <groupId>com.h2database</groupId>
                <artifactId>h2</artifactId>
                <scope>runtime</scope>
        </dependency>
        <dependency>
                <groupId>org.liquibase</groupId>
                <artifactId>liquibase-core</artifactId>
        </dependency>

        <dependency>
                <groupId>org.springframework.boot</groupId>
                <artifactId>spring-boot-starter-test</artifactId>
                <scope>test</scope>
        </dependency>
    </dependencies>

    <build>
        <plugins>
                <plugin>
                        <groupId>org.springframework.boot</groupId>
                        <artifactId>spring-boot-maven-plugin</artifactId>
                </plugin>
        </plugins>
    </build>
</project>
```

Listing 11-10 shows the pom.xml. If you were doing the flyway example, that's the only one you need to comment out or remove and replace it with the liquibase-core dependency. One of the requirements of Liquibase is to have a db/changelog directory and a db.changelog-master.yaml file where you do your migrations. Let's see that file. See Listing 11-11.

Listing 11-11. src/main/resources/db/changelog/db.changelog-master.yaml

```
databaseChangeLog:
  - changeSet:
      id: 1
      author: mrfood
      changes:
        - createTable:
            tableName: person
            columns:
              - column:
                  name: id
                  type: int
                  autoIncrement: true
                  constraints:
                    primaryKey: true
                    nullable: false
              - column:
                  name: first_name
                  type: varchar(255)
```

```
                    constraints:
                      nullable: false
                - column:
                    name: last_name
                    type: varchar(255)
                    constraints:
                      nullable: false
  - changeSet:
      id: 2
      author: mrfood
      changes:
        - insert:
            tableName: person
            columns:
              - column:
                  name: first_name
                  value: Bobs
              - column:
                  name: last_name
                  value: Burguers
```

Listing 11-11 shows the db.changelog-master.yaml file. In this file you have two groups—the first one will create the table with their columns and types and the second group will insert a record in the table. If you need to know about the format and the types, take a look at the Liquibase documentation at http://www.liquibase.org/documentation/. You should have the structure shown in Figure 11-12.

```
.
├── mvnw
├── mvnw.cmd
├── pom.xml
└── src
    ├── main
    │   ├── java
    │   │   └── com
    │   │       └── apress
    │   │           └── spring
    │   │               ├── SpringBootWebActuatorApplication.java
    │   │               ├── domain
    │   │               │   └── Person.java
    │   │               └── repository
    │   │                   └── PersonRepository.java
    │   └── resources
    │       ├── application.properties
    │       ├── db
    │       │   ├── changelog
    │       │   │   └── db.changelog-master.yaml
    │       │   └── migration
    │       │       ├── V1__init.sql
    │       │       └── V2__init.sql
    │       ├── static
    │       └── templates
    └── test
        └── java
            └── com
                └── apress
                    └── spring
                        └── SpringBootWebActuatorApplicationTests.java

19 directories, 11 files
```

Figure 11-12. *Project structure with the db/changelog directory*

Next, you need to make a small change to application.properties. Change the property spring.jpa.hibernate.ddl-auto=validate to spring.jpa.hibernate.ddl-auto=none; this is because you don't want the JPA to generate your table, this now should be handle by Liquibase. And that's it; you can run your application and you will see in the logs that Liquibase triggers the changelog file and there is only one record in the database. Go to http://localhost:8080/liquibase to see something similar to Figure 11-13.

```
[
  ▼ {
        ID: "1",
        AUTHOR: "mrfood",
        FILENAME: "classpath:/db/changelog/db.changelog-master.yaml",
        DATEEXECUTED: 1455660393299,
        ORDEREXECUTED: 1,
        EXECTYPE: "EXECUTED",
        MD5SUM: "7:b8f2ae9c88deabd32666dff9bc5d7f5d",
        DESCRIPTION: "createTable",
        COMMENTS: "",
        TAG: null,
        LIQUIBASE: "3.4.2",
        CONTEXTS: null,
        LABELS: null
    },
  ▼ {
        ID: "2",
        AUTHOR: "mrfood",
        FILENAME: "classpath:/db/changelog/db.changelog-master.yaml",
        DATEEXECUTED: 1455660393307,
        ORDEREXECUTED: 2,
        EXECTYPE: "EXECUTED",
        MD5SUM: "7:febbfe7873884e5e1e8f309ad353f5a0",
        DESCRIPTION: "insert",
        COMMENTS: "",
        TAG: null,
        LIQUIBASE: "3.4.2",
        CONTEXTS: null,
        LABELS: null
    }
]
```

Figure 11-13. `http://localhost:8080/liquibase`

Figure 11-13 shows the result of executing the db.changelog-master.yaml file. So now you have at least two options for database migrations.

/logfile

This endpoint will show the contents of the log file specified by the logging.file property, where you specify the name of the log file (this will be written in the current directory). You can also set the logging.path, where you set the path where the spring.log will be written. By default Spring Boot writes to the console/standard out, and if you specify any of these properties, it will also write everything from the console to the log file.

You can stop your application. Go to src/main/resources/application.properties and add this to the very end:

```
logging.file=mylog.log
```

Now you can rerun your application. If you go to the http://localhost:8080/logfile endpoint, you should have something to Figure 11-14, which shows the contents of the mylog.log file.

Figure 11-14. http://localhost:8080/logfile

/metrics

This endpoint shows the metrics information of the current application, where you can determine the how much memory it's using, how much memory is free, the uptime of your application, the size of the heap is being used, the number of threads used, and so on.

One of the important features about this endpoint is that it has some counters and gauges that you can use, even for statistics about how many times your app is being visited or if you have the log file enabled. If you are accessing the /logfile endpoint, you will find some counters like counter.status.304.logfile, which indicates that the /logfile endpoint was accessed but hasn't change. And of course you can have custom counters.

If you are running the application, you can stop it. Let's create one simple example by reusing the same example application and modifying the main app. See Listing 11-12.

Listing 11-12. src/main/java/com/apress/spring/SpringBootWebActuatorApplication.java

```
package com.apress.spring;

import org.slf4j.Logger;
import org.slf4j.LoggerFactory;
import org.springframework.beans.factory.annotation.Autowired;
import org.springframework.boot.CommandLineRunner;
import org.springframework.boot.SpringApplication;
import org.springframework.boot.actuate.metrics.CounterService;
import org.springframework.boot.autoconfigure.SpringBootApplication;
import org.springframework.context.annotation.Bean;
import org.springframework.web.bind.annotation.RequestMapping;
import org.springframework.web.bind.annotation.RestController;

import com.apress.spring.repository.PersonRepository;

@RestController
@SpringBootApplication
public class SpringBootWebActuatorApplication {

    public static void main(String[] args) {
        SpringApplication.run(SpringBootWebActuatorApplication.class, args);
    }

    @Autowired
    CounterService counter;

    @RequestMapping("/")
    public String index(){
        counter.increment("counter.index.invoked");
        return "Spring Boot Actuator";
    }

    private static final Logger log = LoggerFactory.getLogger(SpringBootWebActuator
    Application.class);
```

```
@Bean
CommandLineRunner findAll(PersonRepository repo){
        return args ->{
                log.info("> Persons in Database: ");
                repo.findAll().forEach(person -> log.info(person.toString()));
        };
}

}
```

Listing 11-12 shows the modified main app. Let's examine it:

- `@Autowired CounterService`. `CounterService` is a service interface that can be used to increment, decrement, and reset a named counter value. The counter instance will be auto-wired by the Spring container.

- `counter.increment("counter.index.invoked")`. This instance method creates a counter variable with the name `counter.index.invoked` (it can be whatever name you want, just make sure it makes sense) and it will increment (by one) its value every time it's executed. So every time the index page is refreshed, the `counter.index.invoked` counter will be incremented by one.

There is also another service interface you can use, especially designed for gauges, called the `org.springframework.boot.actuate.metrics.GaugeService` service interface. It can be used to submit a named double value for storage an analysis. This is very useful when you want to get some statistics. For example, you can create a smart system where you are connected to a climate sensor, and you are displaying the temperature using the `GaugeService`. Then you can set alarms by setting a threshold that automatically increases or decreases the temperature.

You can rerun your application after the change (from Listing 11-12) and if you visit `http://localhost:8080` several times (do a Refresh) and then go to the `http://localhost:8080/metrics` endpoint, you should see something similar to Figure 11-15.

```
{
    mem: 551275,
    "mem.free": 273417,
    processors: 8,
    "instance.uptime": 187055,
    uptime: 196831,
    "systemload.average": 6.123046875,
    "heap.committed": 472576,
    "heap.init": 262144,
    "heap.used": 199158,
    heap: 3728384,
    "nonheap.committed": 81344,
    "nonheap.init": 2496,
    "nonheap.used": 78700,
    nonheap: 0,
    "threads.peak": 24,
    "threads.daemon": 22,
    "threads.totalStarted": 29,
    threads: 24,
    classes: 10514,
    "classes.loaded": 10514,
    "classes.unloaded": 0,
    "gc.ps_scavenge.count": 7,
    "gc.ps_scavenge.time": 110,
    "gc.ps_marksweep.count": 2,
    "gc.ps_marksweep.time": 104,
    "httpsessions.max": -1,
    "httpsessions.active": 0,
    "datasource.primary.active": 0,
    "datasource.primary.usage": 0,
    "gauge.response.logfile": 2,
    "gauge.response.metrics": 2,
    "gauge.response.root": 4,
    "counter.status.200.root": 6,
    "counter.status.200.logfile": 4,
    "counter.status.200.metrics": 3,
    "counter.index.invoked": 6
}
```

Figure 11-15. `http://localhost:8080/metrics`

Figure 11-15 shows the /metrics endpoint. If you take a look at the very last counter, you will see listed that counter.index.invoked has six hits. I think this is a nice way to have statistics and analysis of your application that work out-of-the-box. The only thing you need to do is use the CounterService or GaugeService service interfaces.

/mappings

This endpoint shows all the lists of all @RequestMapping paths declared in your application. This is very useful if you want to know more about what mappings are declared. If your application is running, you can go to the http://localhost:8080/mappings endpoint. See Figure 11-16.

```
{
  ▼ "/webjars/**": {
        bean: "resourceHandlerMapping"
    },
  ▼ "/**": {
        bean: "resourceHandlerMapping"
    },
  ▼ "/docs/**": {
        bean: "resourceHandlerMapping"
    },
  ▼ "/**/favicon.ico": {
        bean: "faviconHandlerMapping"
    },
  ▼ "{[/]}": {
        bean: "requestMappingHandlerMapping",
        method: "public java.lang.String com.apress.spring.SpringBootWebActuatorApplication.index()"
    },
  ▼ "{[/error]}": {
        bean: "requestMappingHandlerMapping",
        method: "public org.springframework.http.ResponseEntity<java.util.Map<java.lang.String,
        java.lang.Object>>
        org.springframework.boot.autoconfigure.web.BasicErrorController.error(javax.servlet.http.HttpServletReq
    },
  ▼ "{[/error],produces=[text/html]}": {
        bean: "requestMappingHandlerMapping",
        method: "public org.springframework.web.servlet.ModelAndView
        org.springframework.boot.autoconfigure.web.BasicErrorController.errorHtml(javax.servlet.http.HttpServle
    },
  ▼ "{[/trace || /trace.json],methods=[GET],produces=[application/json]}": {
        bean: "endpointHandlerMapping",
        method: "public java.lang.Object
        org.springframework.boot.actuate.endpoint.mvc.EndpointMvcAdapter.invoke()"
    },
  ▼ "{[/metrics/{name:.*}],methods=[GET],produces=[application/json]}": {
        bean: "endpointHandlerMapping",
        method: "public java.lang.Object
        org.springframework.boot.actuate.endpoint.mvc.MetricsMvcEndpoint.value(java.lang.String)"
    },
  ▼ "{[/metrics || /metrics.json],methods=[GET],produces=[application/json]}": {
        bean: "endpointHandlerMapping",
        method: "public java.lang.Object
        org.springframework.boot.actuate.endpoint.mvc.EndpointMvcAdapter.invoke()"
    },
```

RAW

Figure 11-16. `http://localhost:8080/mappings`

/shutdown

This endpoint is not enabled by default. It allows the application to be gracefully shut down. This endpoint is sensitive, which means it can be used with security, and it should be. If your application is running, you can stop it now. If you want to enable the /shutdown endpoint, you need to add the following to the application.properties.

endpoints.shutdown.enabled=true

It's wise to have this endpoint secured. You'd need to add the `spring-boot-starter-security` pom dependency to your pom.xml:

```
<dependency>
        <groupId>org.springframework.boot</groupId>
        <artifactId>spring-boot-starter-security</artifactId>
</dependency>
```

Remember that by adding the security starter pom, you enable security by default. The username will be user and the password will be printed out in the logs. Also you can establish a better security by using in-memory, database, or LDAP users; see the Spring Boot security chapter for more information.

For now, let's add the `endpoints.shutdown.enabled=true` and the `spring-boot-starter-security` pom and rerun the application. After running the application, take a look at the logs and save the password that is printed out so it can be used with the `/shutdown` endpoint:

```
...
Using default security password: 2875411a-e609-4890-9aa0-22f90b4e0a11
...
```

Now if you open a terminal, you can execute the following command:

```
$ curl -i -X POST http://localhost:8080/shutdown -u user:2875411a-e609-4890-9aa0-
22f90b4e0a11
HTTP/1.1 200 OK
Server: Apache-Coyote/1.1
X-Content-Type-Options: nosniff
X-XSS-Protection: 1; mode=block
Cache-Control: no-cache, no-store, max-age=0, must-revalidate
Pragma: no-cache
Expires: 0
X-Frame-Options: DENY
Strict-Transport-Security: max-age=31536000 ; includeSubDomains
X-Application-Context: application
Content-Type: application/json;charset=UTF-8
Transfer-Encoding: chunked
Date: Wed, 17 Feb 2016 04:22:58 GMT

{"message":"Shutting down, bye..."}
```

As you can see from this output, you are using a POST method to access the `/shutdown` endpoint, and you are passing the user and the password that was printed out before. The result is the `"Shutting down, bye.."` message. And of course your application is terminated. Again, it's important to know that this particular endpoint must be secured at all times.

/trace

This endpoint shows the trace information, which is normally the last few HTTP requests. This endpoint can be useful to see all the request info and the information returned to debug your application at the HTTP level. You can run your application and go to `http://localhost:8080/trace`. You should see something similar to Figure 11-17.

```
[
                                                                                                    RAW
  ▼ {
        timestamp: 1455683681386,
      ▼ info: {
            method: "GET",
            path: "/",
          ▼ headers: {
              ▼ request: {
                    host: "localhost:8080",
                    connection: "keep-alive",
                    accept: "text/html,application/xhtml+xml,application/xml;q=0.9,*/*;q=0.8",
                    user-agent: "Mozilla/5.0 (Macintosh; Intel Mac OS X 10_11_3) AppleWebKit/601.4.4 (KHTML,
                    like Gecko) Version/9.0.3 Safari/601.4.4",
                    authorization: "Basic dXNlcjoxMzRjN2U4YiliYzY3LTRiNjYtYTIzMC1jYWZkOGQ4NzJmZTQ=",
                    accept-language: "en-us",
                    accept-encoding: "gzip, deflate"
                },
              ▼ response: {
                    X-Content-Type-Options: "nosniff",
                    X-XSS-Protection: "1; mode=block",
                    Cache-Control: "no-cache, no-store, max-age=0, must-revalidate",
                    Pragma: "no-cache",
                    Expires: "0",
                    X-Frame-Options: "DENY",
                    Strict-Transport-Security: "max-age=31536000 ; includeSubDomains",
                    X-Application-Context: "application",
                    Content-Type: "text/html;charset=UTF-8",
                    Content-Length: "20",
                    Date: "Wed, 17 Feb 2016 04:34:41 GMT",
                    status: "200"
                }
            }
        }
    },
  ▼ {
        timestamp: 1455683679356,
      ▼ info: {
            method: "GET",
            path: "/",
          ▼ headers: {
              ▼ request: {
                    host: "localhost:8080",
                    connection: "keep-alive",
```

Figure 11-17. `http://localhost:8080/trace`

Sensitive Endpoints

I mentioned that the /shutdown is a sensitive endpoint, meaning that if you add security to your pom.xml it will be secured by default. Every time you want to access an endpoint, it will prompt you for the username and password.

The only endpoints that are not sensitive are /docs, /info and /health. So, if you want to disable the sensitive feature, you can configure them in the application.properties file. For example, imagine that you already have security and you don't want to be prompted for the username and password for the /beans and /trace endpoints. What you need to do is add the following to your application.properties file:

```
endpoints.beans.sensitive=false
endpoints.trace.sensitive=false
```

If your application is running, you can stop it now and then rerun it to see the changes. Try to access the /beans and /trace endpoint; you won't be asked for credentials. The key here is to set the endpoints.<endpoint-name>.sensitive to false.

Sensitive also means that you can display certain information. For example, if you are not using security, and you set the endpoints.beans.health.sensitive=true, you will only see in the /health endpoint the status UP. But if you set the sensitive=false you will have a little more information. You can get more information about which endpoints are sensitive by default at https://docs.spring.io/spring-boot/docs/current/reference/html/production-ready-endpoints.html.

Changing the Endpoint ID

You can configure the endpoint ID, which will change the name. Imagine that you don't like the /beans endpoint, at the end this is referring to the Spring beans, so what about if you change this endpoint to /spring.

You make this change in the application.properties file in the form of:
endpoints.<endpoint-name>.id=<new-name>. Example:

endpoints.**beans**.id=spring

If you rerun your application (stop and restart to apply the changes), you can access the /beans endpoint using the /spring endpoint instead.

Actuator CORS Support

With the Spring Boot Actuator module, you can configure CORS (Cross-Origin Resource Sharing), which allows you to specify what cross-domains are authorized to use the Actuator's endpoints. Normally this allows inter-application connect to your endpoints, and due to security reasons, only the domains authorized must be able to execute these endpoints.

You configure this in the application.properties file:

endpoints.cors.allowed-origins=*
endpoints.cors.allowed-methods=GET,POST

If your application is running, stop it and rerun it.

Normally in the endpoints.cors.allowed-origins, you should put a domain name like http://mydomain.com or maybe http://localhost:9090 (not the *), which allows access your endpoints to avoid any hack to your site. This would be very similar to using in any controller the @CrossOrigin(origins = "http://localhost:9000") annotation.

Changing the Management Endpoints Path

By default the Spring Boot Actuator has its management in the root, which means that all the Actuator's endpoints can be accessed from the root /. For example: /beans, /health, and so on. Before you continue, stop your application. You can change its management context path by adding the following property to the application.properties file:

management.context-path=/monitor

If you rerun your application, you will see that the EndpointHandlerMapping is mapping all the endpoints by adding the /monitor/<endpoint-name> context path. You can now access the /trace endpoint through http://localhost:8080/monitor/trace.

You can also disable security, change the address, or change the port for the endpoints:

```
management.context-path=/monitor
management.security.enabled=false
management.port=8081
management.address=127.0.0.1
```

This configuration will have its endpoint with the context-path /monitor/<endpoint-name>, the security will be disabled, the port will be 8081 (this means that you will have two ports listening—one is the 8080 of your application and 8081 is for your management endpoints), and the endpoints or management will be bind to the 127.0.0.1 address.

If you want to disable the endpoints (for security reasons), add the following property to the application.properties file.

```
management.port=-1
```

if you stop your application and rerun it with the management.port=-1, you won't see the endpoints anymore.

Using Spring Boot Actuator in a Non-Web Application

Maybe you are wondering if you can use the Spring Boot Actuator module in a non-web application, and the answer is, yes you can! You will sometimes need to create specialty services that do very specific tasks, such as batch processing, or create some integration apps that don't require a web interface.

In this section, you are going to create a simple standalone application from scratch and see how the Spring Actuator works in a non-web environment.

Let's start by executing the following commands:

```
$ mkdir spring-boot-actuator
$ cd spring-boot-actuator
$ spring init -d=actuator,remote-shell -g=com.apress.spring -a=spring-boot-actuator
--package-name=com.apress.spring -name=spring-boot-actuator -x
```

Did you notice what is new? The remote-shell dependency tool is CRaSH (http://www.crashub.org/) and it's a shell for Java. You are going to connect to your application using ssh and you will see how to interact with the Actuator.

Let's start by looking at the pom.xml. See Listing 11-13.

Listing 11-13. pom.xml

```
<?xml version="1.0" encoding="UTF-8"?>
<project xmlns="http://maven.apache.org/POM/4.0.0"
xmlns:xsi="http://www.w3.org/2001/XMLSchema-instance"
        xsi:schemaLocation="http://maven.apache.org/POM/4.0.0
        http://maven.apache.org/xsd/maven-4.0.0.xsd">
        <modelVersion>4.0.0</modelVersion>
```

```xml
        <groupId>com.apress.spring</groupId>
        <artifactId>spring-boot-actuator</artifactId>
        <version>0.0.1-SNAPSHOT</version>
        <packaging>jar</packaging>

        <name>spring-boot-actuator</name>
        <description>Demo project for Spring Boot</description>

        <parent>
                <groupId>org.springframework.boot</groupId>
                <artifactId>spring-boot-starter-parent</artifactId>
                <version>1.3.2.RELEASE</version>
                <relativePath/> <!-- lookup parent from repository -->
        </parent>

        <properties>
                <project.build.sourceEncoding>UTF-8</project.build.sourceEncoding>
                <java.version>1.8</java.version>
        </properties>

        <dependencies>
                <dependency>
                        <groupId>org.springframework.boot</groupId>
                        <artifactId>spring-boot-starter-actuator</artifactId>
                </dependency>
                <dependency>
                        <groupId>org.springframework.boot</groupId>
                        <artifactId>spring-boot-starter-remote-shell</artifactId>
                </dependency>

                <dependency>
                        <groupId>org.springframework.boot</groupId>
                        <artifactId>spring-boot-starter-test</artifactId>
                        <scope>test</scope>
                </dependency>
        </dependencies>

        <build>
                <plugins>
                        <plugin>
                                <groupId>org.springframework.boot</groupId>
                                <artifactId>spring-boot-maven-plugin</artifactId>
                        </plugin>
                </plugins>
        </build>

</project>
```

Listing 11-13 shows the pom.xml. The only new part is the spring-boot-starter-remote-shell dependency. Next, run your application as usual, and there is nothing to do with your main app or adding classes:

```
$ ./mvnw spring-boot:run
```

After you execute this command you will see two things. First, the logs print out a password:

```
...
Using default password for shell access: 7cb536e1-6c2b-4f71-a9ac-d07b3a85d791
...
```

Second, this program never ends. That's because the CRaSH tool is listening by default at port 2000. Open a terminal and execute the following command:

```
$ ssh -p 2000 user@localhost
Password authentication
Password:
  .   ___          _            __ _ _
 /\\ / ___'_ __ _ _(_)_ __  __ _ \ \ \ \
( ( )\___ | '_ | '_| | '_ \/ _` | \ \ \ \
 \\/  ___)| |_)| | | | | || (_| |  ) ) ) )
  '  |____| .__|_| |_|_| |_\__, | / / / /
 =========|_|==============|___/=/_/_/_/
 :: Spring Boot ::   (v1.3.2.RELEASE) on liukang.local
>
```

In the password prompt you will enter the password from the logs output (from this example: 7cb536e1-6c2b-4f71-a9ac-d07b3a85d791). If you type help and press Enter, you should have the following output:

```
> help
Try one of these commands with the -h or --help switch:

NAME       DESCRIPTION
autoconfig Display auto configuration report from ApplicationContext
beans      Display beans in ApplicationContext
cron       manages the cron plugin
dashboard  a monitoring dashboard
egrep      search file(s) for lines that match a pattern
endpoint   Invoke actuator endpoints
env        display the term env
filter     a filter for a stream of map
java       various java language commands
jmx        Java Management Extensions
jul        java.util.logging commands
jvm        JVM informations
less       opposite of more
mail       interact with emails
man        format and display the on-line manual pages
```

```
metrics     Display metrics provided by Spring Boot
shell       shell related command
sleep       sleep for some time
sort        sort a map
system      vm system properties commands
thread      JVM thread commands
help        provides basic help
repl        list the repl or change the current repl
```

Next, use the command endpoint and list all the available endpoints:

```
> endpoint list
environmentEndpoint
healthEndpoint
beansEndpoint
infoEndpoint
metricsEndpoint
traceEndpoint
dumpEndpoint
autoConfigurationReportEndpoint
configurationPropertiesReportEndpoint
```

Now that you now what endpoint you can invoke, invoke the healthEndpoint:

```
> endpoint invoke healthEndpoint
{status=UP, diskSpace={status=UP, total=750046937088, free=20512227328, threshold=10485760}}
```

As an exercise you can experiment with all the other endpoints. As you can see, you have the same behavior as a web interface. If you want to add your own security or change the default port (2000), you can do so by adding all the properties to your application.properties file, for example:

```
shell.ssh.enabled: true
shell.ssh.port: 2222
shell.auth: simple
shell.auth.simple.user.password: password
```

If you rerun your application, you now can connect with the following:

```
$ ssh -p 2222 user@localhost
```

Use password as the password. I covered only basic properties for the shell, but you can get more information about other properties that you can apply by visiting https://docs.spring.io/spring-boot/docs/current/reference/html/common-application-properties.html.

Now you have a good understanding of how the Spring Boot Actuator module works, including what its endpoints are and how to use them. Of course, you can create your own endpoint and health monitor, but I will cover this in a later chapter.

Summary

This chapter showed you how the Spring Boot Actuator works, including what its endpoints are and how customizable it can be. With the Actuator module, you can monitor your Spring Boot application, from using the /health endpoint to using the /trace for more granular debugging.

The next chapter talks about deploying your Spring Boot applications, including how to create JAR and WAR files and use them as a service.

CHAPTER 12

Deploying Spring Boot

During the entire book you have been executing the Maven command `spring-boot:run` and I haven't covered it in too much detail, but when you execute it, you are actually executing the Spring Boot Maven plugin goals. These normally have a particular flow. They will compile your application (classes), execute the unit tests, and run your application taking the `target/classes` (where the compilation phase output all the compiled classes into) directory as the working directory.

This chapter discusses another Maven command that will allow you to create standalone applications or executable JARs. If you prefer, you can create WARs from your web application and run them using an external application container.

Before getting into the details, you need to set up the main project, which will help you understand the Spring Boot deployment better.

Setting Up the Spring Boot Journal App

You have been working with this application throughout the entire book, and you are going to get most of it from Chapter 9. Let's get started.

Execute the following commands in a terminal window:

```
$ mkdir spring-boot-journal
$ cd spring-boot-journal
$ spring init -d=web,thymeleaf,data-jpa,data-rest,mysql,actuator,security,actuator-docs
-g=com.apress.spring -a=spring-boot-journal --package-name=com.apress.spring
-name=spring-boot-journal -x
```

As you can see, you are adding most of the dependencies that you already know. Listing 12-1 shows the resultant pom.xml.

Listing 12-1. pom.xml

```xml
<?xml version="1.0" encoding="UTF-8"?>
<project xmlns="http://maven.apache.org/POM/4.0.0"
xmlns:xsi="http://www.w3.org/2001/XMLSchema-instance"
        xsi:schemaLocation="http://maven.apache.org/POM/4.0.0
        http://maven.apache.org/xsd/maven-4.0.0.xsd">
        <modelVersion>4.0.0</modelVersion>

        <groupId>com.apress.spring</groupId>
        <artifactId>spring-boot-journal</artifactId>
```

```xml
<version>0.0.1-SNAPSHOT</version>
<packaging>jar</packaging>

<name>spring-boot-journal</name>
<description>Demo project for Spring Boot</description>

<parent>
        <groupId>org.springframework.boot</groupId>
        <artifactId>spring-boot-starter-parent</artifactId>
        <version>1.3.2.RELEASE</version>
        <relativePath /> <!-- lookup parent from repository -->
</parent>

<properties>
        <project.build.sourceEncoding>UTF-8</project.build.sourceEncoding>
        <java.version>1.8</java.version>
</properties>

<dependencies>
        <dependency>
                <groupId>org.springframework.boot</groupId>
                <artifactId>spring-boot-starter-actuator</artifactId>
        </dependency>
        <dependency>
                <groupId>org.springframework.boot</groupId>
                <artifactId>spring-boot-actuator-docs</artifactId>
        </dependency>
        <dependency>
                <groupId>org.springframework.boot</groupId>
                <artifactId>spring-boot-starter-data-jpa</artifactId>
        </dependency>
        <dependency>
                <groupId>org.springframework.boot</groupId>
                <artifactId>spring-boot-starter-data-rest</artifactId>
        </dependency>
        <dependency>
                <groupId>org.springframework.boot</groupId>
                <artifactId>spring-boot-starter-security</artifactId>
        </dependency>
        <dependency>
                <groupId>org.springframework.boot</groupId>
                <artifactId>spring-boot-starter-thymeleaf</artifactId>
        </dependency>
        <dependency>
                <groupId>org.springframework.boot</groupId>
                <artifactId>spring-boot-starter-web</artifactId>
        </dependency>
        <dependency>
                <groupId>org.springframework.security</groupId>
                <artifactId>spring-security-taglibs</artifactId>
        </dependency>
```

```xml
        <dependency>
                <groupId>org.thymeleaf.extras</groupId>
                <artifactId>thymeleaf-extras-springsecurity4</artifactId>
        </dependency>
        <dependency>
                <groupId>org.springframework.hateoas</groupId>
                <artifactId>spring-hateoas</artifactId>
        </dependency>
        <dependency>
                <groupId>mysql</groupId>
                <artifactId>mysql-connector-java</artifactId>
        </dependency>
        <dependency>
                <groupId>org.springframework.boot</groupId>
                <artifactId>spring-boot-starter-test</artifactId>
                <scope>test</scope>
        </dependency>
    </dependencies>

    <build>
        <plugins>
            <plugin>
                    <groupId>org.springframework.boot</groupId>
                    <artifactId>spring-boot-maven-plugin</artifactId>
            </plugin>
        </plugins>
    </build>

</project>
```

Listing 12-1 shows the pom.xml that you are going to use. Review in detail this pom.xml and notice that you are adding different dependencies from various chapters. You can copy some of the files from Chapter 9 (from the spring-boot-journal-secure project), because the application will be secure. Even so, I didn't explain that you can use SSL and connect through HTTPS. Now is a perfect time to create it, so when you deploy it, SSL will be integrated.

Take a look at the final directory structure of this version of the journal app, shown in Figure 12-1.

```
.
├── mvnw
├── mvnw.cmd
├── pom.xml
└── src
    ├── main
    │   ├── java
    │   │   └── com
    │   │       └── apress
    │   │           └── spring
    │   │               ├── SpringBootJournalApplication.java
    │   │               ├── config
    │   │               │   ├── InMemorySecurityConfig.java
    │   │               │   └── SecurityConfig.java
    │   │               ├── domain
    │   │               │   └── JournalEntry.java
    │   │               ├── repository
    │   │               │   └── JournalRepository.java
    │   │               ├── utils
    │   │               │   ├── JsonDateDeserializer.java
    │   │               │   └── JsonDateSerializer.java
    │   │               └── web
    │   │                   └── JournalController.java
    │   └── resources
    │       ├── application.properties
    │       ├── data.sql
    │       ├── keystore.jks
    │       ├── static
    │       │   ├── css
    │       │   │   ├── bootstrap-glyphicons.css
    │       │   │   ├── bootstrap.min.css
    │       │   │   └── styles.css
    │       │   └── fonts
    │       │       ├── glyphicons-halflings-regular.svg
    │       │       ├── glyphicons-halflings-regular.ttf
    │       │       └── glyphicons-halflings-regular.woff
    │       └── templates
    │           ├── index.html
    │           └── login.html
    └── test
        └── java
            └── com
                └── apress
                    └── spring
                        └── SpringBootJournalApplicationTests.java

21 directories, 23 files
```

Figure 12-1. *Journal app directory structure*

Figure 12-1 shows the directory structure of the journal app, but which classes will be the same as the ones in Chapter 9? Table 12-1 describes the packages and includes some notes. I don't want to repeat all the code here, just the classes that change and the new additions.

Table 12-1. *Reusable Code Summary*

Package/Directory	Class/File	Notes
com.apress.spring	SpringBootJournalApplication	No changes
com.apress.spring.domain	JournalEntry	No changes
com.apress.spring.repository	JournalRepository	No changes
com.apress.spring.utils	JsonDateDeserializer JsonDateSerializer	No changes
com.apress.spring.web	JournalController	No changes
com.apress.spring.config	InMemorySecurityConfig SecurityConfig	There is a change in both classes
src/main/resources/	application.properties	There are some new properties
src/main/resources/	keystore.jks	This is a new file that you will generate
src/main/resources/static src/main/resources/template	css/* index.html login.html	No changes

■ **Note**   You can find the book's source code on the Apress site. Or you can go to my GitHub account at https://github.com/felipeg48/pro-spring-boot to get the latest code.

Let's start by checking out all the files that will be modified and the new keystore.jks that you will create to use SSL. Listings 12-2 and 12-3 show InMemorySecurity and SecurityConfig, respectively.

Listing 12-2. src/main/java/com/apress/spring/config/InMemorySecurityConfig.java

```java
package com.apress.spring.config;

import org.springframework.beans.factory.annotation.Autowired;
import org.springframework.context.annotation.Configuration;
import org.springframework.security.config.annotation.authentication.builders.
AuthenticationManagerBuilder;
import org.springframework.security.config.annotation.authentication.configuration.
EnableGlobalAuthentication;

@Configuration
@EnableGlobalAuthentication
public class InMemorySecurityConfig {

    @Autowired
    public void configureGlobal(AuthenticationManagerBuilder auth) throws Exception {
        auth.inMemoryAuthentication().withUser("spring").password("boot").roles("USER")
                .and().withUser("admin").password("password")
                .roles("USER", "ADMIN");
    }
}
```

Listing 12-2 shows the InMemorySecurityConfig class, which is very similar to Chapter 9, but now you are changing the username and password and of course the users are going to be in-memory. Of course you can change this to point to a database. (You can do this as an exercise.)

Listing 12-3. src/main/java/com/apress/spring/config/SecurityConfig.java

```
package com.apress.spring.config;

import org.springframework.context.annotation.Configuration;
import org.springframework.security.config.annotation.web.builders.HttpSecurity;
import org.springframework.security.config.annotation.web.configuration.
WebSecurityConfigurerAdapter;
import org.springframework.web.servlet.config.annotation.ViewControllerRegistry;
import org.springframework.web.servlet.config.annotation.WebMvcConfigurerAdapter;

@Configuration
public class SecurityConfig extends WebSecurityConfigurerAdapter{

                @Override
                protected void configure(HttpSecurity http) throws Exception {
                        http.authorizeRequests()
                        .antMatchers("/**").authenticated()
                        .and()
                        .formLogin().loginPage("/login").permitAll()
                        .and()
                        .logout().permitAll()
                        .and()
                        .csrf().disable();

                }

                @Configuration
                static protected class LoginController extends WebMvcConfigurerAdapter{
                        @Override
                        public void addViewControllers(ViewControllerRegistry registry) {
                                registry.addViewController("/login").setViewName("login");
                        }
                }
}
```

Listing 12-3 shows the SecurityConfig.java, which is where you add the HTTP security. As you can see in detail, you are securing everything now and providing a login page and a way to log out. You are also adding a LoginController class that configures just the controller (from spring-security /login) and setting its view (templates/login.html). Also notice that you are disabling the CORS (Cross-Origin Http Request) by using the csrf().disable(). You already know about Spring Security and the entire configuration, so I omit some of the details and continue with the other files.

Next, let's see the application.properties, shown in Listing 12-4.

Listing 12-4. src/main/resources/applications.properties

```
spring.datasource.url = jdbc:mysql://localhost:3306/journal
spring.datasource.username = springboot
spring.datasource.password = springboot
spring.datasource.testWhileIdle = true
spring.datasource.validationQuery = SELECT 1

spring.jpa.show-sql = true
spring.jpa.hibernate.ddl-auto = create-drop
spring.jpa.hibernate.naming-strategy = org.hibernate.cfg.ImprovedNamingStrategy
spring.jpa.properties.hibernate.dialect = org.hibernate.dialect.MySQL5Dialect

spring.data.rest.basePath=/api

management.context-path=/monitor
endpoints.shutdown.enabled=true

server.port=8443
server.ssl.key-store=classpath:keystore.jks
server.ssl.key-store-password=tomcat
server.ssl.key-password=tomcat
```

Listing 12-4 shows the new application.properties. As you can see, it contains all the information from previous chapters, including the actuator management.context-path and the enabling of the shutdown endpoint. It also includes the new server properties with a different username and password. As you can see, it uses the server.ssl.<properties> to enable a secure socket layer, by providing the keystore, the keystore's password, and the key password. Also notice that the server port is 8443, so now you will connect to the https://localhost:8443 URL.

Creating the SSL Self-Signed Keystore

In order to get the SSL working in your application, you need to create a self-signed keystore file. If you already have a CA (Certificate Authority), you can import it as your keystore file.

This example assumes that you will do the self-certificate keystore, so open a terminal window (go to your project's root) and execute the following commands:

```
$ keytool -genkey -alias tomcat -keyalg RSA -keystore src/main/resources/keystore.jks

Enter keystore password: tomcat
Re-enter new password:   tomcat

What is your first and last name?
  [Unknown]:  apress media
What is the name of your organizational unit?
  [Unknown]:  publishing
What is the name of your organization?
  [Unknown]:  apress
What is the name of your City or Locality?
  [Unknown]:  ny
```

```
What is the name of your State or Province?
  [Unknown]:  ny
What is the two-letter country code for this unit?
  [Unknown]:  us
Is CN=apress media, OU=publishing, O=apress, L=ny, ST=ny, C=us correct?
  [no]:  yes

Enter key password for <tomcat>
    (RETURN if same as keystore password):
```

The keytool command comes with your Java distribution, so you should not have any issues. This command creates a keystore.jks and places it in src/main/resources directory. You can add any values for your common name, organizational unit, and so on, but keep in mind that you need to remember the passwords because they are needed in the application.properties file. In this example, the password for the keystore and the key is tomcat.

Testing SSL

All the other files remain the same, so it's time to test the new SSL part. Remember that you need to have your MySQL server up and running. Then, you can run your application as usual:

```
$ ./mvnw spring-boot:run
```

After you execute this command, you should have in your logs information about the Tomcat listening in port 8443. You can go to https://localhost:8443. Since this should be the first time you do this, you should see something similar (depending on your browser) to Figure 12-2.

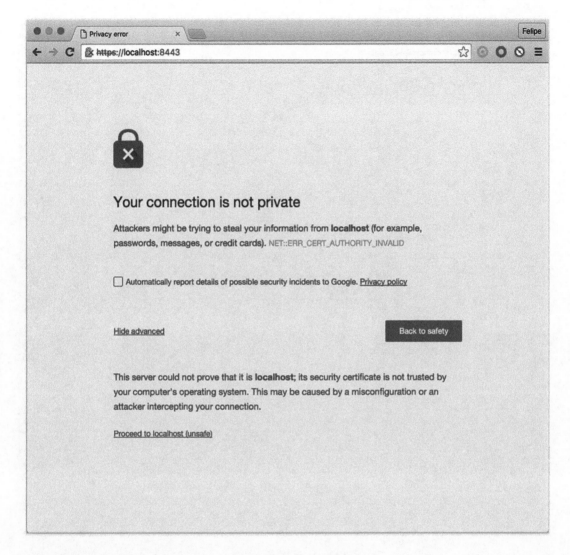

Figure 12-2. Google Chrome's version of https://localhost:8443

Figure 12-2 shows the result of going to the https://localhost:8443, and because there is a cert that cannot be authenticated, you will get that warning. So you can click Proceed to Localhost (depending of your browser) or add a Security exception so you are allowed to use this site. After that, you should see what's shown in Figure 12-3.

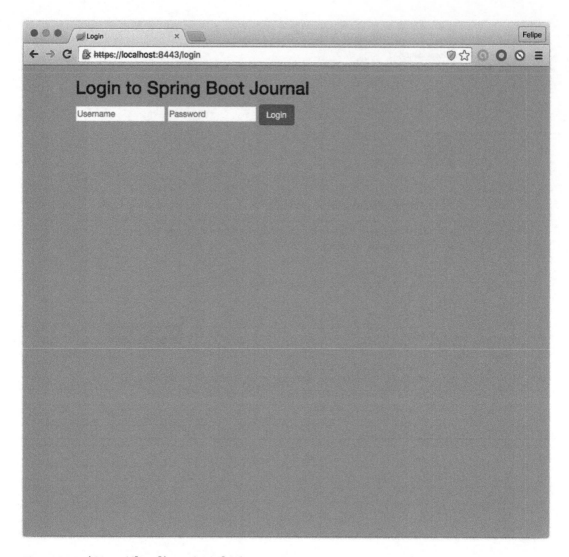

Figure 12-3. *https://localhost:8443/login*

Figure 12-3 shows the /login endpoint and this is because even the index page is secured (it was secured in Listing 12-3), so you need to provide the username and password. You can use the ones you set up in memory for example: spring as username and boot as password. After providing the credentials, you should be redirected to the index page. See Figure 12-4.

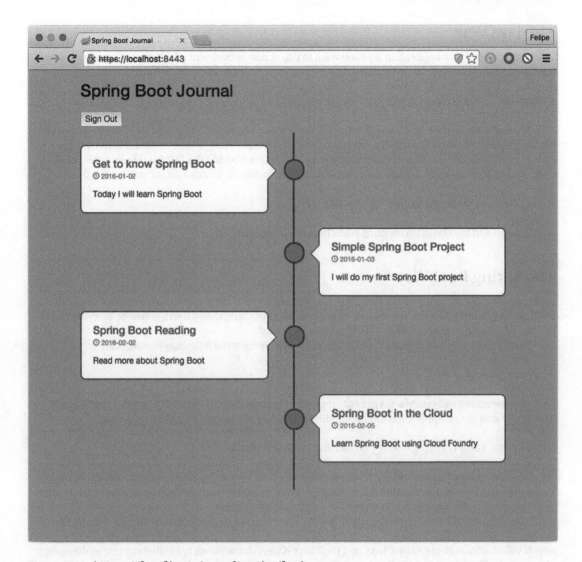

Figure 12-4. `https://localhost:8443` *after the* `/login` *page*

Figure 12-4 shows the index page after you submit your credentials. Now you have a secured web application. Maybe you are wondering why I didn't add this example in the security chapter. Well, right now it makes perfect sense to add it because you are going to start deploying your application and running it in standalone mode or as a service, and what you are looking for is to have your app secured.

Creating Executable JARs

Now that you have your journal app tested and ready, let's create a standalone application. This means that it will be portable and you can ship it knowing that you still need a way to connect to a database. You can think about it as a desktop application that runs in your web browser and can be distributed to different users.

The Java Way

When you create a Java application and you want to run it, normally you need to know about the class that has the `public static void main` method to get executed. You would do something like this:

```
$ java -cp .;lib/3rdparty.jar com.sample.MyApp
```

Normally you specify the classpath with the `-cp` option to get your dependencies (if needed) or if you package your application as a JAR file, you must provide a `MANIFEST.MF` where you need to declare the `Main-Class` declaration. (This declaration indicates which class within the JAR file is your application's entry point.) You also must declare the `Start-Class` declaration, so you can do something like this:

```
$ java -cp .;lib/3rdparty.jar -jar myapp.jar
```

You can add the classpath for third-party libraries (if needed).

The Spring Boot Way

Spring Boot works the same way as Java (but simpler) when you want to create an executable application. It will identify which class has the `public static void main` method and it will generate everything that you need to create an executable app. Let's see how it's done.

To create the standalone and executable journal app, execute the following command:

```
$ ./mvnw package
```

This command will create a `target/spring-boot-journal-0.0.1-SNAPSHOT.jar` file. And that's it! That's your executable application, an executable JAR. Now you can run it with the following:

```
$ java -jar target/spring-boot-journal-0.0.1-SNAPSHOT.jar
```

Your journal application will start. This is awesome. Now you can ship your application to your users so they run it even without any third-party libraries. Wait, what? Remember that the journal app has some dependencies, yet in this command there is no `-cp` (classpath) option.

When you run the Maven package goal, it will package all the dependencies within the same JAR (normally called "Fat JAR") and will create the `MANIFEST.MF` file that has all the information related to your app. It will also include the `Main-Class` and the `Start-Class` declarations set with the name of the main classes that will start up your application.

If you are curious about it, you can see the contents of the JAR file generated with the following:

```
$ jar tvf target/spring-boot-journal-0.0.1-SNAPSHOT.jar
```

(The `jar` command is another tool that comes with the JDK installation.) This command prints out the JAR structure. You can see that there is a `lib/` folder where all the dependencies are and some Spring Boot classes that are helpers to run your application. If you want to see the `MANIFEST.MF` file, you can extract and view it using the following commands:

```
$ jar xvf  target/spring-boot-journal-0.0.1-SNAPSHOT.jar META-INF/MANIFEST.MF
$ cat META-INF/MANIFES.MF
Manifest-Version: 1.0
Implementation-Title: spring-boot-journal
Implementation-Version: 0.0.1-SNAPSHOT
```

```
Archiver-Version: Plexus Archiver
Built-By: felipeg
Start-Class: com.apress.spring.SpringBootJournalApplication
Implementation-Vendor-Id: com.apress.spring
Spring-Boot-Version: 1.3.2.RELEASE
Created-By: Apache Maven 3.0.4
Build-Jdk: 1.8.0_66
Implementation-Vendor: Pivotal Software, Inc.
Main-Class: org.springframework.boot.loader.JarLauncher
```

As you can see from the MANIFEST.MF file, the Start-Class declaration points to your Spring BootJournalApplication class and the Main-Class declaration points to the run helper JarLauncher from Spring Boot that will be in charge of bootstrapping your application.

Now you know how to create a Spring Boot standalone executable JAR.

■ **Note** I know that sometimes you don't want to run the tests when you are creating the executable JAR. You can execute $ ./mvnw package -DskipTests=true to skip the tests.

Creating Executable and Deployable WARs

You now know how to create an executable standalone JAR app—a portable way to distribute your application—but what happens when you already have application servers like Pivotal tc Server, Tomcat, JBoss, or Web Sphere, and are used to deploying WAR files?

With Spring Boot apps, it's really easy. You need to change two things:

1. Modify pom.xml (or build.gradle).

   - Change the <packaging> tag from jar to war (or apply the plugin war if you are using Gradle).

   - Add the spring-boot-starter-tomcat dependency to your pom.xml and set the scope to provided (or in your build.gradle set the name in the configurations section to a providedRuntime if you are using Gradle).

See Listing 12-5 for the pom.xml and Listing 12-6 for Gradle version.

Listing 12-5. Snippet of pom.xml

```xml
<?xml version="1.0" encoding="UTF-8"?>
<project xmlns="http://maven.apache.org/POM/4.0.0"
xmlns:xsi="http://www.w3.org/2001/XMLSchema-instance"
        xsi:schemaLocation="http://maven.apache.org/POM/4.0.0
        http://maven.apache.org/xsd/maven-4.0.0.xsd">
        <modelVersion>4.0.0</modelVersion>

        <groupId>com.apress.spring</groupId>
        <artifactId>spring-boot-journal</artifactId>
        <version>0.0.1-SNAPSHOT</version>
        <packaging>war</packaging>
```

```
            <!-- ... -->
        <dependencies>
                <dependency>
                    <groupId>org.springframework.boot</groupId>
                    <artifactId>spring-boot-starter-web</artifactId>
                </dependency>
                <!-- ... -->
                <dependency>
                    <groupId>org.springframework.boot</groupId>
                    <artifactId>spring-boot-starter-tomcat</artifactId>
                    <scope>provided</scope>
                </dependency>
                <!-- ... -->
        </dependencies>
</project>
```

Listing 12-5 shows a snippet of the journal app's pom.xml, where you change the packaging tag to WAR and then you add the `spring-boot-starter-tomcat` dependency with the `<scope>` tag set to provided. I know that the starter Tomcat is not in the original `pom.xml` because all the Tomcat dependencies are downloaded by the `spring-boot-starter-web` pom, but you are adding the Tomcat dependency here. This means that, when you package your application, all the libraries will now be placed in the `WEB-INF/lib` and the `WEB-INF/lib-provided` for the Tomcat libraries within the "Fat JAR".

This will make your application executable as standalone app and container-ready. There is a reason why in a WAR the tomcat libraries are placed in the `WEB-INF-lib-provided` directory—remember that everything that you add in the `WEB-INF/lib` will be taken by the application container, so if you leave the Tomcat JAR in this directory (`WEB-INF/lib`), the application container will fail because of duplicate JARs. That's why Spring Boot creates `WEB-INF/lib-provided` so it can run outside and inside of a container.

Next, let's see the `build.gradle` changes in Listing 12-6.

Listing 12-6. Snippet of build.gradle

```
// more configuration here

apply plugin: 'war'

war {
    baseName = 'spring-boot-journal'
    version =  '0.0.1-SNAPSHOT'
}

repositories {
    mavenCentral()
}

configurations {
    providedRuntime
}

dependencies {
    compile("org.springframework.boot:spring-boot-starter-web")
    providedRuntime("org.springframework.boot:spring-boot-starter-tomcat")
    ...
}
```

Listing 12-6 shows build.gradle (if you are using Gradle to build and run your Spring Boot apps). You modify the main application to extend from the SpringBootServletInitializer abstract class. This is required because the Spring web is using the Servlet 3.0 support and it's necessary to bootstrap your application when it's being deployed by the container.

Let's see the final version of the main app. See Listing 12-7.

Listing 12-7. src/main/java/com/apress/spring/SpringBootJournalApplication.java

```java
package com.apress.spring;

import org.springframework.boot.SpringApplication;
import org.springframework.boot.autoconfigure.SpringBootApplication;
import org.springframework.boot.builder.SpringApplicationBuilder;
import org.springframework.boot.context.web.SpringBootServletInitializer;

@SpringBootApplication
public class SpringBootJournalApplication extends SpringBootServletInitializer {

    @Override
    protected SpringApplicationBuilder configure(SpringApplicationBuilder application) {
        return application.sources(SpringBootJournalApplication.class);
    }

    public static void main(String[] args) {
        SpringApplication.run(SpringBootJournalApplication.class, args);
    }
}
```

Listing 12-7 shows the main app. This class extends from the SpringBootServletInitializer and it's overriding the configure(SpringApplicationBuilder application) method. That will help to bootstrap the application. Again, this is important if you want to deploy it in application container like Pivotal tcServer, Tomcat, etc.

So, after modifying the pom.xml and the main app, you are ready to create your container-ready journal application. Execute the following command:

```
$ ./mvnw clean package -DskipTests=true
```

Now you will have your target/spring-boot-journal-0.0.1-SNAPSHOT.war file ready to be executed with the following command:

```
$ java -jar target/spring-boot-journal-0.0.1-SNAPSHOT.war
```

After executing this command, you can go to https://localhost:8443. You will be redirected to the /login page. Enter your credentials (spring/boot) to see the home page.

Excellent! You have now a distributable and executable WAR journal app. Next, let's deploy the same WAR to a Tomcat-based container.

■ **Note** As a recommendation, you can always create a WAR file and extend from the `SpringBootServletInitializer` and override the `configure` method in your main application. This way, you can create an executable and container-ready Spring Boot application.

If you want to create a WAR when you are starting a new project with `spring init`, you can execute the following command (your journal app):

```
$ spring init -d=web,thymeleaf,data-jpa,data-rest,actuator,security,actuator-docs
-g=com.apress.spring -a=spring-boot-journal --package-name=com.apress.spring
-name=spring-boot-journal --packaging=war -x
```

The only difference is that you added the `--packaging=war` option, which will configure everything that you need (your pom.xml `<packaging>` tag will be set to `war`). Even the `SpringBootServletInitializer` configuration will be created as separate class file.

Deploying to a Tomcat-Based Server

If you don't have a Tomcat-based server you can installing it by using `brew` (if you have Mac OS/Linux), or you can get the binaries from the Apache Tomcat web site (`http://tomcat.apache.org/`).

```
$ brew update && brew install tomcat
```

I personally recommend the Pivotal's tc server, a Tomcat server on steroids! You can find all the information at `https://network.pivotal.io/products/pivotal-tcserver`. Some of its cool features are:

- You can install Spring Insight, an embedded tool for monitoring and tracing your Spring applications.

- It includes several add-ons such as GemFire (In-Memory Data Grid) and Redis (Key-Value Store Database) for session-management. These are very handy when you have a cluster of servers and want to centralize the session management.

- Highly configurable and very easy to use.

- Excellent documentation found at `http://tcserver.docs.pivotal.io/docs/index.html`.

You can install it with `brew` by executing the following command:

```
$ brew update && brew tap pivotal/tap && brew install tcserver
```

Once the `brew` finishes installing the tc server, follow these steps to deploy the journal app:

- Go to your installation and you should see a `tcruntime-instance.sh` file (`/usr/local/Cellar/tcserver/<version>/libexec/` for the Mac). Execute the following command:

  ```
  $ ./tcruntime-instance.sh create -i . myserver -v 8.0.30.C.RELEASE
  ```

This command will create in the current folder the `myserver` directory with all the Tomcat installation based on the `8.0.30.C.RELEASE` (this version is the same as the name of the Tomcat folder that should be in the current path and you should have at least 2 `tomcat-<version>`).

- Go to the `myserver` directory and copy the `spring-boot-journal-0.0.1-SNAPSHOT.war` in the `webapps` folder with the name `journal.war`.

```
$ cd myserver
$ cd webapps
$ cp ~/pro-spring-boot/ch12/spring-boot-journal/target/spring-boot-
journal-0.0.1-SNAPSHOT.war ./journal.war. Remember that you need to have
your MySQL server up and running.
```

- Next, go to the `bin` directory and start the tc server.

```
$ cd ..
$ cd bin
$ ./tcruntime-ctl.sh start
```

After executing these commands, the tc server should start. Now you can see the logs:

```
$ tail -f ../logs/catalina.out
```

You should see the familiar Spring Boot banner and all the logs about the journal app. Now you are ready to use it. Go to `http://localhost:8080/journal` and you should see the `/login` page (it will redirect to `http://localhost:8080/journal/login`). Enter your credentials (`spring/boot`) and your will see the journal.

Remember that the main context for your app is now `/journal` because you are using an application container. You can start testing all the other endpoints like `/journal/monitor` and `/journal/api`.

Congratulations! You deployed your WAR journal app to an application container. Well done!

Activating Profiles

Have you noticed the difference between running the journal app as standalone app vs. in the tc server? When running the journal app as standalone, you are using the `https://localhost:8443` URL, which is a SSL connection. But when you are using the tc server, you are not using the SSL/HTTPS. Spring Boot will identify when you are deploying to a container and it will omit some of the properties that are valid only when running in standalone mode. This means that if you want to secure the Tomcat server, you need to do it in a different way. If you need more information about securing Tomcat, visit `https://tomcat.apache.org/tomcat-8.0-doc/ssl-howto.html`. This link is generic for all Tomcats version 8.x.

Also, what happens if you want to connect to a different database, such as a production database, or have some other configuration that you want to expose when you are running in a container?

The good thing is that you can use the Spring profiles, something that you read about in earlier chapters. One of the recommended ways is to have several `application-<profile>.properties` files, so you can activate them in standalone mode or in the container.

You can create, for example, a new application-container.properties file. It will be identical to the other. Maybe you can create a new database and use that one as an example. Its contents are shown in Listing 12-8.

Listing 12-8. src/main/resources/application-container.properties

```
spring.datasource.url = jdbc:mysql://localhost:3306/calendar
spring.datasource.username = springboot
spring.datasource.password = springboot
spring.datasource.testWhileIdle = true
spring.datasource.validationQuery = SELECT 1

spring.jpa.show-sql = true
spring.jpa.hibernate.ddl-auto = create-drop
spring.jpa.hibernate.naming-strategy = org.hibernate.cfg.ImprovedNamingStrategy
spring.jpa.properties.hibernate.dialect = org.hibernate.dialect.MySQL5Dialect


spring.data.rest.basePath=/rest


management.context-path=/insight
endpoints.shutdown.enabled=true
```

Listing 12-8 shows the new application-container.properties file. The only changes are the name of the database from journal to calendar (remember that you need to create the calendar database in the MySQL server), and the paths for the rest, from /api to /rest and the management context-path, from /monitor to /insight. The SSL properties are no longer required.

Now, let's package the app and run it as standalone, activating the profile to container.

```
$ ./mvnw clean package -DskipTests=true
$ java -Dspring.profiles.active="container" -jar target/spring-boot-journal-0.0.1-SNAPSHOT.war
```

In the logs you can see (in the first three lines) the legend: "The following profiles are active: container". You can also review all the endpoints and even in your MySQL to see if the journal app created the entry table.

■ **Note**   If you want to run it first, meaning with the spring-boot:run, you can do so by executing $ ./mvnw spring-boot:run -Dspring.profiles.active="container" to activate the container profile.

Now the question is, how can you activate the profiles in a Tomcat-based container? It's as simple as adding the property spring.profiles.active=container in the <tomcat-installation>/conf/catalina.properties file.

If you are using the tc server, you can go to the same path (the following commands are based on a Mac installation):

```
$ cd /usr/local/Cellar/tcserver/<version>/libexec/
$ cd myserver/conf
$ echo spring.profiles.active=container >> catalina.properties
```

This command will append the properties to the `catalina.properties` file (see the double >>). Next you can start your tc server and see the activated logs and the profile container.

■ **Note** Remember that to create a container-ready WAR executable, you need to modify your `pom.xml` and subclass from the `SpringBootServletInitializer`. This is only for containers that support the Servlet API 3.0+ versions. For older version or legacy containers, you can get more info in the Spring Boot reference documentation.

Creating Spring Boot Apps as a Service

Another amazing feature of Spring Boot is that you can run your app as a service. Running a Spring Boot as a service has its benefits. It's easy to install and manage, and if the server restarts, your app will start automatically without you having to do it manually.

If you are using Unix, the only thing you need to do is add a configuration declaration to the Spring Boot plugin in the `pom.xml` file and in `build.gradle`. See Listings 12-9 and 12-10

Listing 12-9. pom.xml

```xml
<?xml version="1.0" encoding="UTF-8"?>
<project xmlns="http://maven.apache.org/POM/4.0.0"
xmlns:xsi="http://www.w3.org/2001/XMLSchema-instance"
        xsi:schemaLocation="http://maven.apache.org/POM/4.0.0
        http://maven.apache.org/xsd/maven-4.0.0.xsd">
        <modelVersion>4.0.0</modelVersion>

    <!-- ...all the previous code -->

    <build>
        <plugins>
            <plugin>
                <groupId>org.springframework.boot</groupId>
                <artifactId>spring-boot-maven-plugin</artifactId>

                <configuration>
                    <executable>true</executable>
                </configuration>
            </plugin>
        </plugins>
    </build>
</project>
```

Listing 12-9 shows the pom.xml file. The only thing that's new is in the <plugin> tag, the <configuration> tag that is making the WAR or JAR executable.

Listing 12-10. build.gradle

```
...
apply plugin: 'spring-boot'

springBoot {
        executable = true
}
...
```

Listing 12-10 shows the build.gradle. The only thing you need to add is the springBoot declaration. Now, when you package your application with the following:

```
$ ./mvnw clean package -DskipTests=true
```

You can execute the JAR directly:

```
$ target/spring-boot-journal-0.0.1-SNAPSHOT.war
```

And it will run! So, if you are running a UNIX environment you can just bind it to the /etc/init.d (in a Debian environment, assuming you have the executable in the /opt folder):

```
$ ln -s /opt/spring-boot-journal-0.0.1-SNAPSHOT.war /etc/init.d/journal
```

Then you can start your application with the following:

```
$ service journal start
```

So simple! You'll probably need to set up the run levels where the app might run. You can take a look at your UNIX distribution to see what else you need to do in order to enable the journal app as a service.

Maybe you are wondering how is this possible. You can take a peek at the file. If you execute the following command:

```
$ head -n 242 target/spring-boot-journal-0.0.1-SNAPSHOT.war
#!/bin/bash
...
...
```

You will see that the first 242 lines of the file are a BASH script. So, that's how it runs.

Spring Boot Apps as Windows Service

If you are looking to do this in a Windows environment, you can take a look at this URL at https://github.com/snicoll-scratches/spring-boot-daemon, which contains all the information you need to create a Spring Boot application and run it as a Windows service.

Spring Boot with Docker

In the past years, Docker has become one of the emergent technologies that is gaining a lot of popularity, because you can have multiple containers that can run a Linux-based OS in the same box. This is very similar to a virtualized environment but without all the footprint of a VM. If you are not familiar with Docker, I suggest reading some tutorials on the web at https://www.docker.com, https://docs.docker.com/mac, https://docs.docker.com/linux and https://docs.docker.com/windows/. Let's get started and create a Docker container that will include your journal app.

Make sure you have Docker up and running. Before you build the image that will contain the journal app, let's use profiles again and add a new dependency to the pom.xml file. See Listing 12-11.

Listing 12-11. src/main/resources/application-docker.properties

```
spring.datasource.url=jdbc:h2:mem:testdb;MODE=Oracle;DB_CLOSE_DELAY=-1;DB_CLOSE_ON_EXIT=FALSE
spring.datasource.username=sa
spring.datasource.password=
spring.datasource.driverClassName=org.h2.Driver

spring.data.rest.basePath=/api

management.context-path=/monitor
endpoints.shutdown.enabled=true

server.port=8443
server.ssl.key-store=classpath:keystore.jks
server.ssl.key-store-password=tomcat
server.ssl.key-password=tomcat
```

Listing 12-11 shows the application-docker.properites. All the spring.datasource properties are new. It has defined the H2 database that will run in-memory and also contains the SSL. Remember that in order to use the H2 database you must include this dependency in the pom.xml file:

```
<dependency>
        <groupId>com.h2database</groupId>
        <artifactId>h2</artifactId>
</dependency>
```

Now, you can create in the root folder the Dockerfile (this file helps create Docker images). See Listing 12-12.

Listing 12-12. Dockerfile

```
FROM java:8
VOLUME /tmp
ADD  target/spring-boot-journal-0.0.1-SNAPSHOT.war journal.war
ENV SPRING_PROFILES_ACTIVE docker
EXPOSE 8443
ENTRYPOINT ["java","-Djava.security.egd=file:/dev/./urandom","-jar","/journal.war"]
```

Listing 12-11 shows the Dockerfile that will be used to create the container. Let's examine it:

- `FROM java:8`. This line pulls a Debian 8 image (jessie) that contains the OpenJDK version 8.

- `VOLUME`. Needed to create a volume, because Spring Boot creates working directories for Tomcat by default.

- `ADD`. Copies the WAR (or JAR) file as `journal.war` (or Jar) in the root of the container.

- `ENV`. Needed to add the environment variable that will activate the Docker profile.

- `EXPOSE`. It's exposing the port 8443. Remember that this is the port for the SSL.

- `ENTRYPOINT`. This declaration determines how the container will execute when it starts up. To reduce the Tomcat startup time, you need a system property pointing to `"/dev/./urandom"` as a source of entropy.

Next, execute the following command to build the Docker image:

```
$ docker build -t springboot/journal
```

This command will build an image with the `springboot/journal` tag name. After it finishes building, you can run it with this command:

```
$ docker run -p 8443:8443 springboot/journal
```

This command will run the container using the `springboot/journal` image. Now you can go to your browser and open the journal app. If you are running this example in Linux, just go to `https://localhost:8443`. If you are using a Mac or a Windows machine, use the Docker IP:

```
$ docker-machine ip
192.168.99.100
```

Now you can go to `https://192.168.99.100:8443` (or any Docker IP) and voilà! You have your journal app running in a Docker container!

Maybe you are wondering if there is another way to automate (at least a little) the creation of the Docker image, and the answer is yes there is. There are Maven and Gradle plugins that incorporate the creating of the images based on a Docker file.

What you need to do is create a Dockerfile (I suggest in the `src/main/resources` folder) and add the plugin to the `pom.xml` (or Gradle) file. See Listing 12-13 for the `pom.xml` example.

Listing 12-13. Snippet of pom.xml

```
<?xml version="1.0" encoding="UTF-8"?>
<project xmlns="http://maven.apache.org/POM/4.0.0"
xmlns:xsi="http://www.w3.org/2001/XMLSchema-instance"
        xsi:schemaLocation="http://maven.apache.org/POM/4.0.0
        http://maven.apache.org/xsd/maven-4.0.0.xsd">
        <modelVersion>4.0.0</modelVersion>
```

```
        <groupId>com.apress.spring</groupId>
        <artifactId>spring-boot-journal</artifactId>
        <version>0.0.1-SNAPSHOT</version>
    <packaging>war</packaging>

    <!-- ... More tags here -->
    <properties>
            <project.build.sourceEncoding>UTF-8</project.build.sourceEncoding>
            <java.version>1.8</java.version>
            <docker.image.prefix>springboot</docker.image.prefix>
    </properties>

    <!-- Dependencies here -->

    <build>
        <plugins>
            <plugin>
                    <groupId>org.springframework.boot</groupId>
                    <artifactId>spring-boot-maven-plugin</artifactId>
            </plugin>
            <plugin>
                    <groupId>com.spotify</groupId>
                    <artifactId>docker-maven-plugin</artifactId>
                    <version>0.4.1</version>
                    <configuration>
                            <imageName>${docker.image.prefix}/${project.artifactId}
                            </imageName>
                            <dockerDirectory>src/main/resources/docker</dockerDirectory>
                            <resources>
                                    <resource>
                                            <targetPath>/</targetPath>

                                            <directory>${project.build.directory}
                                            </directory>
                                            <include>${project.build.finalName}.war
                                            </include>
                                    </resource>
                            </resources>
                    </configuration>
            </plugin>
        </plugins>
    </build>

</project>
```

Listing 12-13 shows the pom.xml and the new declarations, the Docker plugin and the Docker property prefix. The important part of the Docker plugin is the tag <dockerDirectory>, where the Dockerfile will live. Next, let's see the Dockerfile in Listing 12-14.

Listing 12-14. src/main/resources/docker/Dockerfile

```
FROM java:8
VOLUME /tmp
ADD spring-boot-journal-0.0.1-SNAPSHOT.war journal.war
ENV SPRING_PROFILES_ACTIVE docker
EXPOSE 8443
ENTRYPOINT ["java","-Djava.security.egd=file:/dev/./urandom","-jar","/journal.war"]
```

Listing 12-14 shows the Dockerfile that will be used by the Maven Docker plugin. What is the difference between this and Listing 12-12? One of the differences is the ADD declaration and the name, which will be the same as the `artifactId` + `version` + `extension`. The other declarations remain the same. The other difference is that the name of the Docker image will be `springboot/spring-boot-journal`, because it will take only the `artifactId` as a name.

Now you can build it and create the image in the same line with:

```
$ ./mvnw clean package docker:build -DskipTests=true
```

This command creates a new Docker image called `springboot/spring-boot-journal`. Now you can run it with:

```
$ docker run -p 8443:8443 springboot/spring-boot-journal
```

You can go to your browser and take a look at your journal app. Congrats! You "Dockerized" your journal application!

■ **Note** A quick note. In this Docker example you have two Dockerfile files—one in the root and another in the `src/main/resources/docker` directory. The only difference is the ADD declaration. This `src/main/resources/docker/Dockerfile` file will be picked up only by the Docker plugin in your `pom.xml` and it won't affect the other file in the root.

Summary

This chapter explained how to deploy your Spring Boot apps by using the command line, creating executable and container-ready WARs, how to use profiles for deployment, and how to deploy to Docker containers. As a developer, you have a lot of options for deployment.

The next chapter shows you a little more of the deployment, but focuses on cloud environments. It discusses the new technology architectural trend: Microservices.

CHAPTER 13

Spring Boot in the Cloud

Cloud Computing is nowadays one of the most important concepts in the IT industry. Companies that want to be at the edge of the latest technology are looking to be *fast* by increasing the speed of their services, they want to be *safe*, by recovering from errors or mistakes as fast as possible without the client knowing about it, they want to be *scalable* by growing horizontally (typically refers to scaling infrastructure capacity outward such as spawning more servers to shared the load) instead of vertically (refers to the ability to increase available resources (cpu, memory, disk space, etc) for an existing entity like a server); but what kind of concept or technology can provide all these concepts?.

The term "Cloud-Native" architectures is begining to emerge, because allows you as developer follow some patterns that will provide speed, safety and scalability with ease. In this chapter I will show you how you can create and deploy Spring Boot applications for the Cloud by following some of these patterns.

The Cloud and Cloud-Native Architectures

I imagine you have heard about these companies: Pivotal, Amazon, Google, Heroku, NetFlix, Uber that are applying all the concepts I mentioned before; but how these companies have accomplished to be fast, safe and scalable at the same time?

One of the first pioneers of the Cloud Computing was Amazon, which started using virtualization as primary tool to create resource elasticity; this means that any deployed application can have more computer power, by increasing the number of virtual boxes, memory, processors, etc, without any IT person involved. All these new ways to scale an application was the result satisfying all the user demand that has been and keep growing.

How NetFlix can satisfy all these user demands, and we are talking about millions of users daily that are streaming media content? All these companies have now the IT insfrastructure required for the Cloud era, but don't you think that, any application that wants to be part of the cloud needs to be some how adaptable to this new technology? What I mean with this comments is that, you need to start thinking on how scaling resources will impact my application, you need to start thinking more on distributed systems, right? How my applications will communicate to legacy systems or between each other in this kind of environments, what happened if one of my systems is down and how to recover, or how the users (and if I have millions) can take advantage of the Cloud?

The new cloud-native architecture responds to all the above questions. Remember that now your applications need to be fast, safe and scalable:

First, you need to have some *visibility* in this new cloud environment, meaning that you need to have a better way to monitor your applications, by setting alerts, have dashboards, etc. *Fault isolation and tolerance*, where you need to have applications that are context-bounded, meaning that the applications shouldn't have any dependency between each other; if one of your applications is down, the other apps should keep running, or if you are deploying continuously an application, that shouldn't affect the entire system; this means also that you need to think about some kind of *auto-recovery*, where the entire system is capable to identify the failure and recover.

© Felipe Gutierrez 2016

F. Gutierrez, *Pro Spring Boot*, DOI 10.1007/978-1-4842-1431-2_13

Twelve-Factor Applications

Following what you need to create a cloud-native architecture, the engineers at Heroku start to identify a lot of patterns that became the twelve-factor application guide. This guide shows how an application (a single unit) need to be architect focusing on declarative configuration, being stateless and deployment independent; this is what I mentioned before: your application need to be fast, safe and it can scale.

This is the summary of the twelve-factor application guide:

- *Codebase*. One codebase tracked in VCS, many deploys. One app has a single code base and its tracked by a version control system like Git, Subversion, Mercurial, etc. You can do many deployments (from the same code base) to development, testing, staging and production environments.

- *Dependencies*. Explicity declare and isolate dependencies. Some times your environments don't have internet connection (if is a private system), so you need to think about packaging your dependencies (jars, gems, shared-libraries, etc) or if you have an internal repository of libraries, you can declared manifest like poms, gemfile, bundles, etc. Never rely that you will have everything in your final environment.

- *Configuration*. Store config in the environment. You should't hardcode anything that varies. Use the environment variables or a configuration server.

- *Backing Services*. Treat backing services as attached resources. Connect to services via URL or configuration.

- *Build, Release, Run*. Strictly separate build and run stages. Related to a CI/CD (Continuous Integration, Continuous Delivery)

- *Processes*. Execute the app as one or more stateless processes. Processess should not store internal state. Share nothing. Any necessary state should be considered as a *Backing Service*.

- *Port binding*. Export services via port port binding. Your application is self-container, and these apps are exposed via port binding. An application can become another App' service.

- *Concurrency*. Scale out via the process model. Scale by adding more application instances. Individual processes are free to multithread.

- *Disposability*. Maximize robustness with fast startup and graceful shutdown. Processes should be disposable (remember they are stateless). Fault tolerant.

- *Environment parity*. Keep development, staging and production environments as similar as possible. This is a result of High Quality, ensures continuous delivery.

- *Logs*. Treat logs as event streams. Your apps should write to stdout. Logs are streams of aggregated, time-ordered events.

- *Admin processes*. Run admin and managemenr tasks as one-off processes. Run admin processes on the platform: DB migrations, one time scripts, etc.

Microservices

The term Microservices has been around for the last two years, trying to define a new way to create applications. You need to see Microservices just as a way to decompose monolithic applications into different and independent components that follow the twelve-factor app guide and when deployed they just work. See the following Figure 13-1:

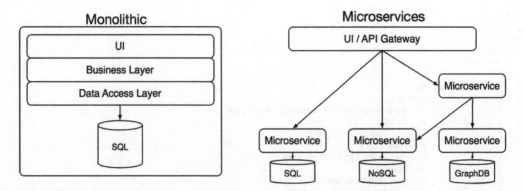

Figure 13-1. *Monolithic vs. Microservices*

I think Microservices has been around since the invention of Unix, because you can use one of the command line tools, like for example: grep, that is just a single unit that do its job well. And if you combine several of these commands (eg. find . -name microservices.txt | grep -i spring-boot) you can create a better app or system; but have in mind that these commands are independent of each other and the way of communication is through the Unix pipe |. This analogy can be the same within your applications.

Microservices help you to accelate development, why? Because you can designate a small team that can work in one and only one feature of the application, with a bounded-context and that follows the twelve-factor application guidelines.

I know there is a lot to say about Microservices and guides on how migrate existing architectures into Microservices, but the idea here is explore Spring Boot and see how can you deploy it into a cloud environment.

Preparing the Spring Boot Journal App as Microservice

What would you need to do in order to convert the Spring Boot Journal App as a Microservice? Actually, nothing! Yes, nothing, because Spring Boot was thought as a way to create Microservices with ease.

So, you are going to use the same Spring Boot Journal App and be able to deploy it to a cloud platform. Which platform? You are going to use Cloud Foundry!

Let's start by generating first our application. Execute the following commands:

```
$ mkdir spring-boot-journal-cloud
$ cd spring-boot-journal-cloud
$ spring init -d=web,thymeleaf,data-jpa,data-rest,actuator,h2,mysql  -g=com.apress.spring -
a=spring-boot-journal-cloud --package-name=com.apress.spring -name=spring-boot-journal-cloud -x
```

from the above command, notice that, just for now you are removing the security (you can add it later). Next, copy all the files that you are already familiar with, all the `src/main/resources/templates` (without the `login.html`), `src/main/resource/static`, `src/main/resources/application.properties` and the Java sources. You should have something similar to Figure 13-2. Don't worry too much, I will tell you if you need to do any change in the files.

```
├── mvnw
├── mvnw.cmd
├── pom.xml
└── src
    ├── main
    │   ├── java
    │   │   └── com
    │   │       └── apress
    │   │           └── spring
    │   │               ├── SpringBootJournalCloudApplication.java
    │   │               ├── domain
    │   │               │   └── JournalEntry.java
    │   │               ├── repository
    │   │               │   └── JournalRepository.java
    │   │               ├── utils
    │   │               │   ├── JsonDateDeserializer.java
    │   │               │   └── JsonDateSerializer.java
    │   │               └── web
    │   │                   └── JournalController.java
    │   └── resources
    │       ├── application-cloud.properties
    │       ├── application.properties
    │       ├── data.sql
    │       ├── static
    │       │   └── css
    │       │       ├── bootstrap-glyphicons.css
    │       │       ├── bootstrap.min.css
    │       │       └── styles.css
    │       └── templates
    │           └── index.html
    └── test
        └── java
            └── com
                └── apress
                    └── spring
                        └── SpringBootJournalCloudApplicationTests.java

19 directories, 17 files
```

Figure 13-2. *Spring Boot Journal project*

Figure 13-2 shows you the directory structure, you can see that there is no config directory anymore, because the security configuration is no longer needed, also notice that there only two properties file, one is the default, the one that you should test (this will have the H2 in memory database). And the other property file has the `cloud` word, meaning that you are going to use it for deploying using the cloud profile.

■ **Note** You can find the example of the chapter in the Book's source code from the Apress Site or you can download it from github at: `https://github.com/felipeg48/pro-spring-boot`.

See Listing 13-1 the default properties file.

Listing 13-1. src/main/resources/application.properties

```
spring.datasource.url=jdbc:h2:mem:tesdb;DB_CLOSE_DELAY=-1;DB_CLOSE_ON_EXIT=FALSE
spring.datasource.driverClassName=org.h2.Driver
spring.datasource.username=sa
spring.datasource.password=
spring.datasource.testWhileIdle = true
spring.datasource.validationQuery = SELECT 1

spring.jpa.show-sql = true
spring.jpa.hibernate.ddl-auto = create-drop
spring.jpa.hibernate.naming-strategy = org.hibernate.cfg.ImprovedNamingStrategy
spring.jpa.properties.hibernate.dialect = org.hibernate.dialect.MySQL5Dialect

spring.data.rest.basePath=/api

management.context-path=/monitor
endpoints.shutdown.enabled=true
```

Listing 13-1 shows you the application.properties file (the default profile) that you are going to use to run it locally. So, if your copy is ok, try to run you application; you should have the Journal App up and running. All the data is in Memory. Also, try to get into the /api and /monitor endpoint, just to make sure they work.

Next, let's review the application-cloud.properties file. See Listing 13-2.

Listing 13-2. src/main/resources/application-cloud.properties

```
spring.data.rest.basePath=/rest

management.context-path=/insight
endpoints.shutdown.enabled=true
```

Listing 13-2 shows you the contents of the application-cloud.properties. This would be cloud profile. Notice that, there are no datasource properties, only the rest base path and the actuator management.context-path declared. There is a meaning for this, but you are going to see why in the next sections.

Before you deploy this to the cloud you need to know more about the Platform you are going to use.

Cloud Foundry

Cloud Foundry has been around since 2008, a PaaS (Platform As A Service) company that was acquired by Spring Source and that Spring Source was itself acquired by VMWare, and since then, Cloud Foundry was and still is the most used Open Source PaaS. It's worth to mention that Cloud Foundry as an open source solution has the largerst community support and it's backed up by several large IT companies, like IBM (with BlueMix), Microsoft, Intel, SAP and of course Pivotal (with Pivotal Cloud Foundry) and VMware among others.

Cloud Foundry is the only open source solution that you can actually download and run it without any problems, it just work! You can find two versions of Cloud Foundry, the open source: https://www.cloudfoundry.org/ and the commercial version: http://pivotal.io/platform. If you are interested in download the commercial version, you can actually do it without any trials or limited time: https://network.pivotal.io/products/pivotal-cf, actually is a free version, but if you want to have support or help on how to install it, that's when you need to contact a Pivotal sales representative.

Cloud Foundry

Cloud Foundry is built on Open Architecture, and it offers the following features:

- *Router*. Routes incoming traffic to the appropriate component, usually the Cloud Controller or a running application on a DEA node.

- *Authentication*. The OAuth2 server and Login server work together to provide indentity management.

- *Cloud Controller*. The cloud controller is responsible for managing the lifecycle of application.

- *HM9000*. Monitors, determines and reconciles application to determine their state, version and number of instances, and redirects to the Cloud Controller to take action to correct any discrepancies.

- *Application Execution (DEA)*. The Droplet Execution Agent manages application instances, tracks started instances and broadcasts state messages.

- *Blob Store*. The blob store: resources, application code, build packs and droplets.

- *Service Brokers*. When a developer provisions and binds a service to an application, the service broker for that service is responsible for providing the service instance.

- *Message Bus*. Cloud Foundry uses NATS (this is different from the network nats), a lightweight publish-subscribe and distributed queueing messaging system, for internal communication between components.

- *Logging and Statistics*. The metrics collector gathers metrics from the components. Operators can use this information to monitor an instance of Cloud Foundry.

Pivotal Cloud Foundry Features

Pivotal Cloud Foundry®, powered by Cloud Foundry (Open Source), delivers a turnkey PaaS experience on multiple infrastructures with leading application and data services.

- Commercially supported release based on Cloud Foundry open source.

- Fully automated deployment, updates and 1-click horizontal and vertical scaling on vSphere, vCloud Air, AWS or Openstack with minimal production downtime.

- Instant, horizontal application tier scaling.

- Web console for resource management and administration of applications and services.

- Applications benefit from built-in services like load balancing and DNS, automated health management, logging and auditing.

- Java Spring support through provided Java buildpack.

- Optimized developer experience for Spring framework.

- MySQL Service for rapid development and testing.

- Automatic application binding and service provisioning for Pivotal Services such as Pivotal RabbitMQ and MySQL for Pivotal Cloud Foundry.

what is the difference between the Open Source from the Commercial version? Well, all the features listed above. In the Open Source version you need to do everything manually, using the command line mostly (to install, configure, upgrade, etc), but in the Commercial version, you can use a Web console to manage your infrastructure and run your applications. It's important to know that you can install Cloud Foundry in Amazon AWS, Open Stack and VSphere.

Cloud Foundry CLI - Command Line Interface

Before you start using Cloud Foundry, you must install a command line tool that will be useful for deploying and do a lot of other tasks. If you are using a Windows OS you can get the latest version from https://github.com/cloudfoundry/cli#downloads.

If you are using Mac OS/Linux you can use brew:

```
$ brew update
$ brew tap cloudfoundry/tap
$ brew install cf-cli
```

after you install it, you can test it by running:

```
$ cf --version
cf version 6.15.0
```

now you are ready to use Cloud Foundry. Spoiler alert coming! As a final example, you will use the Pivotal Web Service platform, this is the commercial version of Pivotal Cloud Foundry.

Development Enviroment - PCFDev

I've just given you the spoiler alert; you will use the Pivotal's public PaaS. You can think of as a production environment for your applications, but maybe you are wondering if there is something in between, I mean, you want to test first your application, right? So, it should be something that emulates the Cloud environment. Of course you are ready to probe that, by creating profiles and adding your database connections to a properties file or even putting some variables in the environment variables' OS; or by installing Cloud Foundry (but for that you need to have ready your infrastructure and read about the Cloud Foundry internal before installing it); and again, it should be easier way to deploy apps into a local machine.

I'm glad there is. The Pivotal Cloud team did a very hard work to bring a Vagrant file with a VM ready to use, that is actually a micro-instance of the actual Cloud Foundry; no need to pull off your hair trying to install Cloud Foundry, just use the PCFDev (Pivotal Cloud Foundry Dev) and deploy your applications in your local machine.

PCFDev is one of the latest iterations of the Pivotal Cloud team, before *PCFDev*, it was: *Lattice* (http://lattice.cf/) and before that: *BoshLite* (https://github.com/cloudfoundry/bosh-lite - this is still very active in the community, but is more related to the internal parts of Cloud Foundry, related to the *BOSH* technology) and before that: (part of the VMware team) the *Micro Cloud Foundry* (https://micro. cloudfoundry.com/ - That url is no longer valid, it will re-direct to the Pivotal Platform. This was also a VM image). So, as you can see it's being a lot of hard work to get into this point, where you can have an amazing technology running in your local machine.

Installing PCFDev

What are the requirements?

- Vagrant 1.7+ - https://www.vagrantup.com/

- Cloud Foundry CLI (you already have this) - https://github.com/cloudfoundry/cli

- Internet Connection required (for DNS)

- Around 3 to 4GB of Disk space free.

- One of the following:

  - VirtualBox: 5.0+ - https://www.virtualbox.org/

  - VMware Fusion: 8+ - https://www.vmware.com/products/fusion

  - VMware Workstation: 11+ - https://www.vmware.com/products/workstation

---

■ **Note**   VMware requires the Vagrant VMware plugin that is sold by Hashicorp. https://www.hashicorp.com/.

---

after you install the requirements from above, you can now install PCFDev:

- Download pcfdev-<version>.zip from: https://network.pivotal.io/products/pcfdev

- Unzip the pcfdev-<version>.zip

- Open a terminal and go to the pcfdev-<version> folder.

- Run: vagrant up --provider=<provider> where <provider> can be: virtualbox, vmware_fusion or vmware_workstation.

- (Optional) There are already some scripts that can be used instead of the previous command. These scripts optimized the resources needed for your environment. These scripts are:

  - start-osx/stop-osx for Mac Users.

  - start-windows.ps1/stop-windows.ps1 for Windows users.

if you are using VirtualBox, then you do:

```
$ vagrant up --provider=virtualbox
```

After you run the above command, you should have in the last lines the following output:

```
Bringing machine 'default' up with 'virtualbox' provider...
==> default: Importing base box pcfdev/pcfdev'...
==> default: Matching MAC address for NAT networking...
==> default: Checking if box pcfdev/pcfdev is up to date...
...
...
==> default: Waiting for services to start...
==> default: 0 out of 48 running
==> default: 3 out of 48 running
...
==> default: PCF Dev is now running.
```

```
==> default: To begin using PCFDev, please run:
==> default: cf login -a api.local.pcfdev.io --skip-ssl-validation
==> default: Email: admin
==> default: Password: admin
```

the first time it will take a few minutes (well, around 15 to 45 minutes depending on your system), and this is because the PCFDev is downloading, setting everything up, so be patient! The above output tells you that your PCFDev vm is up and running, so let's start playing around with it.

Login into PCFDev

Let's login into the PCFDev. Execute the following commands:

```
$ cf login -a api.local.pcfdev.io --skip-ssl-validation
API endpoint: api.local.pcfdev.io

Email> admin

Password>
Authenticating...
OK

Targeted org pcfdev-org

Targeted space pcfdev-space

API endpoint:   https://api.local.pcfdev.io (API version: 2.54.0)
User:           admin
Org:            pcfdev-org
Space:          pcfdev-space
```

the cf login command sets the target api url, this means that every subsequent command using cf will use that URL by default. This is a one-time only command (this will change when you target the public Pivotal Web Services or if you company already has Pivotal Cloud Foundry, you can target your provided api url). The output above shows you that you successfully have logged in.

■ **Note**   Just for the curious, once you set the target URL and login, the cf command will write into your home directory in the ~/.cf/config.json file. You can take a look at it (but don't modify it), you will see the target URL and some other keys. Now you are ready to deploy.

By default PCFDev will assign a target *Organization* (pcfdev-org) and a target *Space* (pcfdev-space). You can see the organizations and spaces as way to structure your development. You can have as many organizations as you want. Every organization has one or more spaces. For example, you can create a "Journal" organization and have "Prod", "QA", "Dev" spaces attach to the "Journal" organization.

Now, I'm assuming you test you application before, so let's package the Journal app with:

```
$ ./mvnw clean package -DskipTests=true
```

the above command will create the target/spring-boot-journal-cloud-0.0.1-SNAPSHOT.jar file. Now your Journal app is ready the be deployed.

Deploying to PCFDev

To deploy your Journal app to PCFDev just execute the following command:

```
$ cf push journal -p target/spring-boot-journal-cloud-0.0.1-SNAPSHOT.jar
Creating app journal in org pcfdev-org / space pcfdev-space as admin...
OK

Creating route journal.local.pcfdev.io...
OK

Binding journal.local.pcfdev.io to journal...
OK

Uploading journal...
Uploading app files from: target/spring-boot-journal-cloud-0.0.1-SNAPSHOT.jar
Uploading 37.2M, 185 files
Done uploading
OK

Starting app journal in org pcfdev-org / space pcfdev-space as admin...
Downloading php_buildpack...Downloading staticfile_buildpack...Downloading ruby_buildpack...
Downloading binary_buildpack...
Downloading nodejs_buildpack...
Downloading go_buildpack...
Downloading python_buildpack...
Downloading java_buildpack...
Downloaded binary_buildpack (8.3K)
Downloaded staticfile_buildpack (2.4M)
Downloaded nodejs_buildpack (44.3M)
Downloading ruby_buildpack failedDownloading go_buildpack failedDownloaded java_buildpack
(239.9M)
Downloaded python_buildpack (254M)
....
....
....
Showing health and status for app journal in org pcfdev-org / space pcfdev-space as admin...
OK

requested state: started
instances: 1/1
usage: 1G x 1 instances
urls: journal.local.pcfdev.io
last uploaded: Tue Feb 23 04:47:47 UTC 2016
stack: cflinuxfs2
```

```
buildpack: java-buildpack=v3.5.1-offline-http://github.com/pivotal-cf/pcf-java-buildpack.
git#d6c19f8 java-main open-jdk-like-jre=1.8.0_65 open-jdk-like-memory-calculator=2.0.1_
RELEASE spring-auto-reconfiguration=1.10.0_RELEASE
...
....
```

the above output tells you that you deployed your app to PCFDev, but let's see what actually happen. First you executed this command (Do not execute this command, Im explaining what you did):

$ cf push journal -p target/spring-boot-journal-cloud-0.0.1-SNAPSHOT.jar

the syntax for pushing an application is:

```
$ cf push <app-name> [-p <path>]
```

so, you are pushing your application by given a name: journal, and you are telling where to get the file, by the -p parameter passing the relative path of the jar, in this case: target/spring-boot-journal-cloud-0.0.1-SNAPSHOT.jar. Then the PCFDev responds by entering into the internal deployment process. It will download the necessary tools (buildpacks) that will identify the type of application (in this case a Spring/Java app) and it will try to run the journal app by assigning a URL, in this case: journal.local.pcfdev.io.

Now, you can go to your browser and see your Journal app in action. Congratulations, you just deploy your app in your local Cloud environment, PCFDev!

Cloud Profile

Did you try to go to the /api and /monitor endpoints? Did you get an error? If you packaged the Journal app with the two properties files, application.properties and application-cloud.properties, you should get an error going to the /api and /monitor endpoint, but why?

By default, when you deploy to PCFDev or Pivotal Cloud Foundry, the active profile is set to "cloud", this means that your Journal app will use the application-cloud.properties file, then, your endpoints are different, remember? Your application-cloud.properties file sets the rest endpoint to: /rest and the actuator endpoint set to: /insight. So, you can go to your browser and see that the endpoints work.

If you want to see that actually these endpoints are mapped to the /rest and /insight, you can execute the following command:

```
$ cf logs journal --recent
```

with the above command you can review all the logs of your app.

Adding a new entry to the Journal

Let's try to add a new entry to the Journal app through the /rest endpoint. So far you have only 4 records, the ones taken from the src/main/resources/data.sql file.

To add a new record, in your terminal window execute the following command:

```
$ curl -i -X POST -H "Content-Type:application/json" -d '{ "title":"Cloud
Foundry","summary":"Learn about Cloud Foundry and push a Spring Boot Application","creat
ed":"2016-04-05"}' http://journal.local.pcfdev.io/rest/journal
```

317

the above cURL command will add a new record to your Journal through the endpoint http://journal.local.pcfdev.io/rest/journal. You can now go to the home page and refresh, you should see the new record added.

Backing Services: Creating and Binding Service Instances

If you stop your Journal app from the PCFDev with the command:

```
$ cf stop journal
```

and start it again with the command:

```
$ cf start journal
```

or you can do a simple:

```
$ cf restart journal
```

you will find out that the recent entry you posted is now gone, why? Because Spring Boot recognized that you have in your dependencies the H2 (in-memory DB) so it will use it; but how about using the MySQL, because you have that dependency too. One of the good things is that you can create a Backing Service (remember from the twelve factor app guide?), this means that you can create a MySQL service and use it within your application.

What is the difference here about using MySQL? First of all, Cloud Foundry offers you services that are plugin into the platform, ready to be used. You don't need to worry about installation or anything like that, just use them and that's it, and MySQL is one of those services that Cloud Foundry offers your that work out-of-the-box.

How can you use these Services, and in this case the MySQL service? You need to create an instance of that MySQL and give it a name; this means that Cloud Foundry will create a dedicated Database instance ready to be used. After creating the service instance, you need to bind it to your application.

Let's start by seeing that Services the PCFDev has. Execute the following command:

```
$ cf marketplace
Getting services from marketplace in org pcfdev-org / space pcfdev-space as admin...
OK

service plans description
p-mysql 512mb, 1gb MySQL databases on demand
p-rabbitmq standard RabbitMQ is a robust and scalable high-performance multi-protocol
messaging broker.
p-redis shared-vm Redis service to provide a key-value store

TIP: Use 'cf marketplace -s SERVICE' to view descriptions of individual plans of a given
service.
```

from the above command you can see that PCFDev has 3 available backing services with their plans (plans are a way to control what you consume from a service, for example if you choose a plan with 1GB, you only have that storage size for your persistence, and if you pass that threshold you won't be able to persiste data anymore) and description, ready to be used. The Marketplace is where normally you will find all the available services for Cloud Foundry. Now, let's create the MySQL service instance with the following command:

```
$ cf create-service p-mysql 512mb mysql
Creating service instance mysql in org pcfdev-org / space pcfdev-space as admin...
OK
```

the syntax to create a service instance is:

```
cf create-service SERVICE PLAN SERVICE_INSTANCE [-c PARAMETERS_AS_JSON] [-t TAGS]
```

where the SERVICE=p-mysql (name from the marketplace), PLAN=512mb and SERVICE_INSTANCE=mysql (any name you want). The above command will create a "mysql" service instance from the "p-mysql" backing service.

If you execute the following command:

```
$ cf services
```

it will list the service you just created. Next, let's bind the "mysql" service instance to the journal app with the command:

```
$ cf bind-service journal mysql
Binding service mysql to app journal in org pcfdev-org / space pcfdev-space as admin...
OK
TIP: Use 'cf restage journal' to ensure your env variable changes take effect
```

the syntax for binding a service instance is:

```
cf bind-service APP_NAME SERVICE_INSTANCE [-c PARAMETERS_AS_JSON]
```

where the APP_NAME=journal (this is the app name from the cf push command) and the SERVICE_INSTANCE=mysql. The above command will bind the mysql service instance to the Journal app. Because you bind a service to an application it's required to restage the application to take the changes. To restage the Journal app execute the following command:

```
$ cf restage journal
Restaging app journal in org pcfdev-org / space pcfdev-space as admin...
....
```

after it's re-stage you can go to the home page of your Journal app. You should see something similar to Figure 13-3.

Figure 13-3. *Journal App home page after restage*

Figure 13-3 shows you the Journal app after restage, but what happen to the data? Because you have bound a service (MySQL service), and because the `application-cloud.properties` doesn't have any of the `spring.jpa.*` properties declared it will get the defaults, making the table drop every time you start/restart the Journal application.

Let's fix that. Add the following properties to your `application-cloud.properties` file:

```
spring.jpa.hibernate.ddl-auto=create
spring.jpa.generate-ddl=true
```

the above properties will create the table once, without droping when stop or restart. After that change, you need to repackage the Journal app:

```
$ ./mvnw clean package -DskipTests=true
```

then, you need to push your app back again:

```
$ cf push journal -p target/spring-boot-journal-cloud-0.0.1-SNAPSHOT.jar
```

refresh your browser (you should see still Figure 13-3), then you can try to insert an entry:

```
$ curl -i -X POST -H "Content-Type:application/json" -d '{ "title":"Cloud
Foundry","summary":"Learn about Cloud Foundry and push a Spring Boot Application","creat
ed":"2016-04-05"}' http://journal.local.pcfdev.io/rest/journal
```

after executing the above command you can refresh the home page. You should see something similar to Figure 13-4.

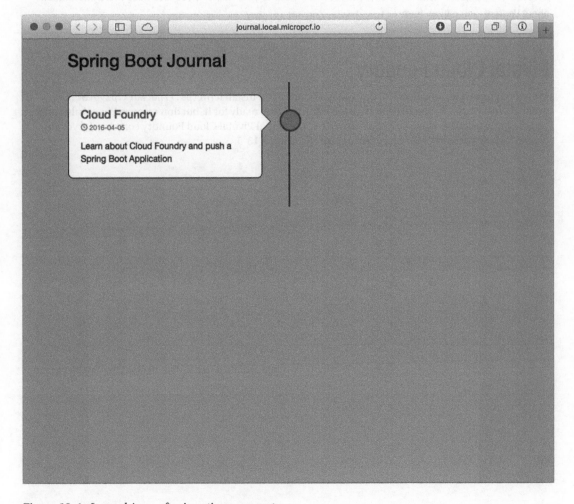

Figure 13-4. *Journal App - after inserting a new entry*

Figure 13-4 shows you the result of adding a new entry using the cURL command. Now if you stop and start the Journal app:

```
$ cf restart journal
```

and refresh your browser, you should still have your entry you previously added. Congrats! Now you push an application that has a backing service!

■ **Note**   If you want to know more about the Cloud Floundry CLI, just execute the command: `$ cf help` this will bring a very well documented commands. Or, you can execute: `$ cf help <command-name>` to get detail help about a particular command. So, remember, `cf help` is your friend. If you also need more information about Vagrant, you can go here: `https://www.vagrantup.com/`.

Pivotal Cloud Foundry

Even though you can download Pivotal Cloud Foundry and install it (`https://network.pivotal.io/products/pivotal-cf`) you need to have the infrastructure ready for it, but don't worry; Pivotal also offers you the infrastructure where you can make use of the actual Pivotal Cloud Foundry commercial version, Pivotal Web Services `http://run.pivotal.io/`. See Figure 13-5.

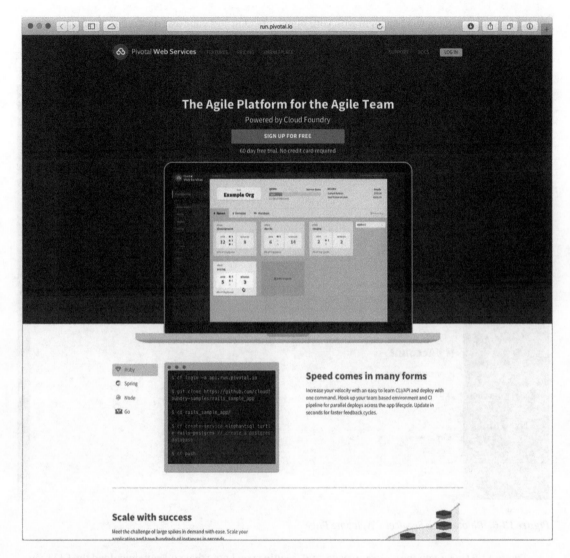

Figure 13-5. *Pivotal Web Services* `http://run.pivotal.io/`

Pivotal Web Services offers you a 60 trial, I think enough to get to know the power of Cloud Foundry. You can sign up for it. In order to get the frial trial, you need to add your Mobile Number, because Pivotal require SMS verification for claiming free trials to ensure responsible use of their platform and protect all the current users. Your number is only used for claiming your free trial, and it will never be distributed to third-parties or used for marketing purposes.

■ **Note**   Users are limited to one free trial org per user account. If you have any issues or questions, please contact support@run.pivotal.io.

Once you signed up, you will login with your email provided and your username, and the first screen that you will see, will be something similar to Figure 13-6.

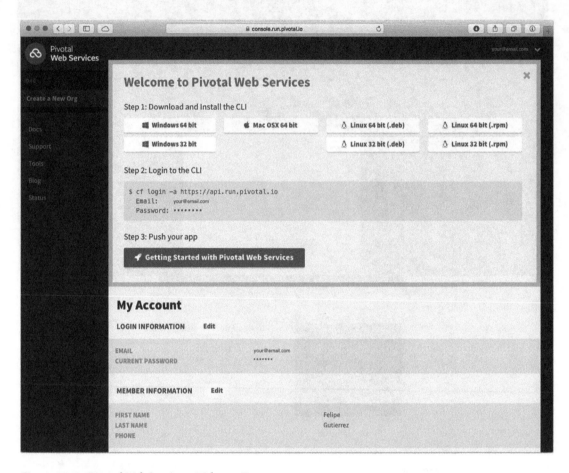

Figure 13-6. *Pivotal Web Services - Welcome Page*

Figure 13-6 shows you the welcome page, and is letting you know that you can download the CLI (you already did) as Step 1, and in Step 2, you can see the commands that you need to execute in order to login into Pivotal Web Services, as shown below:

```
$ cf login -a https://api.run.pivotal.io
  Email: <your email>
  Password: <your password>
```

Now, you are ready to use Pivotal Web Services, the commercial version of Pivotal Cloud Foundry. As you already know, Pivotal Web Services offers you a Marketplace that allows you to add/bind services to your applications. You can choose Market place from the left menu, and see what is available for you, or you can go directly to this url: `https://console.run.pivotal.io/marketplace`. See Figure 13-7.

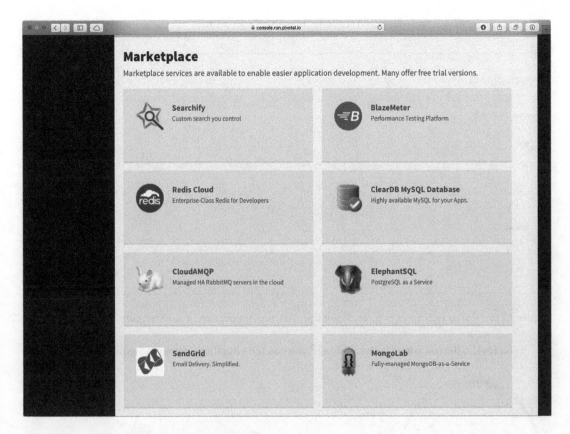

Figure 13-7. *Pivotal WebServices Marketplace*

Figure 13-7 shows you the Marketplace. You can use the ClearDB for testing your MySQL, similar what you did with the PCFDev where you added the service instance and bind it to the Journal application. Here, you can either use the command line (as before) or use the Web ui.

Deploying to Pivotal Web Services

You are already logged in into Pivotal Web Services, now you can follow the same steps from the PCFDev deployment, with just a small change:

```
$ ./mvnw clean package -DskipTests=true
$ cf push journal -p target/spring-boot-journal-cloud-0.0.1-SNAPSHOT.jar --random-route
```

the above command will push your Journal app to the Pivotal Web Services, but notice the --random-route, you need to add that, because the **the url must be unique**. By default, Pivotal Web Services will generate a URL in the form of: https://<app-name>.cfapps.io for every single application hosted there (of course you can bind your own domain) and because there are a thousand apps running, probably the name "journal" (URL: https://journal.cfapps.io/) is already taken, and probably you will have some collision names. That's why you need to add the --random-route (until you register your own domain and point to the app), this will generate a URL of the form: https://<app-name>-<random-name>.cfapps.io/. In the example about the URL was: http://journal-glenoid-anticlericalism.cfapps.io/, so you can go ahead an dive into your app.

After you push you app you should see something like Figure 13-8.

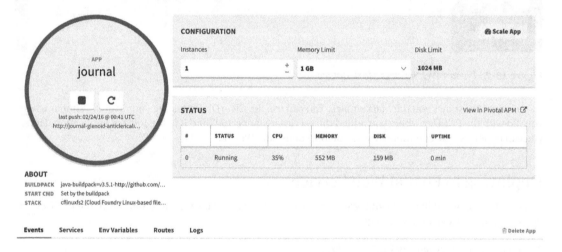

Figure 13-8. *Pivotal Web Services (CloudFoundry) - Journal Application up and running*

if you click in the row where it says: *"journal"*, you can see something similar to Figure 13-9.

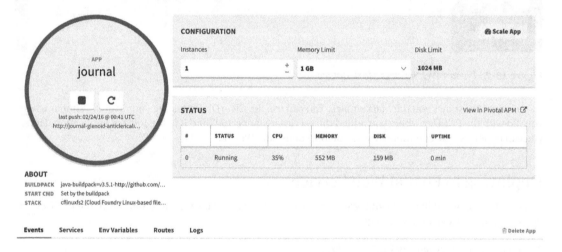

Figure 13-9. *Journal App*

Figure 13-9 shows you your app and some other details. If you click below, in the *"Services"* tab, you should have something similar to Figure 13-10.

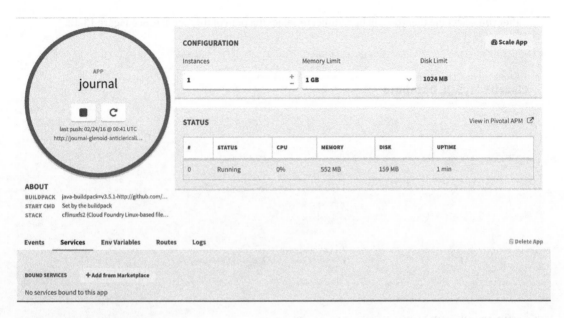

Figure 13-10. *Services tab detail*

Figure 13-10 shows you the "*Services*" tab, and as you can see there is no Backing Service bound to the Journal app, so, go ahead an click the "*+ Add from Marketplace*". You will see the Marketplace. Select the *ClearDB MySQL Database* tile. ClearDB (https://www.cleardb.com/) is a company that optimize MySQL for cloud infrastructure providing its services to Cloud Foundry and other cloud services like Heroku. See Figure 13-11.

Figure 13-11. *Marketplace - ClearDB MySQL Database tile*

after you select the tile, you will be redirect to select the plan of this Service. See Figure 13-12.

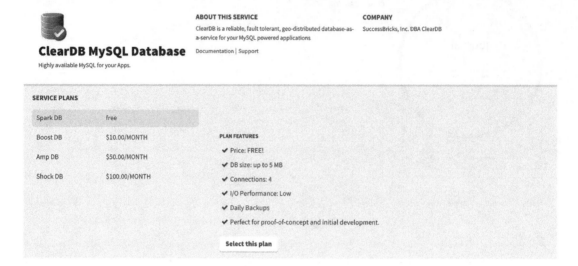

Figure 13-12. *ClearDB MySQL Database Service Plans*

Figure 13-12 shows you the Service Plans. Select the "*Spark DB free*" plan. After you select the plan, it will take you to fillout some information about it, the *Instance Configuration*. See Figure 13-13.

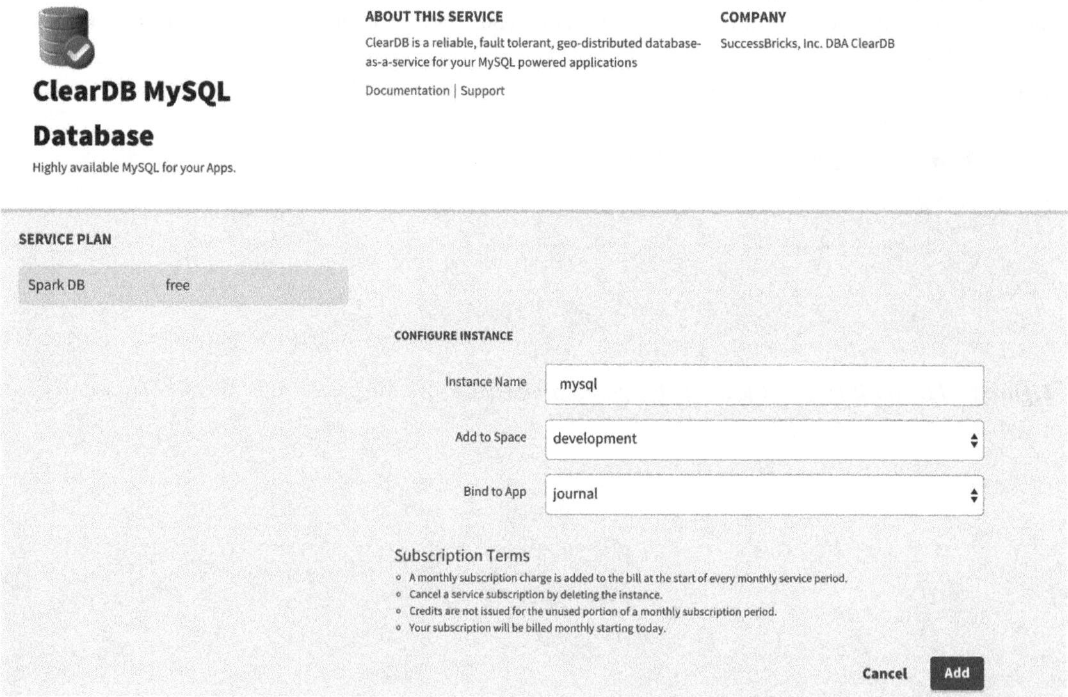

Figure 13-13. *ClearDB MySQL Database - Instance Configuration*

Figure 13-13 shows you the Instance Configuration form. As you can see you need to add the Instance Name: `mysql` and choose the default values. It will bind to the `journal` automatically. Click the "*Add*" button. See Figure 13-14.

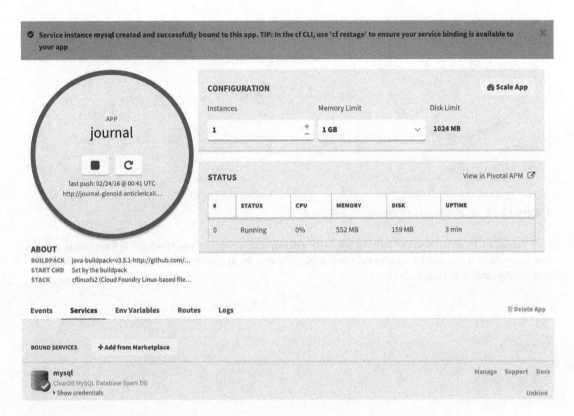

Figure 13-14. *Journal App after the Service Instance was created and bound*

Figure 13-14 shows you the Journal app after you created the mysql service instance. Now is necessary to restage. So, go to a terminal window and execute the following command:

```
$ cf restage journal
```

while the above command is executing, you can see your Journal app going down. See Figure 13-15.

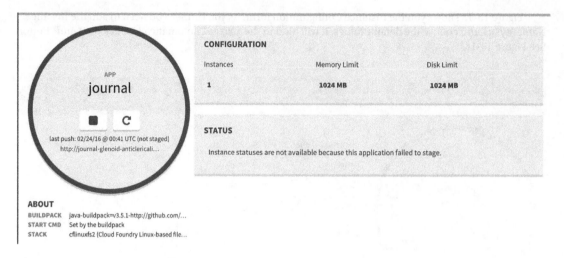

Figure 13-15. *Journal app in a restage status*

Figure 13-15 shows you the Journal app with a down status because the "restage" is happening. After a few seconds, you app will be up and running. Add some entries to your Journal App, and you should have something similar to Figure 13-16.

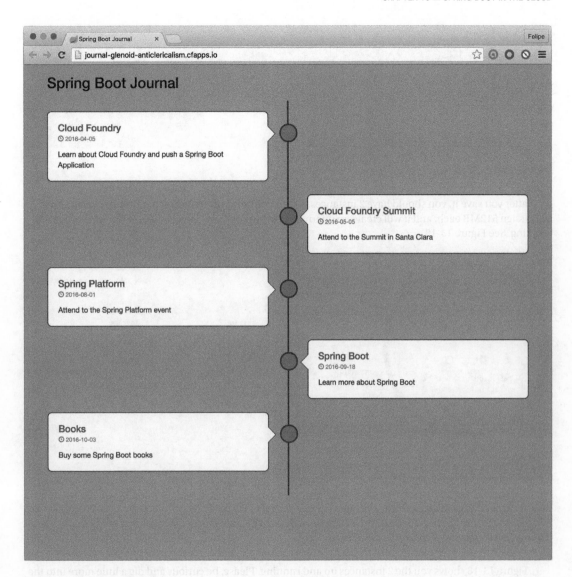

Figure 13-16. *Journal App*

Of course you can do everything in the command line as before. You just did it using the Pivotal Web Services console. And of course this is not the end, there is still more to learn about the Cloud Foundry. For example, imagine that you have a lot of users for the Journal app, and you realize that you need more instances and more memory for each instance. So, you can actually increase the number of instances by going into the upper corner of the Journal app, where it says: "Scale App". So, scale it to 2 instances and reduce the memory to 512MB each(this is just to no exceed the quota, by default as a trial user you only have 1GB of memory available) See Figure 13-17.

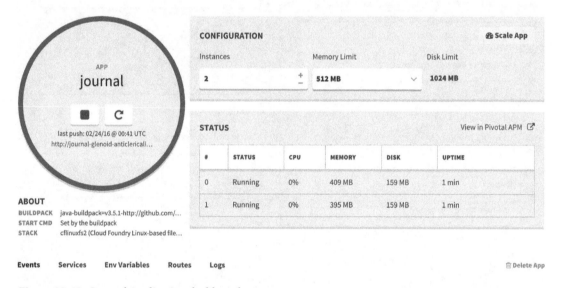

Figure 13-17. *Scale App*

after you save it, you should have 2 instances. Cloud Foundry will create 2 separated instances and it will assign 512MB each, and it will create an internal router so you have a load balancer out-of-the-box and working. See Figure 13-18.

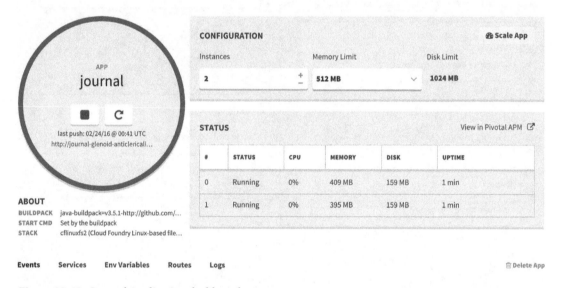

Figure 13-18. *Journal Application dashboard*

Figure 13-18 shows you the 2 instances up and running. Please, be curious and dig a little more into the Pivotal Web Services console. You have a lot of power using the Cloud Foundry Platform.

If you or your company has Pivotal Cloud Foundry, I totally recommend that you install more Services and test them, specially the Spring Cloud Services tile (from `https://network.pivotal.io/products/p-spring-cloud-services`) a new way to bring Spring app into a new level. The Spring Cloud Services brings a Configuration Server, Service Registry and , Circuit Breaker pattern. After you have a small taste of them, you won't go back. You can get more info at: `http://docs.pivotal.io/spring-cloud-services/`.

I know that this chapter was a small taste of what Pivotal Cloud Foundry is, or maybe I missed to mention other solutions, but by far, Cloud Foundry is the best Cloud PaaS out there, there is no comparison to make.

Summary

In this chapter I talked about the cloud and what you need to do in order to create you application as native-cloud. I mentioned also about the twelve-factor application guidelines that are just a patterns that you can apply for developing for the cloud.

I also talked about one of the best open source PaaS solutions, Cloud Foundry. I mentioned some of the features and difference between the open source and the commercial version.

I showed you how to deploy your Spring Boot application into Cloud Foundry, first by using the PCFDev as development tool and then to the Pivotal Cloud Foundry. Also, I mentioned about the Spring Cloud Service and how you can use them to get most of the Platform.

In the next chapter I will show you how to extend Spring Boot by creating your own starter and health endpoint.

Extending Spring Boot Apps

Developers and software architects are often looking for design patterns to apply, new algorithms to implement, reusable components that are easy to use and maintain, and new ways to improve development. It's not always easy to find a unique or perfect solution and it's necessary to use different technologies and methodologies to accomplish the goal of having an application that runs and never fails.

This chapter explains how the Spring and Spring Boot teams created a pattern for reusable components that are easy to use and implement. Actually, you have been learning about this pattern in the entire book, and especially in the Spring Boot Configuration chapter.

This chapter covers in detail the auto-configuration, including how you can extend and create new Spring Boot modules that can be reusable. Let's get started.

Custom Spring Boot Module

As you already know, the `spring-boot-starter-<module>` is an important piece for the Spring Boot engine to auto-configure your application based on the dependencies that the starter that you defined brings to the applications. This section discusses how you create your custom starter.

Imagine for a moment that your Spring Boot journal app has a very good acceptance between your colleagues and now you want to create a journal starter pom. How can you do that? You are going to create a special project where you include three modules:

- `spring-boot-journal`. This is the project that you have been working on during the book. I will show you which pieces you need to include in the following sections.

- `journal-spring-boot-starter`. This is your definition of your journal module. Every time you want to include part of the journal in a new application, you need to use this starter.

- `journal-spring-boot-autoconfigure`. This project brings the journal module to life because you will create a special auto-configure configuration to set everything up when another project includes `journal-spring-boot-starter`.

The spring-boot-journal Project

You are going to use the journal app as a module. Choose a directory and create a folder named `spring-boot-journal`. Use the well known Spring Initializr command:

```
$ mkdir spring-boot-journal
$ cd spring-boot-journal
$ spring init -d=web,thymeleaf,data-jpa,data-rest,h2,mysql -g=com.apress.spring -a=spring-
boot-journal --package-name=com.apress.spring -name=spring-boot-journal -x
```

© Felipe Gutierrez 2016

F. Gutierrez, *Pro Spring Boot*, DOI 10.1007/978-1-4842-1431-2_14

Next you can copy some of the files that you have been using during the chapters. Don't worry too much; I'll tell you what to include. You need to have the structure shown in Figure 14-1.

```
.
├── pom.xml
└── src
    ├── main
    │   ├── java
    │   │   └── com
    │   │       └── apress
    │   │           └── spring
    │   │               ├── SpringBootJournalApplication.java
    │   │               ├── domain
    │   │               │   └── JournalEntry.java
    │   │               ├── repository
    │   │               │   └── JournalRepository.java
    │   │               └── utils
    │   │                   └── JsonDateSerializer.java
    │   └── resources
    │       ├── application.properties
    │       ├── data.sql
    │       ├── static
    │       │   └── css
    │       │       ├── bootstrap-glyphicons.css
    │       │       ├── bootstrap.min.css
    │       │       └── styles.css
    │       └── templates
    │           └── journal.html
    └── test
        └── java
            └── com
                └── apress
                    └── spring
                        └── SpringBootJournalApplicationTests.java

18 directories, 12 files
```

Figure 14-1. *The spring-boot-journal directory structure*

Figure 14-1 shows the files that you need to copy over this new structure. The JournalEntry, JournalRepository, and JsonDateSerializer classes haven't change at all. Just make sure that your JournalEntry has the @Entity annotations because that's what you will use. The contents of the applications.properties file is simple, as shown in Listing 14-1.

Listing 14-1. src/main/resources/application.properties

```
spring.data.rest.basePath=/api
```

The journal.html page is identical to the index.html of the other versions; there is no security enabled. I will explain why you needed to rename it later. The data.sql contains some of the records for the entry table. See Listing 14-2.

Listing 14-2. src/main/resources/data.sql

```
INSERT INTO ENTRY(title,summary,created) VALUES('Get to know Spring Boot','Today I will
learn Spring Boot','2016-01-02 00:00:00.00');
INSERT INTO ENTRY(title,summary,created) VALUES('Simple Spring Boot Project','I will do my
first Spring Boot project','2016-01-03 00:00:00.00');
INSERT INTO ENTRY(title,summary,created) VALUES('Spring Boot Reading','Read more about
Spring Boot','2016-02-02 00:00:00.00');
INSERT INTO ENTRY(title,summary,created) VALUES('Spring Boot in the Cloud','Learn Spring
Boot using Cloud Foundry','2016-02-05 00:00:00.00');
```

■ **Note**   Remember that you can get all the code from the Apress web site or from the GitHub repository at
https://github.com/felipeg48/pro-spring-boot.

If you run this app:

```
$ ./mvnw spring-boot:run
```

You won't see the home page, but why? The web controller class is missing (JournalController),
but there is a reason for that and I will discuss it in the next sections. You can still go to the REST API, but
remember that it is included because you added (data-rest) in the Spring init command . So you can go
to http://localhost:8080/api/ and it should give you a result. (Remember to test it in the Chrome web
browser with the JSONView add-on installed, so you can see the response JSON+HAL.)

The journal-spring-boot-starter Project

Now you are going to define a starter that any new project will use to include the journal functionality.
Remember that you are in the spring-boot-journal directory, so go back one level and create the directory
journal-spring-boot-starter and add a pom.xml.

```
$ pwd
/journal/spring-boot-journal
$ cd ..
$ mkdir journal-spring-boot-starter
$ cd journal-spring-boot-starter
```

Now copy the pom.xml file shown in Listing 14-3. You'll need it for your starter.

Listing 14-3. pom.xml

```
<?xml version="1.0" encoding="UTF-8"?>
<project xmlns="http://maven.apache.org/POM/4.0.0"
xmlns:xsi="http://www.w3.org/2001/XMLSchema-instance"
        xsi:schemaLocation="http://maven.apache.org/POM/4.0.0
        http://maven.apache.org/xsd/maven-4.0.0.xsd">
        <modelVersion>4.0.0</modelVersion>
```

```
<groupId>com.apress.spring</groupId>
<artifactId>journal-spring-boot-starter</artifactId>
<version>0.0.1-SNAPSHOT</version>
<packaging>jar</packaging>

<name>journal-spring-boot-starter</name>
<description> Spring Boot Journal Starter</description>

<properties>
        <project.build.sourceEncoding>UTF-8</project.build.sourceEncoding>
        <java.version>1.8</java.version>
</properties>

<dependencies>
        <dependency>
                <groupId>com.apress.spring</groupId>
                <artifactId>journal-spring-boot-autoconfigure</artifactId>
                <version>0.0.1-SNAPSHOT</version>
        </dependency>
</dependencies>

<build>
        <plugins>
                <plugin>
                        <groupId>org.springframework.boot</groupId>
                        <artifactId>spring-boot-maven-plugin</artifactId>
                </plugin>
        </plugins>
</build>

</project>
```

Listing 14-3 shows the pom.xml that defines only one dependency this time. The journal-spring-boot-autoconfigure dependency is the project that you will create in the next section.

For creating a starter, that's it, you just define the project that you have the dependencies on and that's pretty much what you will be doing here. Of course, the important part is to have the dependencies ready. The journal functionality is defined in the journal-spring-boot-autoconfigure project.

Before you go to the next section, did you notice the name of the project? The Spring Boot team already put in place a naming convention for any new starter project pom. This naming is in this form: <module>-spring-boot-starter. If you are creating an auto-config project, the conventions is <module>-spring-boot-autoconfigure. This is because some of the modules are based on this naming convention.

The journal-spring-boot-autoconfigure Project

This project will contain configuration that will allow the journal functionality to be active in any new project that includes the `journal-spring-boot-starter`. Let's start by creating the folder and initializing the project with the Spring Initializr command.

```
$ pwd
/journal/journal-spring-boot-starter
$ cd ..
$ mkdir journal-spring-boot-autoconfigure
$ cd journal-spring-boot-autoconfigure
$ spring init -d=web,thymeleaf,data-jpa,data-rest,h2,mysql -g=com.apress.spring -a=journal-spring-
boot-autoconfigure --package-name=com.apress.spring -name=journal-spring-boot-autoconfigure -x
```

Next you need to add an extra dependencies to the `pom.xml` that you just created by executing the previous command. See Listing 14-4.

Listing 14-4. pom.xml

```xml
<?xml version="1.0" encoding="UTF-8"?>
<project xmlns="http://maven.apache.org/POM/4.0.0"
xmlns:xsi="http://www.w3.org/2001/XMLSchema-instance"
        xsi:schemaLocation="http://maven.apache.org/POM/4.0.0
        http://maven.apache.org/xsd/maven-4.0.0.xsd">
        <modelVersion>4.0.0</modelVersion>

        <groupId>com.apress.spring</groupId>
        <artifactId>journal-spring-boot-autoconfigure</artifactId>
        <version>0.0.1-SNAPSHOT</version>
        <packaging>jar</packaging>

        <name>journal-spring-boot-autoconfigure</name>
        <description>Demo project for Spring Boot</description>

        <parent>
                <groupId>org.springframework.boot</groupId>
                <artifactId>spring-boot-starter-parent</artifactId>
                <version>1.3.3.RELEASE</version>
                <relativePath/> <!-- lookup parent from repository -->
        </parent>

        <properties>
                <project.build.sourceEncoding>UTF-8</project.build.sourceEncoding>
                <java.version>1.8</java.version>
                <journal.version>0.0.1-SNAPSHOT</journal.version>
        </properties>

        <dependencies>
                <dependency>
                        <groupId>org.springframework.boot</groupId>
                        <artifactId>spring-boot-autoconfigure</artifactId>
                </dependency>
```

```xml
<dependency>
        <groupId>com.apress.spring</groupId>
        <artifactId>spring-boot-journal</artifactId>
        <version>${journal.version}</version>
</dependency>

<dependency>
        <groupId>org.springframework.boot</groupId>
        <artifactId>spring-boot-starter-data-jpa</artifactId>
</dependency>
<dependency>
        <groupId>org.springframework.boot</groupId>
        <artifactId>spring-boot-starter-data-rest</artifactId>
</dependency>
<dependency>
        <groupId>org.springframework.boot</groupId>
        <artifactId>spring-boot-starter-thymeleaf</artifactId>
</dependency>
<dependency>
        <groupId>org.springframework.boot</groupId>
        <artifactId>spring-boot-starter-web</artifactId>
</dependency>
<dependency>
        <groupId>com.h2database</groupId>
        <artifactId>h2</artifactId>
        <scope>runtime</scope>
</dependency>
<dependency>
        <groupId>mysql</groupId>
        <artifactId>mysql-connector-java</artifactId>
        <scope>runtime</scope>
</dependency>
<dependency>
        <groupId>org.springframework.boot</groupId>
        <artifactId>spring-boot-starter-test</artifactId>
        <scope>test</scope>
</dependency>

<dependency>
        <groupId>org.springframework.boot</groupId>
        <artifactId>spring-boot-configuration-processor</artifactId>
        <optional>true</optional>
</dependency>
</dependencies>
```

```
        <build>
                <plugins>
                        <plugin>
                                <groupId>org.springframework.boot</groupId>
                                <artifactId>spring-boot-maven-plugin</artifactId>
                        </plugin>
                </plugins>
        </build>

</project>
```

Listing 14-4 shows the pom.xml that you will be using in your journal-spring-boot-autoconfigure project. Next let's create a class that will hold some properties that will part of the configuration for the journal functionality. See Listing 14-5.

Listing 14-5. src/main/java/com/apress/spring/config/JournalProperties.java

```java
package com.apress.spring.config;

import org.springframework.boot.context.properties.ConfigurationProperties;

@ConfigurationProperties(prefix="journal")
public class JournalProperties {

        private String contextPath = "/spring-boot-journal";
        private String banner;
        private String apiPath;

        public String getContextPath() {
                return contextPath;
        }

        public void setContextPath(String contextPath) {
                this.contextPath = contextPath;
        }

        public String getBanner() {
                return banner;
        }

        public void setBanner(String banner) {
                this.banner = banner;
        }

        public String getApiPath() {
                return apiPath;
        }

        public void setApiPath(String apiPath) {
                this.apiPath = apiPath;
        }

}
```

Listing 14-5 shows the JournalProperties class. You are already familiar with this type of class, because I showed you in the first chapters that you can externalize your custom properties and can use your own prefix. In this case you will have three properties:

- journal.context-path. Sets by default the context path of the journal home page, which in this case is reachable at /spring-boot-journal. You give your users of the journal-spring-boot-starter a chance to change the context path by setting this property in the application.properties file.

- journal.banner. Displays a banner about the journal being configured. I know that this functionality won't be a real value, but it just proves the point that you can do a lot with the auto-configuration feature that Spring Boot provides. This property accepts the location of the journal.txt file; the default is at /META-INF/banner/journal.txt. You will create this file later. This allows your users that create their own banners and use them with this journal property.

- journal.api-path. Sets the REST API context path. Remember that by default you have the spring.data.rest.basePath when you include the spring-data-rest pom and that you can change its path. Here you will expose the option to your users to modify the path as well, but using your custom journal property.

The next code example shows that all these properties will be used to configure the journal functionality. The JournalAutoConfiguration class is the most important class in this project, as shown in Listing 14-6.

Listing 14-6. src/main/java/com/apress/spring/config/JournalAutoConfiguration.java

```
package com.apress.spring.config;

import java.util.Properties;

import javax.servlet.http.HttpServletRequest;
import javax.servlet.http.HttpServletResponse;

import org.springframework.beans.factory.InitializingBean;
import org.springframework.beans.factory.annotation.Autowired;
import org.springframework.boot.Banner;
import org.springframework.boot.ResourceBanner;
import org.springframework.boot.autoconfigure.condition.ConditionalOnClass;
import org.springframework.boot.autoconfigure.condition.ConditionalOnProperty;
import org.springframework.boot.autoconfigure.condition.ConditionalOnWebApplication;
import org.springframework.boot.context.properties.EnableConfigurationProperties;
import org.springframework.context.annotation.Bean;
import org.springframework.context.annotation.Configuration;
import org.springframework.core.env.Environment;
import org.springframework.core.io.DefaultResourceLoader;
import org.springframework.core.io.Resource;
import org.springframework.core.io.ResourceLoader;
import org.springframework.data.rest.core.config.RepositoryRestConfiguration;
import org.springframework.data.rest.webmvc.config.RepositoryRestMvcConfiguration;
import org.springframework.util.ClassUtils;
import org.springframework.web.servlet.ModelAndView;
```

```
import org.springframework.web.servlet.handler.SimpleUrlHandlerMapping;
import org.springframework.web.servlet.mvc.AbstractController;

import com.apress.spring.repository.JournalRepository;

@Configuration
@ConditionalOnWebApplication
@ConditionalOnClass(JournalRepository.class)
@EnableConfigurationProperties(JournalProperties.class)
@ConditionalOnProperty(prefix = "journal", name = { "context-path", "banner" },
matchIfMissing = true)
public class JournalAutoConfiguration extends RepositoryRestMvcConfiguration {
        private final String API_PATH = "/api";
        private final String BANNER = "/META-INF/banner/journal.txt";

        @Autowired

        JournalProperties journal;

        @Autowired
        Environment environment;

        @Bean
        InitializingBean simple() {
                return () -> {
                        Banner banner = null;
                        ResourceLoader resourceLoader = new DefaultResourceLoader
                        (ClassUtils.getDefaultClassLoader());
                        Resource resource = resourceLoader.getResource(BANNER);

                        if (null == journal.getBanner()) {
                                banner = new ResourceBanner(resource);
                        } else {
                            Resource _resource = resourceLoader.getResource(journal.getBanner());
                                if (resource.exists()) {
                                        banner = new ResourceBanner(_resource);
                                }
                        }
                        banner.printBanner(environment, environment.getClass(), System.out);
                };
        }

        @Override
        protected void configureRepositoryRestConfiguration(RepositoryRestConfiguration config) {
                if (null == journal.getApiPath())
                        config.setBasePath(API_PATH);
                else
                        config.setBasePath(journal.getApiPath());
        }
```

```
@Autowired
JournalRepository repo;

@Bean
AbstractController journalController() {
        return new AbstractController() {
                @Override
                protected ModelAndView handleRequestInternal(HttpServletRequest request,
                                                               HttpServletResponse response)
                                throws Exception {
                        ModelAndView model = new ModelAndView();
                        model.setViewName("journal");
                        model.addObject("journal", repo.findAll());
                        return model;
                }
        };
}


@Bean

public SimpleUrlHandlerMapping urlHandler() {
        SimpleUrlHandlerMapping handler = new SimpleUrlHandlerMapping();
        handler.setOrder(Integer.MAX_VALUE - 2);
        Properties mappings = new Properties();
        mappings.put(journal.getContextPath(), "journalController");
        handler.setMappings(mappings);
        return handler;
}

}
```

Listing 14-6 shows the main class that will be picked up by Spring Boot auto-configuration pattern. It will try to configure the journal app to work as was specified by the properties and other configurations. Let's examine the class:

- @Configuration. As you know, this annotation will be picked up by the Spring Boot auto-configuration.

- @ConditionalOnWebApplication. This annotation will tell the auto-configuration to execute the configuration only if it's a web application. If not, it will skip it. This is useful when you have an application that doesn't have the spring-boot-starter-web pom.

- @ConditionalOnClass(JournalRepository.class). This annotation tells the auto-configuration that this configuration will be accepted only if in the classpath exists the JournalRepository.class. Note that the JournalRepository will be configured as a REST endpoint through the spring data-rest auto-configuration, so that's why you are adding this particular condition.

- @EnableConfigurationProperties(JournalProperties.class). This annotation tells the auto-configuration that you will be using the JournalProperties as a custom property. Remember that you have access at all times by using the @Autowired or the @Value for a specific property.

CHAPTER 14 ■ EXTENDING SPRING BOOT APPS

- `@ConditionalOnProperty(prefix = "journal", name = { "context-path", "banner" }, matchIfMissing = true)`. This annotation tells the auto-configuration that if you don't have the `journal.context-path` or the `journal.banner` properties defined, it can execute the configuration anyway.

- `RepositoryRestMvcConfiguration`. The `JournalAutoConfiguration` class is extending from the `RepositoryRestMvcConfiguration` class, which is helpful because you are going to override the REST endpoints by using your `journal.api-path`.

- `API_PATH, BANNER`. These are the final variables that will be the default values for the `journal.api-path` and `journal.banner` properties, if none is provided in the `application.properties` file.

- `@Bean InitializingBean simple()`. This method will be executed when this class is created. This method will print out the banner at the console based on the `journal.banner` property. If none is provided, it will print out what you have in the `/META-INF/banner/journal.txt classpath`.

- `configureRepositoryRestConfiguration(RepositoryRestConfiguration config)`. This method belongs to the `RepositoryRestMvcConfiguration` class and it's overridden by setting the REST endpoint's context path based on the `journal.api-path` property. If none is provided in the application properties, the default is `/api`.

- `@Bean AbstractController journalController()`. This method is the replacement of the `JournalController` that you didn't use in the journal application. Here you are returning an `AbstractController` instance and you are overriding the `handleRequestInternal` method by adding the journal view (this will be from the journal project at `templates/journal.html`; this page is not an `index.html` page, because you don't want to have a collision name for other projects; I will explain this later). You are also adding the model setting its value with the `repo.findAll()` method call. The repo instance is the result of the `@Autowired JournalRepository`. This means that you should have the `JournalRepository` class in your classpath.

- `@Bean SimpleUrlHandlerMapping urlHandler()`. This method will set the handler for the final context path where the `journal.html` will be requested. You are returning a `SimpleUrlHandlerMapping` instance that sets the correspondent mapping, the URL (based on the `journal.context-path` property). and the controller (the `journalController` method call). It's very important to mention that in order to create your own URL handler programmatically it's mandatory to add this call: `handler.setOrder(Integer.MAX_VALUE - 2);`. This is because the mappings are in order, so they have the lowest order making the `ResourceHttpRequestHandler` (this resource handler takes all in `/**`) to have precedence over your mapping. That's why it's necessary to set the order in that way.

Before you continue, take moment to analyze this more in detail. Try to look the meaning of every class. Now, it's worth mentioning that there are more `@Conditional*` annotation that allow you to execute the configuration class.

How does Spring Boot load this auto-configuration class? In order to use the power of the auto-configuration, you need to create it in the `META-INF/spring.factories` file. You specify the class that holds the auto-configuration. See Listing 14-7.

Listing 14-7. src/main/resources/META-INF/spring.factories

```
org.springframework.boot.autoconfigure.EnableAutoConfiguration=\
com.apress.spring.config.JournalAutoConfiguration
```

Listing 14-6 shows the contents of the spring.factories file. You need to specify the class that will be picked up by the EnableAutoConfiguration class. This class imports the EnableAutoConfigurationImportSelector that will inspect the spring.factories and loads the class and executes the declaration. That's the secret behind the auto-configuration. If you see the source code of spring-boot-autoconfigure module itself you will find out that it contains a lot of the auto-configuration classes defined. Here is a sneak peak of the spring-boot-autoconfigure spring.factories contents:

```
# Initializers
org.springframework.context.ApplicationContextInitializer=\
org.springframework.boot.autoconfigure.logging.AutoConfigurationReportLoggingInitializer

# Application Listeners
org.springframework.context.ApplicationListener=\
org.springframework.boot.autoconfigure.BackgroundPreinitializer

# Auto Configure
org.springframework.boot.autoconfigure.EnableAutoConfiguration=\
org.springframework.boot.autoconfigure.admin.SpringApplicationAdminJmxAutoConfiguration,\
org.springframework.boot.autoconfigure.aop.AopAutoConfiguration,\
org.springframework.boot.autoconfigure.amqp.RabbitAutoConfiguration,\
org.springframework.boot.autoconfigure.MessageSourceAutoConfiguration,\
org.springframework.boot.autoconfigure.PropertyPlaceholderAutoConfiguration,\
org.springframework.boot.autoconfigure.batch.BatchAutoConfiguration,\
org.springframework.boot.autoconfigure.cache.CacheAutoConfiguration,\
org.springframework.boot.autoconfigure.cassandra.CassandraAutoConfiguration,\
org.springframework.boot.autoconfigure.cloud.CloudAutoConfiguration,\
org.springframework.boot.autoconfigure.context.ConfigurationPropertiesAutoConfiguration,\
org.springframework.boot.autoconfigure.dao.
PersistenceExceptionTranslationAutoConfiguration,\
org.springframework.boot.autoconfigure.data.cassandra.CassandraDataAutoConfiguration,\
org.springframework.boot.autoconfigure.data.cassandra.
CassandraRepositoriesAutoConfiguration,\
org.springframework.boot.autoconfigure.data.elasticsearch.ElasticsearchAutoConfiguration,\
org.springframework.boot.autoconfigure.data.elasticsearch.
ElasticsearchDataAutoConfiguration,\
...
...
```

Remember that you can use --debug when you running your application. You can run it to see if your starter is being picked up by the auto-configuration engine.

Package and Install the Journal Project

Now you have your three projects ready to be packaged and installed in your computer; but first let's create a pom.xml that will treat the three projects as modules. Go one level up and create a pom.xml file. See Figure 14-2.

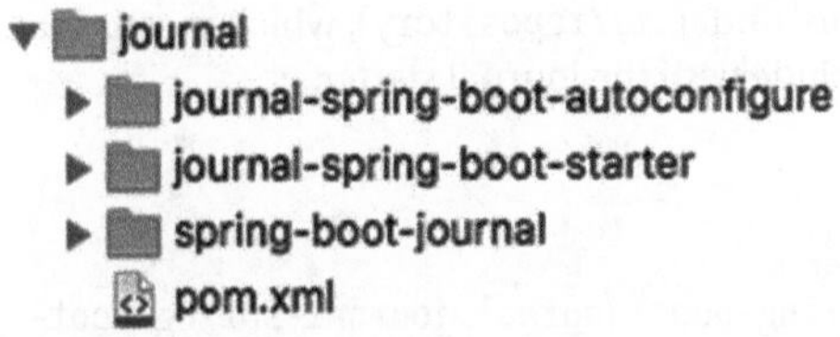

▼ 📁 journal
  ▶ 📁 journal-spring-boot-autoconfigure
  ▶ 📁 journal-spring-boot-starter
  ▶ 📁 spring-boot-journal
    📄 pom.xml

Figure 14-2. *The directory structure*

Next, let's see the pom.xml. See Listing 14-8.

Listing 14-8. pom.xml

```xml
<?xml version="1.0" encoding="UTF-8"?>
<project xmlns="http://maven.apache.org/POM/4.0.0"
xmlns:xsi="http://www.w3.org/2001/XMLSchema-instance"
        xsi:schemaLocation="http://maven.apache.org/POM/4.0.0
        http://maven.apache.org/xsd/maven-4.0.0.xsd">
        <modelVersion>4.0.0</modelVersion>
        <groupId>com.apress.spring</groupId>
        <artifactId>journal</artifactId>
        <version>0.0.1-SNAPSHOT</version>
        <packaging>pom</packaging>
        <name>Extending Spring Boot</name>

        <modules>
                <module>spring-boot-journal</module>
                <module>journal-spring-boot-autoconfigure</module>
                <module>journal-spring-boot-starter</module>
        </modules>

</project>
```

Listing 14-8 shows the master pom that includes the three projects as modules. This will allow you to package and install them. If you have Maven already installed, you can skip this part. If not, remember that you are using the Spring init and this brings the Maven wrapper that you don't have in the journal folder. You have only the pom.xml, so in order to use the maven wrapper, execute the following commands:

```
$ pwd
/journal
$ cp -r spring-boot-journal/.mvn .
$ cp spring-boot-journal/mvn* .
```

If you have now the Maven wrapper, execute the next command to package and install the journal project:

```
$ ./mvnw clean package install -DskipTests=true
```

Or if you have Maven installed, just execute this command:

```
$ mvn clean package install -DskipTests=true
```

That will install the three projects (in your home directory under .m2/repository), which means that you are ready to use them in any new project you want to include with the journal starter.

The spring-boot-calendar Project

I know that I told you about creating only three projects—spring-boot-journal, journal-spring-boot-starter, and journal-spring-boot-autoconfigure—but of course you need to test them too. You need to see if the auto-configuration really accesses the JournalAutoConfiguration class.

You can create a new project that can be outside of the journal solution (the three projects) and create just a default Spring boot app using the spring init command:

```
$ pwd
/journal
$ cd /
$ mkdir calendar
$ cd calendar
$ spring init -g=com.apress.spring -a= spring-boot-calendar --package-name=com.apress.spring
-name= spring-boot-calendar -x
```

This command will create your calendar project. Basically, this project will use the journal-spring-boot-starter and that's it. The project will only have an index page just to make the point that you can create any application and use the journal starter. The final pom.xml for this project is shown in Listing 14-9.

Listing 14-9. pom.xml

```xml
<?xml version="1.0" encoding="UTF-8"?>
<project xmlns="http://maven.apache.org/POM/4.0.0"
xmlns:xsi="http://www.w3.org/2001/XMLSchema-instance"
        xsi:schemaLocation="http://maven.apache.org/POM/4.0.0
        http://maven.apache.org/xsd/maven-4.0.0.xsd">
        <modelVersion>4.0.0</modelVersion>

        <groupId>com.apress.spring</groupId>
        <artifactId>spring-boot-calendar</artifactId>
        <version>0.0.1-SNAPSHOT</version>
        <packaging>jar</packaging>

        <name>spring-boot-calendar</name>
        <description>Demo project for Spring Boot</description>

        <parent>
                <groupId>org.springframework.boot</groupId>
                <artifactId>spring-boot-starter-parent</artifactId>
                <version>1.3.3.RELEASE</version>
                <relativePath/> <!-- lookup parent from repository -->
        </parent>

        <properties>
                <project.build.sourceEncoding>UTF-8</project.build.sourceEncoding>
                <java.version>1.8</java.version>
        </properties>
```

```
<dependencies>
        <dependency>
                <groupId>com.apress.spring</groupId>
                <artifactId>journal-spring-boot-starter</artifactId>
                <version>0.0.1-SNAPSHOT</version>
        </dependency>

        <dependency>
                <groupId>org.springframework.boot</groupId>
                <artifactId>spring-boot-starter-test</artifactId>
                <scope>test</scope>
        </dependency>
</dependencies>

<build>
        <plugins>
                <plugin>
                        <groupId>org.springframework.boot</groupId>
                        <artifactId>spring-boot-maven-plugin</artifactId>
                </plugin>
        </plugins>
</build>
```

</project>

Listing 14-9 shows the pom.xml that you will use for the calendar project. See that you are only including the journal-spring-boot-starter. If you run it right away, you should be able to see the banner (with the legend Journal) and all the default endpoints (/api, /spring-boot-journal). Remember that these default values now can be overridden, and that's what you going to do in the next sections. You can run your app as usual:

```
$ ./mvnw spring-boot:run
```

After running the calendar project just make sure that the journal is working. Now, let's create a controller in the main app and start adding some other details like an index.html page (that's why you have a journal.html in the spring-boot-journal module, so it won't collide with this one).

Listing 14-10 shows the main application.

Listing 14-10. src/main/java/com/apress/spring/SpringBootCalendarApplication.java

```
package com.apress.spring;

import org.springframework.beans.factory.annotation.Autowired;
import org.springframework.boot.SpringApplication;
import org.springframework.boot.autoconfigure.SpringBootApplication;
import org.springframework.web.bind.annotation.RequestMapping;
import org.springframework.web.bind.annotation.RequestMethod;
import org.springframework.web.bind.annotation.RestController;
import org.springframework.web.servlet.ModelAndView;
```

```
import com.apress.spring.config.JournalProperties;

@SpringBootApplication
@RestController
public class SpringBootCalendarApplication {

        public static void main(String[] args) {
                SpringApplication.run(SpringBootCalendarApplication.class, args);
        }

        private static final String VIEW_INDEX = "index";

        @Autowired
        JournalProperties journal;

        @RequestMapping(value="/", method = RequestMethod.GET)
        public ModelAndView index(ModelAndView modelAndView){
                modelAndView.setViewName(VIEW_INDEX);
                modelAndView.addObject("journal", journal);
                return modelAndView;
        }
}
```

Listing 14-10 shows the main application. You basically already know all the annotations in this class, but it's good to mention that the JournalProperties instance is available and you will be using it to access its values in the index page.

Next, let's see the application.properties. Remember that you can now override those properties as well. Its content is shown in Listing 14-11.

Listing 14-11. src/main/resources/application.properties

```
journal.api-path=/myapi
journal.context-path=/myjournal
```

Listing 14-11 shows the application.properties that you will use in this second run to see if the defaults can be overridden. For now it doesn't have the journal.banner property (with the value /META-INF/banner/journal.txt); you can play around with it later.

Now let's see the index.html page (you need to create the templates folder). See Listing 14-12.

Listing 14-12. src/main/resource/templates/index.html

```
<!DOCTYPE html>
<html lang="en" xmlns:th="http://www.thymeleaf.org">
  <head>
    <meta charset="utf-8"></meta>
    <meta http-equiv="X-UA-Compatible" content="IE=edge"></meta>
    <meta name="viewport" content="width=device-width, initial-scale=1"></meta>
    <meta name="description" content=""></meta>
    <meta name="author" content=""></meta>
    <title>Spring Boot Calendar</title>
    <link href="css/bootstrap.min.css" rel="stylesheet"></link>
    <link href="css/cover.css" rel="stylesheet"></link>
  </head>
```

```
<body>

  <div class="site-wrapper">
    <div class="site-wrapper-inner">
      <div class="cover-container">
        <div class="masthead clearfix">
          <div class="inner">
            <h3 class="masthead-brand">Spring Boot Calendar</h3>
            <nav>
              <ul class="nav masthead-nav">
                <li class="active"><a href="#">Home</a></li>
                <li><a th:href="${journal.contextPath}">Journal</a></li>
                <li><a th:href="${journal.apiPath}">API</a></li>
                <li><a th:href="${journal.apiPath} + '/journal/search'">Search</a></li>
              </ul>
            </nav>
          </div>
        </div>

        <div class="inner cover">
          <h1 class="cover-heading">Spring Boot Calendar</h1>
          <p class="lead">This is a small Calendar application, showing the power of
          Spring Boot auto-configuration features.
          This Calendar application also provides you a full access to the Journal Web UI</p>
          <p class="lead">
            <a th:href="${journal.contextPath}" class="btn btn-lg btn-default">Journal</a>
          </p>
        </div>

        <div class="mastfoot">
          <div class="inner">
            <p>Spring Boot Calendar, powered by <a href="http://projects.spring.io/
            spring-boot/">Spring Boot</a>.</p>
          </div>
        </div>

      </div>

    </div>

  </div>
</body>
</html>
```

Listing 14-12 shows index.html and the important part is the usage of the journal object that is sent from the controller (the JournalProperties instance). Regardless of which path you add for the API or the journal you will be always have the right endpoint.

Before you run it, you need to have the cover.css file that is located in the static/css folder (you need to create the static folder as well). The bootstrap.min.css is being picked up from the journal module, so you don't need it here. You can get this code from the Apress site. (Or you can get it from the GitHub at https://github.com/felipeg48/pro-spring-boot).

Now you are ready to run it:

```
$ ./mvnw spring-boot:run
```

If you go directly to the root at http://localhost:8080/, you will see something like Figure 14-3.

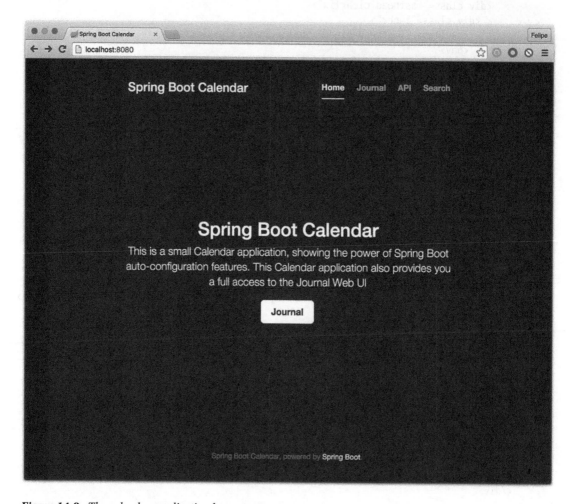

Figure 14-3. *The calendar application home page*

Figure 14-3 shows the calendar app. You can test the links declared in the index.html file and see if the endpoints actually work because they should have taken the values of the properties specified in the application.properties file. So, click the Journal button and you should get sent to the /myjournal endpoint. If you click at the top of the page in the navigation bar, the API menu option, you should be sent to the /myapi endpoint and be able to read all about the RESTful services.

Congratulations! You have just created your custom Spring Boot starter!

Custom Health Indicator

Another way to extend your Spring Boot application is to add your own health indicator when you are using the spring-boot-actuator module. It would be nice to have a way to monitor specific requirements; for example, imagine that you want your calendar be able to monitor how many entries you have in your journal. In other words, you can have customers who want to use your calendar application and you want to limit the entries per journal. You'll build a quota health monitor for that purpose.

You will continue using the Calendar project. The spring-boot-starter-actuator is missing in your pom.xml in order to activate the health endpoints. So add this to your pom.xml:

```xml
<dependency>
        <groupId>org.springframework.boot</groupId>
        <artifactId>spring-boot-starter-actuator</artifactId>
</dependency>
```

Next, let's create two classes that will define the quota monitor. The first class is a standard exception handler. See Listing 14-13.

Listing 14-13. src/main/java/com/apress/spring/health/QuotaException.java

```java
package com.apress.spring.heatlh;

public class QuotaException extends Exception {

        private static final long serialVersionUID = -1L;

        public QuotaException(String ex){
                super(ex);
        }

}
```

Listing 14-13 shows a simple class that extends from exception and overrides the constructor with a String parameter; this is nothing new that you don't already know. Next is the most important part to create the monitor. See Listing 14-14.

Listing 14-14. src/main/java/com/apress/spring/health/QuotaHealthIndicator.java

```java
package com.apress.spring.heatlh;

import org.springframework.beans.factory.annotation.Autowired;
import org.springframework.boot.actuate.health.Health;
import org.springframework.boot.actuate.health.HealthIndicator;
import org.springframework.stereotype.Component;

import com.apress.spring.repository.JournalRepository;
```

```
@Component
public class QuotaHealthIndicator implements HealthIndicator{

        private static final Long QUOTA_MAX_SIZE = 10L;

        @Autowired
        JournalRepository repo;

        @Override
        public Health health() {
                long size = repo.count();
                if(size <= QUOTA_MAX_SIZE)
                        return Health.up().withDetail("quota.entries", size).build();
                else
                        return Health
                                .down()
                                .withDetail("quota.entries", size)
                                .withException(new QuotaException("Quota Exceeded. Max
                                allow: " + QUOTA_MAX_SIZE + ". See your Administrator
                                for Quota policies."))
                                .build();
        }

}
```

Listing 14-14 shows the QuotaHealthIndicator class. Let's examine it:

- HealthIndicator. This is the main interface that you need to implement in order to create your custom health monitor. You need to implement the health method that returns a health instance.

- Health health(). This method is an implementation method from the HealthIndicator interface, and it returns a health instance. This instance has a fluent API that allows you to create the necessary response for your monitor. Take a look at the code and see that you can set the health up or down depending on your own business rules. Also note that you are using the JournalRepository instance (repo) and using just the count() method that will bring the number of records you have. This will help to decide what to do in your health monitor.

As you can see, is very trivial to create a custom health indicator or monitor. You only need to implement the HealthIndicator instances. As a naming convention, you need to append the HealthIndicator postfix to your class, so the Actuator can use the name. In this example the quota name will be used in the response of the /health endpoint. In order to make this work, you need to annotate this class with the @Component annotation so that the Spring engine can recognize the health actuator endpoint.

It's worth mentioning that there is another class that can be extended from: org.springframework. boot.actuate.health.AbstractHealthIndicator. You need to implement the abstract method called doHealthCheck. See the Actuator's documentation for more information about this class.

Now it's time to run it:

```
$ ./mvnw spring-boot:run
```

After executing this command, you should see the Actuator endpoint displayed. You can go to the `http://localhost:8080/health` endpoint. See Figure 14-4.

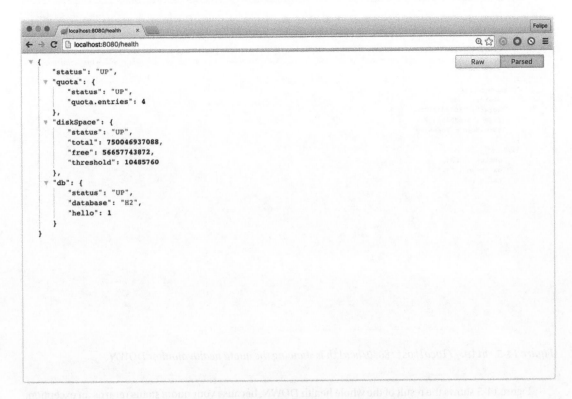

Figure 14-4. `http://localhost:8080/health` is showing the quota health monitor UP

Figure 14-4 shows the result of going to the /health endpoint, and as you can see you have your own quota health monitor where the status is UP with the quota.entries key and a value of 4. I'm assuming that you still have the data.sql in one of your projects, which is why you have the four entries.

Now, if you don't want to add more entries, and want to see the monitor status change to down, you can set the variable QUOTA_MAX_SIZE to 3 and then rerun the application. Then you can refresh the endpoint and see the results shown in Figure 14-5.

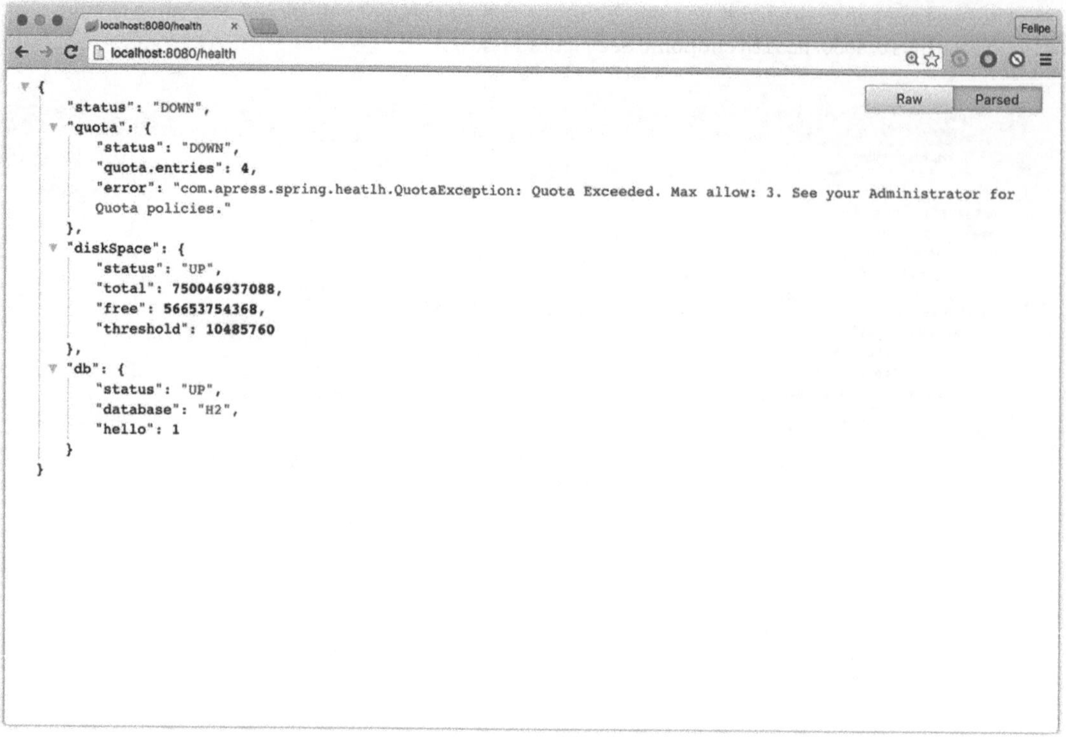

Figure 14-5. http://localhost:8080/health is showing the quota health monitor DOWN

Figure 14-5 shows the result of the whole health DOWN, because your quota status returns an exception. Congratulations! You created your own quota health monitor!

■ **Note** Another alternative is to use the STS IDE and import the projects—in this case the journal master (the one that contains the modules) and the calendar—so you can test better and use the code completion that the IDE offers you. Also you don't need to package and install the project every time you do a modification; just make the change and the IDE will take care of the rest.

Summary

This chapter showed you how to create a module for Spring Boot by using the auto-configuration pattern. It showed you how to create your custom health monitor. As you can see, it's very simple to extend Spring Boot apps, so feel free to modify the code and experiment with them.

We didn't do much if any unit or integration testing and it would be good homework for you to practice all the detail that I showed you. I think it will help you understand how Spring Boot works even better. Repeat and you will master!

APPENDIX

■■■

Spring Boot 1.4.x

Spring Boot 1.4.X Release Notes

Upgrading from Spring Boot 1.3

Executable Jar Layout

The layout (the directory structure) of executable jars has changed. If you are using Spring Boot's Maven, Gradle, or Ant support to build your application this change will not affect you. If you are building an executable archive yourself, please be aware that an application's dependencies are now packaged in BOOT-INF/lib rather than lib, and an application's own classes are now packaged in BOOT-INF/classes rather than the root of the jar.

Deprecations from Spring Boot 1.3

Classes, methods and properties that were deprecated in Spring Boot 1.3 have been removed in this release. Please ensure that you aren't calling deprecated methods before upgrading.

In particular, log4j 1 support has been removed following Apache EOL announcement.

DataSource Binding

Prior to Spring Boot 1.4, auto-configured datasources were bound to the spring.datasource namespace. In 1.4, we only bind the common settings to spring.datasource (see DataSourceProperties) and we have defined new specific namespaces for the four connections pools we support (in that order):

- spring.datasource.tomcat for org.apache.tomcat.jdbc.pool.DataSource

- spring.datasource.hikari for com.zaxxer.hikari.HikariDataSource

- spring.datasource.dbcp for org.apache.commons.dbcp.BasicDataSource

- spring.datasource.dbcp2 for org.apache.commons.dbcp2.BasicDataSource

If you were using specific settings of the connection pool implementation that you are using, you will have to move that configuration to the relevant namespace. For instance, if you were using Tomcat's testOnBorrow flag, you'll have to move it from spring.datasource.test-on-borrow to spring.datasource.tomcat.test-on-borrow.

If you are using configuration assistance in your IDE, you can now see which settings are available per connection pools rather than having all of them mixed in the spring.datasource namespace. This should make your life much easier figuring out what implementation supports what features.

© Felipe Gutierrez 2016
F. Gutierrez, *Pro Spring Boot*, DOI 10.1007/978-1-4842-1431-2

Jta Settings Binding

Similarly to DataSource binding, JTA provider-specific configuration properties for Atomikos and Bitronix were bound to `spring.jta`. They are now bound to `spring.jta.atomikos.properties` and `spring.jta.bitronix.properties` respectively; the meta-data for these entries has been greatly improved as well.

@ConfigurationProperties Default Bean Names

When a `@ConfigurationProperties` bean is registered via `@EnableConfigurationProperties(SomeBean.class)`, we used to generate a bean name of the form `<prefix>.CONFIGURATION_PROPERTIES`. As of Spring Boot 1.4, we have changed that pattern to avoid name clashes if two beans use the same prefix.

The new conventional name is `<prefix>-<fqn>`, where `<prefix>` is the environment key prefix specified in the `@ConfigurationProperties` annotation and `<fqn>` the fully qualified name of the bean. If the annotation does not provide any prefix, only the fully qualified name of the bean is used.

Jetty JNDI Support

The `spring-boot-starter-jetty` "Starter POM" no longer includes `org.eclipse.jetty:jetty-jndi`. If you are using Jetty with JNDI you will now need to directly add this dependency yourself.

Analysis of Startup Failures

Spring Boot will now perform analysis of common startup failures and provide useful diagnostic information rather than simply logging an exception and its stack trace. For example, a startup failure due to the embedded servlet container's port being in use looked like this in earlier versions of Spring Boot:

```
ERROR 24753 --- [           main] o.s.boot.SpringApplication              : Application
startup failed
java.lang.RuntimeException: java.net.BindException: Address already in use
    at io.undertow.Undertow.start(Undertow.java:181) ~[undertow-core-1.3.14.Final.
        jar:1.3.14.Final]
    at org.springframework.boot.context.embedded.undertow.UndertowEmbeddedServletContainer.
        start(UndertowEmbeddedServletContainer.java:121) ~[spring-boot-1.3.2.RELEASE.
        jar:1.3.2.RELEASE]
    at org.springframework.boot.context.embedded.EmbeddedWebApplicationContext.
        startEmbeddedServletContainer(EmbeddedWebApplicationContext.java:293)
        ~[spring-boot-1.3.2.RELEASE.jar:1.3.2.RELEASE]
    at org.springframework.boot.context.embedded.EmbeddedWebApplicationContext.finish
        Refresh(EmbeddedWebApplicationContext.java:141) ~[spring-boot-1.3.2.RELEASE.
        jar:1.3.2.RELEASE]
    at org.springframework.context.support.AbstractApplicationContext.refresh(Abstract
        ApplicationContext.java:541) ~[spring-context-4.2.4.RELEASE.jar:4.2.4.RELEASE]
    at org.springframework.boot.context.embedded.EmbeddedWebApplicationContext.refresh
        (EmbeddedWebApplicationContext.java:118) ~[spring-boot-1.3.2.RELEASE.
        jar:1.3.2.RELEASE]
    at org.springframework.boot.SpringApplication.refresh(SpringApplication.java:766)
        [spring-boot-1.3.2.RELEASE.jar:1.3.2.RELEASE]
    at org.springframework.boot.SpringApplication.createAndRefreshContext(SpringApplication.
        java:361) [spring-boot-1.3.2.RELEASE.jar:1.3.2.RELEASE]
```

```
     at org.springframework.boot.SpringApplication.run(SpringApplication.java:307)
        [spring-boot-1.3.2.RELEASE.jar:1.3.2.RELEASE]
     at org.springframework.boot.SpringApplication.run(SpringApplication.java:1191)
        [spring-boot-1.3.2.RELEASE.jar:1.3.2.RELEASE]
     at org.springframework.boot.SpringApplication.run(SpringApplication.java:1180)
        [spring-boot-1.3.2.RELEASE.jar:1.3.2.RELEASE]
     at sample.undertow.SampleUndertowApplication.main(SampleUndertowApplication.java:26)
        [classes/:na]
Caused by: java.net.BindException: Address already in use
     at sun.nio.ch.Net.bind0(Native Method) ~[na:1.8.0_60]
     at sun.nio.ch.Net.bind(Net.java:433) ~[na:1.8.0_60]
     at sun.nio.ch.Net.bind(Net.java:425) ~[na:1.8.0_60]
     at sun.nio.ch.ServerSocketChannelImpl.bind(ServerSocketChannelImpl.java:223) ~[na:1.8.0_60]
     at sun.nio.ch.ServerSocketAdaptor.bind(ServerSocketAdaptor.java:74) ~[na:1.8.0_60]
     at org.xnio.nio.NioXnioWorker.createTcpConnectionServer(NioXnioWorker.java:190)
        ~[xnio-nio-3.3.4.Final.jar:3.3.4.Final]
     at org.xnio.XnioWorker.createStreamConnectionServer(XnioWorker.java:243)
        ~[xnio-api-3.3.4.Final.jar:3.3.4.Final]
     at io.undertow.Undertow.start(Undertow.java:137) ~[undertow-core-1.3.14.Final.
        jar:1.3.14.Final]
     ... 11 common frames omitted
```

In 1.4, it will look like this:

```
ERROR 24745 --- [           main] o.s.b.d.LoggingFailureAnalysisReporter   :

***************************
APPLICATION FAILED TO START
***************************


Description:
Embedded servlet container failed to start. Port 8080 was already in use.

Action:
Identify and stop the process that's listening on port 8080 or configure this application to
listen on another port.
```

if you still want to see the stacktrace of the underlying cause, enable debug logging for org.springframework.
boot.diagnostics.LoggingFailureAnalysisReporter.

Test Utilities

spring-boot-starter-test now brings the Assert4J assertions library. Test utilities from the
org.springframework.boot.test package have been moved to a spring-boot-test dedicated artifact.

New and Noteworthy

You can get all the new changes at this address: https://github.com/spring-projects/spring-boot/wiki,
look for the Release Notes and the section New and Noteworthy.

Index

■ T, U, V

■ W

■ X, Y, Z

Get the eBook for only $5!

Why limit yourself?

Now you can take the weightless companion with you wherever you go and access your content on your PC, phone, tablet, or reader.

Since you've purchased this print book, we're happy to offer you the eBook in all 3 formats for just $5.

Convenient and fully searchable, the PDF version enables you to easily find and copy code—or perform examples by quickly toggling between instructions and applications. The MOBI format is ideal for your Kindle, while the ePUB can be utilized on a variety of mobile devices.

To learn more, go to www.apress.com/companion or contact support@apress.com.

Apress®
THE EXPERT'S VOICE™

CPI Antony Rowe
Chippenham, UK
2017-02-24 10:39